First published in Great Britain in 2010

British Library Cataloguing-in-Publication Data
A CIP record for this title is available from the British Library

Standard edition ISBN 978 0 85704 075 6
Limited edition ISBN 978 0 85704 077 0

HALSGROVE
Halsgrove House,
Ryelands Industrial Estate,
Bagley Road, Wellington, Somerset TA21 9PZ
Tel: 01823 653777   Fax: 01823 216796
email: sales@halsgrove.com

Part of the Halsgrove group of companies.
Information on all Halsgrove titles is available at: www.halsgrove.com

Printed and bound in China by Toppan Leefung Printing Ltd

CONTENTS

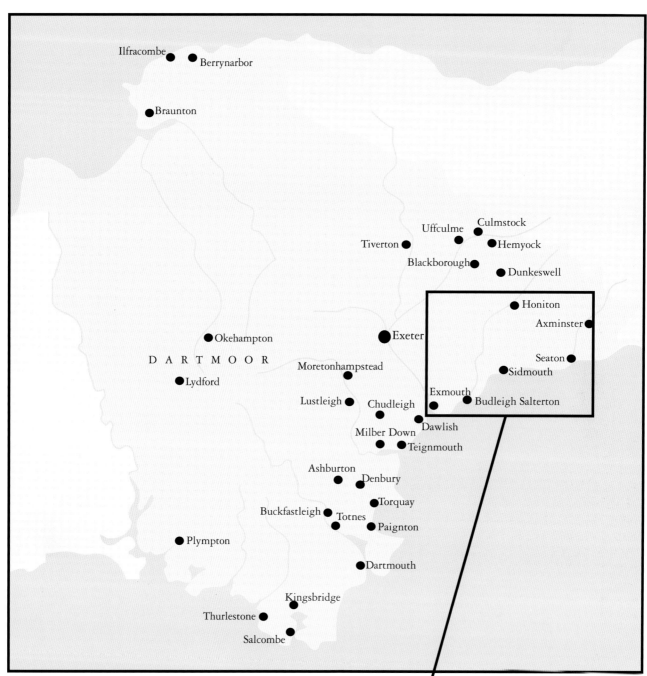

**PLACES MENTIONED
AND ILLUSTRATED
IN THE DIARIES**

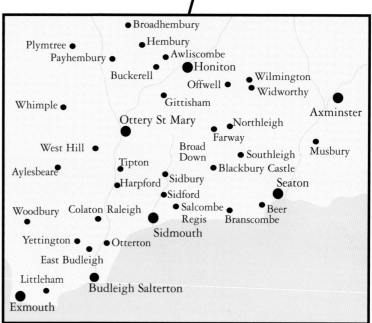

INTRODUCTION

'Not having quite run our course, and finding from twenty years experience and more that our antiquarian expeditions constitute a very pleasurable part of our existence, Mr Heineken and myself started out again today'. So writes POH in a diary entry for July 5, 1872 at the age of 62 as he set out with his friend on yet another strenuous exploration of the antiquities of South-east Devon. His previous expeditions are related in *Travels in Victorian Devon* (Devon Books 2000) in which a short biography of Hutchinson and a description of his writings appear in the introduction. The present volume continues the record to 1894, three years before his death, when Hutchinson finally decided not to continue his diary any further.

King Arthurs Chromlech, Glamorgan. 1833

Although Hutchinson had a general interest in ancient sites in his earlier years, as the water colours in the margin show, it was a casual walk across High Peak with its prehistoric embankments in 1848 which really stirred his imagination. The hills and heaths were then far more open than today before the clearance of new enclosures and plantations obscured the landscape, and much that was then accessible is now hidden or lost altogether. Some amateurish digging here initiated a lifelong interest in the subject and he soon developed a more scientific approach that was far ahead of many of his contemporaries. After attending a roughly conducted excavation by the Rev. R. Kirwan on High Peak, he comments in a letter to the Society of Antiquaries 'I have a great reluctance at the idea of digging further, for an incautious hand might easily destroy valuable evidence to science' (September 18, 1871). He was far more interested in the significance of the location of any finds he made than in collecting objects for his cabinet, and strongly disapproved of the contemporary hobby of barrow digging. At that time prehistoric studies in Britain were still in their infancy but with true Victorian energy Hutchinson was determined to try to solve some of the minor mysteries which the local antiquities presented. Were the linear banks in the vicinity of some of the hill forts defensive outworks or evidence of attacks by besiegers, or perhaps not even contemporary at all? Did the ancient Britons use the slingshot before the Romans arrived, a question posed by Hutchinson's knowledge that many of the pebbles he found shattered by impact in the vicinity of these fortifications did not come from the immediate neighbourhood? Were palaeolithic tools really not to be found west of the Axe valley except in the bone caves as Evans remarked in 'Ancient Stone Implements', a query first satisfactorily decided by a friend who, though 'smiling at my simplic-

Druidic Circle near Selma. 1838

v

Chromlech near Gorey, Jersey.   *1852*

ity', presented him with a 'stone implement' he had found on Salcombe Hill (April 22, 1873). By carefully mapping the hill forts, tumuli and other earthworks of south east Devon, he attempted to answer these questions and others, but 'work, instead of diminishing always seems to increase' (April 16, 1872) as further possibilities presented themselves   Along with the results of occasional judicial excavations his conclusions were regularly reported in the Transactions of the Devonshire Association and to the Society of Antiquaries, as well as in the regional newspapers.   Eventually though, with Heineken 'feeling age creeping upon him' and some years later at the age of 78 having to admit that he was 'not the active boy I was a few summers ago', his more energetic investigations came to a close.

Other useful observations such as the legends associated with some of the monuments and the gradual destruction or even complete loss of them, such as the Mutters Moor stone circle, the stones of which ended up in Bicton Park rockery, would have gone unrecorded but for the entries in his Diaries and in the remarkable, and largely unpublished, 'History of Sidmouth'.   He encouraged the local farmers to inform him of any finds they might make in their fields with a cash incentive, and when gossip reached him of some new find or old memories he invariably traveled to interview those concerned in order to ascertain the facts. Together with the splendid illustrations in the sketchbooks these records form an invaluable resource for researches into the history and prehistory of Devon, which would be much the poorer but for his contribution. (Most recently, Jones, A.M. and Quinnell, H. 2008; Tilley, C. 2009)

The text is taken from Hutchinson's diaries with contributions from the History of Sidmouth (in the West Country Studies Library) and letters, and the illustrations from the six volumes of the sketchbooks in the Devon Record Office.   As in the earlier volume, practically all entries and drawings referring to Devon are included, together with some of the more star-

Roman Amphitheatre near Dorchester.

tling or amusing events from the wider world which Hutchinson thought interesting enough to record.   The diaries are not confined to Hutchinson's archaeological pursuits however, but contain much more of general interest, such as those local customs that were then fast dying out, the annual mayhem accompanying November the fifth celebrations and tales of body snatching, strange accidents, robbery and worse.   Though originally intended to be seen by no one but himself they are written in such a clear and naturalistic style as if to entertain a reader, and provide a fascinating chronicle of life in a provincial town throughout much of the Victorian era.

1871

New Years Day 1871. *Sunday January 1, 1871.* The New Year comes with all its hopes, like others before. (*Diary*).

Moon eclipse. *Friday January 6, 1871.* Eclipses are as plenty as blackberries, indeed much more so, at this season of the year. Only a fortnight ago *there was* an eclipse of the sun and now *there is* an eclipse of the moon. I was struck with the similarity in appearance, owing to nearly the same amount of obscuration but making due allowance for the different arrangement of the three great heavenly bodies engaged in the performance. (*Diary*).

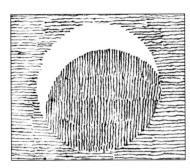

71/1/6 Eclipse of the moon (Diary)

New will. *Saturday February 11, 1871.* The death of my brother in Australia *on* August 3 1870 and of my sister's husband *on* October 11, have altered my plans. Made a new will, leaving my houses in Sidmouth to my sister. Also stock and money and my land Section 18 at Port Victor. (*Diary*). *This was John Robertson, his sister's second husband. Her first husband, Charles Rumley, with whom she had emigrated to South Australia in 1849, had died in 1855.*

71/3/7 Egg, Edge, or Hedge, Branscomb. From a sketch taken Aug. 2. 1847 (Soc.of Antiq. Ms 250)

Further destruction of diary. *Tuesday March 7, 1871.* Destroyed my diary from February 1849 back to 1840. I had previously destroyed it back to 1832. I may yet have another spell at destroying and lop off another decade or two. The early part I thought contained a great deal of childish nonsense. Some few entries would have been worth retaining had they stood alone but as they did not outweigh the trash I condemned the whole together. I observed under date -

Monday August 2, 1847. Mr. Heineken and myself went over to Branscombe to examine the interesting old house at Edge Farm. *A few details of this visit together with the accompanying sketch are preserved in the Library of the Society of Antiquaries:* Egge, Edge or Hedge, a massively built house in the parish of Branscombe, has a secret chamber on the lower story accessible only through a hole in the thickness of the wall. If the window seat of an upper window be taken up (the window against which the ladder is being placed) there is revealed a square hole like a chimney shaft which descends downwards in the thickness of the wall, past the room

71/3/7 Site of ancient mill at Mill Cross

below and into the cellar beneath. This secret chamber measures (as the farmer said) about eight feet by sixteen. There is no other communication with it except a small hole sloping downwards through the wall on the higher side, down which food might have been passed. The chamber or dungeon, or whatever it may have been, was accidentally discovered a few years before my visit (August 2, 1847) when I made the sketch reproduced here. (*Soc. of Antiq. Ms. 250, p.26*).

Wednesday September 8, 1847. I dined at Salcombe Lodge when the company were alarmed after dinner at seeing a great blaze over the town of

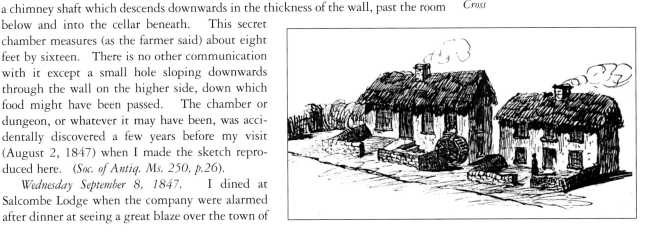

Sidmouth. About a dozen houses were burnt down at Mill Cross opposite the Unitarian Chapel and Mill Lane, now foolishly altered to the sentence 'All Saints Church Road'. The remains of the monk's and Adam de Radway's old mill with the adjoining houses were destroyed. The fire was caused by a man going into a stable with a candle and setting the hay and straw alight through carelessness. (*Diary*). It was the driver of the mail cart, the worse for liquor, who set the straw on fire. One man who went back to try to find some sovereigns lost his life. (*History of Sidmouth V, 160*). *The accompanying sketch of the ancient mill was done 'from recollection'.*

Wednesday January 12, 1848. H. Ponsford on the cliff of Salcombe Hill, fell over and was killed. He was ferreting rabbits and a dead ferret was found in his pocket. My late mother and myself, walking on the esplanade, saw his body brought home in a boat. (*Diary*).

Branscombe expedition. *Friday March 24, 1871.* Beautiful day, *the* wind north-east fresh and pleasant *and a* brilliant sun. Mr. Heineken and myself drove over to Branscombe. Went up Trow Hill, past Slade to Higher and Lower Bulstone, to enquire more about the coffin made of slabs of stone with bones in it said to have been found many years ago by a labouring man near a hedge. Could get no information whatever, either there or *from some* old men elsewhere. Drove into Branscombe *and* went again into the old house called 'The Clergy' near the church with the loophole and trapdoor over the entrance (*see June 22, 1855*). *Then* went to Castle Close on the hill over Culverhole or Trafalgar Cottage (see July 9, 1861). The lintel of the hole where the lime is withdrawn from the upper kiln (now in ruins) is a sandstone block three feet long and nine inches thick. (Query – the stone taken from the destroyed tumulus?). The corresponding hole of the lower kiln is buried in rubbish. We ate our sandwiches and bread and cheese, and drank our beer and cider as we sat on the grass enjoying it all amazingly. We entered the chalk quarry, which is now worked out and abandoned, *and* then scrambled up to where the filled-in trenches of the supposed camp were. I dug *into* the end of the southern one. It had been nine feet deep and about the same width at top. The portion remaining of the trench (or agger or vallum) is sixty-five feet long, then turns at a right angle and goes fifteen feet to the edge of the quarry. Having been filled in and all on the level, nothing is seen but the ends of the trenches in the face of the cliff. Bones, pottery, etc., having been met with by the quarrymen suggested my digging at the end, but I had neither time nor tools to do much. We found beach pebbles like sling stones in the fields above, which may or may not be genuine, *and* near the kilns we saw many flint flakes, evidently modern. Perhaps gun flints used to be made there.

71/3/24 (Diary)

We then went on to Branscombe church. There is no proper font. John Parrat, who is seventy-nine and has been sexton for fifty to fifty-five years, told us that the old font had been used as a pump trough within his memory, and taking us to the garden at the east end of the churchyard he showed us a fragment of it about eighteen inches long, being the curved segment of the outside. *This fragment has been rescued and brought within the church.* On the altar tomb of Joan, the wife of Ellis Carter of Weston, 1699, opposite the south porch, is a rhyming stanza of four lines which stands as I copy it out here: -

> WHEN I LY DOWN MY AGED HEAD
> AND DEATH DOTH CLOSE MY EYS
> AN ANGELL WAITE ABOYTE MY BEED
> AND GIDE ME IN HIS WAIS

71/3/24 (Diary)

About half a mile out of Branscombe, as we were returning home, we met a man with a donkey cart, and as the lane was very narrow we stopped to let him pass. The cart was loaded with faggots of sticks on which was perched a boy of ten or twelve. Willing to have a joke, I cried out in a Devonshire accent, 'I zay! What'll 'e zell the lot ver, sticks and boy and all?' 'I should be very glad to zell the boy', said the man, 'but I can't pairt wi' the sticks'. This caused a great laugh all round, in which the boy joined. (*Diary*).

Peak Hill rusement. *Friday March 31, 1871.* The frost and rains of winter loosened the cliff *below* Peak Hill, and recently there has been a large 'rusement' or fall of the sea face nearly in line with Peak Cottage. I have seen many such occurrences but never on so large a scale. So much fell down as to make a little promontory in the sea. Of course, this will not last long as the soil is soft. Such a cliff-fall is locally termed a rusement, rhyming with amusement. *Unde derivatur?* (*Diary*). *The accompanying coloured sketch of an earlier rusement that occurred in much the same place shows* the present road by the edge of the cliff and the two former roads which have successively fallen away. (*Sketchbook D*). *On April 10, Hutchinson went to stay at Wareham for a week, visiting Bindon Abbey, Corfe Castle, examining the British trackway at Wareham, etc., returning to Sidmouth on April 17.*

Broad Down again. *Tuesday April 4, 1871.* Wishing to have a thorough examination of Broad Down, Mr. Heineken and myself spent the day there. We drove to Sidbury, passed the vicarage where I *spent* many a pleasant evening in the time of Mr. Fellowes, the former vicar. Some twenty-five years ago (I hazard a rough guess) the vicarage was burnt down and the two old volumes in vellum of the parish register were virtually destroyed. They looked like two lumps of charred wood. About an inch of the outside was burnt, the centre being untouched, but the skin was so dried, twisted and contracted that I could not open them. I had several articles in *Notes and Queries* on singed vellum about a dozen years ago. It is strange to me that the old registers are not collected and preserved in the government record offices, *as* there is not one clergyman in ten who can be trusted with the custody of them. (*Diary*). *Hutchinson had taken on the task of rescuing them.* A few years ago the vicarage house of an adjoining parish burnt down. The parish register, consisting of several old volumes in vellum, received considerable injury. At the first glance they have the appearance of masses of charred wood. The edges of the leaves, for half an inch to an inch inwards, have been burnt away and the remainder of each volume, although not destroyed, has been rendered useless by the action of the heat. These leaves, instead of being flat and smooth as heretofore, are now curled, twisted, contracted, contorted, involuted, convoluted and crumpled together so densely and so rigidly that they resist all attempts, except violence, to separate them. But violence is destruction, because the heat and the dryness have rendered them brittle. Any attempt to unfold them from their present involutions only cracks them. The writing is brown with age as in other MSS of equal date, but has received no manifest injury from the fire. (*Notes and Queries 1854*).

71/3/31 Rusement, or fall of the cliff, near Peak Cottage, Peak Hill, Sidmouth. August 31, 1847. Coloured on the spot. (DRO, Z19/2/8D/39)

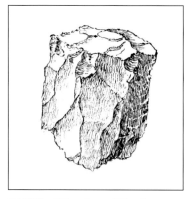

71/4/4 *Flint Core* (Diary)

We ascended the lane up to Sweetcombe Common, now cultivated, and got out near Roncombe's Girt. We first traversed Seven Barrow Field, as I call it, where the cup and little cylindrical vase full of calcined bones were found in 1868. On the surface, which had recently been ploughed, I found a core from which flint flakes had been struck, but as the flint, which is not black, did not seem to have split kindly, perhaps for that reason it had been thrown away. It is roughly cylindrical, three inches high *by* two and a quarter across.

We plotted down all the barrows on the north, some of which were new to us, *and* then skirted the eastern side of the Down. We looked into and admired the deep chasm at the head of one of the streams running down to Wiscombe. Near it we discovered three barrows. We pushed on westwards till we came out into the road, a rough track for the carriage, *and* then walked north and again visited the two large ones. The eastern one is a bowl barrow, flat or rather dished or slightly hollowed on the top. We made the top or platform seventy feet in diameter *and* the slope of the sides thirty feet. The whole diameter is thus one hundred and thirty feet. We were indeed inclined to think that instead of a barrow, this may have been a speculum or miniature fortress of a circular form in advance of Farway Castle. It is to be lamented that Mr. Kirwan has obtained unlimited permission to dig over as many barrows as zeal may invite. One barrow at a time opened and examined carefully and deliberately would give far more satisfactory results than tumbling over a great many and leaving the workmen too much to themselves. The annexed plan may assist.

Coming home we saw, just after sunset, a peculiar yellow light over the sun. It was the same width as the diameter of the sun and rose to the height of nearly fifteen degrees. It continued steadily for twenty minutes. I reported it to Professor Airy. (*Diary*).

On April 10, Hutchinson went to stay with Heineken's daughter Mrs Lloyd at Wareham for a week. Whilst there he took the opportunity to visit some of the ancient sites in the vicinity, including Lulworth Castle, Bindon Abbey and Corfe Castle.

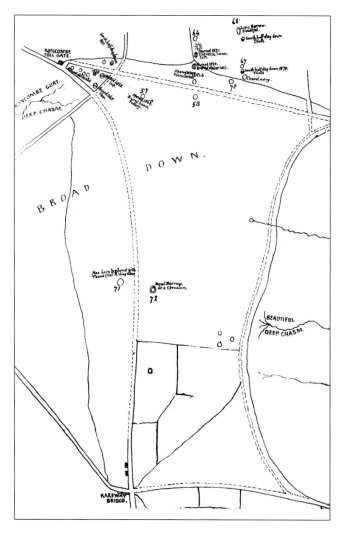

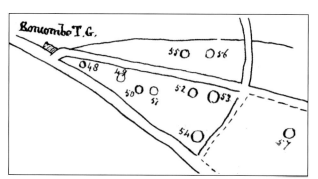

Above: 71/4/4 (Diary)

Left: 71/4/4 Map of Broad Down (Diary)

Below: 71/4/4 (Diary)

Bushy Knap and Buckerell Knap again. *Monday May 8, 1871.* Mr Heineken and myself wished once more to examine Bushy Knap and Buckerell Knap, which has all the appearance of being an outwork like a promontory in advance of Hembury Fort, overlooking the Icknild between Honiton and Exeter. We drove through Sidbury to the top of Honiton Hill. We got out at the six mile stone and walked a few score yards eastwards over the heath to revisit the three barrows opened in 1869. We went on and made a short cut to Awliscombe by crossing the great road a mile or two west of Honiton. We discussed our sandwiches in a shady place near the mill at Mardles and then mounted the flank of the hill. This peculiar hill is a long narrow ridge and seems to have been regularly fortified by an earthwork all round. I took several measurements and made a more correct plan than my former one of June 6 1859, which appeared in the *Journal of the Archaeological Association.* Some old writers say there was a sacrificial stone on this hill. We renewed our enquiries, but no one had ever heard of it. The defences at the north end are certainly very peculiar and interesting. If this place became untenable, the garrison would retire upon Hembury Fort along the ridge, discernible nearly all the way. In my *History* I have stated why I now believe Hembury to have been Moridunum.

After this we made a divergence to Buckerell. The Rifle Volunteers were being drilled in the village. The Volunteers of this place made themselves quite famous as marksmen a few years ago. Went into the church. The wall behind the communion table is covered with odds and ends of old oak panels, as if the carved fronts of old oak chests, etc., etc. The late vicar had it done we were told and the effect is not bad. There is a black oak open screen, I presume original. Thence to Feniton. In the churchyard on the south side of the tower there is an altar tomb recording John Pierce, 1620. The screen in this church has been cut in two; one half has been pushed back and fixed against the east wall behind the communion table and unfortunately painted white and blue, whilst the other half runs at right angles to it between the chancel and south aisle. There is also a small bit across the south aisle.

We returned home through Fenny Bridges, Ottery, Bowd and Bulverton. Out from 11 AM to 9 PM. *(Diary). The coloured sketch of Bushy and Buckerell Knaps was done some years later, in October 1880, but with no accompanying Diary entry.*

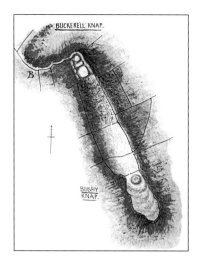

71/5/8 Buckerell Knap (Hist of Sid. I,50a)

71/5/8 The Hill called Bushy Knap and Buckerell Knap, near Honiton. October 1880. (DRO, Z19/2/8F/27)

Runaway apprentice. *Wednesday May 10, 1871.* This morning I was in the Blue Room over the Hall of the Old Chancel when I heard a great outcry. On looking out of the window I saw a boy caught on the spikes of the iron railings under the elm tree in front of No. 4 Coburg Terrace. By the time I had got down he had extricated himself, but he had badly pierced the palms of both his hands and also one of his arms. I asked him why he tried to climb the railings? He said he was running away from his master who, for some offence, was going to give him 'a good walloping'. He was bleeding and in great pain, so I took him into the kitchen of No. 4, made the cook get him some warm water and, after he had washed his hands, I bound them up with rag and gave him some diacolon plaster. *(Diary)*

Broad Down expedition. *Thursday June 1, 1871.* Mr. Heineken and myself drove again to Broad Down, our chief object being to explore the western portion to see if there are any tumuli in that quarter. We ascended Salcombe Hill and turned into a field on the left at the turn off to the lane. The land was first enclosed some twelve to fifteen years ago, when the labourers found a quantity of beach pebbles like the sling stones of Sidbury Castle. I went up at the time but Mr. Heineken had not seen the spot. We observed from forty to fifty lying about within a radius of perhaps thirty yards of the great stone, as if some ancient fight had taken place there. Mr. Heineken took two or three but I left them (see January 7, 1873).

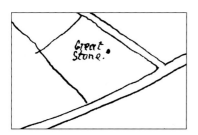

71/6/1   (Diary)

We passed Thorn Farm, then the pound and glanced at the Ordnance mark on its east side. We got out at Trow hamlet and looked into some of the cottages to see if they had any old oak furniture, but they had not. On the Lyme road we observed the Ordnance marks on the mile stones, the elevations *of which* I have. We turned off north and descended at Rakeway Bridge *on* the southern part of the Down. Mr. Heineken explored the south-east corner whilst I went away north on the east of the centre road *where* I observed traces of an old trackway, perhaps used before the *present* road was made. This portion was enclosed about 1820. I noted down two tumuli, one doubtful. Came out by the two great barrows and returned by the road *where I* joined Mr. Heineken and we then proceeded to take another look at the Lovehayne tumulus, or rather, of the eastern portion which is all that remains. Standing on it, Mr. Heineken turned up a fine thumb flint with his stick. Returning through the field to the road I found another, and then another, the last not being well made. He then picked up a core. We think there must have been a manufactory of flint weapons here, for we have always seen numerous indications in this field. We now proceeded to the great western triangle, *going* north from Rakeway Bridge a few score yards and then turn*ing* in to the left westward and over the hedge. There is a large expanse of heath beyond. I went further west leaving him to explore in a northerly direction, but on surmounting the next hedge there was still another expanse of wild heath. No wonder this Down got the name of 'Broad'. Finding no tumuli I veered away northward, then into some plantations, then out over the hedge towards Seven Barrow field, then back till I met Mr. Heineken , when we proceeded to the great barrow in the middle of the Down on which some years ago he met with a thumb flint, now in the Exeter Museum. With his stick today he turned up a flake, apparently intended for a thumb flint but not completed. I measured the north and south diameter of the barrow and made it 140 feet. There is no fosse round it.

71/6/1   (Diary)

It was now time to return home. We drove north, stopped and walked round Farway Castle, proceeded to Hunter's Lodge, Sidbury, Sidford, and home before nine. A hard day *with* much rough walking in the heat, *but* the flints we found repaid us. (*Diary*). *A long letter relating the discoveries made on this and previous expeditions, entitled 'The Tumuli on Broad Down', appeared in the Exeter Daily Telegram on June 12.*

Forgeries. *Tuesday June 13, 1871.* The iniquities of this world are monstrous and they take every variety of form. The annexed are rubbings of false antiques made of brass, very ingeniously corroded with vinegar and acid and *smeared* all over *with* dirt, mortar and verdegris to make them look old, and very old they look. They have been forwarded to me for examination by Rev. H. T. Ellacombe, Rector of Clyst St. George. They are said to have been found near Budleigh. He warns me to be on my guard lest any designing person bring the like to me. I have shown both sides of the two preceeding. The two last are hollow, being apparently of two stamped plaques soldered together. The bishop is four inches high, the heart three and a half inches. (*Diary*). *Also illustrated is a gold coin of Elizabeth dated 1571. Given to me June 13, 1871 by the Rev. H.G.J.Clements, Vicar of Sidmouth and now in Exeter Museum. (History of Sidmouth I, 99).*

71/6/13   (Diary)

On July 28 Hutchinson went over to Dawlish for a few days and whilst there walked out to places of archaeological interest in the neighbourhood. His investigations resulted in two long articles in the Exeter and Plymouth Gazette (July 7 and 14) entitled 'Camp on Little Haldon' and 'Lidwell Chapel, Dawlish'. He was back in Sidmouth on July 3.

Barrows on Farway Hill. *Tuesday July 18, 1871.* Whilst I was at Dawlish, Mr. Heineken paid a visit to Farway Hill and informed me that he had hit upon five more barrows which we had not before noted down. To verify this we went up again today. We drove through Sidbury and having mounted the hill, turned into the plantation

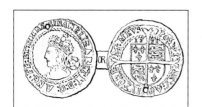

71/6/13   Gold coin of Elizabeth (Hist of Sid. I,98a)

and the fields on the right a half mile short of Hunter's Lodge Inn. We walked all up through the plantation to search for barrows. We then got out upon the moor and proceeded eastwards. *We* visited most of the barrows we had known before *and* also Ring-in-the-Mire, now an oval pond full of water. *We* found a small egg-shaped beach pebble, probably a sling stone, between this and the fourteen-milestone from Lyme and then made for Farway Castle. We sat on the agger on the north side and eat our sandwiches. Before we left, we measured the height of one of the fir trees growing within the circular area and made it 56 feet. This camp is very like that on Little Haldon, only smaller. The diameter of that is about 124 yards, this is 210 feet; the slope of the agger of that is 15 or more feet, whereas in this it is not half so much.

We then proceeded further eastward, almost as far as the road that branches off north to Offwell, to measure and jot down the new barrows we had come to examine. There are three in this region, a small one with the furze burnt off (or it would not have been seen) measuring 28 feet in diameter and 3 high; a large one 100 feet from it eastward, 7 feet high and 98 in diameter with a bond stone on the top of it; and east of this a smaller one 20 feet from it, 3 feet high and 30 in diameter. On this I accidentally disturbed a partridge's nest, scared away the old birds and scattered the little ones. The young ones were scarcely larger than sparrows and very pretty. I left them to recover themselves. There may be many more barrows about the hill but the furze bushes are so high that it is impossible to say. The others we visited are close to the lane leading down to Roncombe. The one close on the west side of the road has had most of the middle cleared out but the circumference remains. It is 30 feet in diameter and about 3 high. The other, close on the west side of it, is 23 feet in diameter and 2½ high. These two last may perhaps be looked upon as rather doubtful. When near the one crowned with the boundary stone we went into a field on the south, where there is a beautiful view down the valley towards Sidmouth, and hunted about the recently ploughed land. Mr. Heineken found a small beach pebble and I found a large one. It is hard to imagine how they got here on this recently enclosed land, unless they had been sling stones used by ancient tribes on the hill.

We returned home via Sweetcombe Common (pronounced Swetcombe) and Sidbury. Out from 11 AM till 9 PM. (*Diary*).

Artillery Corps disbanded. *Thursday August 3, 1871.* Today an order was received from the War Office disbanding the Sidmouth Artillery Corps. The reason alleged is that there are no commissioned officers attached to it and have not been for a long time. Gentlemen do not like to undertake the trouble and the expense, besides which it is very difficult in a small place like Sidmouth to find gentlemen among the permanent residents free to accept commissions. The order came quite unexpectedly and has caused general regret. (*Diary*).

Tumuli west of Hunters Lodge. *Monday August 7, 1871.* Mr. Heineken and myself went to explore Chineway Head and search for tumuli in that direction. We got on the Honiton coach. Mr. G. Gordon, curate of Sidmouth, was there, on his way to London for a month. Saw corn cutting for the first time this year, *as* owing to the continued cold and showery weather since the beginning of June the harvest is very backward. In Sidbury Mr. Parker, the curate there, joined us. We mounted Honiton Hill and admired the beautiful view over the valley on the left going up. At Putt's Corner, sometimes called 'Hare and Hounds' or 'Hunter's Lodge', we got down *and* here we turned west. Mr. Heineken took the road and kept his eyes over the southern hedge, the ground being more open, whilst I turned to the plantations on the other or north side. I observed traces of an old trackway from six to eight feet wide and from one to two feet below the general surface. There are several portions of old hedges in this plantation running more or less parallel with the road. In the north-west corner near a cottage and a cottage garden, I came upon what appeared to be a large tumulus, *so* I hailed Mr. Heineken and got him over the hedge to examine it with me. He agreed that it had all the appearance but it had been disturbed, perhaps for the sake of the flints to build the cottage. It measured twenty paces in diameter. We returned to the road, *where* I got into the next plantation near the milestone. The walking was very rough, difficult and tiring owing to the thick undergrowth of weeds, fern and bramble, as well as the tangled branches of the trees. I nearly stepped on a viper with a V on his head,

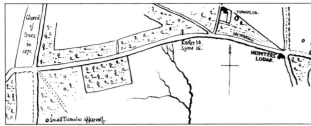

71/8/7 Vicinity of Hunters
Lodge (Diary)

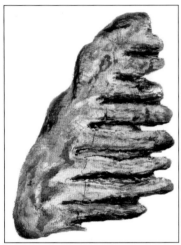

Above: 71/9/2 *Fossil elephant's
tooth, found on Sidmouth beach in
Jan. 1871* (Hist of Sid. I,23b)

Below: 71/9/2 *Crown of tooth*
(Hist of Sid. I,23b)

about eighteen inches long and about as thick as my finger. I was struck with the grace, rapidity and easy gliding motion with which he passed over the grass making for a rabbit hole, into which he vanished. I made my way all through the plantation and came out at the western road. I think there are no tumuli there, though it would not be difficult to overlook them in so dense a foliage.

Tired and hot and thirsty, we sat on the slope of the hill to eat our sandwiches and admire the splendid view over the valley of the Otter and the country beyond. I never saw the colouring finer nor the distant view clearer. Every stranger ought to get to the top of Ottery East Hill, especially in the forenoon, to enjoy this view. With the telescope we could see Exeter Cathedral and the houses of Heavitree easily.   On Dartmoor we clearly saw the cairn on Cawsand Beacon, Blackaton Rock, Haytor and the road down to the quarries with other peaks and mountains.

We then walked half a mile south *where* I got over the east hedge and found a small tumulus, apparently. Then we proceeded to return along the Chineway Head road to Hunter's Lodge, making observations all the way. Sat on the 'Witch's Stone' at the carfoix in front of the Inn. We went eastward as the coach had not arrived and re-examined the nearest tumuli. The coach arrived, we got up and soon got to Sidmouth. (*Diary*).

Russian guns moved. *Friday August 25, 1871.* Went into Exeter to see my banker. Brought back 175 sovereigns in a bag. Drove to Ottery Road and took the rail. Returned by coach over Aylesbeare Hill. Spent an hour in the Exeter Museum, *as I* wished to examine some of the flints, cups, bones and bronzes found on the Honiton and Farway Hills and other neighbouring places. Took a turn on Northernhay *and* looked at the Acland and Dinham statues. I observe that within a few months the two Russian guns taken at Sebastopol in 1855, which used to stand on the platform close to the back of the court house, have been transferred to a platform in Queen Street close to the railway station. (*Diary*).

Plague of earwigs. *Friday September 1, 1871.* For the past month or more there has been a plague of earwigs in Sidmouth.   About five or six summers ago I recollect a great many, but not so many as this year.   They have found their way all over the houses *and* everything must be examined, food, clothes, and beds, for they have been met with everywhere.   Some people have a great horror of them and are afraid of them running into their ears, which they think they have a tendency to do.   I imagine they are no more likely to enter a person's ear than any other hole where they would seek concealment.   Should such an accident occur, the best thing is to drop a little sweet oil into the ear, when it could be drawn out with tweezers or even with scissors. (*Diary*).

Second fossil tooth. *Saturday September 2, 1871.*   Not being able to go to the meeting at Bideford of the Devonshire Association for the Advancement of Science, Mr. Pengelly was good enough to read a short paper of mine.   It was a notice of the find of a second fossil tooth here. (*Diary*).

Excavated section on High Peak. *Saturday September 9, 1871.   On the previous Saturday, the Exeter Field Naturalists Club had been invited to examine the newly discovered 'bone bed' at High Peak Camp (see letter September 18).   They were met on the summit by a local committee, including Hutchinson.   After an introductory talk by Kirwan, the latter and Mr. D'Urban, curator of Exeter Museum, proceeded to dig out bones, pottery and charcoal from the deposit in front of the assembled audience.*   Walked to High Peak and deliberately examined the spot where the bones were found.   There was too much hurry-skurry last Saturday *and I was* grieved to see the excavations conducted in too hurried a manner.   Made a careful drawing of the section of the deposit to show the order in which the objects lay *and* found the lower leg bone of a fowl or other bird with the boney core of the spur attached to it complete (see my *History of Sidmouth* I, 32). (*Diary*).

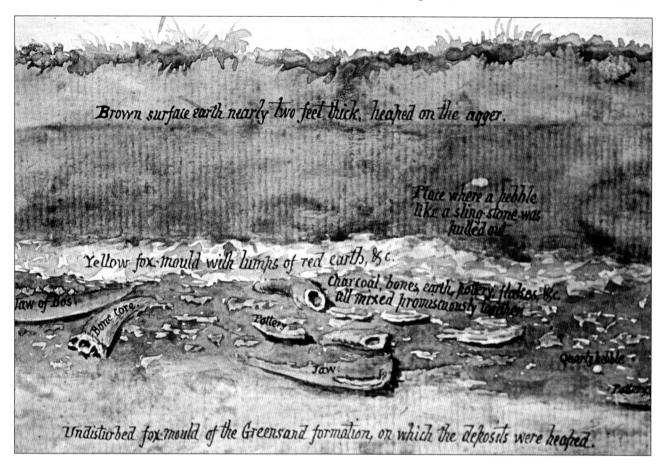

Above: 71/9/9 *Front view, or perpendicular section of the bone bed on High Peak Hill.* Sep 11,1871. (Hist of Sid. I,31)

Right: 71/9/9 Cores from above. (Hist of Sid. I,31)

Below: 71/9/9 (Hist of Sid. I,31a)

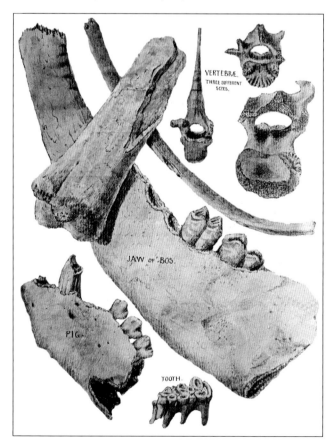

Below: 71/9/9 *Bones of bird.* (Hist of Sid. I,32)

Bottom: 71/9/9 Bones and *white quartz pebble.* (Hist of Sid. I,32)

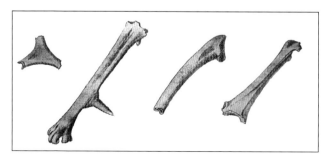

Bone bed on High Peak. *Monday September 11, 1871.* Went again to High Peak. Dug a little as possible, for the deposit is more valuable here than if removed. By picking my way carefully I got another section of the ossiferous bed about a foot thick, made up of bones, charcoal, broken pottery and earth all mixed together. Made another careful drawing *as* important deductions may be drawn from this. (*Diary*).

Wednesday September 13, 1871. Again at High Peak. (*Diary*).

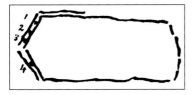

71/9/13   Bury Camp   (Diary)

Bury Camp revisited. *Friday September 15, 1871.* Mr. Heineken and myself revisited Bury Camp after a long interval. Mr. Chick drove over in another carriage and took two labourers. Our object was to dig in the bottom of the fosse, remembering that when the quarrymen were digging away the fosse of what appeared to have been a camp at Castle Close, they came upon bones, pottery and old metal (July 9, 1861). We sank four different holes in the bottom of the fosse (at figures 1,2,3,4) *and* at the depth of nearly three feet the tough yellow clay was reached. In *pits* 1,2,3 some beach pebbles like sling stones, one here, another there, at depths in one or two instances nearly down to the maiden soil, or original bottom, were met with. Four of them from different places had been broken as if by the force with which they had struck something hard, perhaps a large flint in the agger of the camp. It may be inferred that they had been hurled at the camp and, having hit some obstacle, had fallen into the ditch. Some fifty or more yards on the Sidmouth side of the camp, running inwards from the cliff to the three great stones, are traces of a double bank, thirty-five feet dividing, about the same as the aggers of the camp. They may have been an advanced work for protection or defence. The numerous stone heaps along this part of the cliff are remarkably like genuine tumuli. The one we examined on September 8, 1858, produced nothing conclusive but perhaps the examination was not complete (see my ms. Hist. of Sidmouth, I, 58). (*Diary*).

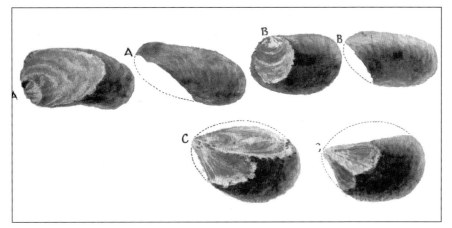

71/9/13 *The above are examples grouped in twos, or pairs, or two images of each stone. The point of impact, or place where the stone struck, is marked by the letters.* (Hist of Sid. I,57a)

High Peak bone bed again. *Monday September 18, 1871.* Again on High Peak. I scrambled down the face of the cliff below the bone bed, as I heard that some bones had been found there which had fallen down. Picked up the femur of a small animal like a hare, and also the core of the hoof of an animal about the size of a red deer. (*Diary*). *A long article written by Hutchinson appeared in the Exeter Gazette for September 29 entitled 'The bone bed on High Peak Hill' and the excavations were again described in a letter to C. Knight Watson at the Society of Antiquaries:*

Dear Sir. Twenty-three years ago I was drawing up a paper on Moridunum and had to say a great deal about the remains of a camp on High Peak Hill. One day when I was examining the spot I pulled some bones out of the side of the agger, but being comparatively young and inexperienced the force of the incident was lost upon me and I neglected to follow up the search and make an excavation. But I brought home the bones and put them in a box, together with some charcoal extracted from another part of the agger. These I have kept by me to the present time. A month or two ago Mr. Aubrey Strahan of this place visited the hill for geological purposes and owing to the wearing away of the cliff and the appearance of other bones brought to the surface, he communicated what he had seen to the Rev. R. Kirwan. The latter at once dug down part of the agger and extracted flint flakes, bones and fragments of pottery. During the past fortnight I have several times visited this well-known spot, not for the purpose of further digging for I am aware that too free a handling of the tool may destroy valuable historical evidence, but for the sake of studying the appearance revealed. By considering the relative positions of the various objects with respect to each other, noting what objects are lowest, what next above them and what above these last, a chronological idea of the sequence of their deposition can be got, and having observed all these facts certain conclusions can be arrived at. I had thought that the flint flakes, ostensibly the oldest, would be the lowest but Mr. Kirwan informs me that he did not remark any order in the way in which the objects lay, for they seemed to be thrown confusedly together. This remark agrees with the observations which I had myself made afterwards.   The bed in which these things are found is in some places about a foot thick and it may be traced horizontally along the side of the agger for twenty feet or more.   It consists of sandy earth stained black by ashes and smoke mixed with pieces of charcoal in which the grain of oak and fir are easily discernible, of flint flakes and of the bones of various animals such as the ox, pig, deer and others as small as the hare.   I also succeeded in extracting several of the bones of a bird about the size of a pheasant, a leg bone having the osseous core of the spur attached, the vertebrae of quadrupeds of three or four differ-

ent sizes, the jaw bones of an ox nearly a foot long and many cores of horns, one of them six inches long and eight inches in circumference at the base.   Among some fragments of pottery of red and buff-coloured clay, I made out sixteen different patterns, all of them being ring patterns (Saxon?), produced by holding the point of a tool or the end of a stick against the outside surface of the vessel whilst it was revolving on the wheel. There were also several white quartz pebbles the size of large hazel nuts perhaps used as

71/9/18 *Pottery, together with the sections or edges of the fragments. Most of the foregoing objects are in the Exeter Museum.* (Hist of Sid. I,32a)

counters to play some sort of game with, two oblate spheroidal hammers or pounding stones, one showing abrasion from use round the edge and the other split by heat in the fire, two sling stones one of which was split, and a piece of flat sandstone about six inches long with longitudinal scratches on one side as if it had been used as a hone. There were no human remains.   Most of these things were extracted by Mr. Kirwan. On top of this bed earth had been heaped to the thickness of two to three feet, apparently for the purpose of heightening the agger.   I have a great reluctance at the idea of digging further, for an incautious hand might easily destroy valuable evidence to science.   The following conclusions suggest themselves:

1. That there is nothing sepulchral in the deposit.

2. That the materials of it were not originally thrown by little and little where we now see them but were brought from some other place.

3. That they were brought from some place inside the camp, as they appear to lie rather on the inside of the agger.

4. That they are the materials of an old fire place and rubbish heap scraped together and thrown upon the agger when it was repaired and heightened.

5. That the flint flakes and the pottery are not contemporary, supposing the former to have been made in the stone age.

6. That the pottery much resembled pottery of known Saxon character.

I beg to remain Dear Sir, Yours faithfully, P. O. Hutchinson.   (*Letter to C. Knight Watson, Soc. of Antiq. Ms. 250*).

More recent excavations have been carried out on High Peak, by Carter in the 1920s and by Pollard in 1961 and 1964.   Pollard established that the original construction was neolithic, possibly a causewayed camp, radio-carbon dated to around 3000 BC.   The pottery was much later in date as Hutchinson recognised, and has been identified as Mediterranean amphora ware of around 500 AD.   (Pollard 1965, 1966).

New railway project. *Saturday September 23, 1871.*   Railway meeting in the Town Hall, Mr. Kennaway MP in the chair.   The Trustees of the Manor, who are mainly promoting it, were present.   The terms seem fair and liberal and I trust that the project may be carried out. (*See July 6, 1874*).   The authorised capital is £66 000 in 6 600 shares of £10 each *and* the greater part of the money is already secured.   The line will leave the London and South-western near Feniton and come down by Ottery, Tipton, Harpford Wood, Bowd and Bulverton to near Broadway. (*Diary*).   From some remarks in Lethaby's Sidmouth Journal for April 1865, it appears that five Acts of Parliament had been obtained in four years.   All of them however seemed rather intended to blind or mislead or decoy people into venturing their money instead of producing any substantial good.   All these schemes were promoted by strangers, sharp men of business, whose only aim, as soon became evident, was to prey upon the too easy and confiding inhabitants.   There was no resident gentleman who had sufficient influence or wealth to take the lead and direct the affairs of the place or act as a check against the machinations of the adventurers. (*History of Sidmouth IV, 175*).

Monday October 2, 1871.   Attended another railway meeting at the Town Hall, the vicar in the chair. The chief business was to appoint a committee to canvass the inhabitants for shares.   I was asked if I would join the committee.   I excused myself, first because I have come to the conclusion that the less people have to do with parish affairs the better for their peace and comfort, and secondly my studies and other occupations at home keep me fully employed and suit me better. (*Diary*).

Tumuli on Ottery East Hill and the Gray Stone.   *Tuesday October 10, 1871.* Though there was a cold north-east wind blowing, Mr. Heineken and myself drove to the top of Ottery East Hill, first to see if we could discover any outworks to Sidbury Castle as a protection against surprise on the Ottery side, and secondly to search the top of the hill for more tumuli.   We went to Sidford, then west along High street, then north along the lane behind Core Hill till we attained the ridge at A *on the map*. We discovered three small barrows where the heath and furze had been burnt off a portion of the hill at B.   The nearest, at seventy-three paces from the road, is five yards in diameter.   The next, touching it, is eight in diameter and the third, twenty-three paces further, is only three yards in diameter.   They are low and small and made of the soil of the spot.   They have all the appearance of being tumuli, though this could not be proved without examination. At C, down on the slope of the hill, we were told of a cairn of dry flints, or 'stone-burrough' as they are commonly called, and some others in the neighbourhood are said to have been destroyed. Going down the lane below A, we were shown the remains of the cairn D on the steep side of the hill but above the cultivated land among the heath and furze.

From A, proceeding northward along the high ridge, from which a splendid view towards the west is obtained and which everyone ought to *see*, we looked for some outwork where the lane from Sidbury Castle comes up, but in vain. Further north a large grass field called 'The Plain' was pointed out to us, on which the soldiers at one period used to exercise. We walked over this and remarked seven low mounds rather oval in figure. At first we thought they might be tumuli, but from their form and from the order in which they are placed, being three on the south side of the field and four on the north, we gave up the idea. The cairn E we had discovered before (see July 20, 1869). It is apparently of dry flints and a little on the side next the road has been dug down. The next, F, on the open heath was a new discovery. It is also of flints, and also on the west side unfortunately some of it has been dug down and taken away. The iron pits over Lincombe Farm I had visited before, but I was anxious to take Mr. Heineken to *see* them. I think there cannot be less than from eighty to a hundred in two or three groups. They are however much smaller pits than those we examined near Wolford Lodge (October 1862 and July 24, 1865). We then passed the

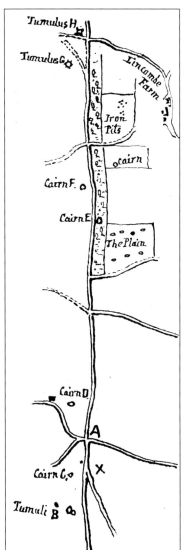

71/10/10 Tumuli on Ottery East Hill (Diary)

two tumuli G and H and turned eastward down the steep lane passing Lincombe Farm. A mile further, at a fork in the roads, we stopped to examine 'Gray Stone', as it is called. I made a sketch of this about 1863, but I see that some Goth with a heavy hammer has *since* struck off the north-east corner. (*Diary*). The maenhir, (literally Longstone), the single column or block of stone, where found on the wild hills gener-

ally commands a certain amount of respect, if not of superstitious fear, from the country people. This feeling may have come down from a very remote origin, but in some districts it no doubt exists in the present day. About half a mile to the north-west of Sidbury on what is now cultivated land,

71/10/10 *Gray Stone, Sidbury.* (Hist of Sid. I,119)

and at a bifurcation of the lane leading to Lincombe Farm, there is a large block of sandstone commonly known as Gray Stone. It measures five feet long by four broad and is about eighteen inches out of the ground on the north side. Some Goth or Vandal, about the year 1870, knocked off the north-east corner with a sledge hammer. The figure in the sketch has placed the point of his stick on the spot. This is one of

71/10/10 *Gray Stone. Between Sidbury and Lincombe.*   Not Dated. (DRO, Z19/2/8E/181)

the stones believed by the peasantry to turn itself round three times, or to go down into the valley to drink, when it hears the clock strike twelve at midnight.   It may be remarked that Mr. Trollope, in his *Summer in Brittany*, mentions the same superstition connected with the large blocks of stone as existing in that part of France amongst the Keltic population.   We may infer therefore that it has come down from ancient British times.   (*History of Sidmouth I, 119*).

We drove home through Sidbury and Sidford, much pleased at having added five tumuli to our list.   (*Diary*).

Sidbury parish register again.   *Tuesday October 24, 1871.*   The Rev. Mr Parker, curate of Sidbury, came to me with part of the burnt parish register and began to tell me a long story about its destruction twenty years ago.   I told him I knew all about it, that I lamented over it at the time, that I urged the late vicar to try and get it repaired, that I had written one or two articles in *Notes and Queries* in 1854 how singed vellum could be restored, and that I had corresponded with the late Dean of Exeter on the subject.   If the Sidbury people would undertake the work, I said I would write to Mr Haydon of the Record Office (son of Haydon the painter) and enquire for a competent person who would smooth out the injured leaves and rebind the two volumes.   (*Diary*).

Sidbury Castle and the Bunch.   *Thursday October 26, 1871.*   Some new question relative to the antiquities of this neighbourhood is frequently starting up, and although Mr. Heineken and myself have visited Sidbury Castle times out of number we resolved to go again.   Sidbury Castle occupies the crown of a hill semi-detached from a spur of Ottery East Hill called, I believe, the Clump or Mump, A *on the plan*, or more commonly the Bunch.   We thought that if Sidbury Castle had ever been besieged, an enemy might have posted himself on A opposite the entrance, to watch the occupiers of the camp.   We found *it* an admirable position.   At B there is a long hollow like a fosse, partly natural, but perhaps utilised as a protection.   All along at C there is a steep bank perhaps fifty feet deep with swampy ground at the bottom.

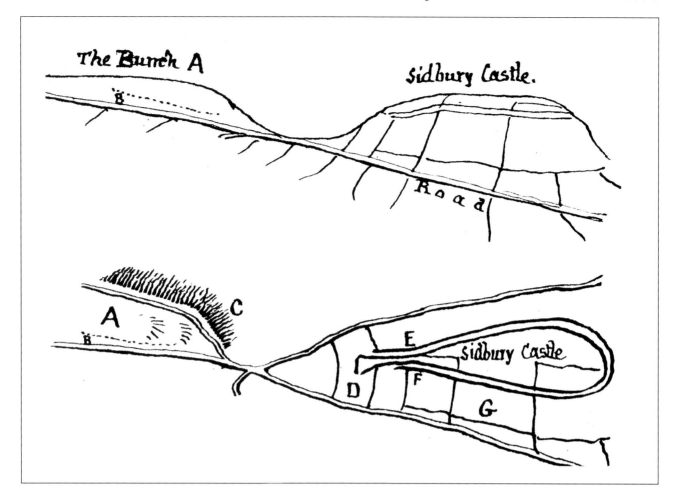

This is natural but may have been improved by artificial means. It is easy to imagine that this place had been fortified. We found two beach pebbles in the lane near C, exactly like the sling stones in the camp and probably the same thing. In the field D in front of the entrance we picked up seven sling stones, one split and broken by the violence with which it had been hurled, and two were large (one a Budleigh pebble), much larger than the usual size. At E on the outside of the outer agger, I measured the steep banks and made it forty-two feet. F is the spot where the cavern full of sling stones was found in March 1864 and where many still lie about. It is fifty-two feet from the hedge. In the steep field G, only partly cultivated, we picked up eight sling stones, one starred and fractured. I also met with two flint flakes, each showing the 'bulb of percussion'.

We then went on to Ottery East Hill, drove northward and once more examined the iron pits. I dug in the bottom of one and came to yellow clay and flints. By some mistake, the man drove the carriage away out of sight and we walked nearly a mile, full of uncertainty, before we found him. We got in and went further north to examine the hill, though it was getting dusk. We passed along Chineway Head to Hunter's Lodge or Hare and Hounds and then returned via Sidbury and Sidford. (*Diary*).

71/10/26 Sidbury Castle
(Diary)

Above left: 71/10/26 *The large sling stone.* (Hist of Sid. I,43)
Above right: 71/10/26-3 *Section through AB.* (Hist of Sid. I,43)

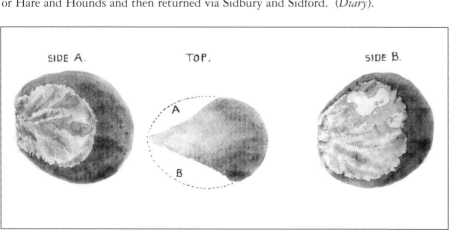

71/10/26 *Broken Sling-stone from field G, south flank of Sidbury Castle. From the point of impact it is splintered off on both sides, A and B.* (Hist of Sid. I,42a)

71/11/6 (Diary)

November the fifth 1871. *Monday November 6, 1871.* For several years past the rioting of the lower orders on the evening of the fifth has been a disgrace to the place. They have taken the occasion as an excuse for carrying about tar barrels and fireballs, and have used these dangerous things to alarm and even threaten any persons against whom they had any supposed cause of offence. The fireball is made of tarred cord or old rope dipped in pitch and bound together with wire *and* is about as large as a man's head. A chain about a yard long is attached to it, by which it is held. When this is lighted and swung about it becomes a formidable weapon, and when a dozen rough fellows in masks parade the streets with them, striking at doors and shutters and destroying the paint with hot pitch, threatening people if they interfere with them, they make rather a striking show. Fifty policemen we had down from Exeter and a hundred special constables sworn in. This force overawed them. They however, burnt a linhay in a field a short distance from the town. (*Diary*).

Margaret of Goole stranded. *Saturday November 18, 1871.* On the 4th during a south-westerly gale, the Margaret of Goole, a Dutch-built cutter, was driven ashore a mile east of Sidmouth. Crew two men and a boy, who took to the rigging when she struck. The men got to land, but a heavy sea shook the boy out of the rigging onto the beach *and he was* much hurt by the fall. She lay there high and dry, *and* on the 13th I walked over and looked at her. She was laden with wheat, which was saved, *and* was sold at auction. Mssrs Ellice and Maeer bought her for fifty pounds. Today they launched her *when* the steam tug came and towed her to Teignmouth. The tug came three times *at* five pounds a time, *and* this and the launching I am told cost thirty pounds. Report says that a hundred and twenty pounds were offered for her at Teignmouth, but refused. (*Diary*).

71/11/18 *The Margaret of Goole, blown on shore near Salcombe mouth, November 4, 1871. Sketched on the spot.* (DRO, Z19/2/8E/205)

Sidmouth Limekilns. *Monday December 4, 1871.* Went down to the beach west of Sidmouth and made a drawing of the old limekilns, most of which has fallen into the sea, together with much cliff and the steep road up which the limestone from Babbacombe used to be drawn in carts to be turned into lime. We have had no lime burnt at Sidmouth since 1855. All the lime I used in building the Old Chancel, I was obliged to get from the kilns at Budleigh Salterton. (*Diary*). See the view of the same made June 3, 1851 and compare the difference. Quantities of the cliff have fallen into the sea with half the limekilns. Also the road washed away and a step ladder used instead during the *last* twenty years. (*Sketchbook E*).

71/12/4 *Remains of the old limekilns near the Chit Rocks, Sidmouth. Dec. 4.1871.* (DRO, Z19/2/8E/207)

1872

Third fossil tooth. *February 1872.   Illustrated is the* portion of tooth, much worn, found on Sidmouth beach about a mile westward from the town and nearly opposite where the first was procured.   *It was* bought by Mr. Aubrey Strahan FGS, for 2/6 *and* in March 1883 he gave it to the Exeter Museum.   (*History of Sidmouth I, 23c*).

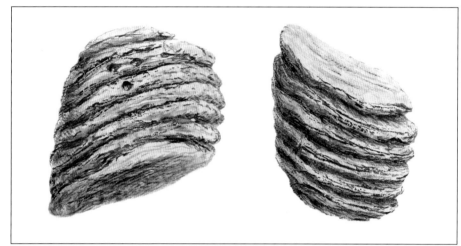

Right: 72/2/?   *Portion of tooth*   (Hist of Sid. I,23c)
Far right: 72/2/?   *Another view* (Hist of Sid. I,23c)

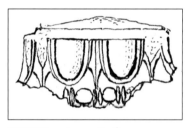

72/2/17   Acropolis fragment (Diary)

Acropolis fragment. *Saturday February 17, 1872.*   The Buttermers at the Elms, amongst a number of other curiosities they have, showed me a fragment of one of the Temples on the Acropolis at Athens.   It is about nine inches long and five deep *and* it appears to have come from the moulding under the feet of the Caryatids in the temple of the Erectheum.   Captain Henry Harston, Mrs. Buttermer's brother (with whom I was at school at Tiverton circa 1824), visited the Piraeus in the Brittania in 1831 and went to the Acropolis at Athens, *where* a Turk broke off this piece of marble and gave it to him.   If it were mine I should take it to the British Museum.   There is no doubt about the beauty of the work (see November 8, 1876). (*Diary*).

72/2/27   Roman coin   (Hist of Sid. I,96)

Roman coin from Sidmouth beach. *Tuesday February 27, 1872.*   This morning a boy called Thomas Salter brought me a second brass, considerably rubbed but with a fat face on the obverse somewhat resembling Vespasian.   He told me he had found it on the sand about three hundred yards west of the old limekilns.   I gave him sixpence for it. (*Diary*).

Safe keeping. *Wednesday March 6, 1872.*   Went over to Belmont Villa, Dawlish, for a few days.   Took coach to Exeter *and* went into the museum in Queen Street. Enquired what are the regulations with respect to readers in the library and whether there is a good supervision over the readers, so that readers, either by carelessness or through design could not have the opportunity of injuring books or manuscripts which they might consult.   For nearly forty years I have had the entrée into the British Museum reading room and in spite of the number of attendants and the care taken for the safety of the books much mischief has occasionally been done.   Books have been purloined and the thieves punished before the magistrates, and I remember a case where a reader was detected cutting passages out of a book in order to save himself the trouble of copying.   According to my present will, my manuscript

History of Sidmouth is left to the British Museum, but if due care is taken for its safety, and if there are good guarantees for the permanence of the Exeter Museum, I should prefer leaving it to the latter.

At the St Thomas's Station I fell in with Mr. W.G.Ormerod, now of Teignmouth but formerly of Chagford, who promoted the restoration of the Shilstone cromlech. (*Diary*).

Roundabout return. *Saturday March 9, 1872.* Returned to Sidmouth by a very pleasant route in fine weather. Went by rail to Starcross, *where* men are now employed in making a double line instead of a single one as hitherto. Took a boat for a shilling and had a pleasant run down to Exmouth. The sailors told me that there is about twenty feet of water in the channel near Exmouth at low water spring tides and that they do not think the channel is filling up, but they think that the rest of the river is getting shallower. The sand banks seem to be accumulating. As the conveyance to Budleigh Salterton would not start for an hour and a half, I started and walked all the way to Sidmouth. (*Diary*).

Tidwell to Littleham. *Thursday March 21, 1872.* The weather has been drier latterly and Mr. Heineken and myself have been looking out for a day suitable to make the first antiquarian excursion of the season. This morning there was a north-east wind and *it was* somewhat cool, but the sky was cloudless and the sun hot. Reasoning from analogy and probability, Mr. Heineken has been disposed to think that, first*ly*, Woodbury Castle is too far from the sea to observe the approach of an enemy from that hill fortress, and secondly that it would be necessary in common prudence *for* the occupiers of that station *to* keep watch on the coast and mouth of the River Exe. He thought it likely that if we examined the southern end of the Woodbury range well, where the ridge of the hill runs out to the cliff between Budleigh Salterton and Exmouth, we might hope to find traces of some camp or outpost on the edge of the cliff in connection with Woodbury Castle, from which intelligence could have been transmitted. In these views I concurred.

We drove over Peak Hill, passed Otterton *and* Budleigh and stopped for a few minutes at Tidwell to see the alterations recently made which I noticed when I returned home on the 9th (see June 7, 1855). The farmhouse, the old dwelling of the Arscotts I presume, is gone and two new cottages dated 1868 occupy the place. The great brick house just beyond has become the farmhouse. The fishponds across the road have been mostly drained and many sad changes made, *though* the terraces in the orchard may still be traced

We passed Knowle and looked north up the road towards the Daleditch of the Otterton Cartulary, now misspelled Daylidgh. Attained the ridge of the hill where there is a fine view over the Exe valley, stopped to examine the Budleigh Salterton pebble bed in the gravel pit at this point *and* then went towards the cliff. About a quarter of a mile from the gravel pit there is a very conspicuous tumulus, visible both on the Sidmouth and on the Exmouth sides of the hill to great distances. In modern times a trench has been cut round it. It seems to be composed of peat earth and pebbles, the soil of the hill, but the interior does not seem to have been examined. The diameter, measuring outside the trench from where the mound begins to rise (between the two figures in the sketch) was sixty feet *and* the height about five. It would be very interesting to find a thumb flint or arrow head or flint flake here because this is not in the flint district like Broad Down, but the wind was so strong and so cold that we could not delay to look. It is useless to search for spherical sling-stones here because all the pebbles of the hill (unlike Broad Down) are round. We then went out to the last field near the cliff and ate our sandwiches in a warm corner in the sun, enjoying the splendid view towards Dawlish, Teignmouth, Babbacombe, the Ore Stone and Berry Head, all of which were before us, and watched the manoeuvres of several vessels making for the mouth of the River Exe. How can people fritter away their days in wearisome idleness when so much enjoyment awaits them on the wild hills?

We then examined the crown of the hill which rises all the way from the gravel pit to the cliff, so that a most extensive prospect is obtained on all sides, both inland and towards the sea. Such an advantageous point could never have been overlooked or neglected, either by the holders of Woodbury Castle or by the Count of the Saxon Shore.

72/3/21   (Diary)

Mr. Heineken remembers that forty years ago this place was called 'West Down Beacon', so that there was probably an ancient beacon here, as well as at the mouth of the river where 'Beacon Place', Exmouth, stands; but we hoped to find the remains of earthworks, as of a small camp or outpost. There are some hedges enclosing a piece of ground where there was a look-out station at the commencement of the present century when a French invasion was apprehended, but these hedges do not appear to occupy the place of any ancient earthworks. We crossed and re-crossed all the ground for some distance but could not discover any inequalities or undulations as if aggers or fosses had been levelled or filled in. It seems scarcely likely that the cliff should have fallen away so much as to have carried any former works into the sea? This has well nigh happened at High Peak certainly, but there is no evidence to go by here. The sky became overcast, and one or two smart snow storms fell, so that we were fain to desist.

72/3/21   *Littleham Church*
(Diary)

We went on and looked at Littleham Church. The oldest part is the chancel where there are two arches, the mouldings plain chamfer of two orders carried from the floor to the top without capitals. The rest is perpendicular, with barrel roofs. There are some fragments of good old coloured glass in the north aisle amongst which is a portrait with a cap on like those in representations of Henry VII, the old painting for instance in Kensington Palace. There is a carved oak screen all across, with colouring and gilding on it. In the south aisle of the chancel there are monuments to Lord Nelson's widow, etc., *and at the* east end of the north aisle, called Spratshayes aisle, are Drake monuments. On the south side *there is* a coloured window to Captain Agassis and his wife. *There are* five bells in the tower.

Returning home it snowed furiously and was very cold. We could scarcely have chosen a worse day and yet we enjoyed it. (*Diary*).

Church pinnacles again. *Thursday April 4, 1872.* Attended a vestry meeting *and* produced a model of the proposed new pinnacles for the corners of the church tower. This subject has been talked of so long that I am becoming tired of it and care little whether it is carried out or not. I suggested it last year and made the model, but it was then received indifferently. It was even sharply criticised and condemned by some wiseacres who did not know a pinnacle from a handspike. (*Diary*).

72/4/4   *The church tower as it is* and *as proposed to be.*
(Hist of Sid. IV,121)

Broad Down. *Wednesday April 10, 1872.* Mr. Heineken and myself, wishing to look up some of our old haunts on Broad Down, started at eleven. We went over the old stone bridge at Holway Foot near the Salcombe Fields to Stephen's Cross (Carfoix, near the bottom of Trow Hill), up Trow Hill and after proceeding about two miles turned northward towards Long Chimney. Here the horse cast a shoe so we turned back a mile out of our way and drove to the Three Horseshoes Inn, near which there is a smith's forge. This however gave us the opportunity of again walking over the Cross-dyke running over the fields to the north of the Inn. The plough is doing its best to level the agger, once from twelve to fifteen feet high as some old men told us some years ago. We hunted about for sling stones and flint flakes in the fields and found many, one or two of which we brought away as specimens *though* I am always loathe to take away these things as I think they lose their value by removal. I cannot doubt that these are genuine sling stones, first because they are all so exactly the size, shape and character as those found in the cave in the agger at Sidbury Castle, about which there can be no doubt. Secondly, because I have no way of accounting for the presence of these oviform beach pebbles lying on the ground so high above the sea, and in some cases so far inland, except by supposing that they had been carefully collected by the ancient inhabitants and then distributed either at their enemies or at wild beasts. Dr. Kendrick of York Museum asserts that we have no evidence to prove that the ancient Britons used the sling. That the Romans and the subsequent possessors of the soil did, we have abundant proof, *but* this point can only be fully ascertained by constant observation on the interiors of undoubted British tumuli.

We now turned our attention to what I have before called a sunk road. It runs east and west through the grass field to the west of the Three Horseshoes, at about fifty yards north of the public road and parallel with it. Whether this was ever a wide ditch or any other work of defence connected with the Cross-dyke I cannot with any degree of confidence say. I have not detected any ditch or sunk road of similar character in the field on the south side of the road. Thus done, we turned back and veered away northwest a mile or two to Rakeway Bridge, then eastward and had our luncheon on the southern verge of Broad Down. Like giants refreshed, we searched over the field A where I had found the two 'thumb flints' on the first of last June. We saw several sling stones and flakes of black flint, easily discerned among the white chert of the hill. Then on to tumulus B. On this Mr. Heineken turned up the 'thumb flint' last June the first. Having taken light tools, I set to work on the crown of what remains and raked the loosened earth well. I found nothing but a sling stone partly washed clean by the winter's rain., but it was a sling-stone that surprised us both. It is an Aylesbeare Hill pebble from beyond the River Otter. The sling-stones are commonly the flint or chert pebbles such as abound on the beach from Sidmouth eastwards. One of the missiles that we met with on the 26th of last October at Sidbury Castle was an Aylesbeare Hill stone, perhaps hurled at the camp by some enemy from Woodbury Castle, and the circumstance astonished us a good deal at the time. The finding of another today, which is a dark red stone from the Silurian or Devonian deposit of the Budleigh pebble bed, still further removed from its original place, furnished us with more food for reflection. It is true that such pebbles are to be met with on the beach, but they are so sparse and so few that I can scarcely take this circumstance into account.

Leaving this we proceeded towards Blackbury Castle, for some labouring men told us they had seen many round pebbles in the fields in that direction when ploughing. We hunted over the large field C but saw only a few, all precisely like the others in character, and scarcely a single flake. I found however, a stone hammer rudely chipped out of a flint the size of an orange. The bruises on one side are very plain where it had been used. I have little doubt that it is a genuine hammer, but as I did not find it in the tumulus perhaps it is not worthy of Exeter Museum. The vitreous glaze of antiquity is strong upon it. I also found a fragment of a Budleigh pebble which had been as large as the hammer before being broken and conclude it had been a heavy missile.

Then we turned back and steered northwards all along the eastern side of the Down, looking into those wonderfully deep chasms as we passed them. The road, or rather track, was so rough and full of ruts and holes that the carriage could not proceed with us, so we were obliged to walk and *let* the carriage jostle on the best way it could. Last year I remarked some springs of water on this side of the Down and I thought that possibly the ancient inhabitants might have built their wigwams near them, and if so heaps of kitchen middens might be found under the turf. I dug in one or two places but had not the time to proceed far enough. After that we went out beyond the northern hedge on the Down to look again at the tumuli. I was grieved at the rough and unscientific way some of them had been opened and the way in which they had been left. Since I was here last year I was sorry to see that the circle of detached stones round the most northerly tumulus but one has been carried away, perhaps to build some wall or mend some road. We got over the hedge and looked at the others but could not espy a flake or sling stone upon them

We drove home *with* Roncombe Gurt on our right, down to Sidbury and were in Sidmouth by eight. (*Diary*).

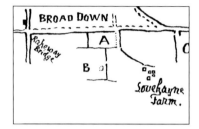

72/4/10 Site of tumulus near Rakeway Bridge (Diary)

72/4/10 *Flint drill or borer – found by me in field north of Stone-Borough plot, April 10,1872.* (Hist of Sid. I,121)

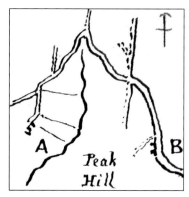

72/4/16   *Peak Hill*   (Diary)

72/4/16   (Diary)

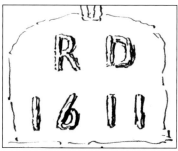

72/4/16   (Diary)

72/4/16   *Tidwell*   (Diary)

72/4/16   *Arscott & St Cleere at Tidwell*   (Diary)

Knowle Hill and vicinity. *Tuesday April 16, 1872.*   The weather being fine, we determined on going again to Knowle Hill. Whilst mounting Peak Hill we stopped at the two cottages where the road is steepest, at B, and enquired for a man named Pyle who some years ago found two coins in the field at A. He *now* only had one, apparently of James I and of silver *and* on the reverse side is a harp. He was glad to sell it to Mr. Heineken for a shilling. We then went on and stopped at the bottom of Otterton, *where* there is an ancient-looking garden near the river on the north side of the road. We entered it at an old doorway of Salcombe sandstone, formerly much used; the old quarries may still be seen to the east and south of Salcombe Regis church. Exeter Cathedral is said to have been built from there. Outside the west wall near the river are the initials of Richard Duke, 1611, as sketched in the margin.

We stopped again at Tidwell and saw Mr. Bastin the tenant, a gentlemanly and intelligent young man, *who* took us across the road to the spot where the swamp had been drained. There is an old culvert that I copied and a little further on the well itself as here in the margin. It is now merely a spring rising through a hole in the ground, roughly walled round and from fifteen to eighteen inches in depth. The water now escapes over a small weir or ledge, *but* whether it still ebbs and flows as of old, Mr. Bastin did not know. We went to the great brick house and in the hall he showed us some scraps of old oak removed from the other when it was pulled down in 1865. I annex the coat of arms, being the second branch of the Arscott of Annery with the St. Cleere shield of pretence. The majority of coats I do not recognise; they may not be Devonshire families. The whole affair has been fresh painted, and mostly in the wrong colours.

We then made for the tumulus on Knowle Hill. There was a bright sun but a cold north wind. We sat on the south side of it enjoying the splendid view and eating our dinner. We searched the surface of the mound well and dug slightly in places but were not so fortunate as to find a flint flake. I was the more *hopeful* because this is not in a flint district. We then searched the ground as far as the cliff edge but to no purpose. It is useless to look for sling stones for all the pebbles of the district would answer that purpose. We then proceeded to the point of the cliff, searching the ground but to no purpose. This commanding site would never have been forgotten by the holders of Woodbury Castle as a look-out station, *as* it not only commands the sea but nearly all the land *thereabouts*. We measured the flagpole there, by an angle of forty-five degrees, and made it forty feet high.

This done, we directed our course inland to examine some inequalities which attracted our notice many years ago on the open moor but which we could not then pursue as we were going to measure Woodbury Castle (May 27, 1858). We got on the heath and then descended to the mill above Dayligh, or anciently Dalditch or Daleditch. I presume this is the place mentioned in the Otterton Cartulary circa 1260, *though* there is however another Daleditch near Luppit. Continuing north we came to a pond or reservoir where the water has been stopped back, and a short distance above this are three barrows close together in a line nearly north and south (*see map May 3, 1872*). They have been tampered with but not properly examined. I should like to try the ground in this neighbourhood and see whether traces of hut circles or other ancient habitations could not be discovered, and possibly kitchen middens or rubbish heaps. From the east side of the three barrows we proceeded north up an old trackway which pointed towards Woodbury Castle, but veering away towards Yattington (or Yettington) we came upon the ridges over the moor of which we were in search. As we looked westwards we could see them running over the hill, like an agger and ditches. We noticed them May 27, 1858, when we were going to measure Woodbury Castle and have often talked of examining them. When I looked at this work today, I first thought of the 'Duke of York's Ditch' on the Malvern Hills, which I traced many years ago, and then of Offa's Dyke which that Saxon king made on the western marches of Mercia to keep the Welsh in check somewhere about 790. I have a sketch of part of Offa's Dyke which I made so long ago as May 16, 1840, when I was making a walking tour through the midland counties. Being late, we were now obliged to turn homewards, but as this earthwork looks important we resolved to devote another day to it soon. Work, instead of diminishing always seems to increase. (*Diary*).

Fourth fossil tooth. *Monday April 22, 1872.* Gave four shillings to William Ware, a lad of about sixteen, for an immense fossil tooth he procured from the bottom of the River Sid last Tuesday. He told me he was wading in the water for lamprey eels when he found it. At this time of year it is usual for the fishermen to seek lampreys (which look something like eels) in the river. They put them alive into a bottle of water and preserve them as a good bait for whiting pollock. I then saw the father and he corroborated the story about the finding of the tooth *and* I can have no reason to doubt it. Unfortunately the tooth has been very much abraded by the gravel of the river, though there can be no question as to what it is. This is interesting from a geological point of view, for I imagine it must have come from the bed of alluvium that lies at the bottom of this valley, from fifteen to twenty feet thick and composed of sub-angular pieces of flint and chert, gravel, sand and earth. The tooth must have been immense, and the mammoth or other animal to which it belonged of huge proportions *since* what remains of it weighs nearly 12lbs 53/4ozs. I shall give it to the Exeter Museum. This is the fourth tooth from the neighbourhood. Number 1, dredged up from the 'Tortoiseshell Reef' a mile or more west of Sidmouth in February 1869, weighed four pounds *and* I gave to the Exeter Museum. Number 2 was found by a Mrs. Walker on Sidmouth beach in January 1871. She took it to Liverpool. Number 3, a round piece about the size of an orange, *was* all that remained of a tooth found on the beach near the same reef in February 1872. Mr. Aubrey Strakan of Blackmore Hall bought it for 2s. 6d. Number 4 is the great one. (*Diary*).

72/4/22 Rubbing of fossil tooth found Tuesday April 16 1872, in the bed of the river Sid at Sidmouth by William Ware, a fisherman who sold it to P O Hutchinson, who destines it for the Exeter Museum (Hist of Sid. I,23d)

East Budleigh Common. *Friday May 3, 1872.* Acting upon the resolution made on the 16th of last month, Mr. Heineken and myself went to Woodbury Hill today. We drove over Peak Hill, through Otterton and reached Yettington without delay. At the west end of the village we took the left hand road which leads over the wild hill direct to Lympstone. On arriving upon the open heath the commencement of the earthworks is soon seen on the left hand or south side of the road, *though* the actual commencement is obliterated by enclosures and disturbances of the ground. There is the hedge and ditch, A of the section *annexed*, and the two ditches with the hedge between them, B. These run westwards nearly parallel with each other for about a thousand feet, when a branch of the road takes a turn to the south. Here there are three small circular plantations, and the earthwork B abuts against one of them and is lost. On the other side, where it ought to reappear, it seems to have been obliterated by the road, and the road, in short, seems to occupy the place of it. The southern earthwork A however, continues all along over the hill for a mile or more, until it reaches point C (in the plan) where the land on the south is enclosed and cultivated. Here the agger A (in the sections) seems to have been made use of to form the hedge on the south side of the road, and so continues onwards. As the hedge H proceeds in the same direction across the field, one is almost invited to imagine that even this hedge may be a continuation of the same structure. This earthwork certainly has all the appearance of antiquity, whatever it really may have been. It is hard to resist the conviction that it was a great cross-dyke drawn over the ridge of the hill from the Yettington valley on the east

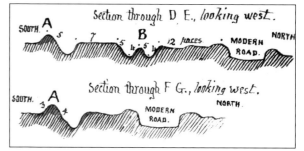

72/5/3 (Diary)

to that of Lympstone on the west; and as to its purpose, it looks as if it had been an advanced work made by the occupiers of Woodbury Castle as a check against the advance of marauders that might land at Exmouth. As the Danes are known to have frequently entered the River Exe and to have committed great devastation along its banks, it is difficult to avoid the conclusion that it had been made by the Saxons at a time when those pirates were infesting the coast. This work is worth examination. Towards its western end, on its north side, there are a number of oval, square and circular pits and platforms. I believe these are the 'soldiers pits', made at the same time and for the same purpose by General Simcoe as those on Aylesbeare Hill.

Much of the massive linear earthwork, its bank up to six metres wide, can still be traced alongside the minor road from Yettington to Lympstone. It certainly appears to be an ancient construction though whether prehistoric or Dark Age is open to question, but with the major ditch on the north side it would seem unlikely to have been an outwork of Woodbury Castle. The two enormous fir-topped tumuli a short distance from Woodbury Castle remain unexcavated but are presumably burial mounds (Grinsell: Woodbury Common N. 1 and 2). The sketch map

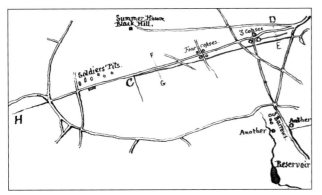

72/5/3   (Diary)

is also of interest in showing five barrows on East Budleigh Common not apparently recorded elsewhere.

Having plenty of time, we drove northwards to Woodbury Castle. In places there were patches of furze in full bloom, acres and acres of it, all one splendid mass of yellow. I never saw it finer. In some places also there were large gravel pits in the side of the hill where good sections of the Budleigh Pebble Bed could be obtained. We had not been to Woodbury Castle for fourteen years. We found that the keeper's cottage had been 'done up', as they say, and looked new. The keeper's wife and children were there, of the name of Woodleigh. They had not heard of any antiquities found there. We walked around the rampart, over our old ground *and* I measured the slope of the agger on the south side and made it forty feet. On the east side it is more. On the slope of the hill to the north-east is a spring of water with a bank or covered way running down towards it called 'Red Slew', where tradition says a battle took place and where the blood of the slain tinged the water. On looking at it in the present day, I should say that the water is strongly impregnated with oxide of iron and is very red in consequence.

We proceeded northwards to the great tumulus, 114 feet in diameter and about 15 feet high, *which* appears never to have been disturbed. Perhaps it was a Teut hill, speculum or look-out station, and not a burial place. Thence north-east to another tumulus, not so large, *which* measured 78 feet in diameter. We espied several ancient trackways across the moor and we decided we ought to walk down them and trace them out. They might lead to important points or to hut circles, refuse heaps or the like. Work never ends, but it was now time to return home. We descended the Hockland valley and through the hamlet of that name to Newton Poppleford, then up the long hill and so to Sidmouth. (*Diary*).

Sid valley. *Wednesday May 15, 1872.* Owing to the finding of the great fossil tooth in the bed of the River Sid (April 22), I walked up the river today in order to examine the banks. The winter floods were unusually high and have washed out great portions of the banks on both sides. In this valley there is a bed of alluvium lying to a depth of from fifteen to twenty feet above the red rock. It is composed of sand, gravel and sub-angular stones, in some places cemented together by earth or clay. I

72/5/15 *Sidmouth Valley* (Diary)

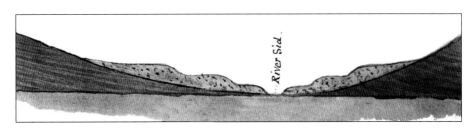

examined the banks all the way up, nearly as far as Sidbury. I got over the parapet on the north side of Sidford Bridge and on looking under the bridge I observed that at some period since its first erection, probably a long time ago, it had been widened several feet on the north side. I observed also that they are engaged in building the chancel of Sidford church, the nave having been erected four or five years ago. Following the river through the fields, I searched over the banks of gravel and stones that the floods had scattered about, but was not fortunate enough to discover any indication of a tooth or fossil bone, or worked flint. I was surprised to see the number of logs and trunks of trees lying about that had been uncovered and washed out, and portions of others partly exposed. They looked very old, but I presume not as old as the drift. One of them however, struck me more than the rest, a log of oak about eight or ten feet long and eighteen inches through, as black as ink, all charcoal. The district below Ebdon Farm has always been called 'Burnt Oak'. Was an oak ever struck here by lightning and burnt? I have now been told that the Manor mill below Sidbury was burnt about 1800. (*Diary*).

72/5/15 *Burnt Oak* (Diary)

Woollcombe manuscript. *Wednesday May 22, 1872.* Went into Exeter to examine two or three things in the Museum. Procured two of the new catalogues of the library, one for Mr. Heineken and one for myself. Then went to the Institution in the Cathedral Yard to examine the Woollcombe manuscript, being a work in two volumes quarto. There is a great deal in one volume about cromlechs, with sketches and plans, and in the other about many of the hill fortresses. I was not as satisfied with the inspection as I had hoped. *(Diary).* *Nevertheless, Woollcombe's unpublished manuscript 'Some Account of the Fortified Hills in the County of Devon', 1839, has become a valuable record of many archaeological sites in Devon now damaged or destroyed.*

Enquiries at Seaton. *Friday June 14, 1872.* Having heard of some antiquities eastward, Mr. Heineken and myself started off to make enquiries. We stopped at the Three Horseshoes, where we were on the 10th of last April, for we had heard of a bronze celt. Mr. Carter, the tenant, was weeding corn in the middle of the field at the north end of the cross-dyke, *so* I went to him and heard all the story. He said that last year he was digging earth in the ditch outside the hedge in the lane on the north side of the gate going into the field, at about sixty paces north of the old barn (now being removed), throwing the earth with his spade up onto the hedge. He threw the celt up with the earth, but did not see it at the time. The rain afterwards washed it clean when one of his men noticed a 'piece of old brass', but paid no regard to it and left it there. As we had charged him to preserve any pieces of old metal he might find (the proximity of the cross-dyke and Blackberry Castle being likely places) he went out and brought it into the house. After negotiating for a short time I bought it off him for two shillings, intending it for the Exeter Museum, but as Mr. Heineken had a fancy for it, I transferred it to him for the same sum and he will send it to the same place. There is no reason to doubt *Mr. Carter's* story or the genuineness of the celt. It is a flat piece of bronze about five sixteenths of an inch thick, four and a half inches long and two and three eighths of an inch wide at the widest end. It weighs seven and a quarter ounces. Its chief peculiarity is that it is marked on both sides with a number of longitudinal cuts or lines, perhaps intended for ornament. (I read a paper on it at the Athenaeum in Exeter on Thursday August 1, 1872, and then placed it in the Exeter Museum. *History of Sidmouth, I,63).*

We then went into the fields at the south end of the dyke across the road to see if any sling-stones could be found, as we had found them at the northern part before. We observed many and as the flints of the hill are angular they are apparent at first glance. I brought away three, one very large and two broken by force. Having satisfied our curiosity on this point we proceeded to the hills overlooking the Axe. We went through a field to Seaton Down and looked at the earthworks, *and on* returning by the field we saw two or three sling-stones, one very large. Thence we journeyed south towards Seaton, but we turned into a field to have our luncheon, for we were hungry and thirsty and it was very warm.

When we were on the beach, we saw the cone of Membury Castle, distant as they said twelve miles, crowned with trees rising up towards the north as per rude sketch. We examined the great mound on which a fort was built to keep off pirates. I made it a hundred and fifty paces in diameter and Mr. Heineken made it about twenty-five feet high, *though* they say it was once twenty feet higher. It is a heap of red earth *and* the esplanade is now carried over it. From this place we went to the river and crossed over by the ferry. At the ferry house we found an intelligent man called Stark, or Start. For some years we have tried to learn something definite concerning the great stone laid down between twenty and thirty years ago by some savants to mark the level of the spot, similar levels having been placed at intervals all across the county northward to the neighbourhood of Bridgewater. (The stone was placed here in 1838). It has been suspected that the land was slowly undergoing some changes of level, and by repeating the levels from time to time along these fixed points, any change will be ascertained. We found the stone inside the warehouse. We entered the western large door (shaded black) and found it at the right hand further corner. It was a block of granite measuring five and a half feet long, two feet four inches wide and apparently one and a half feet deep lying on the ground, or perhaps there is a bed of concrete under it. In the middle of its western or outer end there is inserted a brass or copper bolt, green with verdigris, about two inches in diameter, and from the centre of this I presume that the level was taken. We were both rather surprised

72/6/14-1 Map of vicinity of Three Horseshoes (Diary)

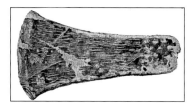

72/6/14 *Bronze celt* (Hist of Sid. I,63b)

72/6/14 *Membury Castle* (Diary)

72/6/14 *The mound of the old Fort, on the beach, looking towards the west.* (Diary)

72/6/14 *Ferry-house, warehouse, Haven cliff, and mouth of Axe River.* (Diary)

72/6/14   Warehouse stone
(Diary)

however, at not finding a horizontal cut across the head of this bolt, as usual in the Ordnance bench marks to mark the exact level. On scratching the bolt with my nail, I fancied I could feel an indentation, but I believe it was nothing but an accidental scratch. Perhaps, as afterwards suggested by Mr. Heineken, there may be a cap soldered on the head of the bolt to preserve such a cut from injury, if it should be there. To protect this stone from being meddled with, a massive arch of masonry has been turned over it. We could not learn where the next stone northward was placed. There is a copper bolt in the front of Axmouth Church (on tower) put there I believe by Ordnance surveyors, like those at Salcombe, Newton Poppleford and other places to make elevations above the sea, but whether this was in connection with the great stone we could not learn. We enquired for the 'bone bed' mentioned in geological books. The man believed it was nearly a mile to the east where the lias crops out and the undercliff comes down to the beach. The masonry and harbour works, promoted at great expense by the late Mr. Hallet, are being allowed to fall into disuse, as the mouth of the river is too narrow for ships to enter.

We were told that the 'Dungeon' of which we had heard was an old packhorse road between Seaton and Beer, now destroyed, and that 'Eye Well' was near it. We were also told that sometimes in the winter, traces may be observed of the square salt pans on the banks of marshes by the river. They have been pointed out to me at Starcross. Many years ago there was an old anchor with a long shank and of peculiar pattern dredged up off Seaton, of which Mr. Heineken sent an account (Lon. & Ed. Ph. Mag., X, 10). We were told that a similar one has been recently fished up off Beer. We enquired where 'Scale Wall' or 'Castellum Stead' might be, and whether it was the same with Hawkesdown Hill Camp, but we could not learn. Steadcombe is just below the camp.

We then drove to Colyford and Colyton but did not find the persons at home whom we sought, so we returned to Sidmouth. We did not get home till nine, having been out eleven hours. (*Diary*).

Lucky find. *Friday June 28, 1872.* Mr. Kirwan informs me that Mr. Drewe told him they had been pulling down an old house near the Grange and had found a wooden bowl containing twenty-seven Henry VII guineas. (*Diary*).

Sidbury Castle and Lincombe Farm iron pits. *Friday July 5, 1872.* Not having quite run out our course, and finding from twenty years experience and more that our antiquarian expeditions constitute a very pleasurable part of our existence, Mr. Heineken and myself started out again today. We first proceeded to Bunch, in front of the entrance to Sidbury Castle (see October 26, 1871). We wanted to re-examine the deep escarpment with the swamp at the bottom, thinking that if this place had ever been held by an enemy attacking the camp, probably the escarpment had been artificially made. We were soon convinced however, when we had picked our way all along its base and scrambled up into the lane above, that this precipitous bank of foxmould is due to the springs of water that come out between it and the red marl, and merely produce effects such as we see on the flanks of most of the hills in this neighbourhood. Thus satisfied we came away. We then searched over some plots of arable land below the road on the south side of the Bunch, to see if we could detect a chance beach pebble sling-stone, not however with much confidence as being rather far from the camp. We could not find any, though Mr. Heineken picked up a spherical white quartz pebble about three quarters of an inch in diameter from Aylesbeare Hill, and probably it may have been devoted to such a purpose..

72/7/5   Lincombe Farm iron pits
(Diary)

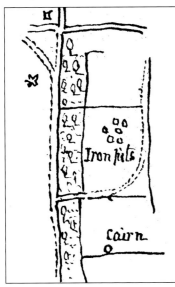

We then pushed on to have another examination of the iron pits over Lincombe Farm. We flattered ourselves with the hope that we might find the place of a forge or bloomery in the bottom of one of them - but no. Perhaps the smelting place was in the valley where wood and charcoal would be more abundant *and* we must enquire if any pieces of scoria or cinders have been met with there. We counted about a hundred pits. Digging to the bottom of several, we only met with pieces of bog iron or haematite. When smelted with charcoal, this yields malleable iron at once (see October 10, 1871).

Owing to the heat and the motion of the carriage the cork flew out of the beer jar, though the loss was not great *as* I had a wine bottle full of water with me. The exercise on the hills on a warm day in July causes a great waste of water in the system, *and* to replace this with beer would make me heavy and sleepy and unfit for work. We had our dinner in a field, enjoying the fine view towards Sidbury and could see the horizon of the sea over all the hills between Sidmouth and Beer Head. When this was over we descried a tumulus about a quarter of a mile to the south of the iron pits *so* we proceeded thither. It was a cairn of dry white flints, which we had not noted before, *and* measured fifty-seven feet in diameter. All the centre portion had been removed and what appeared to have been the large stones of the kist-vaen we found built into the base of the hedge close by. We were told that this hedge was made and the land reduced to cultivation about 1830. We then proceeded north to Chineway Head *where* we met two children with basketfulls of whortleberries. The vaccinium however is not so plentiful as it used to be, as much of the wild land has been reclaimed. We went north to look for a place called Belle Vue and a tumulus of which we had heard, but did not find either. The holes in the plantation at the north-west point of the hill are much like iron pits.

Returned home by the Hare and Hounds and Sidbury. I never saw the foxglove so abundant and so fine. It made some places quite crimson. (*Diary*).

Donations to Exeter Museum. *Tuesday July 16, 1872.* Went to Taunton to see my ancient friend G.E.Hamilton, formally an engineer and architect in Staffordshire. I took the opportunity of carrying into Exeter several objects of antiquity for the Museum, *including the* calcined bones from the Lovehayne tumulus, thumb flints or scrapers, bones from High Peak Hill, the Dunscombe skeleton and the contents of the stone coffin at Bury. Also six quartzite weapon points from Africa. *Whilst in Taunton, Hutchinson went to the museum there and was much impressed with the displays. He noticed a celt on display, 'very coppery' like the one recently found near the Three Horseshoes (see June 14):* And this suggests to me a new idea, namely that if these objects of this early type turn out to be of copper when further investigation has been made, I shall then venture to declare that there was a copper age preceding the age of bronze. The idea is my own and quite new, but more examples must be discovered before the point can be established. (*Diary*). *Hutchinson did indeed propose the idea of a 'Copper Age' at the next meeting of the Devonshire Association.*

Devonshire Association meeting 1872. *Thursday August 1, 1872.* *On July 30, Hutchinson went to Exeter for a week to attend the Devonshire Association meetings, staying in Dawlish.* Went again (*to Exeter*) after breakfast. During the day I read three papers, one was on the celt procured on June 14, the second on iron pits and the third was on the fossil teeth, especially the great one mentioned on April 22. After the readings were over, I deposited in the Museum the celt and teeth. (*Diary*).

Swan and Cygnet . *Friday August 2, 1872.* The work in Exeter being over, I did not leave Dawlish till the afternoon, and then set out to return to Sidmouth. As I passed Starcross, I could not help smiling at that strange piece of naval architecture called the Swan, with its boat in the same form. It is large enough to contain many people. It is generally anchored off Starcross where the owner, Mr. or Captain Peacock, lives. Some say it ought to be painted like a peacock instead of dead white. There are two sails for it resembling wings but it is a poor sailor. (*Diary*). *Launched in September 1860, Captain Peacock designed the 'Swan of the Exe' to accommodate fifteen persons 'in every possible comfort and luxury to be had afloat'. It was seventeen feet six inches long, seven feet six inches wide and sixteen feet from the waterline to the top of the head. The exterior was coloured 'perfectly white picked out with gilt' and the interior was 'completely lined with morocco or delicately painted'. The sketch shows the white Venetian blinds covering the windows and the gilt neck ring supporting 'the gilded blocks through which ran the halliards for hoisting and lowering sails which rise from the bird's sides shaped and proportioned according to the wings of a real swan'. To assist the sails there were oars and a rudder shaped like the tail of a fish, and for extra propulsion two levers through the hull worked the swan's feet. For added versatility this extraordinary vessel could double as a land carriage by substituting a coach box after unshipping the neck and adding a set of wheels. (Exeter and Plymouth Gazette September 15, 1860).*

72/8/2 *The Swan, Starcross.* (Diary)

Musbury Castle and Newenham Abbey. *Friday August 9, 1872.* When Mr. Heineken and myself went to Seaton on the 14th of June, we observed by means of a telescope that some men were ploughing part of the side and the interior of Musbury Castle. We resolved soon to go and search over the newly-turned ground for sling stones, flint flakes or something better if possible, *and* we went today. We ascended Trow Hill and stopped at the Three Horseshoes to enquire whether any more celts had been turned up. We *then* proceeded to Hangman's Stone, dismounted and examined it to reconsider whether it might have ever been one leg of a chromlech or 'Hanging Stone'. I never noticed till today that on the south side of it is an Ordnance bench mark, much overgrown with lichen. In a field on the opposite side of the road, or rather to the north-west, we observed a ridge like another cross-dyke, but there was not time to examine it today (*see August 23,1872*).

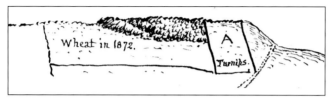

72/8/9   *The west flank of Musbury Castle.* (Diary)

We then drove on to Colyford, crossed the Axe Bridge, and on reaching Musbury passed close to the south side of the church and took the carriage to the top of the first field. There is a farm road all the way *to the summit* and if it had not been so steep we could have taken the carriage right into the camp. The sketch shows the west flank of Musbury Castle. Having first had our open-air dinner under the hedge we ascended the field A on foot. I found a black flint core and a sling stone coming up, *and* as all the stones of the hill are angular and of white chert, they are easily seen. Reaching the summit we searched it well from end to end. Of cores, flakes and sling stones we saw many *but* only brought away a few. The last time we were here was on Tuesday July 14, 1857, fifteen years ago! At that time I bought the tesserae and other remains of the Roman villa at Holcombe, near Uplyme, which were sold at auction in the vicarage at Musbury. I have not yet given these things to Exeter Museum but perhaps they are worth sending. All things considered and allowing for hedges and the great growth of bushes, the plan of the camp given in Mr. Davidson's *'British and Roman Remains in the vicinity of Axminster'* is substantially correct, *though* the square platform near the southern end (the most northerly work there) seems to have been obliterated. The brambles and ferns were so abundant at the entrances at the north-west corner that no examination could be made. The land was stated to belong to Mr. Wills of Borough House.

Having descended the hill we proceeded to Newenham Abbey. We passed Ash (June 14, 1857) where the great Duke of Marlborough was born and the brook called

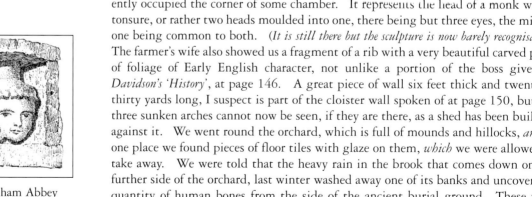

72/8/9   *Lower side of the bridge over War-lake – Aug. 9.1872* (Diary)

War Lake, and going on to within a mile of Axminster we turned down to the left. We reached two farm buildings, the higher and the lower, close to the railway, both of which are on the Abbey grounds, the latter among the ruins. But the ruins are gradually vanishing. The gable with the three-light window of the ancient chapel fell down about 1867, *and* a lithograph of this forms the frontispiece to Davidson's *'History of Newenham Abbey'*. By the side of the farmhouse door in the yard, an old stone fragment has been built in, a sort of corbel that had apparently occupied the corner of some chamber. It represents the head of a monk with a tonsure, or rather two heads moulded into one, there being but three eyes, the middle one being common to both. (*It is still there but the sculpture is now barely recognisable*). The farmer's wife also showed us a fragment of a rib with a very beautiful carved piece of foliage of Early English character, not unlike a portion of the boss given in Davidson's *'History'*, at page 146. A great piece of wall six feet thick and twenty or thirty yards long, I suspect is part of the cloister wall spoken of at page 150, but the three sunken arches cannot now be seen, if they are there, as a shed has been built up against it. We went round the orchard, which is full of mounds and hillocks, *and* in one place we found pieces of floor tiles with glaze on them, *which* we were allowed to take away. We were told that the heavy rain in the brook that comes down on the further side of the orchard, last winter washed away one of its banks and uncovered a quantity of human bones from the side of the ancient burial ground. These were placed in a box and re-buried, *but* I should like to go and dig about there.

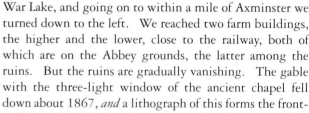

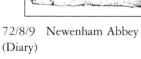

72/8/9   Newenham Abbey (Diary)

We did not leave for home until nearly seven. We heard that a boy had picked up a cannon ball at Musbury Castle and that it was at the toll-gate near Axe Bridge, *so* we halted and enquired for it. The woman brought it out, a four-pound shot. The boy (son of this woman) had been working on the hill, perhaps weeding turnips in the field we ascended, found this ball which he brought back. I examined it, *and* though much rusted *it* was tolerably sound *and* must date about the period of the Commonwealth. From Mr Davidson's little book on the siege of Axminster and from other sources, we learn that the Parliamentary troops once bombarded old Stedcombe House, and there is a field near Honeyditches called 'Bombshot' where they say the guns were planted. At another time some soldiers were posted on Musbury Castle and it is possible that some of the opposite party in the valley below had fired this four-pound shot at them. Mount House was also attacked. Query whether this was the house now called Mount Field House in Musbury.

When we *reached* Colyford it began to rain and continued all the way. We did not reach Sidmouth till half past nine. It was as cold as Autumn, and we warmed our fingers at the kitchen fire. (*Diary*).

Mysterious bank near Hangman's Stone. *Friday August 23, 1872.* The ridge like another cross-dyke, which Mr. Heineken first espied and pointed out to me lying in a field to the north-west of Hangman's Stone, we went to examine today. But we at once perceived that it was not a cross-dyke like that at the Three Horseshoes, because it does not run at right angles to the road *and* nor does it cross it. It runs nearly parallel with the road along its north side, and its eastern end curves away slightly to the north. At Hangman's Stone roads coming from Beer, Colyford and Colyton all converge to a focus, and there is reason to think that this earthwork was thrown up to watch the approaches and hold an enemy in check coming from the east. The people who would do this are not unlikely to have made the cross-dyke, namely those who occupied Blackbury Castle. This earthwork stands between the convergence of these eastern roads and Blackbury Castle, and on the same side of the road. A glance

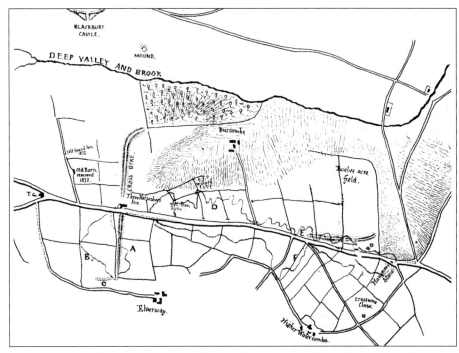

72/8/23 *Cross Dyke and earthworks.* (Diary)

at the *accompanying* map may make these points clearer. The yellow clay lying upon the top of the ridge through the recently ploughed field, contrasting as it does with the dark mould, marked the work as having been artificially constructed. I paced the ridge and made it 180 paces long from west to east, but my paces must not be reckoned quite so much in yards, especially over rough ground. The western end is about 57 paces north of the road and at about one third of its length from this end a gap has been made. This gap is not likely to have been original, for in its perfect state the whole agger is likely to have been continuous. The width of the ridge is 24 paces and is of small elevation. Whilst the western end, as remarked, is 57 paces north of the road, the eastern end is from 80 to 100 because that end trends away somewhat to the north-east. But there is a depression like the traces of a former fosse all along the northern side of the agger, which is not the side I had expected to have found it. As a rule, I have generally held that the fosse of an earthwork or camp or fortified place is on the side of the enemy, so that if an invading enemy was expected from the valley of the Axe, the fosse ought to have been next the road, which it certainly is not. Of late years however, some savage tribes have been noticed in America and other countries who, in their barriers against their enemies, put the ditch on the inside, or on their own side, and jump into it when they have discharged their arrows or other missiles.   Perhaps it is too soon yet to offer any decided theory regarding this work. (*See October 8, 1872*).   I found a flint core and several beach pebble sling stones close to it.   Between the eastern end and the road there are two flattened and partly obliterated tumuli.   These, in connection with the Crossway Close work, indicate a deadly struggle in the neighbourhood (September 26, 1859). We walked to the north end of this large field overlooking the valley, but made no discovery there.   A man called Day who we questioned at the cottage just after passing the brook on the north, told us that this twelve acre field was first taken in hand and partly tilled about 1840, but that it was neglected and allowed to go back into its wild state.   It so remained ever since until about two years ago when it was taken in hand again.   Of the two tumuli, the eastern one is the largest but its crown seems to have been flattened or removed.

We ate our sandwiches, Mr. Heineken sitting upon Hangman's Stone and I lying on the grass beside it under the shade of the hedge.   The sun was intensely hot in the field.   Then we descended the lane northwards, crossed the brook, mounted the next hill, saw something like a cairn of white flints in a plantation up on the left, and pushed on over the hill to Southleigh, or Sailey as they call it.   Then proceeded on to a farm called Hooperhayne.   The termination hayne is very common in this district. Hayes or Hayne is said to signify hedges or enclosures, and was applied to Mr. So-and-so's bit of cultivated ground or farm.   It had been reported that quantities of ancient pottery had been turned up in some parts of the ground, and if this was the case it would be worth while to institute a search.   We were directed into a field where there was a great pit out of which the clay for the pottery was dug, and then to the next field below the cottage.   Here we found plenty of fragments of roofing tiles etc., but they were evidently of modern make.   On enquiry, it seemed that a pottery had been established here about forty years before, but that it had failed and the proprietors had been ruined.   If ancient pottery is really to be met with on this farm , it must be in some other field.

Somewhat disappointed we started for home, where we did not arrive till half past nine, having been out since ten in the morning. (*Diary*).

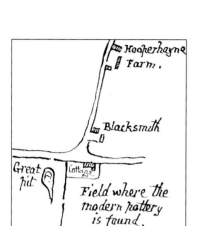

72/8/23   Hooperhayne Farm. (Diary)

Volume one completed.   *Saturday August 31, 1872.*   Finished the first volume of my History of Sidmouth. (*Diary*).

Death of Rev. Kirwan.   *Monday September 2, 1872.*   This afternoon a little before two, whilst I was in the oak room of the Old Chancel, a gentleman, a stranger to me, was announced.   He proved to be a Mr. Andrews, a magistrate of Berkshire residing at Reading.   He apologised for intruding but said he understood I was on friendly terms with the Rev. R. Kirwan,.   I said I was.   He asked whether he had called on me this morning?

I replied, 'No, I had not seen him since we were together in Exeter, at the meeting of the Devonshire Association a few weeks ago'.

He then said, 'I am sorry to inform you that he has met with a lamentable accident, and I am afraid is drowned'.

'Drowned', I exclaimed, 'How do you mean drowned'?   I felt choked, but begged he would proceed.

He then told me that he was a visitor to Sidmouth, that he and some of his family had been taking a walk on the sea shore to the west of the town *and* that at nearly half a mile from the esplanade they observed a gentleman's clothes lying on the beach, but on looking at the water did not observe any person in sight.   He made one of his boys stay by the clothes whilst he took a turn towards High Peak Hill, keeping his eye upon the waves, but on his return *and* still failing to discover any person in the water, he feared that something serious had happened.   *He* therefore examined the clothes and found the name R. Kirwan upon the towel.   He sent his son back to Sidmouth to find the police whilst he tied the things up in a towel.   Some sailors with a net proceeded at once to the spot and commenced dragging the bottom of the sea.

When he left me, I hurried to the vicarage as I had to deliver a book to the vicar. I related the narrative to him, much to his astonishment, and then directed my steps to the same place *where* there was a boat with six men in it and a crowd of people on the shore.   They were dragging a long mackerel net cast out in a semi-circle from

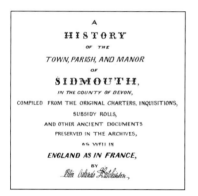

A

HISTORY

OF THE

TOWN, PARISH, AND MANOR

OF

SIDMOUTH,

IN THE COUNTY OF DEVON,

COMPILED FROM THE ORIGINAL CHARTERS, INQUISITIONS,

SUBSIDY ROLLS,

AND OTHER ANCIENT DOCUMENTS

PRESERVED IN THE ARCHIVES,

AS WELL IN

ENGLAND AS IN FRANCE,

BY

Peter Orlando Hutchinson,

72/8/31   Title page to Vol. 1 of the History of Sidmouth

the shore, *which* they did several times but were not rewarded with success. I sketched the scene as it appeared when I arrived. The sea was rough. I remained till five, when they proposed to desist till the tide turned and the current set in another direction. About seven, I heard that the body had been recovered, found by Ware (off whom I bought the great fossil tooth). I was asked to be one of the jury at the inquest, *to which* I consented as I wished to know all the circumstances of the case. (*Diary*).

72/9/2 (Diary)

Wednesday September 4, 1872. Painful as it was, I attended with the others and looked at the body. It had received many scratches and bruises from the gravel whilst it was in the wash of the sea, for it had been thrown on shore by the waves. (*Diary*). *According to the newspapers, the verdict was 'accidentally drowned while bathing'.*

Carving the church pinnacles. *Thursday September 12, 1872.* All this morning I was in the stonemason's yard cutting out the crockets of the new pinnacles for the church tower. After making one or two to feel my way, I found I could advance quicker. I mean however, that Mr. Churchill himself (who did my hall ceiling) should go on with them. (*Diary*).

Earthworks near the Three Horseshoes and C.F.Williams the artist. *Tuesday October 8, 1872.* My old friend C. F. Williams, now a painter in water colours, being for a short time sketching at Beer, I went over to see him. I started at nine and soon after ten got as far as the Three Horseshoes. Ever since Mr. Heineken and myself measured the earthwork in the twelve-acre field across the road from Hangman's Stone on the 23rd of last August, we have been desirous of giving the ground a thorough examination all along the ridge of the hill, feeling that there was still something more to be discovered. Mr. Heineken is just now in Yorkshire, on a visit to his sister Mrs. Horsfall of Hornby Grange near North Allerton, but I resolved to make a search alone. I decided on traversing all the fields on the north side of the road, *so* I dismounted at the Three Horseshoes and told the driver to go quietly on and wait for me near Hangman's Stone. I turned over the hedge and zig-zagged about the fields but could not perceive any traces of a cross-dyke, agger or other old earthwork. The first and second fields on the west side of Burcombe Lane had recently been ploughed. Many flint flakes and two or three cores, as if the ancient tribes had been at work there, I saw and put one or two in my pocket as vouchers to show Mr. Heineken. I then crossed Burcombe Lane and proceeded eastwards. I had soon the pleasure of discovering a long extension of our earthwork a field and a half further west than we had seen before. I had a pencil and a memorandum book in my hands as I went along and the red line on the map of August 22 and 23 is the course I took. This doubles the length of what we had before discovered, *and* altogether it cannot be much less than a thousand feet. It appears to me to have been a breastwork thrown up to watch the road, and Blackbury Castle seems to have been the base of operations in all these works on this hill, the enemy apparently being expected from the south or east or both. I will not say that the fields on my map are quite the proper size or shape on the north side of the road, but those on the south I took from a large map of Branscombe, of which I took a tracing many years ago and still have. Joined the carriage just beyond Hangman's Stone and proceeded to the Dolphin Inn, where I was delighted to find everything very comfortable.

We dined together and then took a walk along the cliff and the beach. Having sat down we talked over some of the pranks of our green boyhood, how many bells we had pulled and run away, how many gates we had un-hung, how many cats we had scared, how many old women we had frightened and so on, and how much we had repented since. I alluded to his late father whom I remember well, and now I was older, was anxious to know something of his residence at Powderham Castle. To this appeal he told me a curious history. His father was the only son of a Mr. Williams who farmed a piece of land of his own near the estate of Sir Watkin Williams Wynne in North Wales. He was intended for the same pursuit but he early showed a strong passion for music. From Sir Watkin's harper and from the harper of another baronet then living in the neighbourhood, he was able to follow his bent. This last baronet had a daughter whom he often had the opportunity of meeting. Some of the neighbours began to suspect that an intimacy was springing up between the young folks and informed the father. He summoned Williams to his room one morning and questioned him on the subject, when the latter admitted he had a preference for her. Upon this the baronet (whose name I forget but think it began with an H) offered him £500 if he would immediately leave the neighbourhood. This he accepted and started for London *where* he lived rather freely for a time, thinking his £500 would be inexhaustible. However, at last it came to an end and he found himself in the midst of a large city without a friend to help him. Matters became worse. He wandered down to London Bridge one day, not knowing which way to turn for a scrap of bread, *and* whilst standing here he heard someone call him by name. He turned round and it proved to be an old acquaintance from North Wales who had been several years in London and was in a good business as an upholsterer. He was then on top of a furniture van *and* made Williams get up, took him home and gave him something to eat. Finding that he was doing nothing but starving and that music was his only chance, he told him he would try and introduce him to Mrs. Salmon, one of the popular singers of the day, that he was going to her house next morning and that *Williams* should go too. This they did. When they got there, Mrs. Salmon was not ready to receive them but she sent word to say that she hoped he would amuse himself with the harp till she came. He therefore did so and he played several pieces after she was in the room. She expressed herself so pleased that she requested he would take part in a concert she was shortly going to give at which she expected the Prince of Wales (afterwards George IV). He took subordinate parts at this concert, but before it was over she desired that he would give the company one of the Welsh airs on his national instrument entirely unaccompanied. He gave them that beautiful air 'The Rising of the Lark', and this sealed his good fortune. When the concert was over Lord Courtenay came up to him and offered him £100 a year to be his harper and reside at Powderham Castle. This he gratefully accepted, and he enjoyed this post in every comfort and luxury for twenty-one years. Whilst he was here he formed an attachment to some young lady and married her twice, the first marriage when she was underage. Who this lady was he would never say. It was suspected she was above him in birth, but some mystery hung over her. She died young bearing one child, a boy, the same who was telling me this story. After the death of Lord Courtenay, the establishment at Powderham Castle was for a time broken up and Mr. Williams came to Sidmouth and took a cottage near my father's residence at No. 4, Coburg Terrace, *and* there I got acquainted with his son who was about my own age. He was fond of drawing and was brought up as an artist. Most of my early attempts at sketching were done with him. He afterwards established himself in Exeter, to which place his father removed. He married a Miss Harvey but this did not turn out well and they have not lived together these twenty years. He had two children, a girl and a boy. The former is married and is now in Russia; the boy married and has since died, leaving no male heir. My friend has for some years lived near Southampton.

Our long gossip passed the time away. We returned to the Inn, had tea and I left. A young moon, about a quarter old, lighted me back to Sidmouth. (*Diary*).

Fast work. *Monday October 14, 1872.* I was a great part of the day in the parish church whilst the white marble tablet to the memory of the late Mrs. Haughton James of Helens was being erected by Signor Monti, the sculptor of 5 Langham Chambers. As Mr. Haughton James was going away (hush – he has gone to be married again and he is only 77) he requested that I would explain to Signor Monti his wishes as to where he would want it placed. It is against the east wall of the north transept. The work is certainly exceedingly good when examined closely. The medallion profile of Our Saviour, placed in the centre, is well done. The price seems very high, but all good work must cost money. Mr. H.J. has already paid £124 and the remainder, being £19 15s., he left with me. This I gave to the little Italian when the work was done and got his receipt. He came and had a look at the Old Chancel and was much amused at my operations. (*Diary*).

Home visit. *Monday October 28, 1872.* I was honoured this morning by a visit from the two Misses Osborne of Cottington and one of the Balmains of Camden, who wanted to look at the Old Chancel. I showed them my building, my antiques and my curiosities. (*Diary*).

Visit to Cottington. *Tuesday October 29, 1872.* I called on the Rev. Lord Sidney Godolphin Osborne at Cottington *and* found him at home *with* Lady Osborne and the two Misses Osborne. They appear to be a clever family. Miss Osborne carves oak capitally *and* she showed me her tools and her work, with which I was much pleased. Lord Sidney's room is full of all such things as a scientific man delights in. I was with him more than an hour. (*Diary*).

72/10/29 Miss Osborne (Diary)

Fishy tale. *Friday November 8, 1872.* I was told an amusing story by a fisherman this morning. Some of our Sidmouth boats have recently been out fishing for whiting. They have to go ten or a dozen miles out where the sea is fifty or sixty fathoms deep and let down long lines. They tell me that the hill they can last discern at that distance is the top of High Peak, the second to the westward of Sidmouth. About a week ago, three or four boats were out in a group and nearly within speaking distance of each other when a rushing noise was heard and something black was for a short distance seen to pass along and then vanish. It was between them and the land and so far off as to appear nearer the land than it really was.

'What was that?' cried one of them.

'I don't know', said another in the nearest boat, 'but perhaps it was the train going down near Dawlish vanishing into a tunnel'.

In a few minutes they were better informed, for an immense black fish 'very like a whale' came up much nearer to them. They did not quite like his proximity but they were next put in a state of great terror by his again coming up, lashing the ocean white and spouting water and making the sea so turbulent as to rock the boats. A boy in one of them, they say, had not ceased trembling when they brought him on shore. This fish has been seen once or twice since. They suppose it is after whiting and pilchards. More recently it has been seen from the esplanade, distant about two miles. (*Diary*).

Musical interlude. *Thursday November 28, 1872.* Went over to General Balmain's at Camden and tried some songs and pieces of music with the young ladies. Having laid aside my music for some time, having been busy in other ways, I have again taken up the flute. In the afternoon I went to a musical party at Captain and Mrs Joliffe's at Woodlands. Those who played and sang were Mrs and Miss Joliffe, Misses Balmain, Misses Strahan of Blackmore Hall, etc. (*Diary*).

Broadway fields. *Saturday November 30, 1872.* I am told that the fields shaded in the plan belonging to Lady Cockburn, widow of the late Dean of York (now married to the Rev. Mr. Wale or Whale) have just been purchased by the Trustees of the Manor for £1250. They comprise about five acres. A month or two ago, they bought back No. 9, Fort Field Terrace, which had been alienated from the Manor in Jenkin's time, I believe. Also, a year or two ago, for £650 I believe, *they purchased* No. 4, which had been alienated in the same way. (*Diary*).

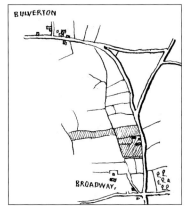

72/11/30 Broadway fields (Diary)

72/12/12 *Stone hatchet* from Peak Hill (Diary)

More beach finds. *Wednesday December 4, 1872.* After storms people go down on the beach to look for treasure. They have picked up recently four gold rings, half a sovereign, a 'spade guinea' of George III, some silver and many copper pieces. None of the money is ancient *and* some think that the rings were lost by ladies bathing. (*Diary*).

Flint implements. *Thursday December 12, 1872.* I have recently been reading Mr. John Evans' book on flint implements, and remembering the few objects of that sort I have picked up on the hills, with the indications of more, I am persuaded that many others are to be met with if we only search diligently for them. I took a walk this morning on Peak Hill with the resolution of having a regular good hunt, and I was rewarded. The day was calm, clear and after the storms, very pleasant. From the cliff-edge I steered inland, zig-zagging about *for* two hours. I saw one flake of black flint, which probably came from Beer Head, a square worked flint of light colour, a leaf-shaped flint of doubtful character, and lastly I was delighted to pounce upon the hatchet or wedge of chert or light flint, of which I give a sketch. I shall keep this for the Exeter museum. Some facets show the polished or glassy look of great age, very different from the dull surface of recent fracture. The core from Seven Barrow Field and the chert hammer from near Blackbury Castle have it still stronger. (*Diary*).

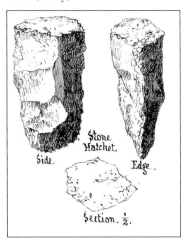

72/12/12   *Found on Salcombe Hill, by Henry Ede Esq. of Lansdowne.* (Hist of Sid. I,121)

Hutchinson took his appointment as Local Secretary of the Society of Antiquaries seriously and frequently sent in reports when he had something of interest to communicate, some of which were printed in the Proceedings. One such was after an unusually long interval:

Dear Sir. I am neither dead, nor ill, nor lazy, nor asleep, though you might suspect me of being in any one of these conditions from the length of time that has elapsed since I communicated anything from this neighbourhood. But I can neither create objects of antiquity nor find them at command, so that I have been obliged to bide my time. However, not to dwell upon a few small worked flints which myself and one or two friends have met with, I have at last come upon an object of larger type. It is a wedge, hatchet or pick of chert or light grey flint, a species of flint common to this locality. Cores and flakes of black flint may occasionally be seen but they come from the chalk district at Beer, about seven miles eastwards. The finding of this object I ascribe to Mr. Evans' new book on flint implements. I have recently been turning over its pages and it instigated me to undertake some determined searches on the higher grounds, both near the hill fortresses in this neighbourhood and in places remote from them. I herewith send a sketch of the pick, representing the side, edge and the blunt top. I found it on Peak hill, a hill that rises on the west side of Sidmouth. I remain Dear Sir, *etc.* P.O.Hutchinson. *Letter to C. Knight Watson dated January 11, 1873. (Soc. of Antiq. Ms. 250, p. 49)*

Names old and new. *Monday December 16, 1872.* The following printed article entitled 'Names , Old and New' I have taken from Lethaby's *Journal.* I save it because it contains a few facts about Sidmouth, and facts are always worth preserving. Very little of fiction is. *The newspaper cutting follows, written as a response to the Local Board's decision to put up street names in the town. To ensure that* the new should not extinguish the old, *Hutchinson had made enquiries* in order to ascertain whether an old name has not already got possession of the spot. *He was particularly concerned that old field names might be lost.* It is a mistake to suppose that the open fields are without names. Go to any farmer and he can tell you the names of nearly all the fields in his occupation, not names of his own giving but what he has learnt by reference to his lease and what are to be found on the parish map. These names ought to be respected. They are often very old, they are generally appropriate to their several localities and being recorded in title deeds, it is confusion to introduce new. *A second article appeared with a further list of names in Lethaby's 'Journal' the following month.*

Field walking on High Peak again. *Friday December 27, 1872.* Took a walk to the top of High Peak Hill, the weather dark and threatening and the ground muddy from the quantity of rain. Hunted about all such fields as were fallow or anywhere bare for flint flakes or implements. Since my find on the twelfth, I am persuaded that diligent searching is likely to meet with something worth having some day. Only found a core and two or three flakes, but this much is encouragement to look again. Observed several beach pebbles like sling stones. If not used in actual warfare it is possible they had been slung by some of the ancient tribes at the rabbits. This is a very likely supposition. The soft soil on the summit of High Peak has been much washed down by the rain, *but* all these cliffs are wearing away fast. The wind was south and so strong that I could scarcely approach the edge of the cliff.

From this lofty station I could see pieces of timber scattered about the beach. For the last two or three days quantities of baulks of deal and fragments of some vessel have been coming on shore, strewed all along from Teignmouth to Beer. Men were engaged in securing them as they were thrown up on the shore. It is supposed that some timber vessel has gone to pieces but as yet no particulars have been ascertained. (*Diary*).

1873

Vessel in distress. *Wednesday January 1, 1873.* A beautiful morning, but as they say 'a fine morning never lasts all day'. This rule has no exceptions. Our lifeboat returned from Beer where the men had slept last night. Yesterday a bark was seen in the offing in distress and our boat went off and took their crew into Beer. It was a French vessel. The wind has moderated and veered from south to west, and the vessel is saved from a lee shore. (*Diary*).

Organist's resignation. *Thursday January 2, 1873.* There has been some dissatisfaction lately about the church choir. A motion was proposed and seconded, and I believe would have been carried, for dismissing the organist had I not stepped in and begged them to refrain from so summary a proceeding. My moderation was approved of and the meeting was adjourned to this day week. I undertook to call on him as a friend and advise him to send in his resignation. This I did.

At the adjourned meeting a letter from the organist was received tendering his resignation. Dr. Robert Haines-Wood is the son of a D.D., and I believe his father's brother was late Dean of Ely Cathedral. He was born to £600 a year but a dishonest trustee defrauded

73/1/1 No title or date.
(DRO, Z19/2/8C/206)

him. He is very sensitive if he is not treated with the respect due to a gentleman. But, alas, people never remember what you <u>were</u> – they only know what you <u>are</u>, and if he has gone down in life he will be treated accordingly by the unsympathising world. But owing to a natural impatience of temperament, he has had the misfortune to offend most of his choir and several of the gentry, and there is the whole secret. (*Diary*).

Sidmouth esplanade damaged by storm. *Friday January 3, 1873.*

73/1/3 *Sketch from the Fort Field, Sidmouth, showing the damage done by the sea to the west end of the esplanade in January 1873.*
(DRO, Z19/2/8E/209)

The sea has knocked a hole in the esplanade wall just opposite the entrance gate to Belmont and the boiling waves, rushing in and back again, have carried away a great quantity of the *structure* and excavated an immense hollow. They are putting in faggots and stones to stop it temporarily. About eleven years ago a similar hole was made a few yards west of this. (*Diary*).

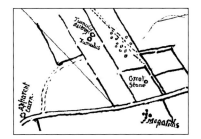

73/1/7   Vicinity of the Great Stone (Diary)

Field walking on Salcombe Hill. *Tuesday January 7, 1873.* Took a walk on Salcombe Hill to look for worked flints, *and* observed some scattered sling stones around the great stone (June 1, 1871). Noticed also several (at least three) pieces of broken sling-stones. These had not been broken by the frost but by a violent blow, as the striae at the point of impact show. I think that this strengthens the idea that a contention once occurred here. I brought back one to show to Mr. Heineken. (*Diary*). *The 'Great Stone'* had probably been placed upright, but it now leans towards the west. About twenty or thirty yards around this megalith a number of spherical or oviform beach pebble sling-stones have been found since the land has been under tillage. Perhaps a fight occurred here. They can still be picked up when the ground is fresh ploughed. (*History of Sidmouth I, 119a*).

Out on the open heath to the north-west of this field I found a large flake having the 'bulb of percussion' very strong. This gives hope of finding something more *here.* (*See May 13, 1873 and* for a correct plan of the hill top see May 1, 1874). (*Diary*).

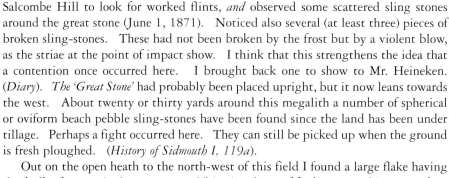

Above left: 73/1/19   *Fossil tooth weighing 6lb 8ozs found on the clay under the shingle of Sidmouth sea beach, just outside the esplanade wall and opposite Belmont, January 18, 1873.* (Hist of Sid. I,23e)

Fifth fossil tooth. *Saturday January 19, 1873.* A lad called Selly brought me a fossil tooth which had been found a little way outside the esplanade wall opposite Belmont, near the west end of the beach. By some carelessness, they broke it into three pieces but I can cement them together with shellac dissolved in naphtha. It is stained a dark grey colour, probably from having lain in a bed of dark clay, which lies under the shingle opposite the Fort Field. This bed of clay had never been uncovered, and never seen by the oldest inhabitant till this winter. I gave him two shillings for it. (*Diary*). *This tooth is now on display in Sidmouth Museum.*

Submerged forest and sixth fossil tooth. *Friday January 24, 1873.* Another tooth! A boy called Frederick Bartlett brought me a much worn tooth also stained dark grey, *which* he said he found lying on the bed of clay. I gave him a shilling for it. Opposite the eastern verge of Fort Field and Fort Cottage the appearance of several stumps of trees rising out of the sand or this stratum of grey or blue or variegated clay, has attracted considerable attention. I have noted their places down and I remember that there seems to be lines of stratification in the clay. The trees appear to have been fir or alder. Must we suppose that there was a forest here in which the mammoth roamed but which has gone down by the sinking of the land? The stumps are uncovered at half tide, the furthest *being* from fifty-five to sixty feet outside the wall (*see March 18, 1873*). I took the *tooth* to the Exeter Museum February 25, 1875. (*Diary*).

Top: 73/1/24   *Portion of fossil tooth found on Sidmouth sea beach, January 24, 1873. I took this tooth to the Exeter Museum Feb. 25. 1875* (Hist. of Sid. I,23f)

Barbarous relic. *Wednesday January 29, 1873.* Took a walk to High Peak Hill. The wind was from the east, 'sharp enough to cut a snipe in two', but exercise soon made me warm. Hunted about some ploughed fields near the cliff and found many flint flakes and cores. On the slopes near the top of High Peak I found a gin tethered to a peg driven into the ground. *It* had gone off, and in its iron jaws it held half of the hind leg of some unfortunate rabbit. The cruelty of such an act cannot be expressed in words. I look upon gins as remnants of the barbarism of the Dark Ages and a disgrace to the period in which we live. If wild animals *must* be caught, catch them, or if they *must* be destroyed, destroy them, but don't lacerate or mutilate them. On a piece of note paper I had in my pocket, I wrote the words 'Think of the cruelty of setting gins', and fixed it to it. These words from an unknown hand and the bleeding evidence I hope may have their effect on the farmer or his labourer when he comes to see what he has caught. In another place I found a looped wire set in a rabbit run, but I undid the loop and went on. (*Diary*).

Diminishing estate. *Tuesday February 4, 1873.* Early this morning about half past three, there was a great fall of the cliff opposite Chit Rocks. Frost and rain are bringing them down. The owner of Sea View has got what I call a diminishing estate. (*Diary*).

Field walking on Pin Beacon. *Friday March 14, 1873.* Took a walk on Peak Hill and the slopes of Pin Beacon beyond, to hunt over some ploughed fields for worked flints. Passed over several fields and found nothing and began to despair *until* I got to a field on the further side of the dip between Peak and Pin Beacon. Near the top I found an area on which I observed many flakes and other pieces, evidently fashioned, though rudely, by the hand of man. In short, here and in some other places, I picked up a core, five scrapers of the thumb flint type more or less discoidal or oval, four scrapers of longer form used at the rounded ends and some of the sides, two hollow scrapers, a half circle scraper, flakes and some others, in all twenty. I must go there again. (*Diary*).

Submerged forest off Sidmouth. *Tuesday March 18, 1873. Hutchinson sent an account of his investigations into the submerged forest recently exposed off Sidmouth to Woolmer's paper.* The storms and gales of wind of January last cleared away the shingle and sand of Sidmouth beach more completely than had ever been witnessed by the oldest inhabitant. The effect of this was to reveal a few geological and archaeological features hitherto unknown. Nearly opposite Fort Cottage the stumps of six or eight trees were visible at low water. As the stumps were at this low level buried under about eight feet of water at every high tide, it was important to discover whether they were really in situ, where they had grown. To ascertain this, one of them, which was sixty feet outside the wall, was dug round and laid bare. The question was settled that it was where it grew, for the stump was upright and several roots diverged from it horizontally, like radii. Two of the roots running seaward were from seven to eight feet long and six inches in diameter. It had grown in a bed of blue clay interstratified with sandy lines of different colours, succeeded lower down by yellow clay and angular river gravel. (*Exeter and Plymouth Gazette March 21, 1873, extract). A rather more detailed account was read at the next meeting of the Devonshire Association in July, pointing out that some of the mammoth teeth were found on the same blue clay ('Submerged Forest and Mammoth Teeth at Sidmouth', 1873).*

Field walking around Pin Beacon. *Thursday March 20, 1873.* Went again to the inland slope of Pin Beacon Hill where I was on the 14[th.] Brought away nothing but a rough and jagged lump of flint about two inches in diameter, which had evidently been knocked out on purpose. It is of black flint whereas the flints of the hill are light coloured, and therefore it has probably been brought from the chalk of Beer Head. Such lumps of flint are likely to have been made for sling stones or other missiles. I have now found nine of them in different places in this neighbourhood.

Returned by striking across the hill to Mutter's Moor. I remember the hollow of Mutter's Moor when it was a picturesque dell, all heath and furze with a spring of water at the bottom. It is now in two fields of about seven acres each. It struck me that the Britons of the Stone Age might possibly have resorted to the brook and chipped flints by the side it, so I took a hasty turn up and down the lower field (which was in turnips) for I had no time today to go to the upper. I saw several flakes in different places and a beach pebble or two, very likely to have been slung at some wild animal, and was gratified at finding a pick or perhaps gouge, nearly four inches long and one and three-quarters in diameter at the butt end. I must go there again. (*Diary*).

Another tooth from Sidmouth beach. *March 1873.* A small portion of a fossil tooth, worn down by the action of the waves and gravel on the sea beach at Sidmouth, was found in March 1873. (*History of Sidmouth I, 23g. No mention in Diary*).

Earthworks near the Three Horseshoes. *Thursday March 27, 1873.* We could not get away on our first archaeological expedition until today, *though* last year we managed it on the 21st. Mr. Heineken and myself went to examine the long earthwork opposite Hangman's Stone (see August 9, 23 and October 8, 1872). We ascended by Trow Hill, *where* there is a large triangular field on the right towards the upper part belonging to the Lord of the Manor of Sidmouth. I got over the hedge and met the carriage on the top. Saw two or three beach pebbles, like sling-stones. I do not see how they could get there unless they were really sling stones, flung perhaps at some wild animal, for they were exactly the pattern of the undoubted sling-stones found in the cave at Sidbury Castle (see May 28, 1864). We then went

73/3/20 *'Pick or gouge'* from Mutter's Moor. (Diary)

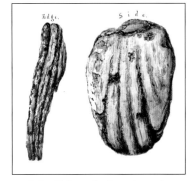

73/3/? Side and edge view of fossil tooth. (Hist of Sid. I,23g)

on to the Three Horseshoes where we alighted, *as* we wanted further to examine the southern half of the cross dyke. We walked down the red line A and returned along B, as shown on the plan at August 23, 1872. We observed many sling stones and flint flakes and secured one or two scrapers. At C there is something like a return or angle in the dyke, but it is too faint to be quite certain about. We then proceeded to explore along the north side of the road, nearly following the red line D, which I traced last August by myself. The west point E of the earthwork is very faint as it is in a field long under the plough, but the eastern point is plainer as the land has only recently been taken in. The end E almost looks as if it curved round towards the road. If it did, it may have proceeded across the road in the direction of hedge F, but it is impossible to say with certainty. This earthwork furnishes food for consideration. After taking all the points of the case into account, it appears to me (and to Mr. Heineken) that the cross dyke 2000-foot long drawn across the ridge of the hill, with the ditch on the east side, was constructed by the inhabitants of the country, and probably those who occupied Blackbury Castle, to keep back an enemy expected from the east, possibly some invader entering the mouth of the Axe. The earthwork on the other hand, flanks the road, and perhaps the west end crossed the road and followed the hedge F. Its ditch was on the north side, which was not without its meaning, and hence it seems that this work, which we can still trace for nearly 1000 feet, was thrown up by the invader pushing his way westwards. They made the ditch on the north side facing Blackbury Castle, and in case of need could secure a retreat to the coast under its protection. The two tumuli near its east end, the British sepulchral urn from Crossway Close (September 26, 1859) and the numerous sling stones and flint flakes we find from the cross dyke to Hangman's Stone, show plainly that this spot was much occupied by early tribes and is likely to have been a field of contention.

We took our refreshment in the open carriage on the Down across the road opposite Hangman's Stone, looking northward up the valley toward Northleigh, for a good view enhances the relish, and in order to be consistent we cut up our sandwiches with flint flakes. We looked at Hangman's Stone, which Mr. Heineken thinks might have been one leg of a cromlech, quasi 'Hanging Stone', and close beside it I picked up a large beach pebble of grey flint about five or six inches long. On examining it I observed that both ends showed abrasion as if it had been used as a hammer or pounder. Mr. Heineken now has it. We then decided on returning. My fellow labourer is not the man he was a few years ago as he has passed his three score and ten, so he kept to the road with the carriage, now and then going into a field to look about. Whilst I, who am still a boy, turned in at Hangman's Stone and followed the red line back over hedge and ditch and joined him near the Three Horseshoes. I made this rough walk to examine the fields to see if I could discover any earthworks on the south side of the road, but did not see any. I found him filling a bottle out of a pond to provide diatoms and rotifers for Lord S.G.Osborne's microscope. We got home by seven P.M. (*Diary*).

73/3/27 *Hammer stone* (Diary)

Flints from around Sidmouth. *Monday March 31, 1873.* *Letter to C. Knight Watson.* Dear Sir. Whilst thanking you for one of the numbers of the 'Proceedings', I take the opportunity of reporting a thing or two about palaeolithic flint implements in Devonshire. In Mr. Evans' excellent book on *Ancient Stone Implements* he remarks that with the exception of those worked flints from the bone caves of Devonshire, no palaeolithic implements have as yet been found further west than Colyton. Living ten miles west of Colyton, the above remark put me on my mettle and I have been searching somewhat assiduously of late. The most likely place to find traces of the ancient inhabitants would doubtless be within the areas of their old camps, but where the land is in grass or where it is still in its wild state and covered with furze or heath, it is impossible to examine the surface for small objects. In default of proximity to old camps, it is necessary to consider what other places are likely to reward a search. The spot where a perennial spring of water issues from a bank is a likely place. Acting upon such reasoning I proceeded a short time ago to Mutter's Moor, a wild dell a mile out of Sidmouth with a spring issuing from the slope at the junction of the greensand upon the red marl and only recently reduced from heath and furze to a fallow field. Here I was rewarded by finding the pick or gouge represented in the sketch, besides sundry flakes. In the same way I have been more or less successful in hunting round two or three depressions or basin-shaped hollows in fields on the flat

Thumb-flint scraper.
Found Mar.14. 1873 on Pin
Beacon Hill, 1½ mile west of
Sidmouth. Nine others have
been found in other places

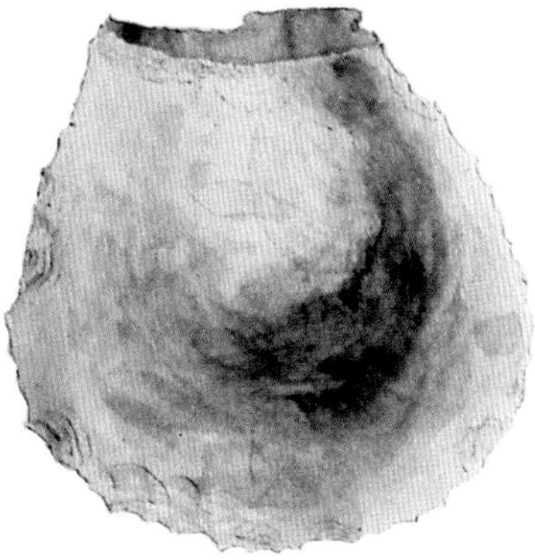

Drill or Borer.
Found near Blackbury Castle in 1871,
five miles NE. from Sidmouth.
Another, 1½ mile west.

Half-moon, or Half-disc Scraper,
Found on Pin Beacon Hill,
Mar.14.1873.
1½ mile west of Sidmouth.

Another.
Found on Salcombe Hill,
one mile NE. of Sidmouth,
Mar.4.1873

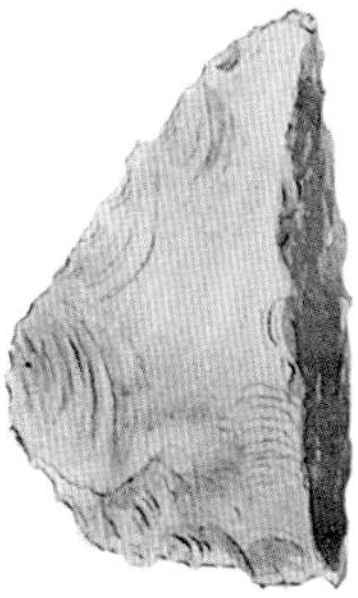

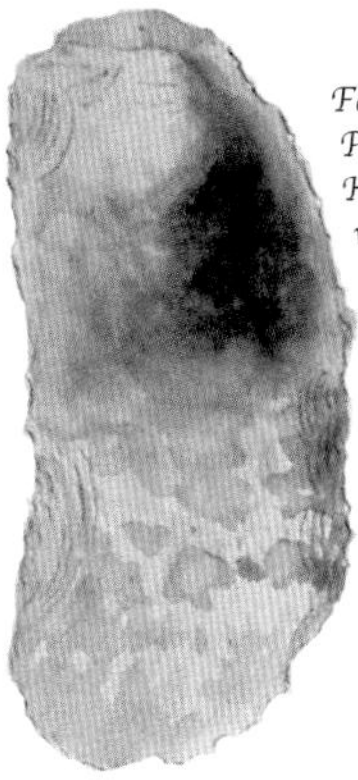

Found on
Pin Beacon
Hill, 1½ m.
west of
Sidmouth
Mar.14.
1873.

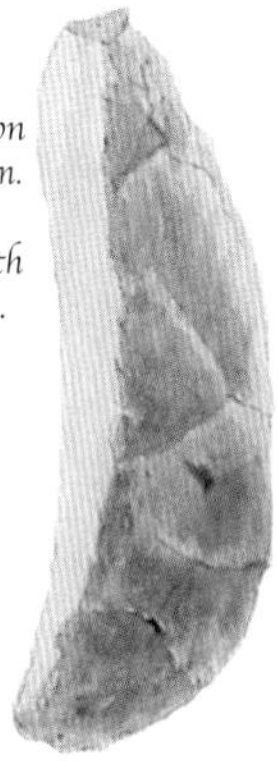

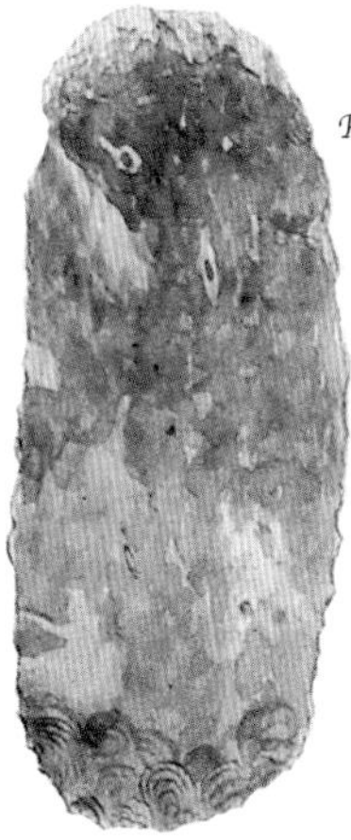

Found on
Pin Beacon Hill,
Mar.14.1873.

Worked all round,
and much
battered
at the ends.

Porcelainous
appearance of
great age well
developed upon
it.

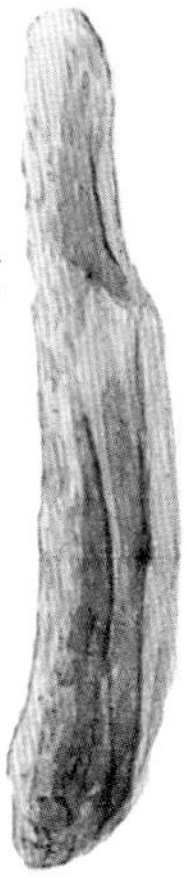

Triangular scraper.
Found on Pin Beacon Hill,
1½m. west of Sidmouth,
Mar. 14. 1873.

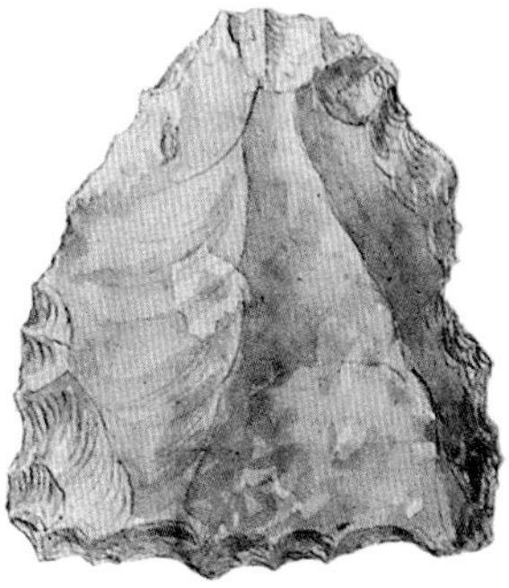

Pick
or Gouge.
From the
hollow of
Mutter's Moor.
1 mile north west
of Sidmouth.
Found Mar.14 1873.

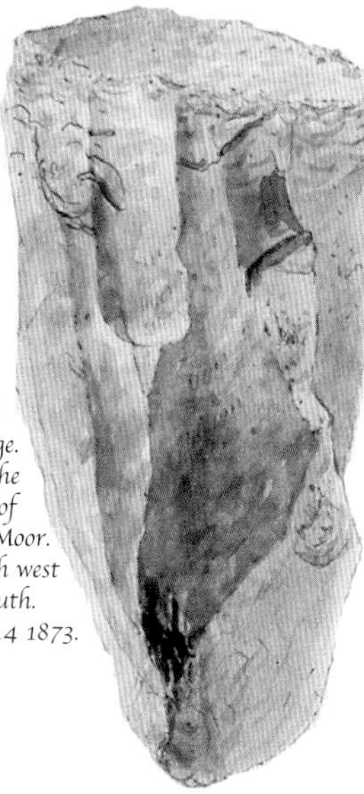

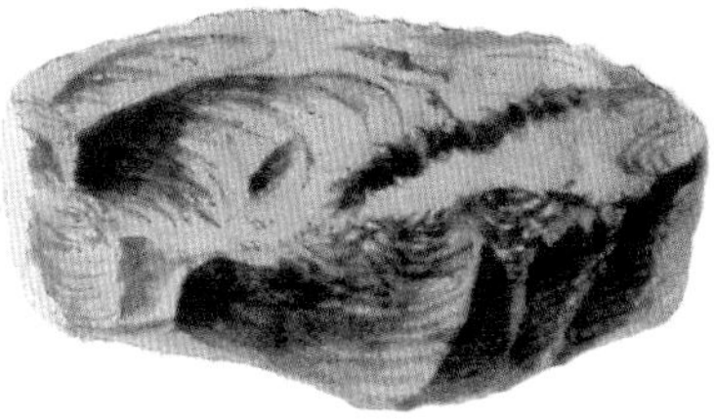

Discoidal Missile, from near Cross Dyke, five miles
north-east from Sidmouth. Found Oct 8. 1872.

tops of some of the hills that surround the valley of the Sid. Another point of attraction to them would be any rock or great stone lying on the moor. There are two or three such on the hills in this neighbourhood and a diligent scrutiny near them has never been altogether in vain. I have only taken up this branch of archaeology within recent times.

I believe that this part of England has never been hunted over but from my own success so far, I am persuaded that there is a great deal to be found if it is only looked for diligently.   The best time of the year is when the crops are off the ground, and the very best is the spring when it has been recently ploughed and harrowed.   The best black flints come from the patch of chalk at Beer about seven miles east of Sidmouth, but all the hills in this neighbourhood are covered with a bed of light-coloured cherty flint.   Though this appears to have been much used by the ancient inhabitants, it does not flake so well as the black flint.   I beg to remain, *etc.*, P. O. Hutchinson.   (*Letter dated March 31, 1873 in Soc. of Antiq. Ms. 250*).

On Mutter's Moor with Miss Osborne. *Wednesday April 2, 1873.*   Accompanied Miss G. Osborne to Mutter's Moor to search for flint implements.   We found a few but nothing very valuable. (*Diary*).

Implement from the Sid. *Tuesday April 15, 1873.*   Walked along the banks of the Sid as far up as Burnt Oak to look for mammoth teeth and flint implements.   Found a piece of chert about six inches long in the bed of the river, one end of which seems to have been chipped round.   If this should prove to be the case, and if it had been washed out of the alluvium through which the river has cut its way, it would be a palaeolith.   But the best proof would be to see it dug out of a gravel pit. (*Diary*).

Devonshire Association at Sidmouth and a chert implement. *Tuesday April 22, 1873. There was a* meeting of the committee at the London Hotel to discuss arrangements for the Devonshire Association next July, as it is arranged to meet at Sidmouth. Most people look upon this as a mistake, *as* in this small place there are neither resources nor accommodation nor public spirit for such a meeting. (*Diary*).

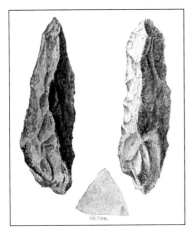

73/4/22   Stone implement of brown-ochre chert, found on Salcombe Hill, about a mile and a quarter NE from Sidmouth, April 14, 1873. (Soc of Antiq. MS 250)

Letter to C. Knight Watson Esq.   Dear Sir.   Some of my friends who are very sceptical on the subject of old flints and smile at my simplicity in hunting for them, have nevertheless had their attention drawn to them.   Taking a walk on Salcombe Hill a few days ago, at a spot about a mile and a quarter or more from Sidmouth, one of these friends picked up on the open heath the implement of which I give a sketch. He was going to throw it away but on second thoughts restrained his hand and retained it for me.   It is made of dark yellow or brown ochre chert, seams of which are found in the greensand beds in the cliff.   The butt end is the old outside surface bleached white.   This specimen, the largest hitherto met with in this neighbourhood, measures seven inches and a quarter long.   It was brought to me on the very day I was indebted to you for Part IV, Volume V of the 'Proceedings', and I presume there was some mysterious connection between the two occurrences.   I remain *etc.*, P. O. Hutchinson. (*Letter preserved in Library of Soc. of Antiq.*).

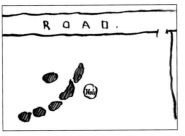

73/4/24   Salcombe Hill stones. (Diary)

Great stones on Salcombe Hill. *Thursday April 24, 1873.*   Mr. Heineken and myself made our second antiquarian excursion this year by going to Harcombe and Blackbury Castle.   We drove via Stephen's Cross, Snogbrook and then up Harcombe Hill, where we hoped to find some tumuli but were disappointed.   On the open heath I picked up a smooth beach pebble, perhaps slung at some wild animal, *and* further on in the ploughed fields I found two or three of those jagged lumps of flint, *such as are* met with on the Sussex Downs and the Yorkshire Wolds, supposed to be manufactured sling-stones or hand missiles.   A blow from one of these would give a very serious wound.   In another field I met with a scraper of the 'thumb flint' type.

We pushed on to the farm called Long Chimney, a corruption of the words *longue cheminee,* from *chemin* a road, alluding either to the long and once dreary Lyme Road or to the track over Broad Down.   We passed Rakeway Bridge, as some think from British *rhac*, a ridge, as in the Ridgeway, and took another look at the Lovehayne tumulus in Stone Barrow Plot.   Then to Blackbury Castle.   Never saw the interior so bare.   Nearly all the trees have been felled.   The field to the west has recently been ploughed for the first time *so I* hunted over this and the field to the south *where I* observed some sling stones and flakes, but the day has not been prolific.

Returning home it was very cold, though I heard the cuckoo on Harcombe Hill. The north-east wind blew sharp with a slight fall of snow.   I stopped and measured the great stones in a curved line in a field on Salcombe Hill.   The line is thirty feet eight inches, and from the side stone to the hole inclusive is twenty feet.   A stone has been removed from the hole. It is to be much wished that the others will be left alone. I am at a loss to know what this *structure* was, if anything. (*Diary*). *The outer stone had been removed a few years previously, perhaps in 1870 when* a great many blocks of stone were taken to Knowle, Sidmouth, to form a rockery. These five stones look too regular to have got there by chance *and* perhaps they are part of a circle. They do not stand upright. (*History of Sidmouth I, 119a*). *Hutchinson's wish was not fulfilled. What remained of the monument did not survive deep ploughing by the Forestry Commission in 1962 (Pollard 1978) and the small slabs of breccia now near the site hardly correspond with the 1.5 m blocks shown on the plan.*

Flint drills. *Saturday April 26, 1873.* Made an experiment this morning at flint drilling. I drilled a hole through one end of an oval eye glass, as in the sketch. I did it with sharp points or splinters of flint, but it was better not to have the point too sharp as it splinters back and becomes blunt. One point of a cube I found to work best. It occupied more than an hour. (*Diary*).

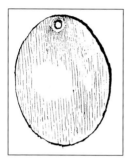

73/4/26 Drilling experiment. (Diary)

Implements from Pin Beacon. *Tuesday April 29, 1873.* Went for the third time to Pin Beacon Hill where I was on the 14th and 20th of last month. I found a roughly worked piece of brown chert like a pick six and a half inches long, some scrapers and many flakes. Went via Mutter's Moor and returned down Stintway Hill. (*Diary*).

High Peak Hill. *Tuesday May 6, 1873.* Took a walk to the top of High Peak Hill. The rains and storms of the past winter have saturated the earth and there have been two falls of the soil. From one of the exposed ends of one of the aggers at the north-eastern end, being the second from the most northerly one, I extracted one of those angular lumps of flint, evidently knocked out on purpose though roughly, supposed to have been used for sling-stones or missiles of some kind. I saw a portion of it exposed in the perpendicular face of the end of the agger towards the sea and fancied I discerned the flaking. This made me determined to get at it, though I had to climb outside.

The *annexed* rough sketch of the hill, looking at it from Sidmouth, exhibits the aggers in an enlarged or exaggerated form. The first or outer agger is like a short outwork. The second, where I got the missile, the same. The third is larger and longer, *and* the fourth is the inner agger of the camp, all the *rest* having fallen into the sea except these remnants. The stone was two feet below the surface and must have been buried there when the agger was made. This is interesting as showing that this worked flint is as old as the camp. The charcoal bed (September 13, 1848) is almost all gone by the falling away of the cliff, and the bone bed (September 29, 1871) is fast going. (*Diary*).

73/5/6 High Peak Hill from Sidmouth. (Diary)

Back to the Great Stone. *Tuesday May 13, 1873.* Mr. Heineken and myself took a walk on Salcombe Hill, to the field of the Great Stone (see January 7, 1873). I got on the stone and ascertained that, elevated in this way, I got a panoramic view and could see the old camps to east, north and west. The ancient tribes may have made use of it in the same way. *The 'Great Stone' remained standing in place into the 1950s, when it was moved to the edge of the field (Pollard 1978). It now lies half buried in the hedge beside Milltown Lane, fated no doubt eventually to become buried completely.*

We looked at the tumuli and decided on attacking the southern or most perfect one, having got leave. Near this, on each side of the trackway (where I have put the small circles on the plan of January 7) Mr. Heineken called my attention to a number of rings about ten to twelve feet in diameter on the open down. First and last we made out nearly fifty. The furze formed the ring but the area inside was mostly heath. At first we considered whether it might be a British village, but decided they were places where peat had been burnt for the ashes (see October 28, 1879). (*Diary*).

Changes at East Budleigh Church. *Tuesday May 20, 1873.* The vicar and Mrs. Clements drove me over to Hayes Farm, *going* over Peak Hill. As we passed Fox's Corner,

I told them the story of my seeing the open grave of the first Mr. Lousada at the top corner of the garden *opposite* where the roads meet – that is the road up Peak Hill and the lane behind Peak House. When we were lads I was one day in the garden with George Guttores (to whom there is a memorial window in the south side of Sidmouth Church). We were slowly sauntering up the path looking for strawberries that grew on each side. This path at last led us to the corner, and the strawberries having ended I looked up, when to my surprise I saw before me an open grave. There were boards around it, if not over it, just like a new-made grave in a churchyard, and I involuntarily gave vent to some exclamation. My companion however, stopped me by saying, rather mysteriously, 'Uncle means to be buried there'. Some time afterwards 'uncle' died. It was, I think, on a 29th of February being a leap year, though which one I cannot now remember. The relations however, did not comply with his whim. The pit was filled up and his body was removed to London to be interred in some Jewish burial ground. He was a very kind old man and though I was but a mere boy he would invite me there to dinner without my father or mother. His late wife I never saw, *as* she was removed before my time. They used to give large balls at Sidmouth, sometimes not very select according to common report. Once when Mr. and Mrs Lousada were at an evening entertainment in London, where they spent a portion of their time, I have been told that a gentleman among the company came up to Mrs. Lousada and entered into conversation with her. She however, was rather distant for she did not recognise him, so he began to explain that he had had the pleasure of being at one of her grand balls in Sidmouth. 'Perhaps so', replied she, 'but we invite rag, tag and bobtail down there'.

On we went over the hill, through Otterton to Bicton Cross where we turned down to the left and soon arrived at Budleigh. We went and looked at the church. On entering the south gate of the churchyard, I missed the old slab of stone that used to lie on the grass to the right of the path, some six to eight yards above the gate. Tradition informs us that one Radulphus Node made himself a pair of wings and tried to fly. He launched himself into the air from the top of the church tower but flew no further than the spot where the slab lay, which marked the place where he fell, where he was killed and where he was buried. It is said that the slab bore the inscription ORATE PRO ANIMA RADULPHI NODE. I could not see any inscription on the top but there might have been one underneath. However, the slab is gone. The sexton's wife told me that it had been used in some part of the grave of a person by the name of Williams, across the path and a little higher up *and* I remarked that there was such a grave there made in 1855. Another bit of carelessness was committed a few years ago in the church, when a portion was re-seated. The date 1537 carved on one of the fine old bench ends, for which this church is celebrated, used to be on the north side of the middle aisle opposite the Raleigh or Rawley tomb but has now been moved to the north transept (or the portion of the interior which answers to the north transept). This is the more to be condemned because it was close to the Rawley slab and it is said that the family occupied that seat. How few clergymen there are who are fit to take care of the property entrusted to their care. They seem to think that they have a freehold and can do as they like. They forget that in reality they have but a short leasehold and that they stand in the place of trustees, to hold the property for the good of their successors. The name of the present defaulter is Adams. Let his name be known. (*Diary*). (*See January 13, 1853 and June 19, 1866 for previous visits to this church*). *The slab commemorating Radulphus Node's early aeronautical experiment, illegible even by Polwhele's time, had previously earned a less than sympathetic comment from Risdon: 'In the churchyard of this parish a stone showeth this inscription, 'Orate pro anima Radulphe Node'. This, as tradition delivereth, was the sepulture of one that presumed to fly from the tower with artificial wings, and brake his neck; which phaethonical fact of his deserves the name of Nody, be the inscription what it is'. (Risdon, Survey of Devon, p.52). Williams's tomb is still there and Hutchinson would have been pleased to know that the carved bench end dated 1537 has been returned to its original position opposite the Raleigh slab.*

73/5/24 Core Hill. (Diary)

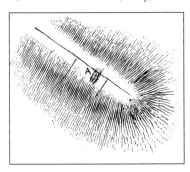

Core Hill. *Saturday May 24, 1873.* Took a walk to Core Hill, *where* I have not been since we 'beat the bounds'. The place where the railway station is to be is now a great brick yard where they are making the bricks for their own works. I made for the point of Core Hill over the fields and hedges after passing High Street. There are traces of an old pond or else some sort of earthwork on the top of the hill at A. It looks something like a ditch and agger, with the agger towards the point of the hill as of a cross-dyke, only it does not descend down the sides of the hill. Near the work, I saw two beach pebble sling stones and picked up five jagged lumps of flint, a scraper and one or two flakes. (*Diary*).

Excavation of tumulus on Salcombe Hil. *Monday May 26, 1873.* There was a partial eclipse of the sun this morning between eight and nine. Though the light of day was not much obscured, there was that peculiar soft colour in it generally accompanying eclipses.

Mr. Heineken and myself drove to the top of Salcombe Hill, *where* he first took a photograph of the megaliths or great stones on the south side of the road and then another of the great stone in the field on the north side (January 7). Then we examined two of the circular patches out of many on each side of the trackway. We had two men with spades and pickaxes and they dug and cleared out two. We wanted to find traces of ancient occupation, whether indeed there had ever been a village here, but nothing whatever was discovered. A new idea suggested itself - whether General Simcoe, when he had his army encamped on Woodbury Hill at the commencement of the century, may have posted a detachment here to watch the valley of the Sid (see June 14, 1861). We propose to examine these places again. We then set the men on the south side of the most southerly of the two tumuli (*B.R. no.89*). The northern one has been cleared away, all but a ring of flints (*B.R. no.88*). A trench was opened and run inwards. It was all flints. There appeared to be a pavement of large flints with traces of charcoal, but we were driven away by showers and violent winds (see June 6). (*Diary*).

73/5/26 *Splendid barrow near Sidmouth! Every preparation made for a thorough examination: but the tenants in possession showed such a hostile determination at resistance, that the attempt was abandoned.* (DRO, Z19/2/8F/73)

Excavations on Salcombe Hill. *Friday June 6, 1873.* Salcombe was again the object of a visit, as we were not satisfied with the last (May 26). The weather was dull and hazy and unfit for photography. We examined two more of the circular patches but did not discover any evidence of occupation or habitation. It is true in one we turned up a broken flint flake and a sling-stone but there was nothing conclusive in this, for both flakes and sling-stones are to be met with on the open heath, left there by the ancient inhabitants. In each circle we dug a trench about eighteen inches wide and deep enough to reach the original soil that had never been disturbed. There was about three inches of black mould *above* six inches of mould with angular flints and we then penetrated nine more into the yellow clay with flints. These circular patches still continue a great puzzle. If they mark the places of ancient huts or wigwams, surely some traces of occupation would be found, such as traces of fire, flint chips or rude pottery. Or, if they are the sites of soldier's tents in more recent times for instance, one might expect to meet with traces of fire also, and perhaps

73/5/26 *There now! Driven off again, and my men scattered. I am tired of this. I am black and blue all over with hard thumps.* (DRO, Z19/2/8F/81)

cinders, pieces of broken pottery or fragments of tobacco pipes. Nothing of the sort however, presented itself in any of the four circles we examined.   Several old men questioned all declare that they never recollect soldiers being encamped on the hill and had never heard of such a thing.   Some remember hearing of the alarm that existed in Sidmouth about the commencement of the present century, when an invasion from France was imminent, at which time General Simcoe had his army on Salcombe Hill.   Mr. Richard Stone the worthy tax gatherer of Sidmouth (whom everyone is glad to see for he always walks into the house so smiling) said he had heard his late father describe the consternation and the preparations made for removing all the women and children inland away from the coast.   Frederich Smith, one of the men working for us, said his grandfather (whom I remember) told him that soldiers were directed to be ready in ambush in a natural hollow that flanks the upper part of the road where it is steepest.   This chasm is now in a cultivated field but *was* then all open heath.

The other man working for us broached an idea that is worthy of attention. He said that perhaps the round patches were spots where they had been burning turf.   It is sometimes the custom, though not very common, for the turf to be pared off to a depth of three or four inches where land is going to be brought into cultivation, and to burn the turf in heaps.   This plan was adopted in Albert Close nearby, belonging to the feoffees, though I think it was not done in the field where the great stone is where sling stones abound.   The process is called 'cutting and burning', though Chappel in his observations on Risdon speaks of den-shiring (or shearing) and implies that the name of the county, Denshire or Devonshire, originated from these words, as if the practise exclusively belonged to this county.   All this we may smile at and put aside.   The circular patches are scattered over an area measuring about 450 paces by about 467, through which the trackway runs over the top of Mill Town lane above Sid (pronounced Seed).   In diameter they vary from six to twelve feet across.   The interior is either grass or heath and it is curious to see how thick the furze grows in a ring all round and yet how persistently absent it is from the middle.   As the root of the furze runs so deep in the ground and is very difficult under ordinary circumstances to destroy, I find it hard to understand how the fire should have killed it so effectively *that it* should refuse to return, though grass and heath do so readily.   The case is somewhat mysterious.

About this time the Misses Osborne came up. I had put up a branch of a tree on the barrow (*B.R. no.89*) which they could see with a glass from Cottingham as a mark.   The trench was proceeded with and carried beyond the centre at A in the plan, *and* at this point Miss Georgina Osborne found an egg-shaped beach pebble like the sling-stones in the cave at Sidbury Castle.   It was not met with in a vase or kistvaen, nor with bones or other remains, but loose among the flints.   If it had been found with *such* remains it would have been important, for down to the present time no sling-stones have been met with in these mounds *linked* with the actual interment. *This is* one circumstance that has led antiquaries to assert that the Ancient Britons did not use the sling.   The case stands this way - there is no proof that they did, but there is no proof that they did not.   Mr. Heineken found one in another barrow, but as this one appears to have been tampered with on the crown and possibly opened, that sling stone may have been thrown in later, as they are met with about the hill. A large Budleigh pebble was picked up at B, where there occurred a bed of charcoal three or four inches thick under a sort of pavement of flints larger than those in the rest of the barrow.   This charcoal was not in the centre *of the barrow* but several feet south of it *and* apparently it had been swept up in a heap, for it only covered a space about two feet in diameter.   This had never been disturbed, for the disturbed part was in the centre.   The great pebble had two pieces split out, perhaps by heat.   We could not discover any remains of bones or bone dust among the charcoal, *which* was of oak and fir. Two white quartz pebbles were met with near the charcoal, one about an inch in diameter and a quarter thick, the other spherical, half an inch through with a small fragment split out and blackened on one side by the fire.   White quartz pebbles were found in the bone bed or refuse heap on High Peak Hill (September 20, 1871) and at other places but their purpose or use is a mystery.

A few yards north of this mound is a tumulus destroyed (*B.R. no.88*. See January

73/6/6   Barrow no. 89.   (Diary)

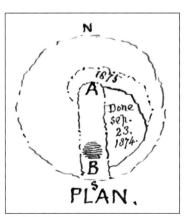

73/6/6   Section of barrow above. (Diary)

7). We set the men to dig in the centre to see if there was anything beneath the surface, but we only met with the soil of the hill. (*Diary*).

Family likeness. *Saturday June 14, 1873.* The Hon. the Lord S.G. Osborne invited me to dinner with him today, and when dinner was over he asked me to go into the next room with him. Here he uncovered a profile medallion of my own face and head looking to the dexter side, about half life size, which he had been modelling in clay at different times without my knowing it. I confess I was considerably surprised. He then made me give him a regular sitting in order to perfect some of the uncertain touches. I did not know my nose was so long. My father had a large nose and I presume some of my ancestors did. One of them, perhaps my great-grandfather the Governor, had been away on some official business and was expected in Boston, Massachusetts, on his return by water, on which occasion some American joker put the following lines in the paper:

'When Hutchinson came the people arose,
To clear a place to land his nose'. (*Diary*).

Otterton, East Budleigh, Hayes Farm and Woodbury Common. *Tuesday June 17, 1873.* Woodbury Hill and our first trip there this year. Mr. Heineken and myself started this morning at ten. Our last visit was on May 3, 1872. Having ascended Peak Hill and attained Otterton, we stopped to look at the new church erected on the foundations of the old one a couple of years ago. We were told that it cost Lady Rolle £13 000. Ham Hill stone is used a great deal in the exterior. There is a nave, chancel, two side aisles and a tower curiously placed at the south-east corner of the building, on the south side of the chancel. The lower portion is now the vestry. In this part of the church there was formerly an old altar tomb to a member of the Courtenay family *which* has since disappeared, *but* from a sketch taken by Mr. Heineken there was a recess or piscina over it. The two brasses once in front of the communion rails fixed in the floor, where I took rubbings of them, are now in the parish chest *but* ought to be re-fixed. One recorded the death of Sarah the wife of Thomas Duke, February 2, 1641, and the other that of Richard Duke, April 19, 1641.

73/6/17   Tomb of James Courtenay   (Diary)

Both the workmanship and the materials of the new church are very good. The columns down each side of the nave are of black veined Plymouth marble some eighteen or twenty inches in diameter, very handsome and of one piece. The capitals are of white stone, the subjects being very well carved. One near the north door represents 'the four ages of women', being four female faces of different ages, one covered with a veil or shroud with the features showing through. I was also delighted with the execution of the pulpit in white stone, the correctness of the forms, the accuracy of the outlines and the sharpness of the angles *having* much to be praised. The roof is of pine stained and varnished, but there is a pleasing absence of those long stiff straight lines that so offend the eye in some churches I could name. All the work is good and of the Second Pointed or Decorated period. In the churchyard there are ten yew trees, the largest and oldest near the south-east corner measuring nine feet one inch in diameter a foot above the ground. I looked again at the altar tomb of Richard Green the ship builder, represented at work on one end of the tomb and a ship on the other. I made a sketch of him in 1849 but he has much decayed since. I saw elsewhere an inscription to Richard Abbott, drowned in the 'great flood' in 1753.

We then went on to East Budleigh and took another look at the church there. According to the sexton's wife, the slab over Radulphus Node (see May 20) was about twelve feet above the top step or sixteen from its centre. Inside the church there is a handsome tablet in white marble to the name of Reade. I regret I did not copy all the coats of arms on the bench ends I observed, *including* Denis, Courtenay and some others. There is an ancient ship at the south-east corner.

We also stopped at Hayes Farm as we passed along (*see April 20, 1864*). The farmer complains bitterly of the trouble, interruption and annoyance that visitors cause him and his family, by calling when they are busy and demanding to see Sir Walter's room. They want to deny everybody and put a stop to it. I told them that it was impossible to destroy the fame of Sir Walter Rawley and that the best way would be to make a profit out of it and charge so much a head for admission. They ought to have busts and portraits of Sir Walter, pictures of his exploits, some of the potatoes he brought back from South America and the very baccy pipe he smoked.

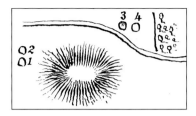

73/6/17 The four newly discovered tumuli. (Diary)

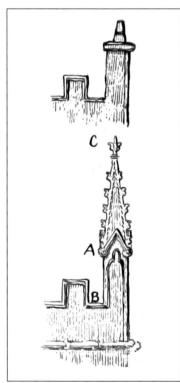

73/7/17-1 Old and new pinnacles. (Diary)

After that we proceeded to the open heath and discussed our sandwiches on a small conical hill near the road. I did the same here on April 20, 1864. The mound has been dug into on the top *but* no one, I imagine, could have mistaken this natural hillock for a tumulus. It was a beautiful situation for luncheon with the wild heath all around. In a little valley with some damp ground to the east, there is an abundance of Drosera rotundifolia or sundew and Eriophorum augustifolium or cotton grass. Attempts, I believe, have been made to spin this cotton into thread but the filaments are too short or otherwise unfit. We discovered four barrows we had not seen before (*see map*). The two to the west of the mound were each about twenty feet in diameter and three feet high. Number three had a trench run in from the north margin but it looked more as if they had been digging for a fox or rabbit than for a kistvaen. Number four is doubtful.

After this we proceeded to the three copses (see May 3, 1872) and then south to the three barrows, *which* seem to be composed of pebbles and earth. They have been tampered with on the top. I dug into the middle one and was surprised to find that most of the pebbles were split and blackened, as if by the action of fire. A careful search also discovered pieces of oak charcoal on, in and about most of the disturbed barrows on these hills, and it is worthy of remark that in the present day the oak does not grow here, or is amongst the rarest of trees. We then espied another *barrow* a little to the west of south, and yet another just across the road to the east, this last forty-four feet in diameter and three feet high.

We have long desired to look for British villages, hut circles, refuse heaps or other traces of ancient habitation on these wild hills and this was one of the points for investigation today. We therefore turned northwards and followed an old trackway across the moor, but could not find any circles or circular patches of different vegetation that might indicate wigwams or huts. We were rather surprised at not discerning, either by eye or by glass, any traces of the sort. Ancient tribes must have abounded here, *for* Woodbury Castle is at hand and their burial mounds are scattered about. Neither could we anywhere discover any flint flakes, though the Sidmouth hills abound with them. It is true that this hill is not in the flint district, but flint implements must have been used here and must have been brought from a distance. Geological maps show patches of Greensand at Black Hill and Woodbury Castle but the only flints here are white chert. On the west side of the trackway, at about 357 yards south of the cross roads (Woodbury Road), we noted down a new barrow apparently untouched. We pushed on to Woodbury Castle and walked around it, but discovered nothing new. I have not learnt of any antiquities of any value have been found there. We turned south to the carfoix (where the four tumuli covered with trees are) and returned home through Yettington. We saw Portland light very bright when coming down Peak Hill, for it was getting dusk. (*Diary*).

Return to Salcombe Hill barrow. *Tuesday July 8, 1873.* Mr. Heineken and myself went to make another examination of the cairn or barrow on Salcombe Hill (the same as June 6). We merely continued in an easterly direction from B to the point C, as in the former plan. We met with a flint flake or two but they may have rolled down from the top, though found at the bottom. (*Diary*).

Sidmouth Church pinnacles. *Thursday July 17, 1873.* The south-east and last pinnacle put up close to the turret. The old pinnacles now removed were put up sixty or seventy years ago by the churchwarden's stone mason in place of the original ones, which were decayed and partly destroyed. These temporary ones were of no known style of architecture. There was a touch of Roman if anything but they were contemptible on a Gothic tower, and yet I was very much abused when I first proposed to remove them and put up new ones of a more correct pattern. And those who talked loudest were those who were most ignorant of the subject. The four new ones were to cost twelve guineas each but the bases were found to be so rotten that new stone was required, increasing the expense. They measure on average, from the lower side of the bars A to the bottom of the embrasure B four foot three inches, and from the lower side of the boss to the summit C nine feet one inch. These measurements may however vary an inch in different pinnacles. They have been given by four residents; the Earl of Buckinghamshire, the Rev. H. G. J. Clements the vicar, Dr. Radford and Mr. Thornton. There is an iron tube down through the centre of each, about an inch and a quarter in diameter and eleven or twelve feet long, *though* I doubt the policy of so long or thick a tube. The holes in the top are stopped. Some people suggest four small vanes stuck in these holes and the removal of the present ugly weathercock (dated 1809) from the turret. The patterns of the bosses consist of ivy leaves, oak leaves and acorns, vine leaves with grapes, etc. The last I did, on the same block of stone with Miss Osborne's at the south-west corner. Over the clock face is a cat with a mouse in its mouth, the subject suggested by a somewhat similar one in the Chapter House at Lichfield. The height of the tower to the top of the battlements is about seventy-five feet though I once made it six inches longer, but perhaps the cord stretched. (*Diary*). *Hutchinson's pinnacles no longer decorate the tower. After just a hundred years they were declared unsafe and were removed. (Whitton and Lane 1997).*

73/7/17 Cat and mouse.
(Diary)

Sidmouth meeting of the Devonshire Association. *Tuesday July 22, 1873.* The Devonshire Association met at Sidmouth today *and* the Right Hon. Steph. Cave, President, read his address. (*Diary*).

Thursday July 24, 1873. Reading papers. I read one on 'Submerged Forest and Fossil Teeth. (*Diary*).

Queen Victoria's flounce. *Monday August 4, 1873.* Went with Lord S.G. Osborne to Miss Radford the lace dealer who lives on the south side of New Street, so called, to see some lace. It consists of a flounce which is being made for some lady of high degree. It is about fourteen or fifteen inches deep, is several yards long *and* is valued at fifty guineas a yard. It is the most beautiful I ever saw. I like it better than a flounce made for one of the Royal Family a few years ago, which I saw at Mrs. Hayman's. I do not know how many yards long that was, but the whole was valued at 300 guineas. (*Later note*: It was for the Queen). (*Diary*).

Hard labour. *Thursday August 7, 1873.* Edward Bartlett, the fisherman, is again in trouble. He has been frequently before the magistrates for being drunk and disorderly *and* this time he has got a sentence of two months imprisonment with hard labour for violent conduct and assaulting the police. He managed to get to the beach where he launched his boat and stood off the town to watch events. The police went down and wanted to follow him but none of the fishermen would launch their boats. Towards evening, he went right off and is believed to be steering for Guernsey. (*Later note:* He got to Guernsey and sold his boat to raise money, but finding he could not get a living there, he came back and quietly went to prison). (*Diary*).

73/9/2 *Two-penny Loaf.*
(Hist of Sid. I,16)

Two-penny loaf. *Tuesday September 2, 1873.* Had an early dinner at Cottington *and* afterwards went fishing in a boat with Lord S. G. O. The wind was north-west and squally but the sea was pretty smooth. The boatman first pulled us over to Ladram Bay where we let out lines for whiting, but my Lord pulled up a mackerel and then I did the same. Thinking that this fish abounded most we took in the lines and threw out others baited for mackerel but then I caught three young gurnards, one after another. We then went on to Chizzlebury or Chesilbury Bay, beyond Ladram Bay, and saw the 'Two-penny loaf', a solitary rock on the reef at the base of the cliff which I had not seen for many years. Passing that we approached Otterton Head, or rather the point this side called 'Brandy Point' because in former days it was one of the usual places where smugglers landed brandy kegs. It is the point seen from Sidmouth beach. We returned after having been out nearly four hours. (*Diary*).

Chairlift. *Thursday September 4, 1873.* Went into the ham or field near the river to see what Mr. Dunning was doing in the matter of the new gas house and coal depot and got into conversation with him. Whilst there, we were much amused at seeing a cow walk out of a neighbouring carpenter's yard with a chair upon her head. She had strayed into the yard through a gap in the fence, and whilst examining the various articles that she met with, she had thrust her nose down through a hole in the seat of an old rush-bottomed chair. In lifting her head, her left horn got caught under the top bar of the back, so that the higher she lifted her head the higher went the chair, so that she could not extricate her nose. The workmen turned out and had a good laugh at her and then took it off. (*Diary*).

73/9/4 *Who stole the chair?*
(Diary)

Dawlish visit. *Monday September 8, 1873.* Went to Belmont Villa, Dawlish. (*Diary*).

Coryton's Cove. *Tuesday September 9, 1873.* After breakfast, I took a walk to the Bishop's Parlour, now called Coryton's Cove. Tradition says that one of the former bishops of Exeter delayed too long and got caught by the tide here, and hence the name. Why are the Dawlish people so silly as to change an old name which has a legend attached to it for a new one which is only the name of an evanescent dweller near the spot? (*Diary*).

Railway damage. *Thursday September 11, 1873.* Walked to the warren by way of the beach *and* observed the damage done to the railway wall last winter. Dawlish station was burnt a month ago, supposed*ly* by the luggage train about ten in the evening. Called at Warren House and saw the Lees who used to live at Sidmouth, had an early tea with them and walked back over the cliff. (*Diary*).

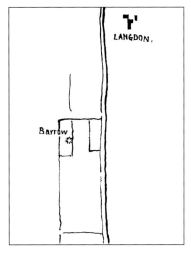

73/9/12   Site of Langdon barrow. (Diary)

Walk to Water Hill barrow. *Friday September 12, 1873.* Took a walk along the ridge of the hill from Dawlish church to Mamhead, to see whether the barrow I have often visited before was still untouched. It is on the left or west side of the lane a quarter of a mile south of Langdon; the field is this year in potatoes. They have been digging around the barrow too closely and thereby encroaching upon it. The diameter is now forty feet and the height seven or eight, *and* there is a depression on the top as if it had been tampered with, though I doubt whether the centre has been reached or disturbed. I hunted all over the fallow or bare fields for flint flakes struck from a core, but could not detect a trace of one. To find anything of the sort here made of black flint would be interesting, because the chalk district from which they must be derived is so many miles distant. Beer Head is the nearest source. The chert or white flint on Haldon would supply them at need but black flint splits or flakes the best.

I returned the same way, that is by taking the field paths along the ridge of the hill above the strand at Dawlish. The twenty-six fir trees on the highest part of the hill are now only twenty-three. (*Diary*).

Back to Sidmouth. *Monday September 15, 1873.* Returned to Sidmouth through Exeter. (*Diary*).

Leasing the Old Chancel. *Thursday September 18, 1873.* Having let my house No. 4 Coburg Terrace to Mr. and Mrs. Merrington for 3, 5 or 7 years commencing on the 29th, I had a sale of my furniture today, the tenants reserving some of the articles and I taking one or two over to the Old Chancel. This reduced the proceeds to £88. 15. 0. (*Diary*).

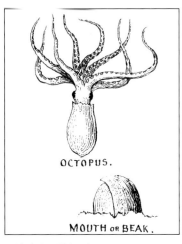

73/9/19   (Diary)

Octopus. *Friday September 19, 1873.* Some visitors here went out in a boat for the purpose of catching blin, a species of whiting, *but* it so happened that they pulled up one of those cephalopods, the octopus. It *squirmed* about so much in the boat that the sailors put their coats over it to keep it down. The party was very much frightened, not knowing what awful creature they had caught and the sailors not having seen one before, so they hurried back to Sidmouth to get on shore. It is furnished with eight arms, which issue from its head, studded with a double row of suckers, *and* in the middle is the mouth having mandibles like a parrot's beak *with which* it is able to break through the shell of a crab. This specimen, about eighteen inches long, is rather smaller than one caught here in 1865, which I saw dissected by Lady Dowling, a friend of Mrs. Maitland who then occupied my house. She dissected out the mandibles and as far as I recollect they were like the sketch. Some of the larger specimens in the tropics are said to attain twenty feet in length, and terrible stories are told of their catching sailors within their long arms. (*Diary*).

Bury Camp again. *Tuesday September 23, 1873.* Branscombe was the place to which Mr. Heineken and myself went today *and* warm and summery was the weather. Mounted Salcombe Hill and stopped at Slade to examine the hydraulic ram recently erected. It is down the valley in an orchard more than two hundred feet below the level of the house, but by little and little it sends the water up and fills the tanks. The only other hydraulic ram I have seen was at Caverswall Castle in Staffordshire. After leaving

Slade, we proceeded to Bury Camp where we had so often been before (May 7, 1858), and examined the earthworks again all round. The most perfect part of the fosse is at the north-west end at A. At B it is also very perfect though less deep, and both A and B are overgrown with bushes. At C it is all in grass *and* at D a modern hedge occupies the dotted line and the fosse is nearly filled up. At E the vallum is all in grass like the interior, but with several breaks and much ploughed down. We then went beyond the hedge F and looked into the chasm leading to the chalk quarries, recently abandoned.

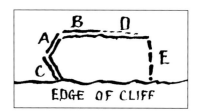

73/9/23 *Bury Camp.* (Diary)

On returning through the camp we gathered a few mushrooms, but I refrained from eating them as I do not wish to be poisoned before my time. But we also gathered and took home a number of large brown puff balls, some nearly as large as my fist. I have heard that they make artificial lightening in theatres with the dust of these things, by puffing them over the flame of a candle (I must try it), and the country people use the soft interior as a styptic to stop the bleeding when they cut themselves.

We then drove on through Branscombe without stopping, and on reaching the lower part of the village we wheeled round to the left and climbed the hill towards the north. We were in search of an earthwork, some said an ancient camp, on one of the hills but our directions were not sufficiently definite so we strayed like lost sheep. And in one of the lanes we *did* meet a fine sheep, covered with beautiful clean wool, which we concluded had broken out of some field. To our surprise it ran up to us and allowed us to stroke its head, for it was quite tame. Some of the views among these steep hills and deep dells were worth coming a long way to see.

Failing to discover what we came for, we got into the great road and returned home, passing near the west end of the earthwork A (see August 23, 1872) and through the cross-dyke B. (*Diary*).

Earthworks above Branscombe. *Saturday October 3, 1873.* Having obtained more information, we started again for the hills above Branscombe. We went by the Three Horseshoes and followed the blue line to D. We took another look at earthwork A and then stopped at C, where an Ancient British sepulchral urn was ploughed up many years ago (see September 26, 1859 and August 23, 1872). We went into this field, called Crossway Close, *where* the plough probably destroyed the remains of a tumulus. The spot was close to the hedge by the lane where there is a rise in the ground, and on pacing I made it some 57 paces above the lower hedge. The pieces of urn were scattered *but* I made a cast of the only fragment I saw. Mr. Power of Elverway had it. We found eleven beach pebbles like sling-stones in this field but only brought some away. Of course, we must always bear in mind that such pebbles might be brought in manure or sea-weed from the beach when that is used, but this spot is rather far for seaweed and a labourer told us that they never brought it there. We also found a few flint flakes

Leaving this spot, we proceeded to Woodhead, where the view is beautiful towards the sea, and then to the east side of earthwork D where we entered on the level. We had been assured that this was an ancient British camp of great importance but the result of two journeys only convinced us that we had come to discover what is called a 'mare's nest'. There is a perpendicular wall of rock, the yellow sandstone of the green-sand formation, about eight to ten feet high, curving round the south point and west flank of the hill. If this had been a camp or hill fortress, this work ought to have been carried all round so as to make an enclosed area, but this does not *as* it is all open on the north and east sides. A labouring man told us he believed it to be only an old stone quarry and appearances seemed to confirm the assertion. We lay on the grass on the crown of the hill and discussed our mid-day meal and the situation. We *also* discussed the nature of the work, walked round it and examined it, picked up a sling-stone or two and one or two flint flakes, and then, not a little disappointed, returned home by the same route as we came. (*Diary*).

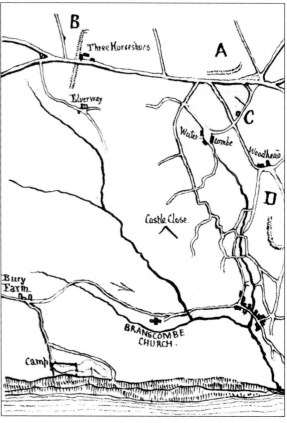

73/9/23 (Diary)

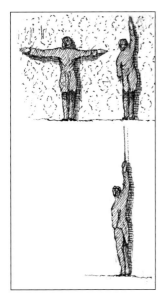

73/10/9   (Diary)

Physical measurements. *Thursday October 9, 1873.* Spending the evening with Mr. Heineken and remembering that we had measured the perpendicular wall of rock at Branscombe by reaching up with a stick, we made some experiments in measuring. I believe I am 5 feet 9½ inches, and by standing with my face to the wall I could stretch *sideways* 5 feet 10 inches, which is a little more than my height. I could reach upwards 7 feet 2 ½ inches to the top of my middle finger and 9 feet 8 inches with a 3 feet walking stick in my hand. The last however, might vary according to how much one grasps in the hand. This of course is not very accurate measuring, but it might do upon certain occasions. In measuring upwards the heels must be on the ground. Mr. Heineken I believe is an inch taller than I am. (*Diary*).

Asherton mansion. *Saturday October 18, 1873.* This afternoon we took a walk out on the Exeter road for half a mile or more, to look at the site of the ancient Asherton mansion, the Ascarton of the Otterton Cartulary six centuries ago and for a time the seat of the Harlewyn family. The late Captain Carslake of Cotmaton told me that Asherton was situated between Brewery Lane to the south and Cox's Lane on the north, though it may not have comprised the whole of this ground. He said there was a rough place in one of the fields where he thought the old house may have stood. Mr. Heineken and myself hunted over two or three fields on the crown of the hill but could not discover any indications. We came out on the west side where the railway station is *being built*. (*Diary*).

Slow progress. *Friday October 31, 1873.* At home writing my History of Sidmouth, which however goes on too slowly. There being so many interruptions *and* visiting runs away with too much valuable time. I have only now got as far as the account of the boundaries. (*Diary*).

New choral society. *Tuesday December 2, 1873.* An attempt is being made to form a new Choral Society here. I delivered nearly fifty circulars inviting people to join. (*Diary*).

Choral practise. *Monday December 8, 1873.* There was the first meeting for practise of the new Choral Society this evening, in the schoolroom by All Saints Church. *There were* present thirty-nine. I hope it will hold together better than the old one did ten years ago. That one was broken up because everybody wanted to play first fiddle, which failing in human nature made some witty person say that there was no instrument in the world so difficult to play as a second fiddle. (*Diary*).

Devonshire cream. *Friday December 12, 1873.* After breakfast I walked out to Parkham, or Parkcombe as some think it should be written, and paid Mrs. Mitchell for some of that stuff that the Phoenicians are said to have introduced into Damnonia peradventure a thousand years before the Christian era, to wit Devonshire cream. It is said it is to be still found in the Lebanon as it is here round Dartmoor. (*Diary*).

Pleasant afternoon. *Wednesday December 24, 1873.* Had luncheon at one o'clock at Cottington, after which the Misses Osborne accompanied me down to the Old Chancel where the afternoon was spent in carving oak by the one and drawing by the other. When it was too dark to see, we wound up with coffee and cake. A very pleasant afternoon truly *and* such are the bright spots in life. (*Diary*).

1873.

1874

New Years Day 1874. *Thursday January 1, 1874.* Being a Thursday, came in mildly, and suggested most of the commonplace reflections that occur on such occasions. This is the time of year when people make good resolutions, and all the rest of the year is the time when they forget them. (*Diary*).

Offer for the Old Chancel. *Wednesday January 7, 1874.* Mr. Sutherland, agent for the Trustees of the Manor, having shown me some interesting old maps of this parish and discussed some of the historical events connected with it, spent the evening with me when we went deeper into these subjects. Talking of harbour projects, I gave him lithographed copies of the plan of 1837, wherein two piers were run out over Chit Rocks to enclose an area of ten acres. He then surprised me by asking whether I would sell to the Trustees the houses and land I had here. They have been buying up many detached pieces of land recently. The alleged reason for the application was that they contemplated forming a handsome road from All Saint's Church to the parish church and that my land stood in the way. I said that I had made the Old Chancel my amusement and did not wish to part with it, that I had not yet even completed my plan and that the only consideration that could induce me to think of parting with it would be that I had no children to leave it to and my late brother's children in South Australia did not seem to care about coming to England. The matter must at all events stand over for the present. (*Diary*).

Sidmouth harbour. *Saturday January 24, 1874.* There is a nice little struggle going on here just now between the Trustees of the Manor of Sidmouth on one side and Mr. Dunning on the other, who recently bought the gas works and afterwards the Ham and is now beginning new gas works near the river. Some say the trustees are vexed at seeing the gas works, which they meant to have bought, slip through their fingers and that we may guess at the reason for their opposition. Mr. Dunning has also put out a plan for the construction of a harbour by means of piers and this is opposed by them too. Having known Sidmouth beach in fair weather and foul for so many years, some of the reasons put forward by new men as to the injury it will do in affecting the accumulation of shingle, appear to me to be very frivolous. It is amusing to see how some people who were praising Mr. Dunning to the skies only three months ago for a liberal and public-spirited man, having discovered that the Trustees must not be offended, have now turned round and are hurling abuse at him. The local board too, by voting strong measures at their meeting recently and then rescinding them at the next, have raised the laughter of the town against them.

74/1/24 Projected plans for harbour at Sidmouth. (Diary)

74/1/24 (Hist of Sid. IV,164)

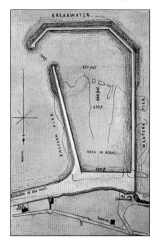

The earliest plan for a harbour in the Ham was long ago described to me as a basin with an entrance between stone piers from the sea. The River Sid could be turned into the back of it. The scheme of 1837 contemplated a basin (like the Cob at Lyme) formed by two arms or stone piers enclosing an area of ten acres. It was over the Chit Rocks at the west end of the beach. Another scheme about 1857 reverted to the Ham *and* this one had the advantage of an inner basin as well as an outer one, and the connection between the two could be closed. For Mr. Dunning's latest harbour plan, see the design in my MS *Hist. Of Sidmouth IV, 170.* (*Diary*).

Siamese twins. *Monday February 9, 1874.* So the Siamese twins are dead, who made such a noise in the world and were shown about in various countries and finally settled down in America. They were born in Siam, closely united side by side with

74/2/9   Siamese twins.   (Diary)

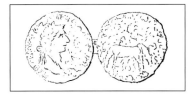

74/3/?   Coin of Nerva.   (Diary)

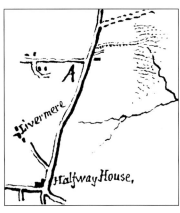

74 /4/21   North of Halfway
House.   (Diary)

a ligature.   After they had been brought as curiosities to Europe it was proposed by some to separate them, but it was decided that their lives would be endangered as a perceptible circulation passed between them.   They made a good fortune by exhibiting themselves.   When I was in New York in February and March 1837, I was walking up Broadway one evening by lamplight, *when* I saw two boys get out of a carriage and walk across the flagstone sidewalk into a house.   I happened to come up to them just at that moment *and* was surprised to see two boys walking so closely together.   I thought they were carrying something heavy between them, for they shuffled awkwardly.   I was told afterwards that they were the Siamese twins.   I had no time to examine whether they were under one coat or two.   The most extraordinary event of their lives was their marriage, or rather marriages, for they married two women, and I believe had families.   It caused much remark and some joking in Europe, *and* I doubt whether it could have been done on this side of the water.   Their domestic arrangements must have been of rather a novel kind.   (*Diary*).

Coin of Nerva.   *March, 1874.*   Brass coin of Nerva.   Profile visible but no inscription.   On the reverse are traces of horses.   Dug up in the middle of old Fore Street March 1874.   (*History of Sidmouth I, 97*).

Lord Rolle.   *Monday March 30, 1874.*   There is a report this afternoon in Sidmouth that Bicton House is on fire *and* were I sure it was true I would hurry to the top of Peak Hill and look, but knowing from experience that false reports are as plenty as blackberries I will wait.   Bicton was anciently Bucketon and Buckinton.   The manor was conferred on the family of Janitor, or doorkeeper, soon after the Conquest for the service of guarding the gate of the gaol at Exeter Castle.   Some people, even our grave historians, have run away with the idea that the gaol was at Bicton but it is time that this notion was abandoned.   Others, by a still more extraordinary mistake, have contrived to place it at Harpford, but how they got this impression I cannot imagine.   The manor afterwards went into the possession of Dennis, and from Dennis to Rolle.   The late Lord Rolle was the last of his name *and* left no children.   I never saw him but once and then he was on horseback.   He had very large feet and there is an old story going about that George III chaffed him on the subject and said his shoes should be fitted out as privateers to cruise against the French.   A rather amusing anecdote is told as occurring in this neighbourhood *when* he was reviewing his volunteer troops on Woodbury Hill.   Some low fellows who were looking on derided his soldiery qualities.   He happened to ride up accompanied by his staff officers and heard a great altercation between two men.   Recognising one of them by his uniform, he demanded to know what the quarrel was about.   The man replied that the other was saying disrespectful things of his Lordship and that he was contradicting him.   'And what did he say of me?' enquired Lord Rolle.   The man hesitated and made excuses saying that his Lordship would be angry if he repeated what was said, but Lord Rolle insisted on knowing.   'Well', answered the man, 'if I must tell, he said you weren't fit to carry guts to a bear'.   'Ho!' cried his Lordship, wincing, 'and what did you say?'   'I zed you was, my Lord'.   (*Diary*).

Venn Ottery earthwork.   *Tuesday April 21, 1874.*   Owing to practising and the work entailed by the concert, and some unsettled weather since, Mr. Heineken and myself did not make our first antiquarian investigation until today.   Last year it was March 27th.   We wished to re-examine an earthwork on Fen Ottery Hill (or Venn as they pronounce it) and also to go to Belbury Castle where we had not been since May 31, 1861.   Starting at 11 o'clock, we proceeded by Knowle, Broadway (the house built there in 1825 by the late Gen. Slessor being now pulled down by the trustees of the Manor, I suppose to build a new one) and so to the station, now nearly completed, and then through Newton Poppleford.   Instead of going up Aylesbeare Hill we turned away to the right at the head of the village, and in time and after a considerable distance, at last struck upon the road that runs from the Halfway House towards Ottery.   *This road is* part of the ancient Portway, starting at the mouth of the Exe and running north-east by Woodbury Castle, Hembury Fort, etc.

At sixty paces north-east from the fork A, a ridge or bank runs away from the road eastwards near some gravel pits across a piece of open moorland.   It may be about ten feet wide and two or three feet high and winds somewhat irregularly, as if thrown up in a hurry or without much supervising care. I paced it and made it near three hundred paces long, its general bearing tending east and west. At its east end the ground quickly descends into a valley with a brook at the bottom. At first I thought it turned south from its east end, but I believe not. Perhaps this work is not much more than seventy years old *as* it is barely a mile in rear of the 'Soldier's Pits' on Aylesbeare Hill, and may have been thrown up by Gen. Simcoe's troops about the commencement of the present century as a retreat in case of necessity. Or, query, peradventure during the civil wars.

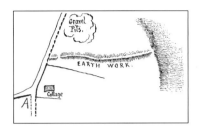

74/4/21 *The same* as the above *but on a larger scale.* (Diary)

We now proceeded half a mile northwards to the crown of a wild hill where there was a fine view, and unpacked our hamper of provisions. The heath has not come out yet but the gorse is one golden mass of yellow blossom. Steering north-eastwards we in time reached Belbury Castle. I got over the hedge at the bottom and walked up the sunken road, the old British trackway. We were anxious to search the interior of this camp to see if we could find any flint flakes. This is important because it is not in a flint district *but on* the Budleigh Pebble Beds *and if* any could be found, it must have been brought from a distance. We could not find any in the camp, but in the field to the east we at last met with a core and four flakes of grey flint and two flakes of semi-transparent chert. This shows that the makers of flint implements had been at work here.

On driving home, we stopped at Bishop's Court. Lysons informs us that this was one of the residences of Bishop Grandisson, that he granted it to his steward John Mercer, that it was confirmed to the Mercer family and that it continued with them until it was carried by an heiress in marriage to the Markers of Coombe. There is a coat of arms cut out of a solid block of oak about a foot square standing loose on the mantle shelf of the room with the panelled ceiling. I do not know the bearing but may be able some day to identify it. (*Diary*).

74/4/21   Unknown bearing. (Diary)

Salcombe Regis Church and some bodysnatchers.   *Friday May 1, 1874.* Walked over Salcombe Hill to Salcombe village. Several children accosted me with green boughs in their hands decorated with ribbons of various colours, asking for something because it was May Day. A single penny on such an occasion made a group of children happy. At Dawlish it is the custom to dress up a doll in a small cradle and carry it about.

Walked a ploughed field on Salcombe Hill and by dint of searching all the way across, I found a tolerably good flint scraper of the 'thumb flint' type. It was at A, north of the cottage. I then went to Salcombe vicarage, got the key of the church and went in *and* took a rubbing of the tablet fixed to the south wall of the chancel. It is in Hebrew, Greek, Latin and English, and was erected in memory of Joanna Avant, a daughter of a former vicar of the parish, who died in 1695. There is a slab to the same name let into the floor below but I did not have time to copy it. Last March, a new memorial window to my late friend the Rev. Basset Mortimer was placed at the east end of the north aisle by his young widow, whom I knew as Miss Stephenson. The window close to it, to the memory of Colonel Gray, I have examined before.

74/5/1   (Diary)

74/5/1   Salcombe Hill. (Diary)

This church was restored some thirty years ago, when the stonework was scraped of the limewash and some neat windows put in, *but* disputes arose on the occasion. This is now commonly the case as questions of High Church and Low Church are too often introduced. A great quarrel also arose owing to the tendency of some of the books in the parish school at Salcombe, introduced by the Misses Morris whose father then lived at Sidcliff. Mr. Christie, who lived at Salcombe Mount, published a pamphlet in which he quoted passages from these books, showing their leaning towards Roman Catholic doctrines and practices though in a school attached to the Reformed Church of England. These charges thus brought against the management of the school were indignantly denied, the Morris family went away and not long after the ladies turned Roman Catholics.

The annexed pen and ink drawings are from sketches made during different visits over the hill to Salcombe. When the chancel was rebuilt in 1869, a solid block of stone of oblong form, supposed to have been the ancient altar, was found embedded in the thickness of the wall. It had a wheel pattern with six rays on various parts of it of Norman character. The workmen,

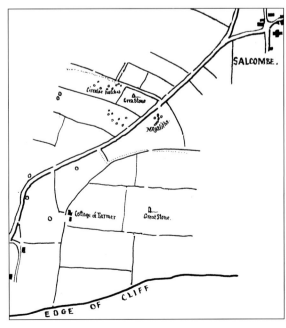

Above left: 74/5/1-3 *font.* (Diary)
Above right: 74/5/1-4 *column.*
(Diary)

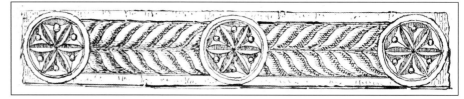

74/5/1   *Part of an ancient stone altar, now in south wall, inside.* (Diary)

not knowing what it was, cut it up and placed one portion in the middle of the south wall of the chancel inside (the sketch) and another portion outside the north wall. The snout of some animal, apparently intended to portray a pig, is a curious feature jutting out from the north wall. As may be here seen, there are fragments of Norman, Decorated and Perpendicular work in various parts of the building. In the angle outside, where the north wall of the chancel leaves the nave, a hole was discovered when the wall was pulled down. On looking into it, which I did, there was a hollow *which* turned out to contain the steps up to the ancient rood loft. It was not further disturbed. (For more about Salcombe refer to July 13, 1869). (*Diary*).

At the south-west corner of the churchyard there formerly was a labourer's cottage and premises, which was occupied by himself with his wife and family. Death robbed him of one of his children, which was buried in the southern half of the yard. Two surgeons of Sidmouth, Mr. Hodge and Mr. Jeffery, set their eyes upon this body and determined that they would try and procure it. Being so long ago it is hard to fix a date to these occurrences, *but* it may have been between the years 1840 and 1850. Experts at 'body snatching', as it was called, did not depend on such simple tools as the spade and pickaxe *but* contrived some sort of apparatus by which they could pull a coffin out of a grave by main force. Part of the earth was first taken out at the head end, then a long iron bar with a screw at the point was forced down and screwed into the lid at its upper extremity and by working a powerful lever the coffin

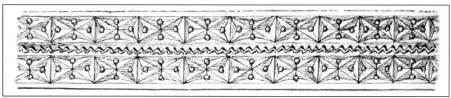

74/5/1   *Over east window – outside.* (Diary)

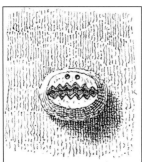

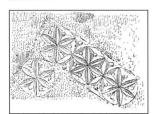

From top: 74/5/1 *Over east window – outside;*
74/5/1 *Label end, east window. Arms of the see;*
74/5/1 *Snout of some animal, outside north wall;*
74/5/1-11 *Outside north wall.* (Diary)

could be pulled out of the ground. On this occasion however these operations were rudely brought to a sudden stop. Whilst the surgeons were busy at work in the obscurity of the night, there was a flash at the cottage window – a report - and they were both severely hit with small shot. Mr. Jeffery received the bulk of the charge in his right side over the region of the liver, *whilst* Mr. Hodge escaped with only a few stray shot. Finding that they were discovered and not wishing to be detained, their only thought was that of immediate escape. They dropped their tools - abandoned the apparatus - and ran for it. They had a mile and a half to go. Jeffery said he felt the blood running down the leg of his trousers and on arriving at Sidmouth, Hodge took him into his house on the east side of the High Street and spent a great part of the night extracting the shot, which fortunately had not penetrated between the ribs. This business was kept very quiet for fear of detection *but* the man at Salcombe did not appear to make any great effort to discover whom he had shot. More than ten years after this occurrence I was with Jeffery one evening and he then told me all about it. (*History of Sidmouth III, 141a*).

74/5/1   *Under east window outside.* (Diary)

 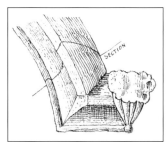 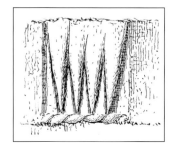 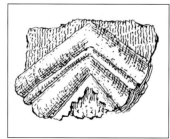

Above from left to right: 74/5/1 *North side, of Perpendicular character*; 74/5/1 *window label, north side, of Decorated character*; 74/5/1-14 *Head of capital, Norman, outside south side*; 74/5/1 *Outside south wall*. (Diary)

This was not the only occasion when Jeffery aroused the wrath of the local inhabitants (see December 3, 1876) nor the first time Hutchinson had heard tales of body snatching. He later recalled an incident whilst his father was a medical student at Exeter Hospital, when bodies for dissection could only be obtained by what some would call rather irregular means. I have heard my father say that they went out one night with tools to possess themselves of this body (*an executed criminal*) but had not been digging long before they perceived soldiers in the dim light of the night getting over the fences, and the discharge of sundry horse-pistols among them made some of the party rather disposed to run for it: they however held their ground when the soldiers came up, and handling them pretty roughly, for they were evidently the worse for liquor, and threatening them with instant death, thrust their swords through the coats of some, and then led them all off to the Guard-room of the barracks where they were temporally quartered. When there they loudly demanded to see the officers, but the officers were at the theatre in Exeter. They were released about midnight, but they laid a strong complaint against the conduct of the men in endangering their lives. The officers made every apology and had the men drawn out in line, when the complainants passed up and down before them, but they found it impossible to identify or swear to any of their assailants.

I have part of the skin of a negro, hanged about this period at Heavitree Gallows and dissected at the Hospital by my father and the other students. It is however not so much the skin as the cuticle and the colouring matter. It is of a deep brown. (*Diary and Letters of Thomas Hutchinson II, 474*).

Old Chancel curiosities. *Friday May 22, 1874.* Three of the maidservants from Lord and Lady Osborne at Cottington came to have a look at the Old Chancel. I showed them my curiosities and the building, and ended by taking them up on the lead roof. They were most amused, or horrified, by the shark's jaws, the pig with eight legs, the Australian skulls, the toad fish, the boa constrictor skin, the bloody swords taken in 1858 during the Indian Mutiny, the oak carving, the panelled ceiling in the oak room with the coats of arms of the lords and lessees of the Manor of Sidmouth painted and gilt by me, the mantel shelf, book case and window cornice carved by me and sundry other odds and ends, good, bad and indifferent. (*Diary*).

Admiral Parker. *Monday June !, 1874.* This day in 1794 the great victory of Lord Howe over the French fleet took place. My mother's father, Parker of Harburn, commanded the Audacious and dismasted the French ship Revolutionaire of superior force, for which he was made an admiral. He was afterwards made a baronet for his share in the Battle of St. Vincent. (*Diary*).

Belbury Castle. *Tuesday June 2, 1874.* Went again with Mr. Heineken to Belbury Castle (see April 21). As there are no flints in that district and we were anxious to see if we could discover any manufactured flint implements or refuse flakes within the area of the camp, because if so, it would be conclusive proof that the ancient inhabitants of that stronghold had brought them from a distance. The area called 'Castle Fields', this summer in potatoes, we hunted over for some time. Whilst so searching, a sketch of Bishop's Court may be given. We had passed by Bowd and Tipton and crossed the river before stopping at the Court, where I rather hurriedly took the sketch annexed. At last Mr. Heineken picked up a half round flint scraper near the middle of the camp and one or two flint chips. Though they were too few to satisfy my craving, they at all events proved the point we desired to ascertain. I would willingly have searched longer, for I

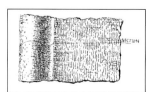

From top: 74/5/1 *Outside south wall*;
74/5/1 *Outside south wall*;
74/5/1 *East end of north aisle*. (Diary)

74/6/2 *Bishop's Court.* (Diary)

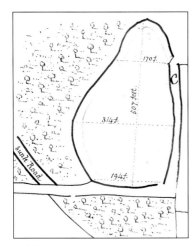

74/6/2   Belbury Castle   (Diary)

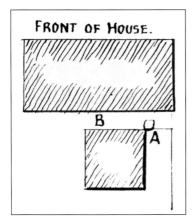

74/6/2   Castle Farm stone
(Diary)

74/6/30   (Diary)

am sure we had not found everything, but we wished to go on to Woodbury Castle before we returned home.   We then measured the camp and made a more accurate plan than that published in the Journal of the Archaeological Association in 1861, which is I believe the only one published.   I walked up the ancient British sunken road, apparently the original approach to the camp, *and* in one place I measured it and found it to be nine feet deep and forty-two wide at the top.   On the south and east sides of this camp the road is in the fosse or ditch.   At C we made the hedges, the old aggers, nine feet high and the width about nine yards, but on the north and west sides the ditch and inner agger were obliterated when the camp was destroyed.   The red line on the plan shows where the old inner agger apparently ran.

The farmer, Samuel White, who lives at Castle Farm just below (son of the old man who first showed us Belbury Castle), told us he had dug up a stone nearly square, about fourteen inches across and six or eight thick, near the middle of the camp and that it was at the farm.   So we went down and examined it.   It is at the back of the house at A, at the end of the passage B.   It seemed to be of blue lias on scraping it with my knife, *and* I think the nearest place to find blue lias is somewhere near Yarcombe.   He also said that it was only a little way below the surface when he found it.   At first I thought it may have been an old hearth stone but as it did not show any marks of fire, I think it may have been used for grinding corn or other grain, especially as the top surface was smooth if not somewhat worn.   He likewise said with respect to the sunken road, that it could be detected at *several* places running northward; by the old sand and gravel pits, the vicarage, the carriage drive of which was partly in it, past Oldridge (Mr. Potter's residence), through Mr. Buller's plantation and so to Streetway Head.

We then drove on south by west along the ancient Portway, past 'Brickhouse' to Halfway House and along over Hockland valley to Woodbury Castle.   *We* called in at the little cottage *but* they had not found anything but a coin in the garden.   It was only a token.   The woman gave my some flowers from her garden and we went on.   We had intended to examine more of the open heath but a shower from a thunder cloud following the heat of the morning stopped us.   We drove home through Yettington and Otterton, having been out nearly ten hours.   (*Diary*).

Firedog.   *Tuesday June 30, 1874.*   For some weeks past I have been occasionally annoyed by the visits of a strange dog, who has made two or three attempts to scratch a hole beside the steps going into the western back door of the Old Chancel.   One day I discovered a great hole nearly as large as a fox hole, with earth, stones and even a brick all scratched out and scattered about.   Surprised at this I made enquiry.   A noise of scratching had been heard in the kitchen, but not suspecting what it was no notice had been taken of it.   I took a spade and threw the earth, stones and brick back again and rammed them all in tight, not expecting I should be troubled again.   Some time after the same thing occurred in the night, and on discovering it in the morning I had to repair it again in the same way.   I now had the curiosity to see what sort of dog it was, and after some time saw a middle sized, saucy, jaunty-looking dog, with his tail impertinently high, run across the garden past the building.   I remember having seen the same dog in the town.   He began the same mischief again and was driven off, *but* I thought it time to devise some plan to frighten him away without hurting him.   After looking at the place and considering my materials, I believed I could do it.   I fixed a pistol to the side of a board and cut an oblong hole opposite the trigger.   I put the end of a stick through the hole and in front of the trigger, the long arm of the lever lying on the ground where the scratching had taken place.   The lever worked easily between two supports, as shown at A B.   The short arm, C, was about two inches in length, the longer fifteen.   I loaded the pistol with a good charge of powder and rammed down plenty of paper.   As the pistol was on one side of the board and the dog could only work on the other, he could not possibly hurt himself beyond a shock to his nerves.   And it succeeded perfectly.   About three in the afternoon, a loud report was heard.   Nobody saw him run away, but if I may judge from his paw marks in the gravel he tore away at no ordinary pace.   On examining the place, I observed that he had scratched a little before moving the lever.   Probably it is the first pistol he ever fired.   (*Diary*).

Railway opened.   *Monday July 6, 1874.*   Today the Sidmouth branch railway was opened.   After having witnessed two or three projects to construct a rail, all of which ended either in failure or swindling, I did not expect to live to see the event that took place. The station is in a field called Whorlands from time immemorial, and for as long as I can remember has been used as a brick field, being about half way between Broadway and Bulverton. The line is 8 miles 12 ½ chains *long* and cost about £70 000. Trains continued to arrive and leave during the day, bringing and taking away crowds of visitors attracted by the novelty. (*Diary*). By the first train at 6.50 many persons, owing to the novelty of the thing, went out to enjoy the ride and returned to breakfast. Later in the day the school children assembled on the beach and then walked in procession to the station to see the 2.45 train depart. The procession had a beginning but seemed to have no end, and people wondered where all the children came from. Great was their wonder, if not alarm, when they saw and heard the engine puffing along and the train following it for the first time in their lives. After the many frauds, failures, swindles and disappointments that had hitherto attended railway undertakings in Sidmouth, I confess I could scarcely believe my own eyes when I beheld it. The children then proceeded in the same way down the lanes towards Sidbrook and had tea and amused themselves afterwards in a field near the river. Judge of the quantity of plum cake consumed when I say that the entertainment cost £44. 18s. 8d. (*History of Sidmouth IV, 176*).

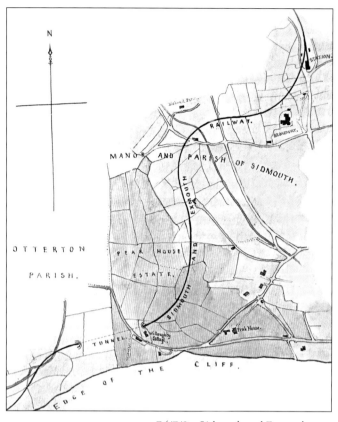

74/7/9 *Sidmouth and Exmouth railway, 1876.* (Hist of Sid. IV, 178)

Celebratory feast. *Thursday July 9, 1874.* Today a feast was given to between 300 and 400 old and infirm people in the grounds of Knowle. They were also carried gratuitously over the new line and very amusing were their remarks, as many of them had never seen a railway before and some old women were terrified of the engine. They had a dinner in tents at Knowle and about 130 gentlemen were wanted to carve. I was asked and of course willingly assisted. Great fun it was. They also had tea, cake and fruit later in the day. Upwards of £150 had been subscribed by the inhabitants to meet all the expenses. (*Diary*). When they left one shilling was presented to every person above 70 of whom there were 145, six pence to every person under that age of whom there were 238, and to the aged and infirm who were unable to come a half crown apiece was given, of whom there were 81. There were left 84 pounds of meat and 24 pounds of plum pudding, and all this was afterwards divided up amongst about 30 deserving families. . . .The opening of the rail soon showed its effect on the value of property in Sidmouth, for at the public auctions both houses and land easily fetched 50, 60 or 70 per cent more than the average selling prices before. In 1876 the Trustees of the Manor were the means of procuring an Act to construct a line to Exmouth. This additional line was to begin from the present station. I subjoin a plan of a portion of the line which I reduced from an official plan put out at the time. (*History of Sidmouth IV, 177*). *The plans for this extension were abandoned in 1879, following the bankruptcy of John Heugh, the senior Trustee of the Manor. An Exmouth link was eventually opened in 1903, but this branched off the Sidmouth line at Tipton before reaching the town.. The lines fell victim to the railway economies of the 1960s.*

74/7/14 *Coggia's comet.* (Diary)

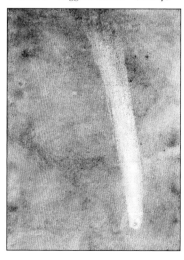

Coggia's comet. *Tuesday July 14, 1874.* The comet is now at its best. Remained up till after midnight and had a good examination but regretted my glass was not more powerful. At midnight it was nearly setting on the northern horizon, and as the elevation of the Pole Star is 51 degrees, the tail of the comet must have reached about 30, for it attained to near the pointers of the Great Bear. The nucleus is small and bright like a star, which is all I could see with my glass. The tail is slightly curved over to the left or west, *whilst* the comet of October 5, 1858 was more curved but in a contrary direction. This gave them the appearance of feathers. The present comet was discovered by M. Coggia of Marseilles and it now goes by his name. It is not certain that it was known before, though it somewhat resembles a comet that appeared about 150 years ago. (*Diary*).

Ottery and Tipton. *Thursday July 16, 1874.* Mr. Heineken and myself resolved to try the new railway, *so we went* to the station in *uno eorum omniborum* (I should like to find the person who can understand that) and took the 12.10 train for Ottery. We found the motion very easy, as if the rails were well laid. It must be said that the situation of Sidmouth station is very rural and picturesque, but as yet no houses are near it. At Bowd there is a very deep cutting, I believe sixty feet, and then we run down through Harpford Wood. We catch a glimpse of Mr. Peppin's new house a few hundred yards to the left or west, see nothing of Harpford village, but come out over the river and descend by a gradient of 1 in 45 to Tipton. After this, along the meadows it is nearly level. At about a mile short of Ottery on the right we espied a sort of cliff, perhaps by the river, with some caves or excavations in it. I imagine that this is the place that goes by the name of 'Pixie Parlour'. The caves however, are not archaic like those near Nottingham.

We stopped at Ottery and went to the church, *where we* noticed the marble font, the recumbent figures of Grandisson and wife, the north aisle, the figure of Cooke of Thorne, the fan-tracery ceiling, some good old black oak bench ends, the organ in the south transept, the curious clock something like that at Exeter, the reredos and the roof rather gaudily decorated in colour, some good modern glass windows, some brasses which we did not have time to copy, the Lady chapel, etc. We were told that a house on the right hand side of the street going down towards the bridge *and* not a hundred yards short of the factory was once occupied by Sir Walter Rawley.

On returning, we stopped off at Tipton. We wished to examine an ancient-looking house I believe called Hayne belonging to Mr. Wreford, which has a stone porch, the head of the doorway a flat Tudor arch within a square moulding or label. *There is* a three-light window of a small room over, with stone mullions. (*Diary*).

Ottery St. Mary church. *Thursday July 23, 1874.* Mr. Heineken and myself took the rail to Ottery, went into the church *and* took rubbings of four brasses – one an inscription and three figures of members of the Sherman family. Also, a brass to (?). I copied the *annexed* coats of arms. The iron handle dated 1575 is on the door of the south porch, the initials I H standing for John Haydon. The wards of the key of the lock (given by him) when held in one position make the letter I and in the other an H. (See June 19, 1877). (*Diary*).

74/7/16 *Hayne House, Tipton.* (Diary)

74/7/23 *Iron handle.* (Diary)

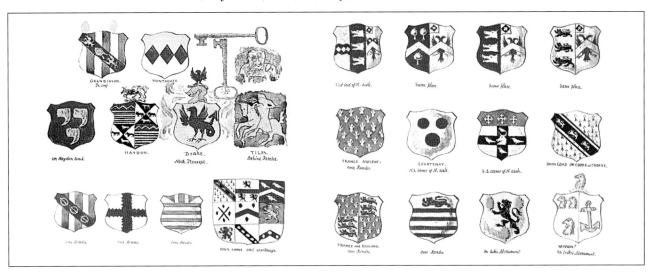

74/7/23 Coats of arms in Ottery St. Mary church (Diary)

Another octopus. *Tuesday August 4, 1874.* Another octopus has been caught in a lobster pot, about the same size as the last of September 19, 1873. A man and a boy carried it about in a tub half full of sea water, *but* the man was too tipsy to understand what he was saying. He spoke of the creature as one of the most wonderful to be found in the ocean *and* said he could get fifteen guineas for it at the British Museum. He turned it over in the water with a stick to show me that it was still alive, and in the most respectful terms he kept on repeating 'He have been dead Sir forty times. If you please Sir, he have been dead forty times'. (*Diary*).

Mammoth mistake. *Tuesday August 11, 1874.* Walked to Sidmouth by way of the Salcombe Fields and 'The Byes'. Went to Mr. Hawkins at the water mill north of the church to see a large tooth (another mammoth tooth as I supposed) which I had been told he had dug up in the gravel. It turned out to be nothing but a great flint! (*Diary*)

Picnic at Hembury hillfort. *Monday August 24, 1874.* After an interval of fifteen years, to the very day as it happened, Mr. Heineken and myself went over to Hembury fort and to the village of Payhembury. We were there on the 24th of August 1859. From an invitation from Miss Venn who was at Sidmouth a few days ago, we went today. We took the rail to the junction where she met us with her carriage and drove us to her home in Payhembury. Here we met Miss Hennell and Miss Seton, both daughters of Colonels in the Army, two young ladies who were staying with her, and having put a hamper of provisions into the carriage we proceeded about two miles to Hembury fort. The little inn at the foot of the hill is now converted into a farmhouse and another inn has been erected a few yards to the south. Whilst the ladies were setting out the dinner, Mr. Heineken and myself took a good ramble beyond the north end of the hill which we had scarcely examined before. The level field to the north of the camp was perhaps a likely fighting ground and an examination here if the place were ploughed might reveal something interesting. There are some stones that may be the remains of a tumulus at A *on the plan.* One of the western aggers runs up to nothing at B, *and* Mr. Heineken wondered whether a sort of sally port had existed there and whether there was not a retreat back into the camp along the bottom of the fosse by a kind of covert way at this point. The heaps and inequalities on the western side of the hill at C and D, Miss Venn said, were where attempts had been made to dig for scythe stones, as they do in the Blackdown Hills above Kentisbeare. She mentioned the case of a man who took a year's lease for ten pounds of her late father, who luckily struck upon a good vein and took out forty pounds worth of scythe stones in a week. In my sketchbook under September 12, 1854, I have a sketch of a man making scythe stones with the peculiarly-shaped tools they employ for the purpose, as I saw him at work when I walked up from Uffculme. We returned back into the Camp through the north-east corner at E, though there is no defined road there now. This series of aggers all along the north end are bold and really grand to look at *and* struck me today more forcibly than before. Every visitor to this place ought to examine and contemplate them. We took no measurements as we had measured everything carefully with the tape fifteen summers ago. I put the old measurements upon the plan *annexed,* and I see that the slope of the agger at one place at the north end is fifty-seven feet. There is an old hedge or ridge at F but we did not go down to examine it. Could it be an outwork or a road?

This hill, an open common, has been claimed by Mr. Drewe of Grange and by Mr. Porter of Hembury Fort House. Three lawsuits, Miss Venn told us, have arisen out of this claim but they have been settled in favour of the Venn family. The Venns own, with few intervals, nearly all the land between here and Payhembury. We dined on the western agger at G where there is a seat, and nicely prepared the dinner was! By way of varying the entertainment, Mr. Heineken put on a false nose unobserved and opened an antique clasp-knife, and I put on a false nose, a pair of large goggle-eyed spectacles and pulled the rim of my felt hat down over my eyes. Drawing a Chinese dagger, I cut up my bread and cheese with it, much to the amusement of the ladies and the astonishment of the boy who attended on us. By the way, the dagger was given to me by Captain Lindsay Brine who was at the taking of the Payho forts near Pekin. It was taken from the body of one of the dead Chinamen found in the fort.

Having returned to Payhembury, we took another look at the church *and* observed that the floor rises or slopes up from the west to the east. It is the same at Awliscombe, at Offwell, at South Brent, at Old Cleeve near Watchet, and at Jumieges in Normandy. There is some good carved work round the south door, a piscina just inside *it* on its east side and another at the north east end. *There are* good solid oak bench ends, something like those at Ottery, *and a* handsome carved oak screen spoilt by being painted blue and white. A hole *has been* cut through the spandrel over the screen where the rood loft was to pass through. The wagon roof *is* now plastered smooth except over the square panel over the pulpit. There is a large monument to Goswell on the north wall within the communion rails. On a seat at the north-east corner on the front of the west gallery there is a coat of arms fretty *and* on the capital of a column in the nave are four coats of arms cut in the white stone: eg. Courtenay. 2 is three leaves which I take to be the three stinging nettle leaves of Malherbe, 3 is three horseshoes on a bend I suppose for Ferrars, and 4 is a saltier between three round discs. We returned to Peyhembury and had tea. Miss Venn has some good specimens of old oak furniture in her house: a fine bedstead, some cabinets, chairs, etc. She drove us to the station and we returned to Sidmouth. (*Diary*).

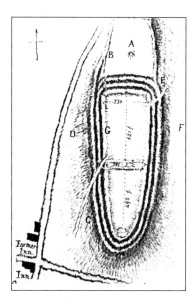

74/8/24 Hembury fort. (Diary)

74/8/24 Payhembury church coats of arms. (Diary)

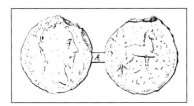

74/9/12 Coin of Commodus
(Hist of Sid. I,97)

74/9/13 *Bronze mortar.* (Diary)

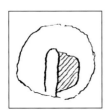

74/9/23 (Diary)

Coin of Commodus. *Saturday September 12, 1874.* Found in the clay under the gravel of the sea beach opposite Fort Cottage, Sidmouth, September 12, 1874. Much defaced. Emperor in a quadriga. (*History of Sidmouth I, 97*).

Bronze mortar. *Sunday September 13, 1874.* Coming out of the churchyard, Mr. Hine-Haycock who has a lease on Belmont, said he had a curiosity to show me and that I must come and look at it immediately. I went with him and madame and Mrs Stewart Gordon residing at Asherton, and he showed me a little bronze mortar but without the pestle. It is rather a rough and rude casting about five and a half inches high. Between two rings around the circumference are cast, in raised lines, a knot and traces of AD and the date 1649 very plain. I think he said it had been dug up at a house occupied by a Mrs. Strickland at Lyme Regis. (*Diary*).

Barrow on Salcombe Hill. *Wednesday September 23, 1874.* This morning Mr. Heineken and myself made another attempt on the barrow on Salcombe Hill, which we had before attacked (see June 1, 1871, June 6, 1873 and August 25, 1875). We drove to the top of the hill and then dismissed our carriage, and here we found Henry McLeod waiting for us with a donkey and cart, tools, etc.. We dug eastwards from the trench, the shaded part *in the annexed sketch but* more clearly shown in the plan of June 6, 1873. In proceeding with our examination, we were anxious to ascertain the exact position in the barrow of any object which we might come upon. When the earth or stones are *disturbed* with a pickaxe, any object lying on the surface (perhaps a recent deposit) could fall to the bottom of the trench and might lead the unguarded to conclude that *it* was *from* the interior and as old as the barrow itself. The sling stone which Miss Georgina Osborne found (June 6, 1873) was at the bottom of the trench, and at first we thought that it may have *fallen* down from the surface, so that *its* position proved nothing. We tried to tear back or scalp off the covering heath and furze with an instrument called a hale, a sort of large rake with three retractable prongs, but it was rather difficult to manage. However we removed the stones carefully. A few stray pieces of charcoal occurred here and there, one being of oak, but there was no deposit. I picked up a large beach pebble which had been used as a hammer stone for it was battered and abraded, pieces *having* been splintered off at its two rounded ends. It was at the bottom of the trench but was clean and I suspect it had fallen in from the top. I also met with a flint flake stained with peat mould and wet *from* the interior and consequently as old as the barrow, but the exact spot I did not see. After a time I came upon a broken sling stone and the exact spot of this I perceived easily, for as I lifted some of the flints it lay between them in some black and wet peat earth, and was itself stained dark. It had six to eight inches of flints over it and I presume it had been covered up when the barrow was made. This leads to no conclusion however, for we do not yet know what people constructed the barrow, whether Saxon, Roman or Briton. (*Diary*).

Beer tradition. *Tuesday October 20, 1874.* Drove over to Beer to spend the day with C.F.Williams, who is again there (October 8, 1872). The weather lately has been very unsettled but I seized on today as it was fine and calm. Of late years many new houses have been built, so that the ancient quaintness of the place is lessened. I was told a tradition in Beer today, which is worth mentioning. I was told that traces of Spanish blood and a Spanish type of countenance are to be observed among the inhabitants of this secluded place, and the story runs as follows. At the time that the plague was raging here in the year 1646 (see April 20, 1870) the panic was so great that many of the inhabitants fled to the neighbouring hills and made tents of sheets or blankets, or ran up huts of such materials as they could collect together. While they were thus encamped on the open down upon Beer Head and other hills, a Spanish ship, being overtaken by a storm, was wrecked on the coast and the crew got on shore at Beer. Going into the place they found half the houses empty and the dead lying in many of them. These they buried and then ensconced themselves in the houses. When the danger was over and the inhabitants returned to their houses, they settled down with the Spaniards and intermarried with them, and the foreigners were well content to remain where they were. The descendants of these people are said still to linger here and to show traces of their foreign origin by their features and the swarthiness of their complexions. On another occasion, if I have the opportunity, I will endeavour to find out whether there are any Spanish names to be met with among them.

Spent a pleasant day and got home by moonlight before nine. (*Diary*).

New pickaxe. *Monday October 26, 1874.* No one knows what he will come to. Today I finished making the handle of a pickaxe for a poor labouring man. I used his pickaxe in opening the barrow on Salcombe Hill (September 23), but it had a villainous handle. In the first place *it was* too short, in the second *it was* round in section instead of oval and in the third there was no swell at the top end so that it was always slipping out of one's hand. These evils *were* corrected, having first made his father-in-law, who is a carpenter, give me a good piece of ash for the purpose. The iron point is put on over the top end and slid down to the lower which expands, so that it cannot fly off. (*Diary*).

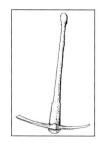

74/10/26   Pickaxe.   (*Diary*)

Further Exeter Museum donations. *Tuesday November 10, 1874.* Went over to Belmont Villa, Dawlish. I took the two Australian skulls to Exeter and gave them to the Museum. Also an old Teignmouth Guide of 1817 illustrated with coloured aquatints, which I gave to the Free Library. (*Diary*). *Hutchinson returned to Sidmouth the following Saturday.*

Exeter mayoral chain. *Thursday November 19, 1874.* When in Exeter the other day, I saw a photograph of the new chain recently given to the Mayor of the City by the Royal Archaeological Institute as an acknowledgement for the courtesy they received from the citizens at their visit in August 1873. It was presented to them on the 19th of October. It weighs 22 ounces of gold and the badge pendent to it 7 ounces. The value is £200. The case is rather interesting, for the former old chain was given to the king in troubled times to relieve his necessities. (*Diary*).

Verses to a lady. *Thursday December 10, 1874.* Not having met a lady of my acquaintance for some little time, I sent her the following: *There follows an amusing eight verse poem written to an unnamed lady Hutchinson was obviously rather fond of. The first verse goes:*
   What is the shape of her nose her nose
   Which hasn't been seen for an age or so?
   No wonder I've no repose repose,
   For whether she's got a nose or no,
   I do not know. (*Diary*).
Hutchinson does not record any response, so it seems he may have been disappointed.

Queen Anne guinea. *Monday December 28, 1874.* About a month ago a Queen Anne guinea dated 1714 was ploughed up in the large field above Peak House. By right of course it belongs to Mr. Lousada as the owner of the land, but the man who found it sold it to another, who sold it again till at last it fell into the hands of a fisherman (one of the many Bartletts) who offered it to me. It was of beautiful gold, of good weight and not at all rubbed or worn. I wrote to the British Museum about it, *but* the answer was that it was not rare and they did not want to buy it. Bartlett sold it to Captain Lousada (brother of the above) for I believe two pounds, or guineas, which must be much above its real value. (*Diary*).

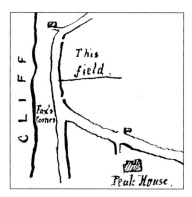

74/12/28   (*Diary*)

Inhabited caves. *Tuesday December 29, 1874.* Read a very interesting account in Mr. Boyd Dawkins' new book on cave hunting and antiquarian exploration. According to him, it does not yet appear proved, though it is probable, that the human race was on the earth prior to the last great glacial period. Lyall calculated from astronomical data that it may be 800 000 years since the commencement of that period. The contents of these caverns have been divided into periods according to their age. The most ancient division is the Pleistocene or Palaeolithic, which is said to be pre-glacial. The next in order is the Prehistoric, comprising the Neolithic and Bronze Ages, and the most recent is the Historic. The earliest is subdivided into: 1.The cave bear period. 2. The mammoth and woolly rhinoceros period. 3. The reindeer period. 4. The bison *period.* (*Diary*).

1874.

1875

1875.

75/1/1   Sidmouth flood.   (Diary)

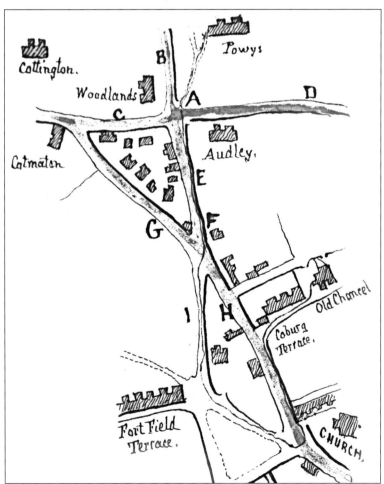

Sidmouth flood. *Friday January 1, 1875.* The wind veered round to the south, a mild rain came on and a rapid thaw. All day long it never ceased. Dined again with the Floyds at Powys *in the company of* William Floyd, Major Henry Floyd, Benjamin Kennet Dawson (married to Miss Floyd) and Mr. Walls. The dinner was in the old English style, the joints being placed on the table and not carved at the sideboard and handed round, a continental practise introduced during the last twenty or thirty years on state occasions. *There was* roast saddle of mutton at one end of the table and boiled turkey at the other, Brussels sprouts, mashed potato, etc. Half-moon shaped plates for salad to put beside the round plate is also a recent introduction *and it is not now the fashion* for port wine to be handed round at dinner. Claret, sherry and champagne are now the usual wines.

I went up in a carriage at seven and there dismissed it, saying I would walk home. About half past ten I left the house and walked down the grounds to the gate at A. To my surprise, I here found a stream of water running down the lane, B in the *annexed* map, and another stream running down C. These divided, one portion going down the lane D and the other down E. I waited awhile not knowing what to do, but finding there was no alternative I made a run and a jump across, not without getting wet in the feet however, and keeping close to the east side of E got down to F. Here was a voluminous meeting of the waters for another stream was rushing down G *and* here I had to stop again and consider what was to be done. Whilst standing there a man came out of a neighbouring cottage with an umbrella over his head, and on my hailing him he waded up to where I stood. I told him I wished to get home but didn't know how, and he told me that he had come out to see whether his house was going to be washed away before he went to bed. He said I could not get down to Coburg Terrace (the lane H) for it was like a river all the way, but that if I could get across and go down to the church I might perhaps manage it by a circuit. So I made a dash across and went down I, and opposite the church where it was narrower I stepped once in and then over. Keeping to the side, I at last got to Coburg Terrace by the red line, the blue being water. I took off my wet things and went to bed. (*Diary*).

Gravel pit on Peak Hill. *January, 1875. There is no mention of the accompanying January sketch in the Diary, but some two months later Hutchinson went again with a companion.* In March 1875 we took a walk up Peak Hill to examine the gravel pits, Mr. Ussher of the Geological Survey and myself. I returned to

Sidmouth but he prolonged his walk and descended by the steep declivity between Peak and High Peak Hills. *Here Mr. Ussher discovered pseudomorphous crystals of chloride of sodium.* I annex a sketch to show the forms they assume, like portions or corners of cubes projecting from the slab (see Trans. Dev. Assoc. II, 383). (*History of Sidmouth I, 17a, 18*).

Left: 75/1/? Crystals (Hist of Sid. I,18)

Below: 75/1/? Section of gravel pit on Peak Hill, near the cliff, shewing apparently contorted strata. January 1875. (DRO,Z19/2/8E/213)

Sir Edmund Prideaux. *Friday February 12, 1875.* So the venerable Baronet, Sir Edmund Prideaux of Netherton Hall has gone at last. People are at a loss to know who is his heir. His first wife I believe was a Miss FitzThomas. I can remember a boy and a girl with a Governess at Sidmouth, but they both died young. His second a Miss Bernard of Cottington *who* caught smallpox at the New London Inn, Exeter, and died at Netherton Hall only three months after her marriage. My late father attended her. It was said that she brought her husband £13 000, but after her death, and I think her mother's, he put in a claim for her alleged reversion of several more, which the Bernards resisted. On this he brought an action at law – but he lost his cause. His third wife was a Miss Irton and his fourth a rich widow lady who had had two husbands before, so the gossips said. She survives him. Is the saying true that 'no man outlives his fourth wife'? Sir Edmund's father it was who was obliged to sell the Manor of Sidmouth to pay off a debt that had accumulated.

75/2/12 *Prideaux of Netherton Hall, Bt.* (Hist of Sid. III,114)

Sir Edmund's father married three times. His first wife was a well-born woman by whom he had no family I believe. His second, I have been told by Farway people, was a farmer's daughter of the neighbourhood and was Sir Edmund's mother. The third wife was only a common apprentice girl. After she was a widow and up in years, she lodged at Sidbury where I knew her well. She was more vulgar and more ignorant than most apprentices have been since. It was fine fun to hear her talk of London life and going to the opera. Her husband however, could not take either of his last two wives into good society. What a position for a gentleman! The following story, long current in this neighbourhood, was told I believe of the second wife, the farmer's daughter. It is said there was one day a dinner party at Netherton Hall and she was sitting at the head of the table with her hands folded listening to the conversation. A cessation occurred in the conversation causing a sudden silence, such as will now and then happen in like cases. A gentleman sitting near her turned and said to her quietly 'Awful pause'. She thought he meant 'paws' and that he glanced at her hands. 'Awful paws', she retorted, 'and yours would be awful too if they had done as much work as mine have!' He was speechless afterwards. (*Diary*)

75/3/11   (Diary)

Unidentified bird.   *Thursday March 11, 1875.*   Weather very cold with a strong north-east wind. Out all morning at work with spade and rake. The weather does not affect me.

A sailor boy brought a bird to me this morning, which I think he had picked up dead on the beach and desired if I could tell him what it was, but I could not. It was not web-footed. After he was gone I made the sketch annexed, but it was only done from memory and I dare say it is not so correct as it might have been. (*Diary*).

Questionable fees.   *Thursday April 1, 1875.*   At a vestry meeting, the churchwardens for the year elected. After which, Lord Sidney Osborne introduced a complaint that several people had made respecting burial and other fees, for notwithstanding a scale of fees was agreed to in 1858, and printed, in which the vicar was to receive half a guinea and the clerk one and sixpence, the 'customary fee' of a guinea to the vicar and half a guinea to the clerk had been received and written receipts given, one of which was produced. The parties declared in their defence that gratuities had been voluntarily offered and that there was no law against receiving presents. But the paying party certainly did not give voluntarily or they would not have complained. We can understand a soft and spoony young fellow presenting the vicar with a liberal sum at a wedding for uniting him with the girl he loves, but fancy a man saying to the vicar after a funeral 'My dear Sir, I know your fee is half a guinea, but as you have put my late friend so securely underground, here's a guinea'. The vicar (*Rev. Clements*), clerk and sexton are rather annoyed about this and from long observation of human nature, I have come to the conclusion that people have no objection to do what is wrong but they hate to be found out. (*Diary*).

History of Sidmouth volume II completed.   *Monday April 5, 1875.*   I finished the second volume of my quarto *History of Sidmouth,* bound in green vellum. If I do not get on a little quicker, I fear I shall not live to complete the work in spite of my youth and good health. I have too many occupations and too many irons in the fire, so that there is too much running from one thing to another. Better give up oak carving, gilding picture frames, gardening and one half of my reading (all just at present in hand) and then there would be more time to attend to fewer things. I thought that three volumes would have completed the work but I now begin to suspect that they will not, so I have just ordered a fourth to be made in London and I shall work away at the third. (*Diary*). *The accompanying sketch, forming the frontispiece to Volume II, is entitled* 'Sidmouth in the 13th Century. Fancy sketch made up from the various sources of evidence in this History'.

75/4/5   Frontpiece to Volume II of the History of Sidmouth.

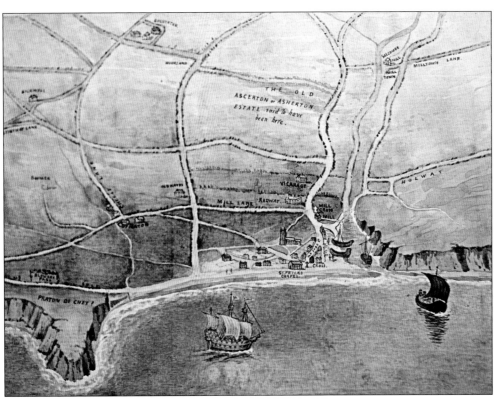

Cross-channel swimmer. *Saturday April 10, 1875.* A Captain Boyton, an American, tried to cross the Channel from Dover to Calais clothed in a waterproof dress inflated with air cells. He paddled and swam and even hoisted a small sail. The papers describe him something like the sketch annexed. He started at 3.20 this morning but after being fifteen hours in the water, that is at six o'clock this evening, he was still six miles from the coast of France having drifted by the current, so he was picked up by the steamer that accompanied him. He proposes to try again. (*See May 31, 1875*). (*Diary*).

Jackdaws. *Monday May 10, 1875.* I was much amused this morning in watching a number of jackdaws pull the hair out of a calf's back to line their nests with. At one time there were six on him all together besides others pulling at him from the ground, but he took no notice of them. (*Diary*).

Catapults. *Monday May 24, 1875.* The catapult is a small engine with an elastic indiarubber band, in the middle of which is a pocket to hold a stone. By pulling this back the missile may be sent with violence to a great distance. The sketch shows its mode of use. It is rather too popular with schoolboys at the present time. (*Diary*). *These remarks were prompted by an incident reported in the newspaper, in which the Princess of Wales and her children narrowly escaped injury from a stone catapulted through the carriage window of a train in which they were travelling.*

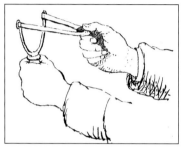

Frightened horse. *Monday May 31, 1875.* We hear that Captain Boyton has crossed the Channel at last, this time from France to England. He left Cape Gris Nez at about three on Friday morning last and landed at Fan Bay near the South Foreland lighthouse at half past two on Saturday morning. It is partly an advertisement to sell these dresses (*see April 10, 1875*).

I was returning from the town this morning, coming up Church Street as far as the lane leading to Westerntown just below the churchyard, when a boy of about fifteen mounted a horse with a basket containing two joints of meat on his arm, from the butcher's shop at that point. He trotted up the road a little way and I stood aside to let him pass. He had not gone twenty yards when a child threw a handful of rubbish out from the shop of Bussel the baker against the horse's legs. The horse shied and started and threw the boy. He fell off on the near side under the horse's feet and I expected every moment to see his brains trampled out by the hoofs. It is rather remarkable that he landed the basket on the ground without spilling the meat. When he let go the bridle the horse started off, breaking the girth and sending the saddle flying. He got up nearly as far as Coburg Terrace when he was stopped and brought back. (*Diary*).

From top: 75/4/10 Captain Boyton. (Diary); 75/5/10 (Diary); 75/5/24 (Diary); 75/5/31 (Diary)

Below left: 75/6/3 Armorials in Whimple church. (Diary)
Below right: 75/6/3 Bench ends in Whimple church (Diary)

Whimple Church. *Thursday June 3, 1875.* After several resolutions which other occupations had interfered with, Mr. Heineken and myself went over to examine Whimple church and neighbourhood. We went to Sidmouth station, took the rail down the steep incline through Harpford Wood, 1 in 41 it is said, stopped at Tipton, sometimes called Tipton St. John, *and* proceeded towards Ottery. Before getting there we saw the holes in the sandbank over the other side of the river which people commonly call 'Pixie Parlour', but which I believe is nothing more than a place where children have been digging out the soft sandstone to sand the cottage floors in Ottery, because they do the same thing in Sidmouth. *We* then stopped at Ottery, went on half a mile, observed the interesting old bridge of red stone over the River Otter and after that the stakes in the fields marking the distances of the rifle range where the Volunteers practice. *At* the junction we took the main line and soon got to Whimple.

The church is noteworthy for a fine range of Perpendicular windows down the nave aisles and a massive tower of no great height. A very pleasing church inside. There is an organ in the north-east corner with eight feet diapason, a good monument to Dr. Heberden who died in 1843 *and* a monument to Newcombe dated 1732, but I am not able to explain the armorials. There is a modern brass to a member of the Buller family, for though Downes may be their headquarters, there are many offshoots scattered about the county. This brass bears the date of 1860. Among the coloured glass windows there is one at the east end of the south aisle bearing the arms of Buller quartered with others and impaled with the wife's. In the south side

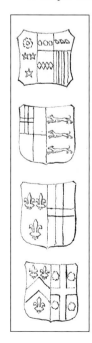

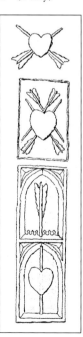

window the Buller family again is seen but this time on the female side, the husband's side being represented by Hughes and the date is 1872. Over the south door there is a large Jacobean monument to Dr. Hickes bearing date 1707. On the south wall there is a brass to E. J. Honeywood, born at Honiton June 26, 1790 and died at Whimple December 12, 1867. Some people do not like brasses because when time wears off the lacquer they begin to tarnish, get dull and look dirty. They could be re-polished and lacquered, *and for* myself, I have rather a liking for them. The arcade down the nave has depressed pointed arches of the Perpendicular period *and* the font is octagonal. The old oak bench ends are also worthy of notice. The strange devices of hearts transfixed by arrows in different lines and directions are novel and fanciful, so I have copied some of them in the margin. (*Diary*).

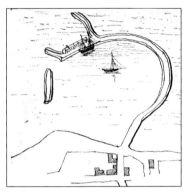

75/6/30   The Cobb, Lyme Regis
(Diary)

Lyme Regis. *Wednesday June 30, 1875.* Mr. W. Floyd and myself went over to Lyme in a carriage, the object being chiefly to examine the piers of the Cobb or harbour. Some well-meaning but I fear rather visionary people in Sidmouth have recently raised the question of constructing a pier or piers on Chit Rocks as a protection to the town, or rather to the west end of the esplanade, forgetting how much money such a work would cost or where it was to come from. The Cobb is a very old work and there are some interesting notices of it in Robert's *History of Lyme.* It is a long pier of massive stonework in an irregularly curved form with branching arms near the end, and a piece from the end (leaving a space of about fifty feet for vessels to come through) extending in a direction towards the shore but stopping short of it. The whole work may be a thousand feet or more long and upwards, and is from forty to fifty feet thick. We lunched at a hotel in the main street and walked about the town, but there is not much to see. The churchyard will fall into the sea some day. The soil of this blue lias district looks cold and barren and very different from the red marl of Sidmouth. (*Diary*).

Further excavations on Salcombe Hill. *Wednesday August 25, 1875.* So Captain Boyton is now eclipsed (see April 10 and May 31, 1875). Captain Webb has crossed the Channel by the strength of his arms alone. It is wonderful that he was not benumbed and chilled to death by being twenty-two hours in the water. Such a feat as this I should think has never been accomplished before in any age or in any country.

Mr. Heineken and myself had another dig at the cairn on Salcombe Hill (see May 26 and June 6, 1873, etc.). We enlarged the trench on the east and north sides, came to some large stones and hoped we were nearing the kistvaen, but were not successful, and so went on disappointed. We picked up a missile of jagged flint from the interior of the cairn and one or two smooth beach pebble sling-stones, which appeared to have been in the interior of the heap and consequently as old as the heap, but not associated with the burial or any sepulchral remains. These missiles and sling-stones, being objects of rude and very early use, may have been thrown about the hill before the cairn was made, and so their appearance does not prove anything. It is alleged that no proof has been brought forward to show that the Britons used the sling, though the Romans and Saxons did, but amongst all those early people it is not possible to say who had thrown these stones. Before we decide the point, we must discover sling-stones actually in the kistvaen along with the remains, and associated with such objects as will prove their nationality (see September 23, 1874). (*Diary*).

Below left: 75/9/10   *Picina and sedilia.* (Diary)
Below right: 75/9/10   *Gundry.* (Diary)
Below far right, top: 75/9/10 *N. Bragge.* (Diary)
Below far right, bottom: 75/9/10 *Drake, and quarterings.* (Diary)

Axminster Church. *Friday September 10, 1875.* In all our antiquarian excursions Mr. Heineken and myself have never been to Axminster, though we had often intended it, but the new railroad to Sidmouth enabled us to do it today. We had long been familiar with the account given by Mr. Davidson of Secktor of the places and objects of interest in the neighbourhood - his plan of the town and the many scraps of its early history. We left by the 10.10 train and got to Axminster at 11.17.

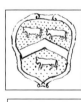

 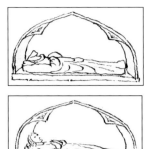   

The church has a central tower with a stair turret. The south aisle runs all along the building, from the west to the east end, the south transept being a portion of it, *and* the same I think on the north. The tower and the south front are covered with rough-cast, but the north face shows all its stonework and has some interesting features. There is a handsome parapet all along with the pattern pierced through. There are also many coats of arms but the stone is so decayed that I could only make out Courtenay and Stafford Knot. There is a good north porch with parvise over. The greater part of the building is Perpendicular work though the chancel is of the Decorated period, but the gem of the building is a Norman doorway at the east end of the south chancel aisle, which I had not time to copy.

In the southern part of the churchyard we saw the following names on tombstones; Gill, Chapel, Robert Lincoln Lendey, Bonner, Hammond, Pilkington of Hilary House, Priddis, Northcotte, Webber, Miller, Edwards, Anning, Gage, Pryer, Pound, Keech, Tytherley, Cox, Linton, Greig, Symes, Cort,

From left to right: 75/9/10   Chancel, north side. (Diary);
75/9/10   Female figure, south side. (Diary); 75/9/10   Priest, north side. (Diary); 75/9/10   (Diary);
75/9/10   Pulpit. (Diary);
75/9/10   Yonge. (Diary);

 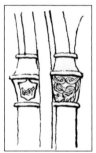  

Perring, Nowlan, Burnett, Bastyan, Hayman, Akerman, Thorn, Robinson, Daniel, Finnemore, Seward, Corner, Willis, Pulman, King, Coombs, Sweetland, Rigney, Gapper, Bucknole, Williams, Naish, etc. There is an Ordnance level mark with copper bolt and horizontal cut across the head of it in the west door jamb of the north porch, about fifteen or sixteen inches above the ground.

The interior was restored and renovated in 1870. The new seats are only of deal but the carving on them is good. *There are* tablets on the south wall of the chancel to Rev. G. Stear, Gunter, and Edward Kennet Dawson and his mother, formerly of Sidmouth. There are two recumbent figures under recesses in the chancel, a female figure on the south side and a male figure on the north with the top half of the head gone. There is a new organ by Dickens of Exeter in the south side of the chancel with sixteen foot G. Two large squints or hagioscopes go through the two eastern supports of the tower, *and* in the south-west support is the newell staircase of the tower. Tablets to N. Bragge, Gundry and Drake, the armorial bearings of which I copy, and to J. Alexander and to Anne his wife, all on the south side of the tower (Gundry's over the door of the tower stairs). There is an old slab in the pavement to the south-west of the tower of fifteen hundred and odd (date broken out) in black letter, with a name something like John Watis. In the nave floor is an old slab with the date worn out recording John Yonge with the arms nearly gone, *and* another near it of 1790 to the local name of Gammes.

The font lined with lead is the old one cleaned, and I fear re-dressed, and perhaps the foot or pedestal may not be original. The arcading down each side of the nave of Perpendicular work is good, and the capitals particularly so. The tablets against the west wall about two feet high are peculiar and of inferior work, *giving* a peculiar smirk to the mouths of both the figures. There is an oval tablet near the pulpit to Benjamin Prince and his wife erected by their son the Rev. John Prince, vicar of Totnes and Berry Pomeroy. It is not often that I admire Jacobean work but I was delighted with the pulpit. Together with the reading desk they were both made out of the old pulpit. The carving is the best in that style I recollect to have seen in Devonshire. (*Diary*).

From left to right: 75/9/10   Font. (Diary); 75/9/10   North side. (Diary); 75/9/10   Alto relievo, west end. (Diary); 75/9/10   Alto relievo, west end. (Diary).

Top: 75/9/10   South side, east end. (Diary)
Above: 75/9/10   North side.. (Diary)

75/9/30 *Eclipse.*
(Diary)

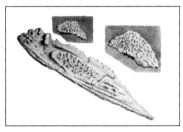

75/9/30 *Organic remains found by Mr. H Lavis F.G.S. on the western side of High Peak Hill, a mile and a half west of Sidmouth, and 60 or 70 feet above the beach in the face of the cliff. Aug. 1875. They may be suspected of being skull bones or plates of saurians or batrachians.* (DRO, Z19/2/8E/217)

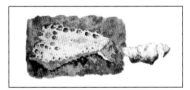

75/9/30 *Specimen found by Rev. S.H.Cook, under old limekilns, Sidmouth.* (DRO,Z19/2/8E/217)

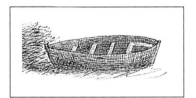

75/9/30-4 (Diary)

Picnic at Blackbury Castle. *Monday September 13, 1875.* Miss Creighton of No. 1 Coburg Terrace gave a picnic to a few friends, the place of meeting being at the cottages close under the south-east end of Blackbury Castle. She drove me there in her carriage. We mounted Trow Hill and just on nearing the summit we passed the spot on the left hand where the old fir tree used to stand in the hedge. When it was felled, or fell down, a few years ago, a young one was planted in its place. I did not observe it today: perhaps it is dead. It was at this place that the apparition of a woman used to terrify the simple folk of bye-gone times according to tradition.

Going along the road for two or three miles, we turned off north to Long Chimney Farm and Rakeway Bridge and then east to Blackbury Castle. We turned in over the wild heath immediately round the east end, and as it was impossible to take the carriage down the steep pitch to the cottages, it was left on the heath and everything carried down. As a dozen or more people were soon expected in a brake or char-a-banc, and as they did not know where to find the cottages, I decided on being in the camp and hailing them when they came near. Besides, I had an eye to business and thought I might poke about and see what I could discover. The calcined flints still continue a mystery, though I have endeavoured to solve it by conjectures. As yet I have only met with them on the south side. I wandered about the area, which has in a great degree cleared of trees but much covered with fern. Wherever I saw a bare spot I examined it for calcined flints, but found none. At last I came to a place, a little south or south-east of the middle I think, where some picnicers or gypsies had made a fire to boil their kettle, and I perceived that the flints among the ashes were all split by the heat. Such appearances might easily deceive and lead to false conclusions, but this fire was quite recent. *The party now arrived and after an excellent lunch on the grass Hutchinson continued his investigations.* I went and examined the mound on the crown of which a pit was sunk some years ago, and I could still see traces of our work.

We had a nice tea in the cottage and after more rambling about we started for home. By way of varying the route we turned eastward *and* came out by Hangman's Stone. The country people are afraid to pass this spot at night. They say that the man who was hanged or strangled there by the sheep comes back once a year to this place on the anniversary of the fatal event, but as nobody knows on what date the event took place, every night in the year has its terrors. We then proceeded home almost in the dark without further incident. (*Diary*).

Sidmouth beach. *Thursday September 30, 1875.* Took a walk along the beach to beyond High Peak and back at low water. The tide was very low for the moon changed yesterday and there was a small eclipse of the sun, which I saw. It began at 11.13, was greatest at 12.02 and ended at 12.51. There will be no eclipse of the sun again until 1880, that is in England. Mr. Lavis, an amateur geologist from London here on a visit, found in the red rocks of Picket Rock Cove where there has been a fall of the cliff, some organic remains like bones or plates of the head of a saurian or batra-chian. I went over to hunt for more but was not successful. Along the beach, I found many hollow bamboo canes five or six feet long, thrown up by the sea and mostly split and broken, gifts of the violent weather we had a few days ago. And one empty boat was picked up off here, which I have been examining on Sidmouth beach, suggesting the occurrence of some fatal wreck. The boat appeared to be French, clumsily built and sharp at both ends. (*Diary*).

Dental expenses. *Thursday October 7, 1875.* Went into Exeter today. Our new branch railway is certainly convenient. Gave Dean Milles' account of finding the Roman penates in Exeter a hundred years ago to the Free Library at the Museum. *I then* went to Mr. Brand the dentist at his new house on the north-west side of Cathedral Yard and had the fang of an incisor taken out. Five shillings! Quickly earned! (*Diary*).

Robbery at Exeter Museum. *Wednesday October 27, 1875.* The Exeter papers this week have the account of a disgraceful robbery by means of false keys of three specimens of native gold in auriferous quartz and a silver coin from the Museum of Exeter. The thief is the son of a clergyman and an undergraduate at Cambridge. I say disgraceful, for the first time he was had up he said to the magistrates, 'I assure you on my word and honour as a gentleman that I know nothing about the robbery'. They have given him six months with hard labour in Exeter jail. More than twenty keys were found on him and in his boxes, some filed into new shapes, two files and a chisel. (*Diary*).

Tuesday November 16, 1875. Hutchinson went to London for a week to transact a little business.

Friday December 3, 1875. Went to Belmont Villa, Dawlish, to see my cousin Mary Roberton. (*Diary*). *He returned to Sidmouth on December 11.*

Kingsteignton Idol. *Monday December 6, 1875.* Went down to Newton Abbot to examine some antiquities which Messrs. Watts, Blake, Bearne and Co. have discovered in the Zitherixon clay works. The chief was a wooden figure 13.3 inches high, resembling the rude and ugly gods carved by the South Sea Islanders, found near the trunk of an oak tree black with age (from which tree they had made the walking stick

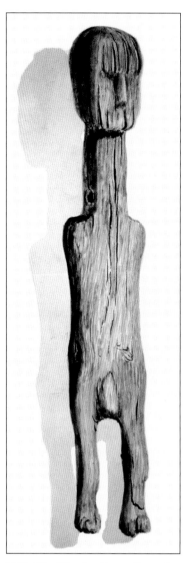

75/12/6 Wooden figure from the clayworks. (Soc. of Antiq. Ms. 250)

75/12/6 Site of Zitherixon clayworks. (Soc.of Antiq. Ms 250)

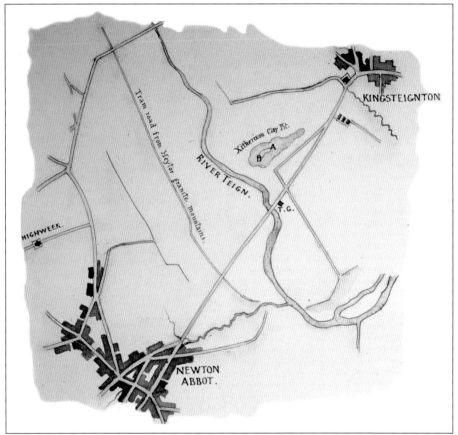

I had in my hand) from twenty-three to twenty-five feet below the surface. There was likewise Roman pottery and a bronze Roman spear head (see Trans. Dev. Assoc. VII, 200 *for Pengelly's account,* where a lithograph is given). Also they have the bones of the face or forehead of an ox (Bos longifrons ?) a leg bone, the femur of a dog apparently, ribs, etc. As I was anxious to collect all the particulars I could in order to send an exhaustive account to the Society of Antiquaries of London, together with photographs and full sized drawings, I expressed a wish to be directed to the spot where they were found. One of them offered to walk out with me. The wind was north-east and sharp enough, the ponds were frozen and the boys were sliding and skating. We went along the road for half a mile towards Kingsteignton, and soon after crossing the River Teign turned up a lane on the left for perhaps three hundred yards or more, at the end of which is a sheet of water several acres in extent with an

75/12/6 *Portion of red clay pitcher with twisted handle, from the Zitherixon clay pit.* (Soc. of Antiq. Ms 250)

75/12/6 *Bronze spear head.* (Soc.of Antiq. Ms 250)

Above: 75/12/6 *Greenstone implement found in the bed of the River Lemon, in July1875.*
(Soc. of Antiq. Ms 250)

Right: 75/12/6 *Greenstone implement found in the bed of the river Lemon, near Newton Abbot, March 1875.*
(Soc. of Antiq. Ms 250)

island in it.   This is the great clay pit, which had long been worked but was abandoned last year, so that the rain and floods had taken possession of it.   There was about twenty feet of 'heading' over the pottery clay, which is disintegrated felspar derived from the decomposed granite of Dartmoor.   The 'heading' is composed of beds of gravel, stones and sand, resting uncomfortably on the clay which here dips to the west. *(Diary). A gap in the Diary here suggests that Hutchinson intended to note down further details of these finds.   His full account, including all the information he could gather on their exact find-spots, appeared in an article in the Proceedings of the Society of Antiquaries the following year.   The wooden figure, one of seven examples known from the British Isles, has been radio-carbon dated to 426-352 BC (Allen and Timms 1996).   His article concludes by describing two further finds, of neolithic axes, made in the vicinity only a few months previously:* On the 26th of March 1875, Mr. Woodward and his nephew Mr. H. F. Barnard were walking through Bradley Vale near Newton when the latter picked up a greenstone celt in the bed of the River Lemon.   On the 24th of July in the same year Mr. Woodward found another not far from the same place but of smaller dimensions.   There is probably little doubt that they are genuine, but the friction they have received in the riverbed has obliterated all traces of the tools of the workman who made them.   *(Proc. Soc. of Antiq. 1876, 41).*

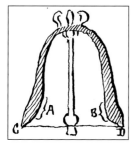

75/12/17 (Diary)

Tuning the bells. *Friday December 17, 1875.* Two more new bells are added to the peal of six in the church tower, thereby making an octave of eight.   During the past week they have been fixing the two highest, the new ones, and they have been chipping them and some of the old ones in order to put them in tune.   In the workshop they would turn off a shaving by machinery, as I once saw at Mears, but in default of that they use the hammer and chisel.   To lower the pitch of a bell, I am told they chip all round the inside at A and B which thins it, but if they require to raise the pitch they cut away round the lower edge at C and D, which makes a smaller bell of it.

I went up to the tower today to see the work and found the two new bells fixed with their mouths upwards.   They had been chipping round their interiors, and the bright brassy-looking shavings lay in the bottoms of the two great basins.   I scooped some up with my hands, as much as I could hold in my two hands together, *and* perhaps I shall be able to cast something out of this metal.   *(Diary).*

1876

Old font at Dawlish. *Saturday January 1, 1876.* New Years Day. Went to the morning service at St. Mark's Chapel, Dawlish, *where the gas lights were all lighted to warm it, and* in the afternoon *went to* the parish church. What remains of the old font stands outside the west door in the cold *and* there was some ice in the bottom of it. At the risk of being told to 'mind my own business', I ventured to plead in its favour, and *inquired* whether some corner under cover and within the walls of the church could not be found for a relic of antiquity. (*Diary*). *The accompanying undated coloured sketch of the east end of St. Mark's Chapel (demolished 1975) was probably done a few years earlier.*

76/1/1   *Old font at Dawlish* (Diary)

75/1/1   *Sketch of the decoration at east end of St. Mark's chapel, Dawlish, Devon.* (DRO, Z19/2/8E/191)

Kingsteignton clay pit again. *Monday January 3, 1876.* Went again to Newton Abbot and walked out to the lake or pond, being the old claypit where the objects were found (*see December 6, 1876*), and made a sketch of it. The wooden figure near the trunk of the oak tree with the bones of animals scattered about, were met with on the northern side of the island. The island is only a heap of gravel thrown aside. Fragments of Roman pottery were also turned up. Towards the south end of the island the elegantly formed bronze spear head was discovered. (*Diary*).

76/1/3   View of the *Zitherixon pottery clay pit, between Newton Abbot and Kingsteignton, Devon,* abandoned in 1875, and now full of water.   (Soc. of Antiq. Ms 250)

Beached whale at Beer. *Tuesday February 1, 1876.* Today one of the fishing boats belonging to Beer, when about four miles off the mouth of the River Axe, espied some large object which, on nearing it, they thought to be the hull of a vessel bottom upwards. They thought so from the appearance of parallel stripes or channels inclining to black and white, looking like planks. But on closer examination it proved to be the dead body of a whale. They made signals to other boats, got a rope around the tail and towed it to Beer. (*Diary*).

Monday February 7, 1876. All the world and his wife have come to see the whale, and every other person I have met on the street during the past week has greeted me with the universal question, 'Have you seen the whale?' I had almost made up my mind that I would not go at all, as I had put it off for so long, and some said I should be poisoned if I did. But what are we to do? The frequently repeated question at last arouses some curiosity, so I thought it better to be poisoned than to resist any longer. But I wanted a companion, *so* I went up to Lansdowne and saw Mr. Ede. 'Have you seen the whale?' 'No'. 'Then you ought'. 'Have you?' 'No', says I. 'What are you going to do?' 'I'll go if you will'. 'Let's take a carriage and go tomorrow morning. The tide will be low about eleven'. He turned to his wife, as all good husbands do when they want an opinion. 'It will be a very nice trip for you' she said, 'only, as the weather is so very cold, you had better take a closed carriage, and Mr. Hutchinson, you must have an early dinner with us on your return. (*Diary*).

76/2/1   *Whale at Beer, near Seaton.*
(DRO, Z19/2/8E/219)

Tuesday February 8, 1876. And we started about half past nine. We mounted Trow Hill and got to Beer by eleven. Leaving the carriage at the Dolphin, we proceeded to the beach. The fish lay opposite the lower end of the street, where they had secured him with a capstan. A high tide once floated him off, so they had to tow him back and secure it better tail first, so that the head was nearest the sea. It is reputed to be Physalus boops, or Rorqual.

We were told it was seventy feet long; some said more, some less, but probably that is about the mark. The sailors had enclosed the flanks and upper or tail end with a cordon of poles and sails, and admitted visitors at three pence each. The lower or head end is washed by the waves at high water, but as we were within a day of full moon we calculated for low water so that we were able to go outside and walk around it without difficulty. I had expected to have found it blue-black in colour like other great fish I have seen, but to my surprise it was ochre mottled with brown. It is true there were a few dark patches about it, but these appeared to have been the scarf-skin which had been nearly all removed by decay and by rough usage on the beach. It was a male fish. The fins and tail were red-brown in tint, like burnt sienna, *though* I could not see what dorsal fin he may have had as he was lying on his back, inclining to his left. The two pectoral fins, answering to the arms, struck me as very small for his size. The fore part of the head was something like a bird's, in so far that the jaws proceeded forwards to a point and curved slightly downwards like a bird's beak. They were a fine yellow colour near the point, becoming fainter in receding. The eye was half closed, *but* appeared to be about the size of a bullock's eye. The underside of the head and thorax was peculiar. The colour was nearly white but the skin was scored longitudinally by black indented channels about four or five inches apart, very much assuming the look of the planks of a vessel, and it was this peculiarity that deceived the fishermen when they fell in with it. The mouth may have been from eight to ten feet at a guess, and in place of teeth the upper jaw was set with a series of plates of slate coloured whalebone fringed on one side, though I think the under-jaw was smooth. About six or eight feet of what seemed to be a tongue hung out of the mouth.

I had brought the sketchbook, colour box and bottle of water with me and I wanted a memorandum of what I had seen. I made an outline sketch and put a wash of colour over it, but the north-east wind was so miserably cold, and my fingers so benumbed, that I was obliged to be content with a slight record to be completed at home.

It had been reported that the fish had been getting rather 'high', so Mr. Ede took a supply of sigarettes to keep off infection. I am not a smoker. It is a year and a half or more since Lord S.G.O. gave me one in his garden, but I took one today. Having completed my examination on the east or windward side, I walked outside his head and round to the other side. There I met a whiff of malaria, but I went on and took a second. Oh my! Thinks I, if that goes into my lungs it is enough to breed fifty plagues and pestilences. I held my nose and hurried back, and getting into fresh air I drew two or three deep inspirations. I drew in the smoke and blew it out through my nostrils, but that persistent fish stuck there for nearly four hours.

We were told that Messrs. Thomas and Co., tallow chandlers of Exeter, had bought the whale for the fat, and it is hoped that the skeleton will be obtained and preserved in the village of Beer as a perpetual attraction to visitors (*see September 19, 1876*). (*Diary*).

76/2/1 A more picturesque version of the whale at Beer. (DRO, Z19/2/8E/221)

Net loss. *Saturday February 19, 1876.* Went into the town *and* on my way I met one of the Bartletts, fishermen, with a large heap of net in a wheelbarrow looking for a place to dry it. After some discussion I gave him leave to hang it on my wire fence, but it never occurred to him or to his wife who was with him, or to me, that some cows belonging to Mr. Lawrence would interfere with it. I proceeded into town *whilst* he and his wife went into the field and hung the net in festoons on the fence.

76/2/19   (Diary)

When I returned about an hour later, I found the neighbourhood in an uproar. It seems that one of the cows, not approving of the net hanging there, got poking at it with her horns until she got her head entangled and then began to back and struggle. I jumped over the fence and got hold of the ropes, the wife screaming and holding the net. I hoped to pull myself up to the cow and so disentangle her, but she pranced and kicked and pulled so hard that I was obliged to let go. *Meanwhile*, the other cows began galloping about the field. Bartlett came running to the rescue but the cow would not let him approach her. Then came Mr. Lawrence whom the cows recognised, so she got the net from her horns. I am afraid the net was very much torn. (*Diary*).

Devonshire Association business, 1876. *Wednesday February 23, 1876.* Went into Exeter by rail to attend a meeting of the council of the Devonshire Association, when the general arrangements were co-ordinated for the meeting next summer at Ashburton. (*Diary*).

Australian offer. *Monday March 13, 1876. Hutchinson had received a number of offers for his land in Australia and now decided to sell.* Well to be sure, and who would have thought it? On the 24th of last September my agent informed me that Mr. Hay had gone up to £600. Since then he has offered successively £700, £800, £900 and lastly has touched the £1000. The deed of conveyance came with the letter which I must execute and return, and I shall have to go into Exeter to get attached to it the signature and seal of office of the Mayor. (*Diary*).

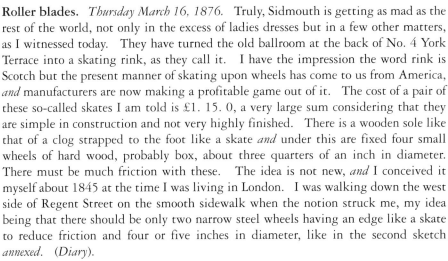
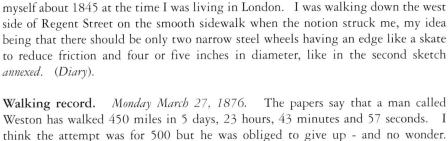
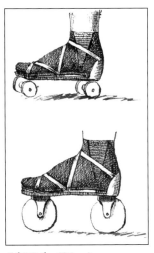

76/3/16   (Diary)

Roller blades. *Thursday March 16, 1876.* Truly, Sidmouth is getting as mad as the rest of the world, not only in the excess of ladies dresses but in a few other matters, as I witnessed today. They have turned the old ballroom at the back of No. 4 York Terrace into a skating rink, as they call it. I have the impression the word rink is Scotch but the present manner of skating upon wheels has come to us from America, *and* manufacturers are now making a profitable game out of it. The cost of a pair of these so-called skates I am told is £1. 15. 0, a very large sum considering that they are simple in construction and not very highly finished. There is a wooden sole like that of a clog strapped to the foot like a skate *and* under this are fixed four small wheels of hard wood, probably box, about three quarters of an inch in diameter. There must be much friction with these. The idea is not new, *and* I conceived it myself about 1845 at the time I was living in London. I was walking down the west side of Regent Street on the smooth sidewalk when the notion struck me, my idea being that there should be only two narrow steel wheels having an edge like a skate to reduce friction and four or five inches in diameter, like in the second sketch *annexed*. (*Diary*).

Walking record. *Monday March 27, 1876.* The papers say that a man called Weston has walked 450 miles in 5 days, 23 hours, 43 minutes and 57 seconds. I think the attempt was for 500 but he was obliged to give up - and no wonder. (*Diary*).

Fatal accident. *Tuesday March 28, 1876.* A young man of seventeen called Charles Dommet died from getting his legs caught and broken in a threshing machine at Slade. Mr. Heineken and myself were there last on September 23, 1873. (*Diary*).

Chaffinches. *Thursday March 30, 1876.* After breakfast between nine and ten, I went into the second room from the front door of the Old Chancel, the sash window of which is thick plate glass. In an instant, a cock chaffinch, chased by another, flew right against the glass with a thump, rebounded and fell on the gravel path on its back, where it lay panting. The other bird hovered over it and then flew way in alarm at what had taken place.   I ran out, picked it up and brought it into the house, *but* after gasping for a few minutes it died in my hand.   I went outside to look at the window.   The sky was then clear and the sun was shining, and every shrub, plant and leaf was reflected as in a mirror, as if the scene was a bright reality.   I have no doubt the unfortunate little bird was sadly deceived and was killed by the deception. (*Diary*).

Monday April 3, 1876.   Another!   This morning, as my servant was preparing the Oak Room just before I came down to breakfast, she was a good deal startled by a sudden thump against the plate glass window.   I went outside and picked up a dead hen chaffinch, a bird with plumage something like the yellowhammer and the linnet but not so yellow.   The reflection in the window of the church tower opposite and the scenery around it was very perfect, especially when the sun was shining. (*Diary*).

Top: 76/3/30   Cock chaffinch. (Diary)

Above: 76/3/30   Hen chaffinch. (Diary)

Sidmouth Church clock.   *Friday May 5, 1876.*   Today, the old clock face that covered the south bell chamber window of the church tower was taken down and a new stone window, made from a drawing by me, is to be put in.   The new clock face will be under it, but too low I fear to be well seen.   It is recorded in Mr Butcher's *Guide* that this window was taken out and the clock face put up in 1808. (*Diary*).

World's richest man.   *Saturday May 6, 1876.*   The papers record the death of a Mr. Stewart who emigrated as a young man from the north-east of Ireland to America, *where he* got a precarious living as a schoolmaster, usher or tutor.   Afterwards he went into business in the drapery and 'dry goods' line, as the Americans say, in the city of New York.   He has now died, having realised the sum of £20 000 000 sterling.   He is described as having been a man of honour and integrity *and* was probably the richest man in the world. (*Diary*).

East Hill iron pits and Gittisham Church.   *Monday May 29, 1876.*   Owing to the extremely cold winds from the north-east which have continued to a very late period this spring, Mr. Heineken, who feels age creeping upon him, was not willing to undertake our first antiquarian excursion until today.   We wanted to look at Gittisham and the neighbourhood, and we began by going to Sidford, then north along the long lane at the back of Core Hill till we got on the ridge of Ottery East Hill and looked down upon the beautiful map of the country beyond.   We kept away northwards where we had often been before, until we got to the extreme end and here we stopped for an hour.   Turning into a field on the left that commanded the view, we sat down to enjoy it and eat our dinner.   When we were here before, Mr. Heineken had remarked certain irregular pits in the plantation at the point of the hill, suspecting that at some former period the diggings had been promoted in pursuit of iron.   The pits and trenches were mostly at B and across the road at C, and the idea was rather confirmed today by our finding many small pieces of bog iron-stone in them.   They somewhat resemble the excavations over Lincombe Farm but are not so large as those beyond Wolford Lodge.

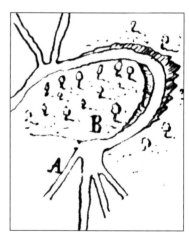

76/5/29   Ottery East Hill (Diary)

With the Ancient Britons iron was not much known, though they used it sparingly, but whether they dug the ore and had learnt the art of smelting it, I do not know.   By smelting bog iron with wood charcoal malleable iron may be at once obtained, ductile and ready to be hammered into arrow heads, which is not the case with our modern processes.   As quantities of clinker or scoria have been found at Churchstanton, and in the neighbourhood of Kentisbear, Tidborough near Hemyock, Bowerhayne Farm near Dunkeswell, etc., it is naturally concluded that bloomeries or furnaces existed at these spots.   Bog ironstone is found in the 'foxmould' on the crowns of the hills belonging to the greensand formation and in the beds of yellow clay and flints that overlie them.   Some suppose that these iron pits, from an unknown beginning, were worked through the middle ages, *when* great quantities of malleable iron were required in the construction of the many churches and castles

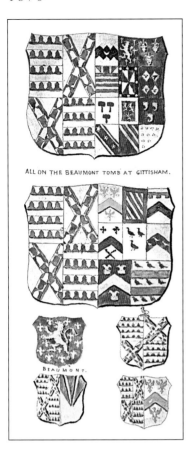

ALL ON THE BEAUMONT TOMB AT GITTISHAM.

BEAUMONT.

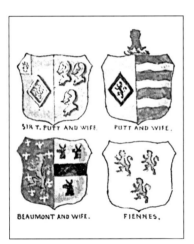

SIR T. PUTT AND WIFE.　　　PUTT AND WIFE.

BEAUMONT AND WIFE.　　　FIENNES.

Arscott & . . . .
See back, Ap. 16. 1872.

76/5/29　Coats of arms,
Gittisham church. (Diary)

then erected. We should be glad to know where the ore dug from the north point of this hill was smelted, for we have not heard of clinkers being ploughed up or lying in heaps anywhere in this neighbourhood.

After completing our examination at B, I went over to C and then we descended the steep hill between two high banks and drove to Gittisham Church. We have visited some thirty churches in our rambles but until now had never come here. It is very prettily situated on rising ground with the pollarded remains of a picturesque old elm in front of the lichgate. The tower is square and is without buttresses except at the lower stage. On its south side, outside, are steps leading up to the belfry and a tablet against the wall to a former Rector named Paul. It contains three bells. The church consists of nave, chancel and south aisle *with* parts belonging to the Decorated and Perpendicular styles. The south wall of the chancel leans in a peculiar way on or against the arcading of the nave. The capitals of the columns of the arcading of the nave are continuous bands in the usual Perpendicular style, like that at Axminster, south side east end (see last September 10), but of good work. The floor of the church rises from the west to the chancel, like Payhembury, Awliscombe and one or two others. The lower floor of the tower seems to be used as a vestry *and* there is in it a long oak chest with three disabled locks. The font is of Perpendicular type, octagonal, and rather like the mutilated one at Dawlish (see January 1), *and* is either new or fresh tooled over. The pulpit I believe was made a few years ago when the church was renovated. Some of the horizontal bands, about four or five inches wide, are effectively carved with good Gothic patterns, and as I at first thought deeply undercut, but on looking closer it appeared that the carved panel was laid over another. There are several poppy heads on the bench ends, very good. The first coats of arms I copied from the Beaumont tomb at the east end of the aisle.

At the north-east end of the south aisle there is a monument in white marble with two white marble vases of inelegant shape on a slab or shelf. The shield and armorial bearings being in marble are without colours. They are to Sir Thomas Putt, Bart., who died in 1686, impaled with those of his wife. In the south aisle there is a tablet to one of the Putt family and to his wife, a Miss Samford of Walford, Somerset, bearing azure, three bars wavy argent. Against the north wall of the chancel there is one to the Rev. Thomas Putt, the last of his name. Also against the north wall, there is an alabaster monument of Jacobean work to Beaumont and his wife, once coloured and very good of its kind, *which* records Joane, daughter of Edmund Green of Exon and wife of Glidd Beaumont. In the south aisle is a tablet to John Fiennes, second son of Lord Say and Seal, who married Susanna Hobbes, 1671, *but* the tinctures on the arms are nearly gone. As the colours are much faded on some of the monuments and I had no time to dwell upon my work, I have only to hope that I have copied all the arms correctly. There is a barrel organ, not in good repair. Against the south wall there is a tablet without coat armour to the memory of the Hon. David Stuart, third son of James Earl of Moray, *who died* June 12, 1784, aged 39 years and 4 months. The tomb of the late Rector, the Rev. R. Kirwan, drowned at Sidmouth (see September 2, 1872) is in the churchyard on the north side of the church. Too inattentive and careless in the accuracy of his writings, he was nevertheless active, industrious and possessed of a great desire for information.

Before we left the village, we went to the sexton's to see a portrait on panel some two or three hundred years old, bought at some sale. It represents a young man but has no great merit as a painting. There is a coat of arms with four quarterings in one corner, rather indistinct but like the annexed. On leaving Gittisham we asked at the Lodge of Combe Park if we could drive through and we easily opened the gate with a silver key. Mr. and Mrs. Marker were not at home. Combe House is very beautifully situated on rising ground backed by a high hill covered with trees. It has some pretensions to Gothic, though not much pretension to anything, and there is a square, ugly building a score yards from it on the north side, very incongruous and inharmonious in the Grecian or peradventure Roman style with a large sash window. We remarked that the trees in this park were neither large nor old. I was once told that the former possessor could not live on £13 000 a year but felled timber and racked out everything *until* obliged to go abroad. When I was quite a young man I recollect dining one day with my late father at the vicarage at Sidmouth, William Jenkins then being vicar, and there was an old lady there whom I understood was a Miss Putt of Combe, the last of her race. I suppose it was her sister who married Mr. Marker, which eventually took the estates into the Marker family.

We drove for more than a mile and a half through the grounds and came out in Chineway Head near Hunter's Lodge, and then returned home through Sidbury. (*Diary*).

Visit to Poole. *Friday June 23, 1876.* Lord Sidney Osborne having been good enough to ask me to go and see his house in Dorsetshire, we started today. We changed trains at Templecombe and proceeded south. On reaching Poole a carriage took us to a rural and quiet spot in the midst of wild heath and trees near Poole Harbour and near the sea. (*Diary*). *Here Hutchinson was as busy as usual, sketching, examining the rock formations, sailing along the coast etc., before returning to Sidmouth on July 5.*

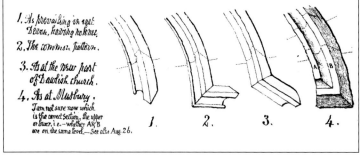

76/7/11 Musbury church, label variations. (Diary)

Musbury Church and Castle. *Tuesday July 11, 1876.* A year or more ago some workmen dug up a jar in the south aisle of Musbury Church. They were making great alterations there, and amongst other things undertook to lower the ground under the floor of the south aisle. The man using the pickaxe struck its point into the bottom of *the jar* and it was further broken by the other men in their eagerness to see what it contained. Stretchley Churchill, a stone mason of Sidmouth (who did the hall ceiling of the Old Chancel and other work for me) was working in the church at the time. He brought me most of the fragments by which I have got a tolerably clear idea of its shape and size. Jars and vases have now been found in many churches, but as their use is unknown some mystery hangs over them. I thought I would bring the subject forward at the meeting of the Devonshire Association on the 25th instant at Ashburton, so I went to Musbury today to make further enquiries. Nothing was

76/7/11 Drake monument, Musbury church (Diary)

found inside it as far as I could ascertain, *but* what I have gathered I shall embody in my paper to read at Ashburton. (see July 27 and August 10 this year).

Had another look at the church – there were men inside and outside still at work about it. The lower ends of the labels over the west doorway caught my eye as peculiar *as* they turn inwards. I give four variations *alongside*. Inside, the church has been renovated and I think the north aisle is entirely new. In the south-east corner is an uncouth monument to the Drake family bearing dates ranging from 1558 to 1643, embellished with six kneeling nearly life-sized figures, three men and their three wives. I was told that they contemplate putting some sort of canopy over them. Near it in the south aisle floor, I observed a slab bearing a name like John Gauarcke in black letter. The organ in the north transept has diapered pipes, *and* the font is new, or new-tooled. The tower floor slopes up from the west. There are five bells. The wall behind and over the communion table is now set off with a large oblong piece of mosaic *depicting* scrolls, leaves and flowers in vitreous-looking tesserae.

76/7/11 *Musbury Castle.* (Diary)

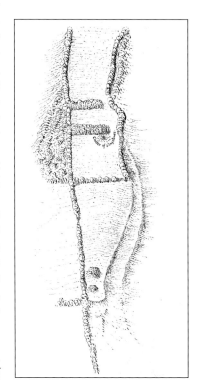

Being so near Musbury Castle I resolved to climb the hill and have another look at the old camp. The last time I was here was on August 9, 1872. The plan I subjoin is taken from Mr. Davidson's book, corrected on the spot to the present time. I cannot say however, that my corrections are very minute, so that they must not be taken as thoroughly exact. As the area is surrounded by hedges and most parts covered with bushes in full leaf, I could not see as many parts of the work as I should have liked. Compared with Mr. Davidson's plan, the changes shown in this one are apparent. The only new thing I have to add is the scattered deposit of beach pebble sling-stones, about the size of small eggs like those at Sidbury Castle (see March 28, 1864, and my *History of Sidmouth I,44*). They had recently been unearthed and scattered by diggings into the cross-hedge, which looked quite fresh. (*Diary*).

Plymtree Church. *Thursday July 13, 1876.* After an interval of sixty years, Mr. Heineken has discovered an old school playmate in the Rev. T. Mozley, vicar of

76/7/13   Plymtree church.
(Diary)

76/7/13   *Pyx.*   (Diary)

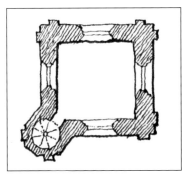

76/7/27   Little Hempston
church. (Diary)

76/8/10   *Jar dug up in Musbury
church, Devon.*   (Diary)

Plymtree, and I accompanied him over there by invitation to spend the day. We took the rail to the junction and Mr. Mozley sent a carriage to take us on, nearly five miles by the winding of the roads. The vicarage house contains many interesting things, *including* some torsos of Roman work and one or two troughs or small stone coffins carved in *alto relievo*, also ancient Roman work. Upstairs there is a representation of the Crucifixion in wood, painted and gilt, about five feet wide and high, brought from Belgium as a quaint curiosity (*and* now in the Exeter Museum upstairs). Built into the wall a few yards above the outer gate there is the shaft of a cross of granite surmounted by an ornament of brown igneous rock. (*The cross shaft has since been re-united with the head, found buried in the 1890s, and re-erected in the churchyard in memory of Rev. Gutteres, the incumbent at that time. The rectory burned down in 1911*).

The tower of the church has a stair turret at the south-east corner that only reaches up to the bell chamber, *where* there are five bells. More than half way up outside the west front of the tower is a sitting figure of the Virgin with Child in a niche under a canopy and nearly as large as life. Strange that this group has escaped the iconoclasts. Inside, the old bench ends are both numerous and good, *and there is a* very handsomely carved, painted and gilt screen all across the church, of fine tracery and *with* rich horizontal bands of foliage over. On the lower portions are painted panels of saints, kings, etc., *and there are* two double doors through it. Beginning at the northernmost door is the Virgin and Child, then Cardinal Morton, as reputed, bare-headed with chalice and paten making obeisance, next Prince Arthur the eldest son of Henry VII holding a pyx, as alleged, the body in the shape of a tun (Mor-ton, *but* why a rebus?). Then King Henry VII, followed by a bishop with mitre and crook in hand. The next I forget, but the one following is a young man with a sorrowful face looking back over his shoulder at an angel in the next compartment. A few panels further on southwards is a figure we were told was St. Sativola who suffered martyrdom by having her head cut off with a scythe, and she is depicted with a scythe by her side and holding her head in her hands. A little further on is a female saint with her eyes torn out, *and* lastly, towards the south, is St. Sebastian pierced with arrows. (*Diary*).

Devonshire Association meeting 1876. *Monday July 24, 1876.* Went to attend the Devonshire Association, which meets this year at Ashburton. Stopped at Belmont Villa, Dawlish. (*Diary*).

Old acquaintance. *Tuesday July 25, 1876.* Took the railroad to Teignmouth *and* called at Seaway to see Mr. Cousins, a handsome old man of 92 with a bushy head of white hair. When I was a child in 1818 and my hip case was on me, my late father and mother rented a house of him. He remembered their sick little boy and he was rather surprised when I told him I was the same, for we had not met since. Then took a turn round the Den *to look at* the shipping, for I am fond of dockyards and ships. (*Diary*).

Ashburton Church. *Thursday July 27, 1876.* To Ashburton again by the same route. The tower of Ashburton church has its stair turret placed in the middle of the north side between the buttresses so that there can be no window in the bell chamber, but a long narrow slit on each side. In that neighbourhood there are one or two other churches on a similar plan but I have not noticed it in east Devon. It was at Little Hempston or thereabouts that I saw a tower with the turret at the south-west corner with buttresses against the turret, *as in the sketch.*

Read my paper on the 'Jar found at Musbury', and returned to Dawlish. (*Diary*). *Hutchinson returned to Sidmouth on August 8.*

Musbury jar again. *Thursday August 10, 1876.* Copied the *annexed* pen and ink sketch of the Musbury jar (July 27) in printing ink onto transfer paper and sent it to Exeter to be transferred to the stone. Four hundred copies are to be printed to illustrate my paper in the *Transactions*. (*Diary*).

Sidmouth regatta. *Wednesday August 16, 1876.* A regatta took place at Sidmouth today. It was a dead calm, and owing to the heat a dense mist covered everything on the water, *but* soon after noon the mist cleared away. The sun was bright and extremely hot and the sea as glassy and smooth as a fish-pond. Some boats started but they only crept along at a snail's pace *and the* three cutter yachts that came lay with their sails motionless and did not move at all. Three steamers came, one large one from Weymouth. The tide was high and the water so smooth *that* she ran her bow aground on the beach and her passengers walked ashore. The calmness of the sea however, was favourable to the rowing matches and these were very good, *but* the best fun was to see the boys try to walk along a horizontal pole fixed to the stern of the committee barge to get a leg of mutton, or fall into the water. I hired a small boat and rowed about for five hours. (*Diary*).

76/10/16 (Diary)

Woodbury and St Johns in the Wilderness Churches. *Saturday August 26, 1876.* Went to Woodbury and St. Johns in the Wilderness with Mr. Heineken. We drove over Peak Hill, through Otterton, passed Bicton Cross and then through Yettingham and over Woodbury Hill. We had not as yet had the opportunity of examining Woodbury Church, so we went there first. It was between one and two when we arrived and the fine air of the hill had sharpened our appetites, so we sat on some altar tombstones in the churchyard near the south porch and there had our mid-day meal, somewhat to the amusement of a few villagers. That done, we walked round the building. The tower is good, high and well built, the battlements at top panelled in quatrefoil but not pierced. On the stages or set-offs of the buttresses are the bases of small quadrangular pinnacles placed diagonally. The west door has a half-round moulding carved in foliage carried all round and a label or hood moulding with unusual ends (see *illustration* July 11, 1876). *There are* good windows in the north wall and half a turret against it that once probably contained stairs to the rood loft. The east window and the south transept window are Second Pointed but new. The interior shows a very rickety church. The arch of the roof has thrust out the north aisle, the colonnade of which is leaning outwards and is only kept up by iron braces across the nave overhead. Most of the south wall, I believe, is new and it looks as if the whole must be new before long. There is a good deal of the Thorverton brown igneous stone used in various parts of this building. The screen is an open, flimsy, Gothic piece of thin woodwork, painted in bright green, red, gold, etc., all rather tawdry. The pulpit is oak and a little carved in the Jacobean pattern. There are two good recumbent figures in carved stone on the north side of the Communion Table, reputed to be John Prideaux and his wife, 1610. On the south side of the chancel there is some oak panelling of the napkin pattern, which is late. The font, cut out

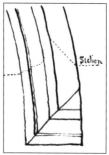

From top: 76/10/26 *Bicton cross.* (Diary); 76/10/26 *Label end to south porch.* (Diary); 76/10/26-3 Font (Diary); 76/10/26 *Holwell. 1716.* (Diary)

76/10/26 *Tomb above ground, or mausoleum, in the churchyard at Woodbury, Devon.* No date. (DRO, Z19/2/8E/229)

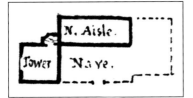

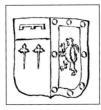

From top: 76/10/26 Polexfen.
1690. (Diary); /6/10/26
(Diary); 76/10/26 Label end.
(Diary); 76/10/26 James Rodd of
Marpool. 1694. (Diary);
76/10/26 On the De Vimes tomb.
(Diary)

of a single block of Beer stone, is of Third Pointed style and apparently original. Two coats of arms, not coloured, I copied from slabs, as here given in the margin. There is a west gallery with organ.

On the north-east side of the churchyard is a singular tomb worth alluding to, of which I made a hasty drawing in my sketchbook. The tradition in the village runs to the effect that the relations of a Prussian named Grackner sought a burial place for the body after landing at or near Plymouth, but could not find a dormitory until they reached Woodbury. It is said further that the deceased had left money by deed to be enjoyed by the survivors 'as long as his body was above ground'. In order to meet the difficulty, four brick walls were built enclosing a small room or quadrangular space, and the coffin was raised above the ground on iron bars placed across for it to rest upon. In this way the coffin was kept above ground, and so I suppose it still remains. Mr. Heineken tells me that when he was at General Lee's at Efford about fourteen years ago, there was a mason at work there called Phillips who told him that his father built this strange mausoleum. It is quite neglected and is a mass of ivy and two young sycamore trees. It may be fifty or sixty years old

We turned down through some lanes southwards and came out upon the open heath. We went into two or three of the gravel pits to break pebbles of the Budleigh Pebble bed and hunt for fossils, but were not successful this time. St. Johns in the Wilderness is in a very pretty and secluded spot. The tower and north aisle of the old church remain but all the rest is gone, a low wall marking the contour of the former nave and chancel. Service is performed there once a month. The features of the tower are Perpendicular, the label end over the west door *being* something like that at Woodbury, *and the* windows on the north side the same in style. The churchyard is quiet, rural, shady and peaceful, and is said to be a favourite spot with the Exmouth people to carry their dead to. Count de Vismes, a French refugee, formerly lived at Sidmouth *and* I was surprised to see his tomb here in the south-east part of the churchyard.

We now turned homewards. We got on Woodbury Common from a new quarter and for a time were completely lost. The driver hurried eastwards however, and we dived into a long lane on the south side of Hayes Wood and came out in the middle of Budleigh. Hence to Sidmouth was a well-worn road. (*Diary*).

Fellow antiquary. *Thursday August 31, 1876.* Mr. Spencer G. Perceval, at present residing at Beer *but* whom I had not known before, did me the favour of a call. He is fond of antiquarian pursuits and has lately been amusing himself by hunting for ancient flint implements on the hills and he showed me several he had found. I showed him my collection, which he looked over. He is the grandson of Mr. Perceval, the Chancellor of the Exchequer under George III, who was shot by Bellingham in the Houses of Parliament, and is I believe a cousin of the present Lord Egmont. He may be about five or six and twenty. He had an early dinner with me and then an early tea before he returned. (*Diary*).

Another look at the Beer whale. *Tuesday September 19, 1876.* The weather has been very unsettled of late, but today being fine I went over to Beer to see Mr. Perceval (see August 31). We met at Hangman's Stone by appointment and by going over the hedge on the northern side of the road (see August 23, 1872) we hunted for flint implements over the fields through which the earthwork runs. In four hours we found one or two picks and several flakes and scrapers. We then drove down to Beer past Bovey House and went to his lodgings.

The whale that I came over to see on the 8th of last February has been retained in the place. After the tallow chandler of Exeter bought the fat, a chemist and bird-stuffer from Seaton bought the carcass and with much trouble and labour (I should think) got the skeleton. This he has set up and articulated within the circuit of a high boarding just above the cemetery and chapel on the west side of Beer beyond the Dolphin Inn. There is an attendant at the gate who admits each person for sixpence. I measured the head (which is almost all jaw) from the occiput to the nose and made it fifteen feet. There was little space for brain. I counted the vertebrae over my head, I think it was 59, by walking down from the head to the tail between the ribs, of which there are 15 long and short. I was told by the attendant that the length of the skeleton was sixty-five feet. The large vertebrae near the shoulders looked nearly a foot in diameter, and they diminish away to about the size of my fist. There is no bony expansion for the fan-like tail as on small fish. This immense tail, which I think was fourteen feet wide, was all gristle and fibre and all removed, the backbone ending in a point. There are two blade bones on the back and the skeleton of the fins somewhat resembles the bones of the human hand. (*Diary*). *Hutchinson was obviously fascinated by this leviathan and returned to take further measurements on November 11.*

Yettington manganese and a case of mistaken identity. *Thursday September 21, 1876.* A beautiful day. Mr. Heineken and myself went to Woodbury Hill. *We* surmounted Peak Hill, went through Otterton, which is not quite so dirty a place as it used to be, and stopped near Bicton to measure the height of the obelisk. This was effected by Mr. Heineken with his apomecometer, *who* made it seventy-seven feet six inches. We stopped at Yettington to enquire about the old manganese diggings which were formerly *worked* in this neighbourhood. A place towards the south was pointed out to us and also that beautiful conical hill covered with fir trees that rises on the north-west called Crook Hill. We stopped just out of the village and ascended this hill nearly to the top *where we* observed places that may have been diggings *and* found some small pieces of black manganese. I am inclined to think that I have made an interesting discovery, in so far as identifying an ancient site mentioned more than six hundred years ago in the Otterton Cartulary. From thence onto the wild and beautiful open common. Many years ago, when Lady Rolle was a trifle younger than she is now (I think she was twenty-six when she was married and her husband was sixty-six) she took a lady friend of hers who was staying at Bicton, out with her one day for a drive on this hill. In order to enjoy the scenery better, they got out of the carriage and walked for some distance across the heath *and* in doing this passed within hail of a couple of labouring men who were at work cutting turf. One of them, not suspecting whom he was addressing, held up his firkin of cider and merrily cried out 'My dear, will 'e have a drop o' zider?' Instead of laughing at this, Lady Rolle was so indignant that she had the man up before the magistrates at Woodbury, where in his excuse he said he was very sorry but he thought they were two lace girls from one of the villages. This only made mattes worse *and* my lady was in a towering passion. The idea that Lady Rolle should be taken for a lace girl!

We joined the carriage in the road and then returned. (*Diary*).

Harpford and Venottery Churches. *Thursday October 12, 1876.* The weather has been very unsettled of late but nevertheless Mr. Heineken and myself took the opportunity of a fine morning for a short trip into the country. We drove down Newton Poppleford Hill to Harpford. The Budleigh Pebble Bed crops out here in the hedge or bank by the roadside, near Mr.Peppin's new house just before descending to Harpford. This is the eastern limit of it. Mr. Peppin is one of the sons of the late vicar of Branscombe, *whose* family has several pieces of property in Harpford parish, including the two little narrow fields in the midst of Harpford Wood.

We went into the church *where* I had not been since I was at the wedding of the Rev. Samuel Walker, Vicar of St. Enodur in Cornwall. The building is very dilapidated, several of the walls are not upright and I should think that the whole must be rebuilt before many years are over. There is a nave, chancel, north aisle and tower *and* there appeared to be a slight rise in the floor from east to west, but not much. The wagon roofs have wooden ribs. Two narrow single-light windows with pointed heads on each side of the chancel *have* First or Second Pointed appearance, *and the* east window is Third Pointed but not old. *There is* a door on the south side of the chancel *and* a small window on the south, perhaps where the rood loft stairs were. The tower arch is pointed, the soffit panelled above the springing. The nave and north aisle arcade of three pointed arches has two plain octagonal columns with two half responds, the east one having a square hole, higher than wide, passing north and south behind it. There is a north door with the Royal Arms over, a yard square. The tower door is fastened by a bar, *the* turret stairs door being on the north side of the tower, inside. The base and central column of the font is old but *supports* an ugly eight-sided basin of Beer stone. Only two old carved bench ends remain in the church, one bearing the initials WH and the other MB TD. The pulpit is very plain *and* the lectern modern, being an ignorant mixture of architectural styles, the stem being of Grecian pattern and the upper or desk of imperfect Gothic. The marble tablets against the wall are to Peppin, Hoskyn and Capt. C. E. Pritchard *who* was the

76/10/12 *Piscina.* (Diary)

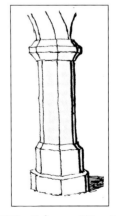

76/10/12 *Column.* (Diary)

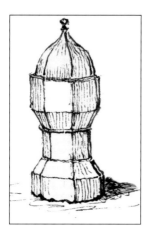

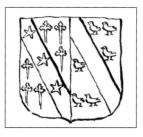

From top: 76/10/12 *Font.*
(Diary); 76/10/2 *Over south porch.*
(Diary); 76/10/12 *Font Ven-
Ottery.* (Diary); 76/10/12 *Arms
of Ayre and wife.* (Diary)

Opposite page, top: 76/12/3
*The sea, Westerntown, behind
Marine Place. Dec. 4. 1876.*
(DRO,Z19/2/8E/235)
Bottom: 76/12/3 *The sea
dashing over the esplanade and
filling the lower part of Fort Field,
between Fort Cottage and the Bedford
Hotel. Sidmouth, Dec. 4. 1876.*
(DRO, Z19/2/8E/231)

husband of Miss Gattey, eldest daughter of the present vicar of Harpford. There is a plain deal west gallery with a small organ having one manual and four stops.

Going outside we remarked that the tower, covered in rough-cast, has no buttresses, but has an octagonal stair turret at the north-east corner. There are three bells in it. On the north side of the churchyard a precipice or deep hollow drops down to an orchard which seems at some former period to have been submerged by the waters of the River Otter. We saw the stump of the granite cross south-east of the church (see April 10, 1870) and Mr. Tucker's tomb to the south in the form of a shrine. West of the churchyard is a new farmhouse rebuilt when the old one burnt down about twenty years ago, *and* it is here that tradition placed an old county jail, afterwards at Bicton. In my little *Sidmouth Guide* and more fully in my manuscript *Hist. Of Sidmouth, I, 169,* I have shown the groundlessness of this notion.

We then went on to Venn Ottery, which in some way is an appendage to the parish of Harpford and served by the same clergyman. We drove to Tipton but on the way we stopped on the crown of the high brick bridge which crosses the railway, and as there is a fine view we here had our lunch. Two or three passers-by were much amused at us and we exchanged jokes on the occasion. We went on, crossed the rail at Tipton at the bottom of the steep incline, 1 in 41, proceeded through Metcombe and reached our destination. Close to the east of the church is a farmhouse belonging to the Yelverton family where we got the key. The Yelverton family, both in Ireland and England, has been at times noted for producing members, both male and female, not over correct in their conduct, carriage or manners, wild, self-willed, ungoverned and sometimes vicious. The church consists of a nave and chancel, only forty-two feet long and eighteen wide I think. The tower at the west end contains an old oak chest and three bells above, its wall at the west door being four foot six inches thick. The tower arch into the nave is circular and devoid of mouldings, and the ceiling is wagon roofed. The small east window of two lights is apparently modern and there is a south chancel door, by some called a 'priest's' door and by others the 'wedding' door. The square Third Pointed window on the north side has cinque-foil heads to the lights. The south door of the nave has an old lock inserted in a clumsy wedge-shaped block of wood two feet long, much like we have seen in other churches. On the north wall is the Royal coat of arms. The High Church party and the Roman Catholics exclude this badge of supremacy. The font is of Beer stone, plain and octagonal. On the south door are some stencil patterns in coarse paint, rudely done, and there was once an open wooden screen painted white, blue and red, for we detected the lower halves of the columns cut off at about four feet high. Near the south door the napkin or linen pattern has been carved on the panels of the pews *and* there are several good old carved oak original bench ends still remaining in the aisle. I regretted I could not copy them by pressing *but* pressing wax is too expensive a compound to be used on a large scale. There are no appliances in a church for warming and softening it before use, but it is a good thing because it hardens afterwards. Some employ pipeclay but it whitens the object and remains soft long afterwards. Red clay has similar disadvantages. Miss Osborne showed me some capital plaster casts the other day of some carvings in Beverley Minster which she had pressed off with new bread squeezed into a lump. On the north side of the chancel there is a tablet to the memory of the Ayre family, and in the floor of the aisle towards the west end a slab records the deaths of Marshal Ayre and Elizabeth his wife, with the coat of arms I have sketched. I am sorry I forgot to take down the dates *but* I think it was about a century ago. (*Diary*).

Unknown disaster at sea. *Saturday October 21, 1876.* The weather has been very boisterous lately, with very turbulent times at sea. Some pieces of wreckage have been washed on shore, and yesterday Samuel Willey, the fisherman, and his companions found the dead body of a young man knocking about on the rocks at the foot of the cliff about half a mile beyond Ladram Bay. Willey tells me that from what remained of the clothes, the body seemed to be that of a foreigner. *He was* buried at Otterton. (*Diary*).

Erectheum fragment. *Tuesday November 8, 1876.* Made a plaster cast in a rude mould of red clay of the fragment of the Erectheum (see February 17, 1872). Dr. Radford of Sidmouth bought the original. (*Diary*).

Flood at Sidmouth. *Sunday December 3, 1876.* Yesterday and today there has been very boisterous and rainy weather, with a violent wind from the east and south. As the full moon occurred on the 1st and we have now the spring tides, great alarm has been felt by persons living near the sea, and not without reason for the waves have been dashing over the esplanade and running into the town. (*Diary*).

Monday December 4, 1876. The wind has continued and the last three or four high tides have been in the town. It is an old grievance for the cellars of the houses near

76/12/3   The sea breaking over the esplanade.   Fort Cottage in the centre with the water near it in the field.   Dec.4.1876.
(DRO, Z19/2/8E/233)

the beach to be half full of water at high tide, for if it does not come in from above it percolates through the gravel and shingle on which they are built, and comes up from underneath.   Some thirty years ago, before the water company brought fresh and wholesome water in pipes down from the spring at Cotmaton, the water in the wells of those houses was occasionally so brackish that it acted on some of the visitors like Epsom Salts, and drove them away to the detriment of the place.   Yet, when Mr. Jeffery, a sensible and clever surgeon who then practised here, declared that the water in those wells was not pure, the townspeople were very indignant and abused him as if he had been a rogue and a scoundrel.   The greatest opposition was thrown in the way of his getting better water brought down to the beach houses, though he was only promoting the general good of the town.   When it had been forced on them, they soon discovered the benefit though they never acknowledged it.   Tongue cannot tell the contempt in which I hold some people.

Well, the waves dashed over the esplanade.   At the west end the water reached the wall of Belmont, the same at Fort Cottage, *and* the corner of Fort Field east of it was like a lake.   The water was up against the Bedford Hotel and Bedford House, and close to Bedford Place and Denby Place. Each side of Marine Place it ran into Westerntown, and I am told that Mr. Pepperell, the dairyman, delivered milk to some of his customers by boat.   Mrs. Churchill, the wife of a mason who used to work for me, unable to come down stairs because the lower part of her house was flooded, was lamenting out of an upper window *when* a neighbour handed her a cup of hot tea from a boat.

I took a few hasty sketches in two or three different places to perpetuate the scene. (*Diary*).

Coin donation to Exeter Museum. *Friday December 22, 1876.   Hutchinson went into Exeter for the day.*   Gave to the Exeter Museum three cases containing about fifty coins, the pick of nearly two hundred found or dug up at Sidmouth and collected by Mr. Heineken and myself.   The Bactrian and Roman ones in case 1 are the most interesting.   (*Diary*).

1877

Porpoise sketch. *January 1877. There is no Diary entry referring to the capture of the* porpoise shown in the sketch.

77/1/? Round headed porpoise, GLOBIOCEPHALUS, caught at Sidmouth, January 1877. (DRO, Z19/2/8E/237)

Swan. *Saturday February 24, 1877.* Went to Dawlish via Exeter. Passing through Starcross I saw the Swan (see August 2, 1872) upon the wharf to be painted. Meeting Captain Peacock at Ashburton last July, he told me it could be used as a floating bath and that it had cost him upwards of £300. (*Diary*).

Clerk Rock, near Teignmouth. *Monday February 26, 1877.* Went to Teignmouth by rail *and* called on Mr. Omerod of Brookbank. His father was an F.R.S. and the author of a '*History of Cheshire*' in three volumes folio. He is a scientific man himself and his house is full of books and works of art. I then called on the Rev. R. Cresswell, a clever man, *whose* wife is a sister of Miss Creighton of No. 1 Coburg Terrace. Walked back along the railway wall *and* approaching the Parson and Clerk tunnel I sketched the rock lying off the point. The neck looks so thin that the head will probably fall off before long. (*Diary*).

77/2/26 Clerk Rock, near Teignmouth – looking east. (Diary)

Early Sidmouth sketch. *Tuesday March 27, 1877.* Finished copying the oldest known view of Sidmouth, a watercolour drawing measuring about seventeen inches by ten *taken from* near the mouth of the Sid looking west. It may be nearly a century old and belongs to Mr. John Pile, ironmonger of Fore Street, Sidmouth. (*Diary*). Beyond the fact that it was bought many years ago at an auction of the effects of a tradesman in the town, very little is known of its history. (*History of Sidmouth V, 7*).

77/3/27 First old view of Sidmouth. (Hist of Sid. V,8)

Good Friday 1877. *Friday March 30, 1877.* Good Friday. I was surprised to see how few people were at the church and how few remained for the sacrament. There is an old but very reprehensible custom still lingering in Sidmouth which ought to be put down. I allude to the practise of football on Good Friday. I have seen it done in the Blackmore Fields, or Church Fields as they are sometimes called, but today it was in the Western Fields over 'The Goyle' below Witheby. Twenty great rough fellows were shouting and using bad language in a way not appropriate to the day, nor indeed to any other day whatever. (*Diary*).

77/4/5   Site of vault (Diary)

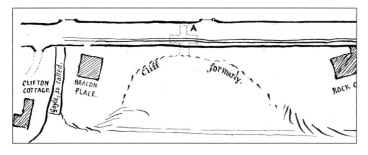

Buried vault. *Thursday April 5, 1877.* The local Board has been engaged in laying the drain up the road at the west end of the beach behind Clifton Place. When the men got twenty-seven paces above Rock Cottage and nine from Beacon Place, they came upon a cruciform vault ten or twelve feet down, at A *on plan*. Some thought it had been a smuggler's cave entered from the beach, but I am told it was made in 1836 when the harbour was projected and gunpowder was kept in it for blasting purposes. (*Diary*).

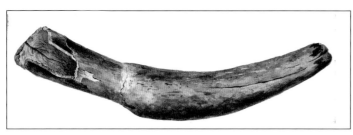

77/6/6   *Mammoth tusk.*
(Hist of Sid. !,10c)

Mammoth tusk. *Wednesday June 6, 1877.* Made a coloured drawing of the mammoth tusk lately found at the mouth of the River Sid probably washed out of the alluvium higher up the valley, which will soon be deposited in Exeter Museum. Taken in conjunction with the teeth, this is an interesting find. I finished the third volume of my *History of Sidmouth.* (*Diary*).

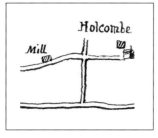

77/6/19   *From Donn's map.*
(Diary)

Ottery St. Mary and Holcombe Barton Farm. *Tuesday June 19, 1877.* Today, Mr. Heineken and myself drove to the neighbourhood of Ottery to look for the remains of an old chapel. In ancient charters of the twelfth and thirteenth centuries, mention is made of a chapel in the parish of Ottery under the name of Ile la Hedreland, or De la Hetheland, *quasi* up among the heather. Bishop Brantyngham in 1388 granted a license for a domestic chapel at Holcombe, about a mile and a half east of Ottery, and I presume this must have been the ancient De la Hetherland under a new regime – at least I do not know where else to look for it. (*footnote* – this appears to be a mistake, and it was near Washfield above Tiverton – see my *Hist of Sidmouth Vol IV, pp 12, 22*).

In Donn's map of 1765 a little chapel is shown. The estates of Higher and Lower Holcombe, comprising about four hundred acres, now belong to Mr. Pidsley. They are farmed by Mr. Page, son of butcher Page formerly of Sidmouth. We were told that the remains of the chapel had been pulled down many years ago and a farmhouse built out of them, parts of which are behind or eastwards of the present dwelling house, which was erected only twenty years ago partly out of the old materials.

77/6/19   *Holcombe Farm,
near Ottery.   June 19, 1877.*
(DRO, Z19/2/8E/239)

When excavating a circular place in front of the new house to make a pond (which we saw), they turned up a quantity of bones, from which they inferred that this spot had been the burial ground.   I went up behind the present dwelling to examine parts of the old house.   There is a large square stone chimney, walls of brown chert well squared out and some good sized blocks of worked Beer stone, such as might have once belonged to an ecclesiastical building.

We then drove through Ottery down to the river *where* there was once a chapel dedicated to St. Saviour, we presumed under the hill or cliff opposite the bridge.   We crossed the bridge and drove to Thorn, a very ancient place.   The original of the painted standing figure in the north aisle of Ottery Church, John Cook of Thorn, lived here.   The house is all modernised, but the old coat of arms cut in stone is over the door (see *illustration* July 23, 1874).   We then drove home.   (*Diary*).

77/6/19   *Cook of Thorn.*   (Diary)

Dorsetshire again.   *Tuesday July 3, 1877.*   Lord Sidney Osborne asked me to go again with him to Dorsetshire and we travelled together today, following the same route as last year (see June 23).   (*Diary*).   *The two friends spent a week cruising up and down the Dorset coast in Lord Osborne's cutter.*

Return of bronze celt.   *Saturday July 21, 1877.*   Mr. Perceval, now staying in Sidmouth, has learnt that Mr W. Toby has sent down from London a bronze celt and a broken piece to his sister, Mrs. Drake of Lower Pinn Farm, Otterton,.   We walked over and procured them for the Exeter Museum.   The story is that they were found 'on or under Woodbury Hill', but when we showed them to Mr. Heineken, he recognised them as what he had seen at the late General Lee's at Elford, near Topsham.   Mathew Lee, the grandfather, got four from the barrow at Lovehayne in 1763 and took them to Elford.   Soon after they were missed from Elford, these same were found in the hands of some workmen near Colyton Rawleigh and, as I was told at the time, one of them called Toby had taken them to London where he had settled as a baker.   This is several years ago.   I got his address and wrote to him but at that time he would not part with them.   Mr. Heineken saw them in the Summer House where other curiosities were kept and there is very little doubt that they were purloined by some workmen.   See November 22, 1861, for Mr. Snook's palstave found in the tumulus at the same time.   In my manuscript *History of Sidmouth I, 78* these things are alluded to.   See also *Transactions of the Devonshire Association II, 647,* for the quotation from Mathew Lee's diary given by Mr. Heineken.   (*Diary*).

Flint donation to Exeter Museum.   *Tuesday July 24, 1877.*   Packed up in a box about a hundred ancient worked flints I have found on the hills during the last seven years and sent them to Mr D'Urban, the curator of Exeter Museum.   Also three spindle whorles, one found by myself and two by Mr. Ede of Lansdowne.   He wished to arrange them at once, as members of the British Association have been invited to Exeter after the Plymouth meeting next month.   (*Diary*).

Devonshire Association meeting 1877.   *Monday July 30, 1877.*   Went to attend the annual meeting of the Devonshire Association at Kingsbridge.   (*Diary*).

Thurlestone Rock.   *Thursday August 2, 1877.*   Reading papers, one *of them* on white ale and I had some at luncheon.   I brought forward my scheme for a history of Devonshire and exhibited the four quarto volumes of my *History of Sidmouth*, which I offered as my contribution, and urged other people to undertake the histories of their several parishes.   I got great praise for my work though the last volume is not finished.   (*Diary*).   *Hutchinson's scheme for a history of the county was certainly practical.*   I see no other plan so likely to ensure success as that of adopting a division of labour . . . and if I may express a wish . . . it is that each one of you, living in each separate place, would undertake to draw up a detailed and careful account of your own parish (*A Scheme for a History of Devonshire*).   *He then produced his own four volumes on the history of Sidmouth for inspection and described its compilation* during a long course

77/8/2   *Thurlstone Rock, Bigbury Bay, near Bolt Tail.   Aug. 1877.* (DRO,Z19/2/8E/ 243)

of years *starting when he* was little more than a child.   *After two voyages across the Channel, numerous visits searching out and transcribing ancient documents in the British Museum and the Record Office in London, twelve years reducing the information to its present form, he was still* far from satisfied.   *Despite their admiration for his monumental industry, Hutchinson's daunting account of his labours can hardly have encouraged the other members to undertake similar projects.*

At five we started in a variety of vehicles, I counted thirteen, to make an excursion south-westwards to Bowringsleigh, a fine Elizabethan mansion which we examined inside and out.   Then we proceeded to Thurlestone, looked at the church and found tea, cake and wine awaiting us on the vicarage lawn.   I discovered that the vicar, Rev. Peregrine Ilbert, was at Tiverton School and I knew him as a boy.   We then went on to the Bay and looked at Thurlestone Rock, here given.   (Diary).

77/8/3   *Salcombe Castle, near Kingsbridge. Aug. 3, 1877.*
(DRO, Z19/2/8E/241)

77/8/3   *From Bolt Head, looking up the inlet of the sea towards Kingsbridge, Devon. Aug. 3 1877.*
(DRO,Z19/2/8E/241)

77/9/4   *Point between Beer and Beer Head.* (Diary)

Kingsbridge and Salcombe. *Friday August 3, 1877.*   This morning we started on a pleasant excursion down the arm of the sea called Salcombe River.   The tide flows up to Kingsbridge and we took the steamer at high water a little below *the town.*   There was scarcely standing room on board.   The views down the estuary were delightful.   We passed the ruins of Salcombe Castle a mile below at the entrance, a half mile in from the sea.   It looks like the outer wall of an octagonal building of no great size, a mere shell half covered with ivy.   It is built on a ledge of rocks at the foot of a cliff on the west side of the harbour.   *From* the edge of the cliff a stone could be thrown into it, yet Cromwell was four months taking it (Ref. *Hist. of Kingsbridge* by Miss S.P.Fox).   Half our passengers landed on the west shore below the castle at a place called South Sands, but the rest remained on board to look at the coast.   First we looked at Bolt Head, *and* then turned eastwards to Prawle Point, through the end of which there is a hole something like Thurlestone Rock.   We got a sight of Start Point further east with its lighthouse and fog horn, and then returned to disembark at South Sands.   The sea was rough outside and most of us were unwell, *but* there was a splendid cold collation laid out on the grass awaiting us which we enjoyed amazingly.   I took a hasty sketch of Salcombe Castle *before* we returned.   The tide was low but rising and about half way back we stuck on a sandbank, *though* in half an hour we floated off and by seven we were in Kingsbridge.   (*Diary*).

Promontory near Beer. *Tuesday September 4, 1877.*   Started in a boat with the same party as last night (*a musical evening at Seafield with Mr and Mrs Vernal and their friends*) to go to Beer, the sea again calm with an easy breeze from the north-west.   The weather was bright and beautiful and the sailing most enjoyable.   The variety of colour in the cliffs between Sidmouth and Beer cannot be exceeded, arising from the red, crimson and purple of the Red Marl, the brown, grey, buff, orange and yellow of the Greensand formation and the white and light black of the chalk.   To these may be added the greens and tints of approaching autumn.   I remarked the dip of the red and yellow strata eastward under Beer Head, rising again near Seaton.

On approaching Beer we saw several pleasure parties in boats.   We landed and soon after mounted the white cliff on the east to enjoy the view. From here the point towards Beer Head looks something like a person sitting with their feet in the water, but we remarked as we passed it that the head looks very tottery as if it would soon fall off. The new church at Beer is progressing, the walls being twelve or fourteen feet high. We had our sandwiches and claret on the hill and took a ramble before descending to the beach. I steered coming home, the wind being rather against us. (*Diary*).

Mars and Saturn. *Thursday September 27, 1877. I was* at Mr. Heineken's this evening, observing Mars and Saturn. Conveniently situated as regards his drawing room window, he got out his astronomical telescope and we examined them for a considerable time. At the south pole of Mars a white spot or patch is distinctly visible *and* this, we are told by astronomers, is supposed to be ice or snow. If so the drift of the argument goes that the climate there would be pretty much the same as ours. As for Saturn, the edge of the ring is turning towards us so that it begins to look a little more than a line of light. I suppose that wonderful ring will one day break up and perhaps add to the number of its satellites. On the 3rd November the planets were close together, only an angle of eleven minutes between them, and looked beautiful. They could both be seen in the field of the telescope together. (*Diary*).

77/9/27   Mars and Saturn. (Diary)

Sketch from the mouth of the River Sid. *October 1877. There is no mention of the annexed view in the Diary. The sketch shows Sidmouth with Peak Hill and High Peak behind and Mr Dunning's harbour works in the foreground.* The work went on slowly, as if it were an amusement for leisure hours (*History of Sidmouth IV, 171*) *and was eventually discontinued altogether in 1879.*

77/10/?   Dunning's plan. (Hist of Sid. IV,170)

77/10/?   *Sidmouth, from the mouth of the River Sid. Coloured on the spot, Oct. 1877.* (DRO, Z19/2/8E/245)

Wreck of the schooner 'Sarah'. *Monday 15 October, 1877. The only entry in Hutchinson's diary for October 14 concerned the weather,* mild and fine with a strong south wind, *but these conditions changed dramatically overnight.* The wind increased last night to one of the strongest gales I can ever remember. The roaring kept me awake for two or three hours. I rose apprehensive lest any of the large terracotta chimney pots on the Old Chancel might be blown over, but they stood well. The salt air has cut and blighted the vegetation and several trees have been blown down. Slates and broken chimney tops lie about the streets everywhere and most of the old thatched houses about the town have been stripped and unroofed. A vessel has been driven ashore a mile eastwards. I walked over this afternoon to look at her and made a sketch, but under difficulties, the wind being strong and cold and showers frequent. She is a round-sterned schooner from Teignmouth *loaded* with pipe clay, bound up-Channel. She lies knocked about in the wash of the sea and will soon go to pieces, for her planks are opening and lumps of pipe clay are coming through a hole in her side.

She became a wreck. Her hull and lower masts were sold at auction for twenty

pounds and her rigging and stores in various lots.   She was called the Sarah of
Yarmouth.   *(Diary).   This Billboy schooner built in 1835, with a crew of four and the*
master's wife on board, was driven ashore a mile east of the town in near hurricane conditions
on a voyage from Teignmouth to Antwerp (The Western Times October 16 and 30, 1877).

77/10/15 Schooner 'Sarah', laden
with pipe clay, driven on shore a
mile east of Sidmouth, Oct. 15,
1877. (DRO, Z19/2/8E/247)

Re-opening Exeter Cathedral.   *Thursday October 18, 1877.*   The ceremony of
opening Exeter Cathedral after its repairs and restoration by Sir Gilbert Scott was
held yesterday and today.   There are some who run after ecclesiastical displays and
delight in seeing troops of clergy in surplices and 'vestments', trying to imitate in an
English church all the gorgeous ritual of Rome.   *(Diary).*

Guy Fawkes Day 1877.   *Monday November 5, 1877.*   A number of lighted tar barrels
and fire balls were carried about the esplanade but the police prevented them being
brought into the town.   Later in the evening however, the police were attacked and
roughly handled, when two or three arrests were with some difficulty made.   The
offenders were afterwards brought before the magistrates and heavily fined.   *(Diary).*

77/11/27   The celestine band is in
the lower half of the carbonate of
lime nodule's band. (Diary)

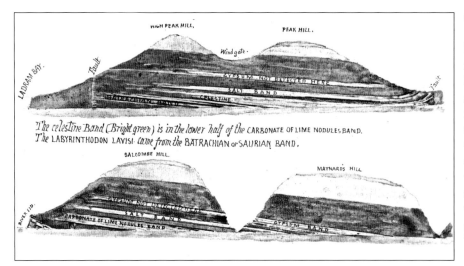

Celestine.   *Saturday November 17,*
1877.   My birthday.   The day
being clear and fine, I started
immediately after breakfast for the
beach under Peak Hill, to look for
some good specimens of celestine
for the Exeter museum.   I have got
one or two pretty good examples of
the light brown crystals, but *none*
of the blue to satisfy me.   I know
they are to be met with, for last
summer Mr. Perceval showed me a
very pretty specimen he procured
from some fallen masses near
Windgate, where the celestine

band runs higher than I can reach.   Perhaps I must wait until another fall of cliff takes place.   (*Diary*).

Tuesday November 27, 1877.   And a fall took place about this time and I have got some bluish crystals.   I have been mapping the face of the cliff lately to see in what order the various strata lie, and the small sections *annexed* may give some indication. The celestine in this locality is mostly in tabular or flat crystals, some of a blue or greenish-blue, others a light brown.   I have *also* procured some almost colourless and nearly as transparent as glass.   (A few feet below the celestine band *is where* I discovered the fossil stems in May, 1878.   See *Trans. Dev. Assoc., XI*).   (*Diary*).

77/11/27   *Celestine crystals on crystals of carbonate of lime.*   (Diary)

Indexing.   *Thursday December 6, 1877.*   Finished making the index to volume IX of the *Transactions of the Devonshire Association*, and sent it to the Rev. W. Harpley, the Secretary.   (*Diary*).

Walk to Peak Hill.   *Monday December 31, 1877.*   The last day of the year.   This morning was calm and bright and the sun shining beautifully, so I took a walk after breakfast on the beach under Peak Hill *as far as* Windgate, to look again for a good specimen of blue celestine.   *Today* I was seeking it at the foot of the Hill but I recently took a pleasant walk over Peak Hill and along the hollow between, where the road was lost when the earth fell away to the beach (in April 1811 I have been told), and then to the top of High Peak.   From this place, looking westwards, I made the sketch of the coast, as shown.   (*Diary*).

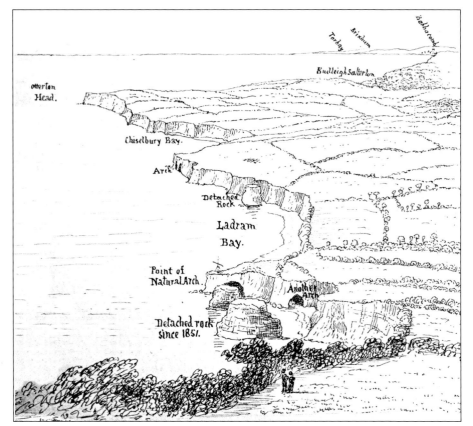

77/12/31   View westwards from High Peak.   (Diary)

1878

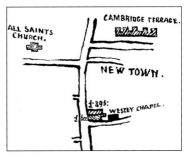

78/1/31 (Diary)

78/5/13 *Fossil stem.* (Diary)

78/5/13 *Sketch of the slab from which I procured the fossil stems.* No date. (DRO, Z19/2/8E/249)

House prices in Sidmouth. *Thursday January 31, 1878. There has been* a sale of houses in Sidmouth. No. 3 Coburg Terrace sold for £340, rent £19.10s., *and* No. 4 next door fetched £355. A small house in New Town as they call it was bought for £130, rent £10. The corner house near the Wesleyan Chapel was bought for £600 by Clode, a baker, *and* the next along by Selkirk, a painter, for £395. A new Wesleyan Chapel has been built opposite. (*Diary*).

Devonshire Association business, 1878. *Wednesday February 27, 1878.* Went to Exeter to attend a council meeting of the Devonshire Association, to make arrangements for the meeting at Paignton in July. (*Diary*).

Family history. *Saturday March 4, 1878.* I have an article today on the Hutchinson family and arms in *Notes and Queries*, in answer to an American correspondent. (*Diary*).

Fossil stems. *Monday May 13, 1878.* Going along the beach under Peak Hill nearly as far as Windgate to try and get a good specimen of celestine for Exeter Museum, I remembered that some fifty tons of the Red Marl had *recently* fallen. One of the great blocks had split with the concussion and one side showed a surface of hardened sand and clay, slightly ripple marked. *There were* a few traces as if annelids or other creatures had crawled over the bottom of a pond and a number of fossil stems about an inch or an inch and a quarter thick with joints every six, seven or eight inches apart lying across one another. The stems were composed of loose sandstone, the bark or outside a thin coating of greenish clay. I extracted one or two pieces and then returned home, but as fossil plants are rare in the Keuper of the New Red, I resolved to go again. (*Diary*).

More fossil stems. *Tuesday May 14, 1878.* I went again taking tools with me and extracted two or three more. Every high tide the waves dash against the block and from its soft nature it will soon be destroyed. I shall note these particulars more fully in the geological chapter of my *History of Sidmouth* (see *Trans. Dev. Assoc. XI, 383*). (*Diary*).

Railway stocks. *Friday May 17, 1878. There was* a meeting of the preference shareholders of the Great Eastern Railway in London, to which I did not think it necessary to go. They decided it would be more advantageous to consolidate a number of stocks with various amounts of interest into one of four per cent. Thus my £2400 at five per cent yielding me £120 per annum *is* altered to £3000 at four per cent, which will yield me just the same. (*Diary*).

Domesday Book. *Friday May 24, 1878.* Finished my portion of extending and translating the Devonshire part of the Exchequer Domesday Book. Some day I must do the same for the Exeter Book. *See October 1, 1878.* (*Diary*). *Nevertheless, he was having some misgivings about the amount of time this project was consuming:* It was showing it at the meeting a year ago (*the manuscript History of Sidmouth, see August 2, 1877*) that got me put on the Domesday Book translation Committee, and I thoughtlessly allowed myself to be put on this Committee not knowing how much work it would involve. I would resign, but I cannot in honour I suppose. (*Letter to Perceval dated September 7, 1878*).

Ottery West Hill, Telegraph House. *Wednesday June 26, 1878.* Went with Mr. Heineken to Telegraph Hill, near Streetway Head. We examined the old wooden house where the telegraph had been. *(Diary). Hutchinson sketched two views of the building:* It was used at the commencement of the present century. A framework with the shutters was raised over it *and* it is built mostly of wood. The holes for the telescope are seen beside the windows. *(Sketchbook).* We returned by Belbury Castle *and* brought home a bottle full of dirty water out of a ditch for Lord Sidney Osborne to put under his microscope. *(Diary).*

Below left: 78/6/26 The old Telegraph House on Ottery West Hill. June 26, 1878. (DRO, Z19/2/8E/251)

Devonshire Association meeting 1878. *Monday July 29, 1878.* Took the rail to Torquay to attend the meeting of the Devonshire Association at Paignton, close by. I got rooms at 2, Abbey Crescent. *(Diary).*

Bishop's Palace, Paignton. *Wednesday July 31, 1878.* Went to Paignton by rail. Torquay station, near Torre Abbey, is being rebuilt in squared limestone with Bath stone dressings. Sat listening to the reading of papers till I was tired. Went out and took a walk around Roundham Head and through the town, looked at the church and made a sketch of the remains of an ancient cross in the southern part of the churchyard. *I also* made a sketch of the old tower overgrown with ivy, being the last remains of the Palace formerly belonging to the Bishops of Exeter. This tower stands at the south-east corner of a large quadrangle enclosed with a massive wall. Looking through a loophole, I could perceive that the interior was bare of buildings, though mounds and ridges indicated where they had stood and the directions the walls had taken. The rest was grass and weeds. *(Diary).*

Above right: 78/6/26 South side of the Telegraph House. The hole for the telescope is seen beside the window. These telegraphs were not used after the battle of Waterloo. (DRO, Z19/2/8E/253)

78/7/31 Remains of cross at Paignton. (Diary)

78/7/31 Tower of the ruined Bishop's Palace at Paignton, Devon. Aug. 1, 1878. (DRO, Z19/2/8E/255)

Thatcher Rock, Torquay. *Friday August 2, 1878.* Put some bread and cheese in my pocket and started after breakfast for a ramble. I went down steep roads and up steep paths towards the sea, and then over many beautiful ups and downs, and downs and ups, gradually descending to the limestone point. From its being scarped and flattened down on terraces, one may judge that this long horn, the northern margin of Torbay, was once worked and quarried for limestone which was put on board ships close up to the rock. There I sat down to enjoy the view. From a survey of the scenery, I took a survey of my bread and cheese. Everything tastes good out upon the wild hills. I had nothing to drink but I enjoyed what I had, for I was hungry enough to eat the limestone rocks of which there was an abundance. Like a giant refreshed I got up and examined the point, until I came across some men working at the outfall of the great sewer from Torquay that is carried underground for a couple of miles or more. The work will be opened for use shortly, when a great demonstration will take place. Getting opposite Thatcher Rock, with Berry Head and Brixham beyond, I stopped to make a sketch of it. It is an immense rock of conical form with serrated peaks at the top looking like the ruins of an old castle *and* on the side a raised beach. I walked on in the hot sun, and hot indeed it was, and in time I reached my lodgings. (*Diary*).

St. Michael's Chapel, Torquay. *Sunday August 4, 1878.* Went to a church built of red rock, walk*ing* a mile or so to examine the remains of the old chapel on Chapel Hill. The tradition is that some devout person who was at sea and in great peril of shipwreck, made a vow that if he should escape death he would build a chapel on the spot of land he should see on approaching the shore. The first land he saw was the top of this hill. (*Diary*).

High Peak and Picket Rock. *Friday August 30, 1878).* Took a walk after breakfast along the beach westwards. High Peak Hill is a beautiful object and would make a splendid study for a painter, especially during the forenoon before the sun gets behind it. By the Ordnance Survey the hill is set down at 513.9 feet high, reduced to mean tide at Liverpool, and I think that Picket Rock, which lies off the point with Little Picket outside, from observation and a rough measurement is about 120 feet, though it looks nothing till you are close to it. Mr. Lavis discovered his Labyrinthodon lavisi amongst some of the cliff that had fallen from a height of sixty or seventy feet, at about three or four hundred yards beyond the point. I had my dinner in my pocket, *so* sat down at the foot of

Top: 78/8/2 The Thatcher Rock in Torbay. This view is looking from the Hope's Nose or Torquay side, due south towards Bury Head and Brixham on the right. Aug. 2,1878. (DRO, Z19/2/8E/259) Above: 78/8/4 Chapel Hill, Torquay. Sketched on the spot August 4, 1878. (DRO, Z19/2/8E/257) Right: 78/8/30 High Peak Hill and Picket Rock. (Diary)

Picket Rock and discussed it. No drink. It takes too much room and weighs too heavy. I stayed for about five hours examining the cliffs. A heavy cloud passed at sea and there was one of the most intense and brilliant double rainbows I recollect ever to have seen. I was once on Little Picket at very low water, spring tide. The

section of the vallum of the old camp on High Peak can be discerned from Sidmouth. (*Diary*).

Exeter Book. *Tuesday October 1, 1878.* Commenced writing out and translating my portion of the Exeter Domesday Book for a committee of the Devonshire Association. (*Diary*).

Salcombe Hill. *Tuesday October 29, 1878.* Took Mr. King to the top of Salcombe Hill and showed him the great stones, the circular patches like a British village and the cairns. (*Diary*).

Exeter Museum exhibits. *Friday November 1, 1878.* Went to Belmont Villa, Dawlish. When in Exeter I took a look at the Museum in Queen Street, which is now becoming a very considerable establishment. The various objects sent there from Sidmouth by Mr. Heineken and myself begin to make quite a show. I also went to the Institution in Cathedral Yard. (*Diary*).

Guy Fawkes Day 1878. *Wednesday November 6, 1878.* Last night three cottages in High Street, Dawlish, were burnt down by way of celebrating Guy Fawkes's exploit. (*Diary*).

78/10/29 Salcombe Hill. (Hist of Sid. I, 86a)

Old Maid Rock, Dawlish. *Saturday November 9, 1878.* Sketched the solitary rock in the Bishop's Parlour (as I believe that cove at the west end of the beach is called), which I am told is called the Old Maid Rock. Why it has got this name I know not, unless from its isolation. Old bachelors are solitary sometimes. I think it is about thirty feet high judging by the size of people standing near it. (*Diary*). *Hutchinson did a larger coloured sketch of the 'Old Maid' the following year. See August 2, 1879.*

Choir and organ in Sidmouth Church. *Sunday December 15, 1878.* The organ having been placed in the new organ chamber in the south-east corner of the parish church, the surpliced choir of eighteen boys and men appeared for the first time today. When the church was rebuilt in 1860, there was a great fight in the parish over this novelty and it was resisted. (*Diary*). *The accompanying sketch shows* the east end of the south chancel aisle in 1878 before the organ chamber was built. (*History of Sidmouth IV, 118*).

78/11/9 *Old Maid Rock, Dawlish.* (Diary)

Cemetery consecration. *Monday December 16, 1876.* The Bishop came and consecrated the cemetery *and* the novelty brought half Sidmouth up there. The day was fine, clear and without wind but the ground was covered in snow. Part of the service was in the south chapel where it was a cram, *and* the pages of our books soon felt damp with the excess of moisture oozing from the new walls. By great efforts the east window, in painted glass by Ward and Hughes (who did the Queens window) was got in. It is dedicated to Lord Sidney Osborne during his lifetime, the arms at the bottom of the middle light *being* done from my drawings. Well - a circuit of paths had been gravelled and cleared of snow round which it was intended to lead the Bishop in his perambulation of the new ground *before going* to the tent in the middle. Vain preparations! When we had formed the procession in the chapel, without waiting to be informed of the route or anything else, off started the Bishop at a good round pace. He went down a side path which had not been gravelled and was deep in mud and half-melted snow and then cut across the grass through the snow direct to the tent, leaving us to follow close behind him. (*Diary*).

78/12/15 *Sketch of the east end of the south chancel aisle in 1878, before the organ chamber was built.* (Hist. of Sid. IV, 118)

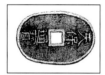

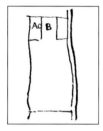

From top: 79/1/29a Gold ring (Diary); 79/1/29b Japanese coin (Diary); 79/3/6 (Diary)

79/3/19 *Facsimile copy of a view of Sidmouth beach. Copied by me in March 1879.* (Hist of Sid. V, 24)

New Years Day 1879. *Wednesday January 1, 1879.* Now then, what will 1879 bring? (*Diary*).

Gold ring and oval coin. *Wednesday January 29, 1879.* A boy brought a gold ring to show me, which he found last Monday on the beach near Chit Rocks. It was eighteen-carat gold and apparently bears a garnet between two emeralds on the broadest part of the loop. He would not sell it. He also found a Japanese oval bronze coin, which he let me have. Many circular Chinese coins have been found there, but this is the first oval one I have seen. I have carefully noted them down in my *History of Sidmouth Vol. I.* The characters at top I think signify the date 1834, as similar characters on china are said to stand for that date. (*Diary*).

Devonshire Association business, 1879. *Friday February 28, 1879. A few days previously Hutchinson had gone to Dawlish to stay with his cousin, and from there* went to Exeter to attend a meeting of the Council of the Devonshire Association. (*Diary*).

Dawlish waterworks. *Thursday March 6, 1879.* Walked to the fir trees on the hill above Dawlish. There are twenty-three trees there *and* it is at this spot I am told that the great tank or reservoir to supply Dawlish with water is to be made. Went to the barrow on the ridge of the high hill a mile off over Langdon (at A *on the map*). (*Later note:* No. The tank is being made at B – see July 23, 1880). (*Diary*).

Dawlish, St. Gregory. *Sunday March 9, 1879.* At St. Marks, the chapel soon to be enlarged with the addition of a south aisle, I believe. *I was also* at the parish church, in the south transept *of which*, in the portion recently rebuilt, is a tablet to the memory of Lady Perryman by Flaxman. There are three or four figures of ladies in light drapery and very short waists with Grecian profiles pouring out a fair measure of grief round an urn, all in white marble. (*Diary*).

Watercolour of old Sidmouth. *Wednesday March 19, 1879.* Mr. Fisher of Blackmore Hall lent me an old watercolour view of Sidmouth beach to copy. It is signed T.W.Upton, 1802, *who* was an Exeter artist. I finished it today. (*Diary*).

New edition of Sidmouth Guide. *Saturday March 29, 1879.* Mr. Lethaby the printer is going to bring out another edition of my *Sidmouth Guide* and has asked me to revise the present one so as to bring matters down to the present time. Though I have no interest in it, my name is on the title page so I have been going over it lately. There are not woodcuts enough, *so* if I can manage it I should like to add a few more for this edition. (*Diary*).

Tuesday April 29, 1879. Finished fifteen small woodcuts to illustrate the new edition of my *Sidmouth Guide,* to be printed soon. I fear I have not made much of a hand of them. (*Diary*).

Find of a ring. *Monday May 5, 1879.* A man brought me a gold ring to look at which he found when pulling down an old house in the Marsh, now by some called Easterntown. It is a hoop, flat on the inside and half round on the outside. Cut with a graver round the inside in a writing hand are the words 'In God and Thee, My joy shall be'. Workmen seem to think that what they find on another person's property is their own. This ring in reality belongs to the Balfours, the old house being on Manor Road. (*Diary*).

79/5/5   Another gold ring. (Diary)

Rose Cottage. *Monday May 19, 1879.* Rose Cottage in Mill Lane, or as they are now pleased to call it All Saints Road, was put up to auction. Mill Lane was the path down which the monks of Otterton Priory came to their mill at the top of the town. *Rose Cottage* was built some seventy years ago by Mr. Stocker, a tallow chandler, who got the nickname of 'The Squire' because he had a great passion for hunting and kept some hounds. But as he could not afford to feed them, they preyed upon the neighbours, robbed all the larders and were the nuisance of the town. One day when my father was living there, one of them got into the larder of No. 4 Coberg Terrace and *stole* a joint of meat, a shoulder of veal I think. There was a great outcry from the street boys as he ran away down the street but he got clear off. On one fine summer morning, doors and windows open and just before we came down to breakfast, one of these prowlers came in and took half a pound of butter off the table. All this was looked upon as great fun. 'The Squire' was the father of the present Dr. Pullin's mother.

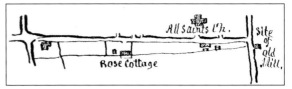

79/5/19   (Diary)

Well – Rose Cottage was put up at £400 and the bidding went up to £514, *but* as the reserved price was £600 it was bought in.   The Rev. Olmius Morgan however, recently from Suffolk, afterwards took it for £575, *but* it was sold again soon. The little bit of ground taken out of the field belonging to the Manor, they pay £1 a year for. (*Diary*).

Committee meeting. *Friday June 20, 1879.* Went into Exeter to attend a committee meeting of the Devonshire Association. About a dozen members met. Mr. and Mrs. Dymond afterwards gave us a very handsome cold dinner at their house at No. 1 Higher Terrace, Mount Radford. (*Diary*).

Dangerous practise. *Wednesday June 25, 1879.* Charles Foyle, an old man of 85, was today thrown and killed (for he died of his injuries soon after) by a bullock on the esplanade.   The butcher's practise of driving cattle through the streets to the slaughterhouses is a grievance long complained of, and I have often heard the remark 'there will be nothing done till someone is killed'. This case is the more reprehensible in that the local board some years ago granted a licence for a slaughterhouse in the heart of the town, the very one to which this beast was being driven.   The bullock also gored and wounded a blind woman of 60 called Julia Russel and pinned a child to a wall with its horns, *though* to the astonishment of everybody the child escaped serious injury. (*Diary*).

Saturday June 28, 1879. The inquest was held on the death of Charles Foyle, but as the butcher had many friends among the jury they brought in a verdict of 'accidental death'. Legal proceedings are however threatened. (*Diary*).

To Ilfracombe. *Monday July 21, 1879.* Left Sidmouth for Ilfracombe to attend the annual meeting of the Devonshire Association and to read a short paper on my fossil stems from Peak Hill (see May 13, 1878). *I had* an hour in Exeter *and then* went on to Barnstaple and Ilfracombe. Near Morthoe station this line attains a height of five hundred feet. (*Diary*).

79/7/24   *Font.* (Diary)

Berrynarbor Church font. *Thursday July 24, 1879.* Reading papers from ten till four. I read mine today and was much praised by Mr. Pengelly of Torquay and by Mr. Ussher of the Geological Survey for my drawings. My fossil stems are supposed

to be calamites though the species was not known to the geologists present.   After this we went by the invitation of the Rev. Treasurer Hawker formerly of Ide, to the rectory at Berrynarbor where we had tea and many good things.   We enjoyed the beautiful views, examined the church *where I* sketched the font as annexed and went over the Manor House, *now* almost a ruin.   We passed Mr. Basset's castle at Watermouth where there is a very pretty little natural harbour and we all went to see the caves, arches and tunnels the waves have made in the cliff.   Everybody ought to see these. (*Diary*).

79/7/25   *Palimpsest brass.*   (Diary)

Palimpsest brass.   *Friday July 25, 1879.*   Made an excursion to Braunston *and* examined the church.   The nave is very wide *and* there is the most perfect set of oak seats with handsomely carved ends that I have seen anywhere.   There is a very interesting small palimpsest brass (loose) on the south side of the chancel, which, from an inscription on another brass below, refers to Elizabeth Bolmer (?), daughter of J. Erle and the wife of Edward Chichester.   On the reverse side are the head and shoulders of a knight in chain armour.   The pulpit is Jacobean, *and* near it, in the splay of a window are traces of fresco painting representing some saint.

On a hill north-east of the church is a tower with pinnacles built in 1833 to commemorate the passage of the Reform Bill. (*Diary*).

79/7/27   (Diary)

Ilfracombe, Christ Church.   *Sunday July 27, 1879.*   In the evening I went to Christ Church in Portland Street, a Free Church conducted by the Rev. Bishop Price.   The prayer book of the Church of England is used and we had a good evangelical sermon.   There is a vessel there used as a font, of dark sandstone apparently, with an interior diameter of perhaps about nine inches (I speak from memory only), *which* stands on a modern pedestal.   We were asked what it originally had been. (*Diary*).   *The font (see August 6, 1880) seems to have puzzled Hutchinson a much as other members of the Devonshire Association, their guesses including a sacred vessel of the Druids, a Roman quern and a medieval piscina (Trans. Dev. Assoc XII, 662-4).*

Repair of the Swan.   *Monday July 28, 1879.*   Left Ilfracombe for Dawlish via Barnstaple and Exeter.   Passing through Starcross, I saw the great Swan hauled up on the wharf under repair with its long neck off. *See August 2, 1872.* (*Diary*).

79/7/30   *The Elephant Rock, Langstone Point, near Dawlish. The head is falling away. Sketched on the spot July 30, 1879.* (DRO, Z19/2/8F/9)

Elephant Rock, Dawlish. *Wednesday July 30, 1879.* The Elephant Rock, which was in its perfect state in 1872 and of which I made a sketch on May 4, 1868, I see is beginning to lose its shape, especially about the head (*see also August 1, 1888*). Walked out to the east side of Langstone Point and made another sketch of it. (*Diary*).

Old Maid Rock, Dawlish, again. *Saturday August 2, 1879.* Made a coloured sketch of the Old Maid Rock, Dawlish. (*See August 1, 1888 for the rock after the loss of its head*). (*Diary*).

79/8/2 *The rock commonly called the 'Old Maid Rock', at the west of Dawlish. Coloured on the spot August 2, 1879.*
(DRO, Z19/2/8F/7)

Presents. *Wednesday August 6, 1879.* Returned from Dawlish to Sidmouth, bringing with me a case of mathematical instruments and a small Orrery which my cousin Miss Roberton told me had not been made use of for forty years. She *is* 80 and gave *them to* me. She. (*Diary*).

Good catch. *Friday August 22, 1879.* Saw a beautiful salmon peal weighing nearly two pounds and a half, caught with an artificial minnow in the River Sid. *The spot was* about sixty yards below the stone bridge in a deep pool called 'Horse's Belly', though for what reason nobody knows. (*Diary*).

Jupiter's satellite. *Sunday September 14, 1879.* Called in the evening to see how Mr. Heineken was. He is in his eightieth year and has never recovered from his illness of last winter. The planets Jupiter and Saturn were very beautiful towards the east, so he wheeled his telescope to the windows. It was a fortunate moment, for after a little observation we saw the satellite C approach the planet and become occulted. This occurred at 8h 13m 13s, so we lost it as in the second sketch. Before we finished, satellite B appeared to have perceptibly approached the great planet. We then turned to Saturn. That wonderful ring! When will it break to pieces? The last time we observed it, the edge was turned towards us so that it was nearly invisible (see September 27, 1877). (*Diary*).

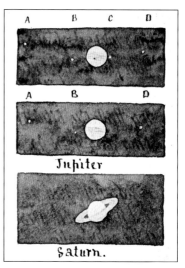

79/9/14 (Diary)

Peak Estate sale. *Thursday September 18, 1879.* The Peak estate was put up to be sold in lots. To see how things go in my parish I generally go to the auctions, *but* today I had an invitation to dine with Mrs.and Miss Soulsby at Salcombe. These ladies are clever at geology and several other sciences and I enjoyed much intellectual conversation. Called also at Sunny Bank and at the vicarage and then walked back.

   The first Mr. Lousada, originally I believe a Spanish Jew and a stockbroker in London, came down about 1790 and bought a house and some ground called the

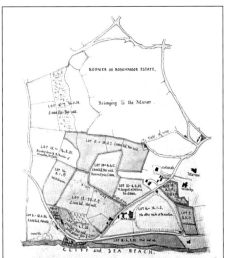

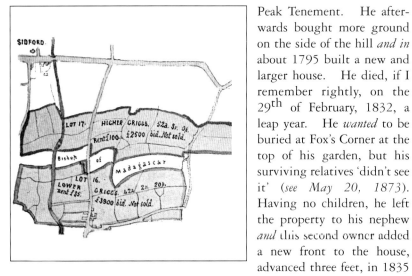

Peak Tenement. He afterwards bought more ground on the side of the hill *and in* about 1795 built a new and larger house. He died, if I remember rightly, on the 29th of February, 1832, a leap year. He *wanted* to be buried at Fox's Corner at the top of his garden, but his surviving relatives 'didn't see it' (*see May 20, 1873*). Having no children, he left the property to his nephew *and* this second owner added a new front to the house, advanced three feet, in 1835

Top: 79/9/14 (Diary)
79/9/18 *Peak House, Sidmouth, Devon. May 1836.* (DRO, Z19/2/8A/129)

Above left: 79/9/18 *The Peak House estate.* (Diary)

Above right: 79/9/18 Higher and Lower Griggs. (Diary)

Opposite, far right: 79/12/10 Sidmouth fires. (Diary)

or 1836. (*Hutchinson's much earlier sketch annexed shows the house around the time of the rebuilding*). He died about 1854, also leaving it to a nephew, the third and last, *but* 'something having gone wrong' *the latter* sold it in 1875 to the Trustees of the Manor. Mr. Heugh, the senior trustee, became bankrupt in 1878 and this property was somehow adjudged liable, and hence the auction.

Two other estates, which had been recently bought in Salcombe parish called Higher and Lower Griggs, were brought to the hammer but were not sold. (*Diary*).

Salcombe Hill circles. *Thursday October 16, 1879.* Had a man dig on Salcombe Hill to try to discover what the circular patches are. Mr. Edward Chick came up. Our dinner was sandwiches and bread and cheese, very enjoyable, and we ate it lying under a hedge as the wind was cold. I was up there surveying with him on September 30, and *again* on October 9 with the man digging. (*Diary*).

Marriage among birds. *Friday October 17, 1879.* In the '*Animal World*' this month is my article headed '*Marriage Among Birds*', giving an account of my observations on rooks. (*Diary*).

Domesday Book progress. *Saturday October 18, 1879.* Finished my second portion of both the *Domesday Books.* Mr. R. J. King's death threw his section upon the rest of the Committee. (*Diary*).

Accident at sea. *Monday October 20, 1879.* Took a walk on Salcombe Hill to look again at the circular patches. It blew so hard from the north-west that I was obliged to tie my hat on. *An* unfortunate accident *occurred* – a man drowned. Boats were out mackerel fishing, one of them with two young men in it called Skinner and Govier *which* capsized in a sudden gust off Windgate (the hollow between Peak and High Peak Hills), a dangerous place. I was nearly turned over myself there once. Govier was drowned. (*Diary*). *The undated sketch perhaps illustrates Hutchinson's near mishap off Sidmouth.*

79/10/20 Fresh breeze, Sidmouth, Devon. Not dated. (DRO, Z19/2/8D/49)

79/11/8 Group of 43 pears on one branch. Old Chancel, Sidmouth. November 8, 1879. Drawn from nature. (DRO, Z19/2/8F/15)

Circular patches on Salcombe Hill. *Tuesday October 28, 1879.* Went to Salcombe again to examine the circular patches. As there are fifty of them in the northern group on the open common at the head of Sid lane and above thirty in the southern group near the road from Sidmouth to Salcombe, mostly clustered near a great pit forty-five feet in diameter and about three deep, they must owe their origin to design and not to accident. Furze bushes grow all round them but not in them, *whilst* grass and heather grow in them but not furze. (*Diary*).

Good crop. *Friday November 7, 1879.* Mr. Colwell the gardener has bought the pears on the tree and he and his son are engaged in removing them with ladders. He allows me ten shillings for them this year and I take it out in vegetables, *though* he once allowed me fifteen shillings. I believe he gets the cream. (*Diary*).

Saturday November 8, 1879. There were a great many pears on the tree this year, though small from want of sun and sufficient heat. Mr. Colwell took away the remainder today, some bags full. He cut a branch off the tree about the size of my little finger loaded with pears like bunches of grapes in a cluster. I counted forty-three and made a drawing of them in my sketchbook. (*Diary*).

Indexing done. *Friday November 28, 1879.* Finished making the index to Volume XI of the Transactions of the Devonshire Association. (*Diary*).

Fire in East Street. *Wednesday December 10, 1879.* This evening, a little before night, I happened to look out and was startled at seeing a bright light and a great volume of smoke rising over the town towards the east. It was a cold, clear, quiet night with a gentle wind from the north-east. On going down I found Fore Street full of people and a quantity of furniture blocking the side walk opposite East Street, now so called. I could not get into East Street for the crowd. About half way down on the left there is a large courtyard surrounded by coach houses and stables belonging to the York Hotel, and half the northern and southern and all the western sides were in a great blaze. I made a circuit round by the eastern streets and found a hearse and a number of carriages ranged all along one side of the street which had been dragged out and saved. A number of horses I was told had also been

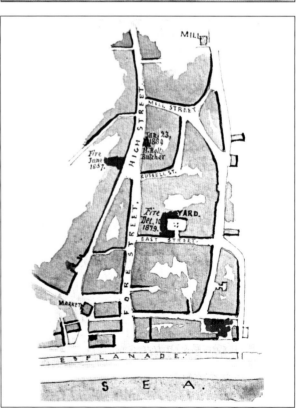

safely rescued.   A pig was so scared by the fire, the noise and the busy crowd that he ran two or three times into the flames, burning himself so much that they were obliged to kill him.   A 'mourning coach', as it is called, was singed and then got out, but I afterwards saw the remains of another coach quite burnt, in short I saw nothing but the charred pole on the ground.   I also saw a quantity of half burnt oats.   The annexed plan will show where the fire was, and two other fires I can remember.   No person could tell me how the fire originated, but probably *it was* a lamp amongst the straw.   If the wind had been strong, half the town may have been consumed. (*Diary*).

History of Sidmouth, Volume IV.   *Friday December 19, 1879.*   This evening I finished the fourth volume of my *History of Sidmouth.*   Owing to a multitude of interruptions, not the least of which was the work on *Domesday Book*, I have been tediously long over it.   On looking back I see that I began this fourth volume on June 7, 1877, and expressed a hope that it would be the last, *but t*he account of the parish church took up so much room that I had not the space left for two or three other subjects which ought to be noticed.   I have also several old engravings and copies of old pictures of different views of Sidmouth and I must either throw them all away or get another blank folio volume, bound in green vellum like the others, to preserve them in.   (*Diary*).   *Hutchinson decided on the latter course and his collection of old prints forms a valuable final volume to the History of Sidmouth.*

Shortest day.   *Saturday December 20, 1879.*   As I sat at breakfast in the Oak Room of the Old Chancel, under the panelled ceiling and the coats of arms of the Lords of the Manor, I observed that at nine o'clock the sun was over the chancel of the church, and an hour later when ten struck, it was over the tower, just clearing the pinnacles. The sun at the shortest day, where we now find ourselves, rises after eight a little to the left of the chancel (as I look at it) but at midsummer it rises at a quarter before four over Salcombe Hill, nearly as far as Trow Hill.   The angle subtended by these two positions of the sun is fifteen degrees.   (*Diary*).

79/12/20 Sunrise. (Diary)

1880

Abandoned harbour works. *January 1880. No Diary entry. The annexed view of Sidmouth from Salcombe Hill, done in January 1880, shows the remains of Mr. Dunning's now abandoned western pier at the east end of town.* The pier was not wide enough, or weighty, or massive or solid enough to withstand the mighty force of the raging sea, so that as fast as the outer end was pushed forward the waves knocked it down. (*History of Sidmouth IV, 171*).

80/1/? *Sidmouth, from the cliff over the River Sid. Jan. 1880.* (DRO, Z19/2/8F/3)

80/1/24   (Diary)

Size matters. *Saturday January 24, 1880.* After a space of five weeks, I observed that at about nine this morning the sun was much higher and further to the left than last month, and at ten it was a good way from the tower. When looking at drawings or paintings in which either the sun or moon is represented, I generally remark that in nine cases out of ten both are drawn too large – far too large. Even our best artists are guilty of this fault. The diameter of both sun and moon is about one half of a degree and every artist ought to bear this in mind. (*Diary*).

New literary project. *Wednesday February 4, 1880.* As I have now finished the fourth volume of my *History of Sidmouth* I have a little breathing time until I can get another folio made. I have been turning my attention to the collection of family papers, old letters, etc., referring to American affairs a century ago, and ironing out and repairing them for the purpose of arranging and binding. I sometimes wish I had laid my Sidmouth history aside and devoted my attention to the compilation of a book from these materials - a sort of fourth volume to Governor Hutchinson's *History of Massachusetts* - a book too long talked of and too long neglected. (*Diary*).

80/2/29   (Diary)

Leap year. *Sunday February 29, 1880.* Being leap year *this* February has twenty-nine days, but what is very extra-ordinary is that there have been five Sundays this month. I heard someone say that this has not occurred 'for hundreds of years' and will not happen again 'for hundreds more'. Whether this is true or not, I have not the time to enquire. The days on which Sunday fell were - 1st, 8th, 15th, 22nd and 29th

At nine and ten o'clock the sun is getting higher and further away. Five weeks more have elapsed since my last observation. (*Diary*).

Lifeboat practise. *Wednesday March 17, 1880.* Went down and saw the lifeboat launched *but* it was not well done. The man on shore who let go the catch so as to free her and let her run off the carriage into the water, was about five seconds too late to meet the wave properly. The wave had *receded*, so that the boat came down upon the gravel and the next wave almost capsized her. I have seen this error committed before. There were ten oarsmen in the boat, *including* one bow-man, two coxswains and Mr. William Floyd the Secretary. The wind was hard from the east, with large waves breaking on the beach. They merely went out for exercise. (*Diary*).

Good Friday 1880. *Friday March 26, 1880.* Good Friday. Hot cross buns for breakfast and salt fish for dinner. My great black tom-cat who sleeps on my bed every night and has his every meal with me, for I never think of sitting down without him, and is as affectionate as a child, thought the buns very good, and my rooks that I feed daily under my window every day considered them excellent. (*Diary*).

Barrow map. *Thursday April 1, 1880.* Finished drawing a map of about six miles around Sidmouth on a smooth lithographic stone. It is a reference map to *accompany* a report on the barrows on the hills near this place for the Devonshire Association. Sent it to Exeter and ordered 575 copies. (*Diary*).

May Day 1880. *Saturday May 1, 1880.* I heard a great talking outside and opened the front door, when I was greeted by a group of six children carrying boughs and branches hung with ribbons and flowers. Soon after that three others came, and then four girls, very vociferous. They soon emptied my pockets of coins. (*Diary*).

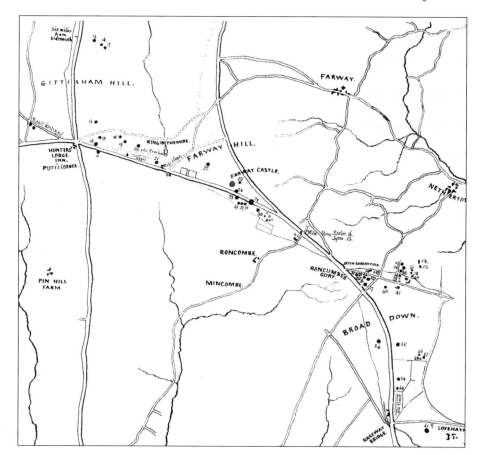

80/4/1 *The map, though by no means accurate, will shew the positions of the principal group of barrows on Gittisham and Farway Hills, and on Broad Down.* (Hist of Sid. I, 68)

Lumpsucker. *Monday May 17, 1880.* Some Sidmouth fishermen brought me a very beautiful little fish to look at, which they had drawn up in their mackerel net at sea. It had a large blunt head tapering away gracefully to the tail - more gracefully than in the horrible sketch *annexed*. It was light green in colour with specks of protuberances of dark green. The eyes were prominent and it turned them perceptibly in different directions, and the pupil was very black (see June 11, 1883).

Today there was a luncheon party of gentlemen and tradesmen at the London Hotel, after which a testimonial with many complimentary speeches were offered to Mr. Richard Stone who has just retired, on account of the weight of eighty winters, from the humble offices of Assistant Overseer and Collector of Taxes. He has always behaved himself so well that he secured to himself many friends. (*Diary*).

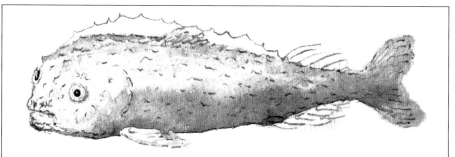

80/5/17 *Fish caught at Sidmouth.* (Diary)

Barrow report. *Tuesday May 25, 1880.* Finished my report on the barrows or tumuli on the hills that surround Sidmouth for the next volume of the *Transactions of the Devonshire Association.* I have a list of no less than ninety-three, all within six miles. It has involved a great deal more work than I anticipated, for I soon saw that the report would be worth nothing unless accompanied by illustrations. I am therefore busily engaged in making some lithographed sketches. (*Diary*). *This article, the most comprehensive of all the seventy-three barrow reports, was abstracted from Hutchinson's History of Sidmouth. A note there advises the reader to go to the printed account in the Transactions (Vol. XII) as* it has been re-written and re-arranged, and in order to make the illustrations as accurate as possible I recurred to the objects found in the barrows now preserved in Exeter Museum. (*History of Sidmouth I, 66a*).

80/5/28 *Kitten.* (Diary)

Siamese kitten. *Friday May 28, 1880.* A short time ago some children brought me a kitten with two perfect faces on one head, as I have endeavoured to represent in the margin. It was in a bottle of spirits. They were the children of Stretchley Churchill, who made the stonework around the entrance door of the Old Chancel and the fan tracery of the hall ceiling. They said that the kitten had lived for a short time after it was born. Such *lusus naturae* however, are too common to excite wonder. (*Diary*).

Bulverton Hill cairn. *Sunday May 30, 1880.* This afternoon I took a walk up to Mutter's Moor and Bulverton Hill. I find that the cairn of flints in the plantation has been taken away since my last visit to this hill. (*Diary*).

Barrow Committee meeting. *Friday June 18, 1880.* Went into Exeter to attend a meeting of the Barrow Committee when my Report was approved and accepted. I spent a good hour in the Museum and deposited there some tessellated pavement and other things from the Roman villa at Uplyme (see July 14, 1857). I hope this museum is properly appreciated by Exeter people, as well as by strangers. (*Diary*)

General election 1880. *Saturday June 19, 1880. As a staunch Tory, Gladstone's victory in the recent elections somewhat ruffled Hutchinson's normally equable temperament.* The new ministry with Mr. Gladstone as Prime Minister has astonished all parties. I wish politicians would be truthful and not so abusive as they are to each other. No doubt the Liberal Party (as they call themselves), take them as a whole, are composed of lower materials than the other party, once called Tories but now usually styled Conservative, so we must make allowances for poor education, low manners, absence of good breeding and indifference to the sense of honour and honesty as we find it amongst gentlemen. (*Diary*).

Longest day. *Monday* June 21, 1880. Where is the sun now? Every day since the shortest, and we have now arrived at the longest, it has been climbing higher in the sky and rising further to the eastward. At nine in the morning on the shortest day the sun was just over the chancel of the church, looking from my Oak Room window, and at ten just over the tower (*see* December 20, 1879). Now indeed, it is 'sky high' and by a rough observation somewhere about where I have endeavoured to place it on this page. I delight in long days and plenty of sunshine, and notwithstanding the serious risk of tarnishing the brightness of my complexion I like to be out in it, and without the use of a lady's parasol. (*Diary*).

80/6/21 (Diary)

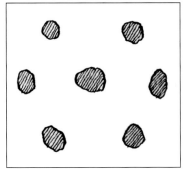

80/6/23 *Mutter's Moor stone circle.* (Diary)

Mutter's Moor stone circle. *Wednesday June 23, 1880.* Having wished to go to Otterton to see an old man called John White, I made the trip light and agreeable by getting into a public vehicle that left Sidmouth this afternoon on its return to Exmouth. Seven o'clock had sounded before I found John White. He remembers the former Druidical monument or circle on Peak Hill, which I first saw on the old map of 1789 belonging to the Lord of the Manor of Sidmouth. I have copied this circle into my Sidmouth Guide at p. 61 of the edition of 1879. *There were six great blocks of stone placed in a circle with a seventh in the middle.* From his description, I understood that they were blocks of breccia of flints and silicified clay so common in this neighbourhood; that the stones were set 'in open order' as he phrased it; that the circle was about forty feet or more in diameter; and that when the rockery was made in Bicton Park these stones along with many others were used. He was working at Bicton at the time. I went over the Bicton grounds and visited the rockery – a beautiful dell with a stream running through it, stopped back by many large blocks of stone. (*Diary*).

Seven Stones discussion. *Wednesday July 7, 1880.* Went over to Otterton by the same vehicle and same route as a fortnight ago. I got down this time at Bicton Church and followed a very beautiful path across the meadows which brought me out near Otterton Bridge. Went to John White's cottage *and* whilst I was talking to him, a man some ten years younger came in. Both of them said they could remember the Seven Stones in their entirety. I gathered from them that the rockery was made in 1830 - or within a year or two after - that a man and his son called Budd or Budge (both since dead) were employed to collect blocks of stone about the hills and bring them to Bicton — and that no orders had been issued for the preservation of objects of antiquity, and in short, that nobody seemed to know any thing about such objects, or care anything about them. (*Diary*).

Natural boulder near Sidford and Sidbury Church. *Friday July 16, 1880.* Mr. Heineken and myself got in a carriage at one and went to Sidbury, to examine the church more fully than we had hitherto before. Getting through Sidford, we turned short round to the left up the Buscombe valley to look at the largest block of stone I have seen anywhere in the neighbourhood. It lies on the south side of the lane and within two or three hundred yards of Brook House Farm. I wanted Mr. Heineken to see it *and* obtained a drawing of it in my sketchbook (*finished on a later visit, see August 20*). It is rather singular in shape, and not only somewhat sunk in the soil but a hedge with bushes has been carried up against the eastern side and partly over the top. The stone is the same flint breccia as the Seven Stones and is very compact and heavy. It measured about ten feet by seven by four feet, *or* 280 cubic feet as the solid contents of the stone, and if we allow fourteen cubic feet to a ton, we find the weight of the stone to be twenty tons.

We then went on to Sidbury and having walked around the church to refresh our memories on the exterior, we commenced operations by eating our sandwiches in the south porch. Apparently there was at one time a stoup for holy water on the right on entering, as a place like a niche has been walled up, and inside the porch high up, on the left of the door going in, is another small niche of irregular shape but for what purpose is uncertain. The ceiling of the porch is supported by four ribs springing from the capitals of four small shafts in the corners *and t*here is a large boss in the centre. I mounted to the room over the porch. The floor is covered with fragments of old oak seats and panelling, and the elements have free entry through two windows where there is no glass. The porch and the turrets beside it are of Perpendicular work, and have been built up against the older church and tower. On the east buttress of the south transept outside *there* used to be an old inscription, as at A, but the letters have now all decayed away; and under the long arched recess between the priest's door and the south-east corner there was once an inscription, as under B, but that has also well-nigh vanished. The checker work pattern under the east window *I give* at C, and the most curious corbel in the corbel table round the outside I give at D. A *second sheila-na-gig like figure, perhaps a corbel, is drawn in the sketchbook.*

   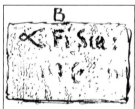 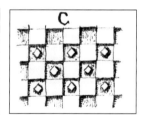

80/7/16 (Diary)

80/7/16 *Carvings under the soffits of two circular headed arches, Sidbury Church, Devon - east end of north and south aisles. July 16 1880.*
(DRO, Z19/2/8F/17)

80/7/16 Sketches from the Diary.

On going inside, it will be seen that the columns of the nave lean outwards owing to the thrust of the roof, and I remark this in most churches. There are two squints or hagioscopes, the north one seen on the west side having a small arch on the outside, G. In the chancel there are two small circular headed windows, north and south. There is a tablet on the north side of the chancel over the vestry door to Huyshe, one on the east wall to Cheek and one to the Rev. Bourke Fellowes's first wife, nee Rocks. On the south wall are brasses to Pearsons and Fellowes and a tablet to Babington; in the north transept to J. Wolcott, to Hunt in the south transept and to Warren at the tower arch. In the corners of the tower, the corbels from which the ribs spring are sculptured with the four subjects in the margin. The nave is barrel-roofed *and* the chancel arch is pointed. The south wall of the chancel was leaning out but in 1860 or 1861 it was pulled up *and* the upper half of the tower was rebuilt about 1853 (?). The two circular arches at the east end of the north and south aisles are beautiful specimens of florid late Norman work - if they are so early *and* I have drawings of them in my sketchbook. The font is of Perpendicular work. There is a pewter flagon, I believe for the water. Mr. Heineken remembers a leather black jack some thirty or more years ago, but the present Sexton knows nothing of such a thing now.

Being at Sidbury, I am reminded of a quatrain in doggerel verse addressed to the fleas and called 'The Sidbury Anthem'. It runs thus:

'Why do those flays torment me zo?
I never did mun wrong
I catch um with my vore vinger
An' kill um with my thumb'.

As I did not wish to get my head broken, I did not repeat them in Sidbury. (*Diary*).

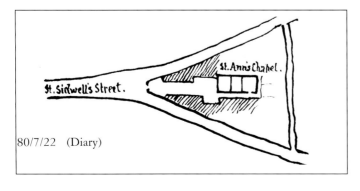

80/7/22 (Diary)

Exeter, St. Ann's chapel. *Thursday July 22, 1880.* Being in Exeter, I went to examine St. Ann's Chapel. The triangular piece of ground is now occupied by eight alms houses. The Chapel remains, but it is divided by cross walls into three portions. The eastern part is still used as a chapel and the two western divisions are converted into abodes for two poor families. *I then* went on to Dawlish. (*Diary*).

Dawlish reservoir. *Friday July 23, 1880.* Walked out to look at the operations at the new reservoir. The works for supplying *Dawlish* with water from the Haldon Hills are in progress. They have excavated a great pit about a hundred feet long, seventy wide and ten or twelve feet deep, and I presume it will be bricked up all round. It is close to the east side of *Water Hill* barrow, an old acquaintance of mine. (*Diary*).

80/7/23 (Diary)

80/7/26 *Totnes Castle, looking north.* (Diary)

Totnes Castle. *Monday July 26, 1880.* Rain. Started for Totnes to attend the annual meeting of the Devonshire Association. I visited the remains of Totnes Castle. They are too much encumbered with trees and surrounding buildings. The plan of the keep is like that annexed, the spectator supposed to be looking towards the north. The circular area, surrounded by the enclosing battlemented wall and now in grass, is about twenty-four yards in diameter. There are steps in the wall to go upon the circular walk all round. The partly decayed parapet wall, pierced for loopholes, is four feet wide and about twelve above the grass plat. A – entrance. B – blocked up. C – steps up to walk. D – doorway into a small chamber in the wall, about seven feet long and six wide. (*Diary*).

Grand reception. *Tuesday July 27, 1880.* Attended the Council Meeting. The Mayor and Corporation gave the members of the Devonshire Association an official reception. We assembled at the Gate House where the arch spans the Fore Street. The chamber over the arch is now used as a reading room. Over the fire place is a small bust of Henry VIII, and another of Anne Boleyn, in a coloured embossed border some eight or nine inches wide that runs all round near the ceiling. A procession was formed in the street. The Mayor in his scarlet robe and gold chain, preceded by the two mace bearers, surrounded by the civic officers and followed by the members, then walked up the street, through the church according to an old custom, entering by the south porch and going out at the north, and then to the Guild Hall. After a formal reception, the Mayor gave us a handsome cold collation in the adjoining room. At eight in the evening we assembled at the Seven Stars Hotel to hear the President's address read. (*Diary*).

Well-deserved praise. *Wednesday July 28, 1880.* The reading of papers continued during the day. There was a garden party on the island this evening but a drizzling rain spoilt it. Here at Totnes bridge the tide rises and falls six to eight feet. I received good praise for my report on the barrows near Sidmouth, which is consolation for a good deal of trouble (see May 25 and June 18, 1880). (*Diary*). *A cutting from the Totnes Times pasted into the Diary described Hutchinson's paper as 'one of the most valuable ever received by the Society, its value enhanced by the beautiful illustrations prepared with very great care and presented free of cost to the Association'.*

Trip down the Dart. *Friday July 30, 1880.* One party went in carriages over the wilds of Dartmoor and another by steam down the Dart. I joined the latter. We had a steam launch with a large boat or barge lashed to it and started from the

Seymour Hotel stairs at half past ten in the morning. The last time I was down the Dart was October 2, 1847, as I see by my sketchbook. This diary does not go back so far as I destroyed all before 1848. *The two accompanying sketches were done on this earlier visit.* We got down in due time, admiring the beautiful scenery all the way and stopping in one place to shout and listen to the echo. We made for the Britannia training ship and went all over her, together with the two-decker attached to her. She is indeed an immense fabric. The cadets were home for the holidays. We then landed at Dartmouth, visited the church - most elaborately decorated - some old houses and a private museum. We embarked and returned well pleased, and I agreed with the opinion of one of my friends in being surprised so few gentlemen's residences to be seen on the banks of the Dart. (*Diary*).

Top: 80/7/30 *On the River Dart. Coloured on the river October 2, 1847.* (DRO, Z19/2/8D/65)

Above: 80/7/30 *Dartmouth Quay. October 2, 1847.* (DRO, Z19/2/8D/67)

Buckfastleigh church. *Saturday July 31, 1880.*   Took the rail at Totnes and went to Buckfastleigh.   The colour of the Dart and of all the streams about Dartmoor strikes me as very brown and quite different from that of the rivers nearer Exeter. Seeing the spire of the church tower, I made for it by the shortest cut, up to the top of a high hill.   There is a small square chamber looking like a dead-house in the churchyard near the south porch. At the east end of the churchyard, about a hundred yards from the church, there are the ruined walls of a small building looking like the remains of a chapel.   The south wall with small doorway and window remains and *is* about thirty-two feet long, but *was* once longer.   The east wall, with the remains of a window but no tracery, *is* some thirty-one feet wide, part of the north wall *survives but there is* no west wall.   A mass of ivy is destroying it.

I was unable to see a habitation or find the town when I got out of the church-yard. I walked some distance and meeting three boys, they told me to keep down-hill towards the south-west and I should find it. The houses are old-fashioned and heavy, and built of stone being the Devonshire slate. There is a limestone quarry east of the church. Towards evening, I returned. (*Diary*).

80/7/31 Churchyard of Buckfastleigh and ruins of an old chapel. July 31, 1880. (DRO, Z19/2/8F/19)

Totnes Church. *Sunday August 1, 1880.* Parish church, *where* there are eight fine-toned bells. There is a very curious archway diagonally across the north-east corner behind the buttress outside, sketching from memory something like the annexed. There was apparently once an entrance into the chancel at that corner. Within a year or two it had been stopped. (*Diary*).

80/8/1 (Diary)

Lydford Castle. *Monday August 2, 1880.* Decided on an excursion round Dartmoor. Went down to Plymouth . . . and then took the rail for Lydford where I stopped for four hours. . . On entering the village, town or city from the south, first there is the church on the left near the road in its churchyard, and then close to it on the north-east the small enclosure containing what remains of the castle. I was woefully disappointed to see so little, and still more so to see such utter neglect. Who has the care of Lydford Castle, or is it purposely consigned to utter extinction? It is nothing but a plain massive keep, about sixteen yards square outside with walls about six feet thick. The masonry is not in courses and the stones are rough pieces of slate of the district or stray fragments of granite.

80/8/2 *Keep of the Castle of Lydford. August 2, 1880.*
(DRO, Z19/2/8F/21)

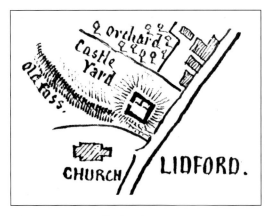

Above: 80/8/2 *Lidford.* (Diary)

Right: 80/8/2 *Lidford Castle.* (Diary)

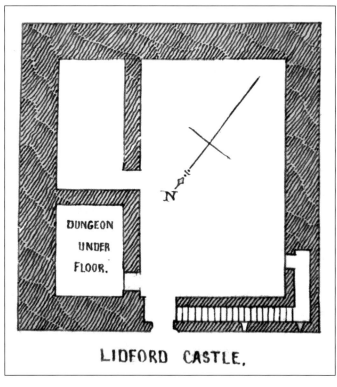

The entrance doorway is in the north-west face. There are three chambers within, a large one and two small, and under one of the small ones is the dungeon. The large chamber is paved with small stones, and some ducks seemed quite at home there in a pool of water that had collected from the recent rains. There are no floors or roof, but I was told in the village that there were both within memory and dances on festive occasions. A few hundred pounds would roof it in as it was. The stairs, immediately on the right on entering, are in the thickness of the wall, and at the top there is a short chamber or passage and a doorway onto the floor when it was there. By means of a ladder access can be had to the upper flight and thence to the top of the walls. The amount of rain that settles upon and soaks into the tops of walls some six feet wide, and the quantity of snow that lodges upon them in winter and melts and percolates through them in spring, is a source of destruction that is always at work. There is a mass of casing at the top of the north-west wall that is bulging out from this cause and will come down before long. Such wilful neglect is much to be lamented and much to be blamed. Walked back to the station, took the train and got to Okehampton before dark. (*Diary*).

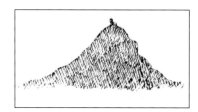

80/8/2   *Brent Tor.*   (Diary)

Okehampton Castle. *Tuesday August 3, 1880.* After breakfast I was impatient to see the ruins of the Castle. At the hotel door my landlady was talking to a gentleman, whom I afterwards learnt bore the name of Saville and was *the* son of a former large

80/8/3   *Arms of Peryam.*
(Hist of Sid. III, 80)

landowner in the neighbourhood and builder of that large square mansion a mile northward from Okehampton and owner of the Castle away westward. He offered to take me to the ruins, and I went. He told me that about forty years ago his late father sold the remains of Okehampton Castle with about five acres of ground to Sir Richard Vyvyan for £2000. Sir Richard died a year or two ago and his nephew Sir Vyal is now the owner. During all these forty years the place has been abandoned to the most utter neglect. The old walls are smothered in weeds, bushes, brambles and a mass of lanky overgrown trees, and their roots together with the uncared-for rain are doing their best to loosen and bring down everything very shortly. Mr. Saville, I believe at his own expense, has had several places repaired and supported with masonry where the massive walls were cracking and opening from these very causes. It is lamentable to see the condition of most of the ruins and the indifference to them manifested by their owners. *I* then walked to the station and took the train. Passed by Crediton, forgetting that I wanted to copy Sir William Peryam's

monument in the church. In Queen Elizabeth's time Sir W. had a good deal to do with Sidmouth and I have his coat of arms in the ceiling of the Oak Room. Arrived in Exeter and finally Sidmouth at half past six. (*Diary*). *Hutchinson's indignation at the neglect of Lydford and Okehampton Castles resulted in a long article 'On the Decay of Ancient Buildings' in the Proceedings of the Society of Antiquaries the following year, condemning the indifference of such owners.*

80/8/6   Old font, Christ Church.
(Trans. Dev. Assoc. XIII, 664)

Christ Church font. *Friday August 6, 1880.* Made a lithographic sketch of the old font at Christ Church, Ilfracombe, (*see July 27, 1879*) for the current volume of the Transactions of the Devonshire Association. It is to illustrate a paper on it by Miss Price. (*Diary*). *The annexed sketch appears in the 1880 volume opposite page 664.*

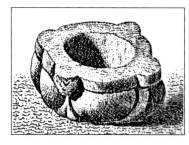

Fire at Rose Cottage. *Monday August 9, 1880.* Between nine and ten this morning, 'Rose Cottage', or as they now call it 'Rose Lawn' (though you might reasonably enquire where the lawn is) was discovered to be on fire. The fire first came out of the thatch near the western dormer window, and I watched it all through until the whole building was destroyed. As the fire began at the top and burnt downwards, there was time to get the furniture out. As to the origin of the fire, one story ran to the effect that one of the ladies sealed a letter at one of the upper windows and thoughtlessly threw the remains of the still burning match on to the thatch. Another declared that it arose from a defect in the kitchen chimney. The house was occupied by Dr. Stokes and his family. *(Diary).*

80/8/9 *Rose Cottage, or Rose Lawn, Blackmore Field, destroyed by fire, Aug. 9. 1880.* (DRO, Z19/2/8F/23)

Sidford, houses along School Street. *Friday August 20, 1880.* Rode to the station *and then* walked to Sidford, *the* sun very hot and roads dusty. Made a sketch of some old houses with stone chimneys on the Sidbury side of the village. Then walked on to the great stone near Brook Farm (see July 16, 1880), got into the field, took out my colour box, sat on the grass and put in the details of the sketch begun a month ago. Walked back. *(Diary).*

Coats of arms. *Monday September 6, 1880.* Sent out to Dr. Edward Oliver of Boston, Massachusetts, the seal that had belonged to his ancestor, Lieut-Governor Oliver more than a century ago. My grandmother was the Lieut-Governor's daughter.

    1.   The second grant of arms to Hutchinson that I know of is this. Granted by T. Flower, Norroy, July 4, 1584, to Hutchinson of Wykeham Abbey, co. York.

    2.   In the heralds visitations of Nottinghamshire 1569 and 1614 the arms of the Owthorpe branch are given thus.

    3.   My own branch thus.

    4.   The Earls of Donoughmore are descended from Richard Hutchinson, a younger brother of William Hutchinson who went to Massachusetts in 1634. The

80/8/20   *Old houses in Sidford.
Sketched on the spot, Aug. 20, 1880.*
(DRO, Z19/2/8F/25)

80/8/20   *The largest block of stone
in the valley of Sidmouth.   It is of
chert breccia, and weighs about 20
tons.   It lies on the south side of the
lane between Sidford and Brook
Farm.   Coloured there Aug. 20,
1880.*   (DRO, Z19/2/8F/11)

elder branch, mine, was ruined in the American revolution.

    5.   Hutchinson of Cornforth and Whitton is described in Burke's *Landed Gentry*. Wordsworth, the Poet Laureate, married Mary Hutchinson of this branch.

    6.   Hutchinson of Carsington, Durham, is also in Burke. This branch, from failure to produce heirs, has now merged into the family of Hutchinson-Synge of Syngefield, co. Cork.

    7.   Foster of Aylesbury, Berkshire, 1650, *who* went to Boston. My great-great-grandfather, Thomas Hutchinson, married Sarah the eldest daughter. I have a right to quarter them.

    8.   Sanford of Boston, Lincolnshire, went early to America. My great-grandfather, Governor Hutchinson, married Margaret the second daughter of William Sanford *and* I have a right to quarter these arms also. (*Diary*).

80/9/6 Hutchinson arms.
(Diary)

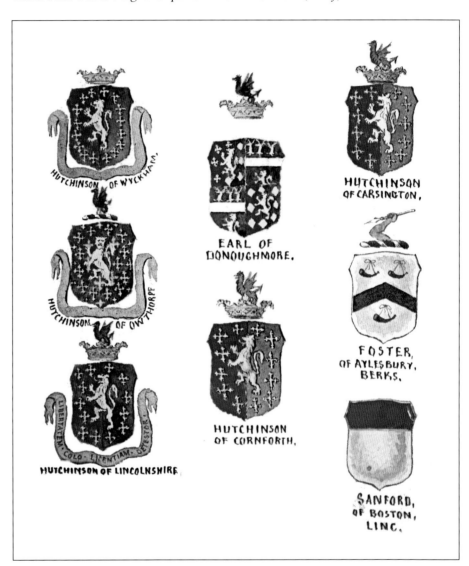

American documents. *Friday October 1, 1880.* Finished binding the five large volumes in blue leather backs and corners and marbled paper sides. The large folio one contains old newspapers and the four small folios are old letters, all referring to America and the Revolution. (*Diary*).

Jesuits in Sidmuth. *Wednesday November 24, 1880.* The arrival of a number of French Jesuits at Sidmouth has taken most people by surprise but Peak House has been for some time empty and tenants were desirable. The tradesmen, who can see nothing beyond how much money they can make from every new arrival are delighted, but the gentry and the educated classes look at this with eyes of a different kind. (*Diary*). *The arrival of the Jesuits followed the closing of their colleges in France by order of the French government.*

Thoughts on marriage. *Tuesday December 28, 1880.* Executed a new will. Owing to my nearest relations, my brother's children, being in South Australia, I find it very difficult to arrange my affairs, houses and odds and ends to my satisfaction.   In spite of the bother and expenses and anxieties of wives and children, as I hear married men say, it is better on the whole for people to marry and make the best of it.   They then have somebody to live for and take interest in, and somebody near them to hand their property over to without trouble.   Had ladies not been such costly people, I would never have remained as I am.   (*Diary*).

80/12/28   *Old Chancel,
Sidmouth, Devon.   1880.*
(DRO, Z19/2/8F/13)

1881

Coffee tavern. *Monday January 10, 1881.* A coffee tavern has been opened at the former Institution Reading Room opposite the London Hotel, promoted by some of the gentry of the place for the good purpose of trying to get people to take tea and coffee instead of intoxicating drinks. There is a lamentable amount of drunkenness here no doubt and I hope this attempt may do good – but! (*Diary*).

Thoughts on the Old Chancel. *Thursday February 4, 1881.* I wish I had the Old Chancel to build again. I would introduce many improvements in plan and construction that I did not think of or know a dozen years ago. (*Diary*).

Guinea from Peak Hill. *Friday March 11, 1881.* John Denner of Coombe Farm, Salcombe, working in a field on Peak Hill yesterday (field lot 12, see *map on* September 18, 1879) turned up a beautiful guinea. It is rather curious that some few years ago a gold coin of Queen Anne was dug up in the same field (December 28, 1874). The guinea, a George III dated 1785, weighs more than a modern sovereign *and* is of fine gold in excellent preservation. *Ob:* GEORGIUS III DEI GRATIA. King's head looking to sinister. *Rev:* 1785 M.B.F. ET H.REX.F.DB.ET L.D.S.R.I.A.T.E. (*Diary*).

81/3/15 Sidmouth in 1796.
(Hist of Sid. V, 18)

Sidmouth's earliest view. *Tuesday March 15, 1881.* I have now got two impressions of the annexed old view of Sidmouth , one in the fifth volume of my *History of Sidmouth* and the other I place here. It is dated July 1, 1796, and is interesting as being the earliest dated view of Sidmouth I have met with. Peak House and the row at the head of the Fort Field had then been only recently built *and* the 'Ram's Horn', a labyrinth of posts and nets on the Chit Rocks wherein fish were entangled and caught and of which I have heard old people speak, is also shown. It was all destroyed in the storm of November 1824. All these old portraits of scenery (which they profess to be but which they are not) would be much more valuable if they were only more correct in outline and detail. (*Diary*).

Artist's influence. *Wednesday March 16, 1881. Hutchinson had strong feelings about the duty of the artist to depict scenes faithfully, judging by his comments on another old Sidmouth engraving he had to hand.* It is wrong in the outlines and in the features of the hills, like almost all other landscapes, and the church tower is faulty since it had no pinnacles in those days. I have known the tower since 1825 and it never had a pyramidal roof with a staff in the middle. Suppose this engraving was brought forward as a proof that it had, consider the falsehood it would establish. Artists never seem to reflect on the responsibility that hangs on the truth of their pencil. This engraving is interesting *however*, in showing traces of the wooden groynes running from the line of the esplanade down to the sea. They were put there in the hope of collecting shingle but the experiment did not succeed. The shingle moved as the wind and waves shifted and the groynes never retained any. I saw them placed there about 1830 and *remember* them some years afterwards when they were falling into disrepair. As they were found to be useless, nothing was done by the town to save them, so that what the waves did not carry away the fishermen stole for wood. (*Diary*).

French conundrum. *Tuesday March 22, 1881.* My late father once wrote down the following capital letters, telling me they must be read off according to French pronunciation, and asked me what they meant. I need only observe that the first two letters indicate the female name Eilene.

LNETDPY
LNAVQ
LAETME
LNADCD. (*Diary*).

New organ for the church. *Thursday March 24, 1881.* There is now a project in Sidmouth for putting a new organ in the parish church at the cost of £800, if they can raise it. The present organ they say will fetch £150. (*Diary*).

Death of Mary Roberton. *Monday April 18, 1881.* My cousin at Dawlish, Mary Roberton, died this morning at 2.30. She was above eighty. She has bequeathed something to me and my sister. (*Diary*).

History of Sidmouth completed. *Friday May 20, 1881. I have* finished the fifth and last *volume* of my manuscript *History of Sidmouth,* written in five quarto volumes bound in green vellum. I conclude the history at the end of the year 1880 by way of closing at a definite point, but if any *further* event occurs in Sidmouth worth recording I shall jot it down in this *diary.* I should have preferred consigning the work to some place in Sidmouth where the inhabitants could read it freely at all hours, but as there is no endowed library institution here to which the public could have easy access, there is no alternative but to bequeath it to the Free Library in Queen Street, Exeter. If I had been a rich man, it would have been my delight to have built and endowed a free library and museum in Sidmouth. The compilation of the book, which is very deficient in many places, has afforded a good deal of amusement for a long time, but the end is very welcome as I want leisure for other things that have been neglected. (*Diary*). *Hutchinson adds a colophon to the end of the final volume:* Two volumes! Two indeed! If life were long enough, how much the whole might be improved by being all re-written again. He who has written it sees faults, or omissions, or acts of carelessness at almost every other page. Be lenient. Such as it is, it must go. (*History of Sidmouth V*).

Having mostly resided at Sidmouth since my boyhood, it was my pleasure to collect at odd times all scraps of information relating to its early and late history. As the Manor had pertained to the Abbey of St. Michael's Mount in Normandy during the long term of 350 years, it occurred to me that there might be documents over there still in existence that referred to its English possessions. With this view I crossed the Channel to France on two separate occasions, for the Abbot was Lord of the Fee, and I was rewarded for my pains. After thirty years of discursive collecting, I threw the materials into consecutive and chronological form and then wrote out a more amplified and historical narrative. Not however being satisfied with this, I procured some blank quarto volumes and began in 1869 to write it more regularly in these. As re-writing anything generally ends in amplification and unforeseen materials crop up to plead for admission, and being anxious to illustrate with maps, plans sketches and such old views as I could procure that seemed worth preserving, the work grew much greater in bulk than I had contemplated. Taking it only at odd times, this transcript was eleven years in hand and has extended to five volumes. As I had some other work in contemplation, I brought it to a close with the end of the year 1880. Never intending to publish it, I have left it to the Free Library of the Exeter Museum in Queen Street, where it may serve as a contribution to a history of the county of Devon, which, as yet, cannot be said to have been written. It is generally supposed that small and remote country towns and parishes have virtually no histories belonging to them, but I have now come to the conclusion that every place, however insignificant it may appear, really has a history if people will only be at the trouble of looking it up. (*Soc. of Antiq. Ms. 309, 1-2*).

Parish bounds. *Tuesday May 24, 1881. The* Queen's birthday. The parish bounds were today perambulated after an interval of fourteen years (*see May 30, 1867*). I walked every step of the way last time but I thought this time that I would take matters more easily, so I rode and walked in turn. (*Diary*).

Donation of fossil stems. *Wednesday June 1, 1881.* Went to Belmont Villa, Dawlish, for a few Days. Took my fossil stems into Exeter (see May 13, 1878) and left them at the Museum. (*Diary*).

Curious legacy. *Thursday June 2, 1881.* Packed up cabinet of fossils, etc., left for me. Amongst the things are three vertebrae of an icthyosaurus stuck together, some old silver coins, tesserae, amber, the claw of the tiger that killed the coach horse near Salisbury Plain about 1816, fossil bones procured by Dr. Buckland and my late cousins from Chudleigh Cavern, etc. (*Diary*).

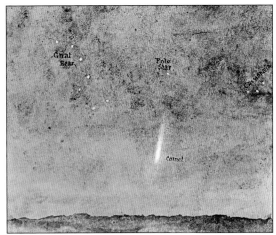

81/6/27 *Comet June 27, 1881.* (Diary)

Comet of ill-omen. *Monday June 27, 1881.* During the past week the appearance of a comet in the northern heavens has attracted the attention of the community *and* sundry old women (of both sexes) are shaking their heads and foreboding all sorts of terrible consequences. One declared in my hearing that it was very lucky the tail was pointing upwards into the sky, for if it had been pointing downwards to the earth we should all have been burnt up. One foretold the speedy end of the world *and* another thought we should only all die of the pestilence. Some ascribed its coming to the spell of hot weather we had at the beginning of the month *and yet* others laid the blame on Mr. Gladstone's ministry, now in power. One wondered what could be so deadly in the tail, a second wanted to know what the tail was composed of and a third said 'you can find out with a pinch of salt'.

I had a good look at it tonight for the sky was clear, but only with a common three-foot telescope. It did not show itself till ten as the daylight lasted so late. Between eleven and twelve it was nearly under the Pole Star, nearly midway between that and the earth but nearer the earth. The tail, about ten degrees long, was pointing nearly to the Pole Star, with the Great Bear to the west and Cassiopeia to the east. A small nucleus was visible. As far as I hear, the comet is unknown and was unexpected. It has passed the perihelion and is now going. (*Diary*).

Transplanted organs. *Saturday July 2, 1881.* A general progress, translation or movement of organs is now going on in Sidmouth. Some six to eight hundred pounds having now been subscribed, a new one by Hill of London is coming down. The *present* church organ is now in course of removal to All Saints, Mrs. Hine-Haycock having presented it. All Saints organ has been sold to the Independents, and they have sold theirs to someone in Exeter. Thus the way is opened for the new one from London. (*Diary*).

Illustrations for Devonshire Association meeting. *Thursday July 21, 1881.* Made an enlarged view of the barrow in Volume 4 of my bound sketches, dated November 17, 1853. (*Diary*).

Friday July 22, 1881. Made an enlarged view of Lidwell Chapel near Dawlish from Volume 5, dated September 22 and 27, 1854. They are to take to Dawlish next week. (*Diary*).

Humerus gift. *Saturday July 23, 1881.* Gave a skull and the bones of a left arm to Dr. Pullin a few days ago. *The skull* was given to me by Dr. Mackenzie when he left *and* had it been a white one I would have kept it, but it was brown and not quite perfect. The arm bones were dug up behind Marlborough Place. (*Diary*).

Devonshire Association meeting 1881. *Monday July 25, 1881.* Went to Dawlish to attend the meeting of the Devonshire Association *and* lodged with the servants of my late cousin in the new house she gave them. (*Diary*).

Tuesday July 26, 1881. Walked out to the new reservoir and looked at the barrow in the field close to the west side of it. We applied for leave to open it but the owner refused permission. The president read his introductory address. (*Diary*).

Luscombe Park. *Thursday July 28, 1881.* Reading papers. *There was* a free pass to the flower show in Luscombe Park. The house, or 'castle', is a paltry attempt at gothic by Nash *but* the flower gardens up beyond the house are extremely pretty. The finest araucaria I ever saw is there *and* I measured the stem at fifteen feet round *some* two feet from the ground. Went again into the chapel *where* they have made a new entrance on the west, a beautiful specimen of gothic by Scott. (*Diary*).

Lidwell Chapel again. *Friday July 29, 1881.* Excursions, one to Powderham, Mamhead, etc., and another to Lidwell Chapel, Haldon, etc. I was deputed to conduct this one as years ago I had collected materials and printed a few scraps on the district. The Rev. R.H.D. Barham who with others had been clearing the ruins, also conducted this party. The base of a wall at B was met with, and at A something like a well within the chapel. It was excavated three feet down but was full of water; with a pole seven feet down only soft mud could be felt. I read my mems. to the company *and w*e then scrambled up the hill to the carriages and proceeded north.

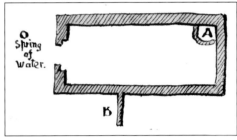

81/7/29 *Lidwell Chapel.* (Diary)

Over Smallacombe goyle, we dismounted and had luncheon on the grass *and* then walked to the circular camp close by. I think I once made it 124 yards in diameter. It is a pity that the division of the land owners, and I believe the parishes, passes right across the middle or diameter of the camp. We then drove three quarters of a mile north by east to the tower. No one lives there now but the door was not fastened and we ascended the staircase to the lead roof. The view was obstructed by the high trees. Thence we returned to near the camp, took the road down towards Dawlish but turned into the Luscombe grounds *where* we drove through the very beautiful woods and made our way to the park in front of the house. The carriages of the other expedition began to arrive and soon after 5 PM we all sat down to a handsome cold collation provided by the Dawlish people as a finish to the meeting. Everything went off very well. (*Diary*).

Harp-lute. *Wednesday August 3, 1881.* Returned to Sidmouth *and* took home a harp-lute in its case. It was invented and very popular to sing to, like the guitar, about the commencement of the present century. I always understood from my late cousin that it had belonged to a Miss Collingwood, I believe a great aunt. This one is marked 'C. Wheatstone, Inventor, 436 Strand, London'. On going into the upper room of the museum, I saw a similar instrument in a glass case. (*Diary*).

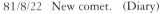

81/8/22 New comet. (Diary)

Buried bones. *Sunday August 14, 1881.* A curious discovery *was* made yesterday in cutting the new road over the high field behind Fort Field Terrace *and* I was asked to go and look at the spot. It was 46 yards up from Station Road towards the top. They were excavating down to the depth of five to six feet below the surface when they came upon a quantity of bones of some animal nearly as large as a donkey. The soil had certainly never been disturbed for the lay of the beds of sandy soil was visible in lines by the side of the pit, the more strange as this was not in a hollow or valley but some way up a hill. The soil showed no traces of dark decaying vegetable matter for the bones were in the clean red sand. I saw vertebrae and leg bones taken out, and also part of a lower jaw with teeth, an os sacrum, portion of ribs and what determined the *nature of the* animal, several pieces of the antlers of a large stag. I have the bones and shall save the best of them. (*Diary*). *In the account Hutchinson wrote for the Exeter and Plymouth Gazette, he suggests the bones were those of a red deer,* a geological deposit of post-Tertiary times.

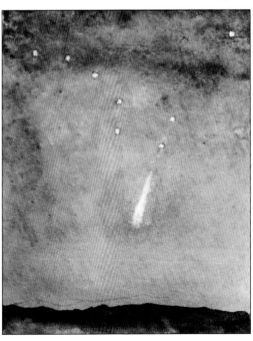

New comet. *Friday August 19, 1881.* Another comet has revealed itself and I believe it was not expected. (*Diary*).

Monday August 22, 1881.   Had a spy at the new comet from my house the Old Chancel.   The nucleus is well-defined *but* the tail is shorter than the former.   A small star was just below it.   It is now at its nearest.   (*Diary*).

81/9/15   Woolbrook Glen.
(Hist of Sid. III, 132)

Woolbrook Glen.   *Thursday September 15, 1881.*   Made a sketch of the Glen and Belmont, or Woolbrook Glen, late the residence of the Duke of Kent, from Clifton Place.   (*See September 1893*). (*Diary*).   The entrance gate to the Glen is between the bridge and the wall of Belmont.   (*History of Sidmouth III, 132*).

Manston Old House.   *Friday September 16, 1881.*   Beautiful weather again after some chilly showers.   As there is a report that they are going to pull down Manstone Farmhouse, one of the oldest houses hereabouts, I walked out to enquire.   It is a mile and a quarter north of Sidmouth, some fifty yards within Sidbury parish, and belongs to Mr. Cave.   This is an interesting old stone house in the gothic style *and* in the south front there is a tablet bearing the half obliterated figures . . . or . . .   I went in and saw Mrs. White*, whose* late husband was one of sixteen.   Some forty years ago or nearly, I walked out *here* one day with my late mother to make enquiries about some hay for two horses we had in the stable.   We went into a room where there were eight children at play.   After a while, by way of saying something, my mother addressed the eldest, a girl of fourteen or fifteen, and said, 'What a number of children!   One, two, three, four, five, six, seven, eight.   I suppose these are not all your brothers and sisters'?

'Ees they be, Mum'.

'Indeed, your father and mother must have enough to do with so many'?

'This is nothing, Mum'.

'Nothing!   Eight children to feed and clothe and put out in the world, nothing.   They have no more of you, I hope'?

'Ees there be, Mum'.

'More!   How many more'?

'Eight more, Mum'.

Oh, you should have seen my mother.   Description won't do.

Mrs. White told me she was sorry the old house was condemned but there was no

Below left: 81/9/16   North door. Manstone Farm, near Sidmouth. September 16, 1881. Below, middle, top: Oak panel in kitchen. Below, middle, bottom: East gable. Below, right, top: Window in east gable. Below, right, bottom: Knocker or handle.   (DRO, Z19/2/8F/29)

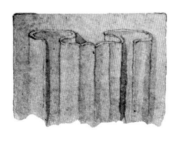

help for it as it was rotten and tottering past saving, and some of the rooms were unsafe and no longer used. Indeed, on carefully looking round, I perceived that the ceilings were swagging downwards and some of the walls were buckling and bending. I copied the linen or napkin pattern on the oak panels of the old seat in the kitchen, and going outside, I made sketches of the north door, east gable, two-light gothic window, etc. They are beginning to build a new brick house near the old one. (*Diary*). *Like a number of other ruinous buildings described and sketched by Hutchinson, not only was this lovely old farmhouse eventually restored but all the features depicted, bar the east gable chimneys, still survive.*

Enhydrite or water-stone. *Monday September 26, 1881.* A friend has given me an enhydrite just brought from Buenos Ayres in South America. It is a hollow petrifaction of chalcedony having a semi-transparent appearance like ground glass *with* corrugations and involutions all over after the manner of Beekite petrifaction. It is half full of some liquid, as may be seen when held against the light. This specimen was found among the pebbles and sand near the waterfall at Sarto, near a hundred miles up the Plata River above Buenos Ayres. I never saw but one other specimen and that belongs to Mr. A. Keily, Manager of the Devon and Cornwall Bank in Cathedral Yard, Exeter, who lent it to Dr. Radford of Sidmount, Sidmouth, where I have seen it. It is rather smaller than mine, not so thick and more irregular in form. European specimens have been met with at Vicenza in Italy. Dr J. Woodward in *Fossils of all Kinds etc.,* p. 16, mentions them. He says 'Liquid: The Fairy's Water Bottle'. Pliny, XXXVII, 12, writes 'Enhydros. Ad motum, fluctuat iutus in eo, veluti in ovis, liquor'. (*Diary*).

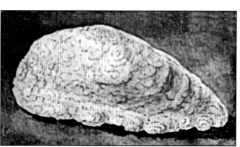

81/9/26 Enhydrite, or water stone. June 12, 1882. (Diary)

Face in the tree. *Saturday October 15, 1881.* This afternoon about three o'clock, as I was sitting in the Oak Room of the Old Chancel writing, the sun shining bright and the remnants of yesterday's gale not yet quite blown out, I was amused at the appearance of one of the large cypress trees in the churchyard across the field between me and the chancel. The masses and lumps of foliage on one side of the tree were very like a large face in outline. As the tree rocked and swung about in the wind the gigantic head seemed to nod, and the tufts forming the eyebrows, nose, lips and chin worked about like a monster busy in the act of mastication. The figure *in the drawing* is pointing at the face. (*Diary*).

81/10/15 (Diary)

Loss of the Fortitude. *Saturday October 22, 1881.* Another gale of wind from the north-east last night and plenty of rain. *There is* scarcely a pear left on the tree and one branch *has* blown off. The newspapers are full of accounts of sad disasters both by sea and land. There is a story in the town that Mr. Dunning's coal vessel, coming with coals for his gas works, has been driven down channel and lost with all hands. (*Diary*). *The story was correct. The sailing schooner Fortitude carrying gas coal from West Hartlepool was finally brought up on a lee shore near Falmouth and wrecked. All five of the crew perished when a large wave swept them from the deck into the boiling surf before there was an opportunity to operate the rocket rescue apparatus from the cliffs above.* (*Exeter and Plymouth Gazette*).

Balloon accident. *Tuesday December 13, 1881.* *There was* a sad balloon accident last Saturday evening. Mr. Powell MP, Captain Templar and Mr. Gardner went up at Bath. Wind to the east of north carried them to Bridport, *where they* descended. *The* car struck the ground and knocked the two last out, but Mr. Powell was carried off to sea with darkness coming on. (*Diary*). *Despite extensive searches at sea, in France and eventually in Spain, nothing further was reported of him.*

1882

New Years Day 1882. *Sunday January 1, 1882.* Whatever hopes we may entertain for the New Year, it seems that every one that passes generally goes through pretty much the same routine of events as the preceding ones. (*Diary*).

Family honours and the site of Moridunum. *Saturday February 4, 1882.* Nearly finished electrotyping from seals on old letters, soldering on handles, tinning (boiling with tin filings and bitartrate of potash), and making labels a number of seals of family coat armour to distribute among my relations, some of them not knowing what arms they have inherited.

This evening I finished writing an article on *The Site of Moridunum* for the next July meeting of the Devonshire Association at Crediton.   Today I received from London seven hundred copies of a map to accompany it, done from my drawings. (*Diary*).   *Thirty-three years after his original article on the site of Moridunum appeared in the Gentleman's Magazine, in which he made a powerful case for its location on High Peak Hill, Hutchinson returned to the subject at the July meeting of the Devonshire Association.   In the intervening years however, the numerous visits described in the Diaries had persuaded him that Hembury hillfort with the outworks on Bushy and Buckerell Knaps was the real site of the Roman Station.*

82/2/4 *Map of Iter XV in Antoninus.   From Calleva to Isca Dunmoniorum.* (Hist of Sid. I, 33)

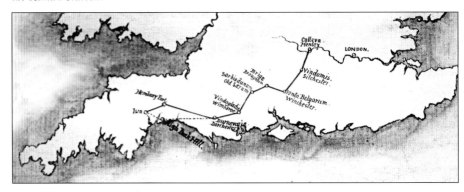

82/2/4 *To accompany the paper on 'The Site of Moridunum' by Peter Orlando Hutchinson.* (Hist of Sid. I, 50a)

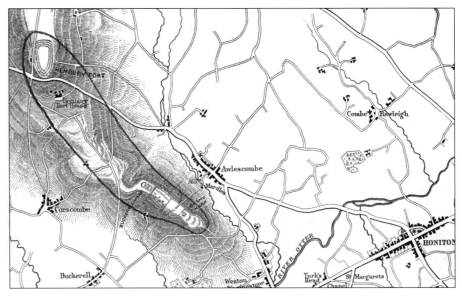

Suspicious Fire. *Tuesday February 14, 1882.* *There was* great alarm of fire in the town last night between nine and ten. A wagon loaded with straw standing in the yard behind the Anchor Inn at the lower end of Old Fore Street was found to be on fire. Men rushed out from the Inn, some *of them* prepared to unload the straw and save the wagon from being burnt. Others were afraid that this would scatter the fire and endanger the houses, most of which at that spot are old and covered with thatch. At last it was decided to seize the shafts and drag it all out. This they did. They drew it through the archway into the street, then past the Market House out upon the beach, on the broad part of the street opposite Marlborough Place and there unloaded it, throwing all the blazing bundles out where they burnt away. It was a fine night and many of the townspeople ran down to see the fire. Suspicion suggests that it was not accidental *and* there is a ten pounds reward to find the incendiary. (*Diary*).

Counter-claims. *Friday February 17, 1882.* *There is* great dissatisfaction in the town because the Board of Trade has put forward a claim to the foreshore and forbidden all persons from taking any sand or gravel from the beach. This was attempted some years ago, about 1870, but caused such a storm that *the proposal* was dropped. Curiously enough, the trustees of the Manor have immediately put in a counter claim and have warned all persons not to take any sand or gravel from the beach without paying them (the Trustees) a shilling a load. (*Diary*).

Silver halfpennies. *Friday February 24, 1882.* Amongst the multitude of coins of all nations and ages, from the Bactrian coin (given to the Exeter Museum) to the present time, no half pennies have ever turned up except for the two annexed silver pieces. They were found and brought to me in February 1879 but have been lying by. I shall record them in the 1882 volume of the *Trans. Dev. Assoc.* and then give them to the Exeter Museum. (*Diary*).

82/2/24 (Diary)

Electrotyping. *Tuesday March 7, 1882.* Intending to electrotype a few more seals, I made a glass cell by scratching a ring and then cutting a quart bottle in half with the point of a red hot poker. (*Diary*).

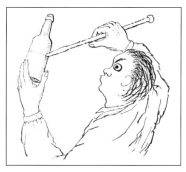

82/3/7 (DRO,Z19/2/8E/147)

Weird floor. *Wednesday April 12, 1882.* The Manor people have pulled down an old house in the middle of the town at the corner of Fore Street and Russel Street, long inhabited by George Russel, a baker. They came upon an ancient floor of the shank bones of oxen or some large animal, driven into the ground on end so as to form a pavement. This was discovered under two separate lime-ash floors. They are building a new house there of red brick. (*Diary*).

82/4/12 (Diary)

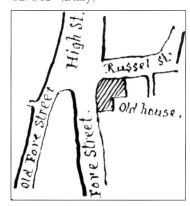

Curious fish. *Wednesday May 17, 1882.* Some sailors brought me a curious fish to look at which got entangled in a mackerel net. It was alive in a large tub of water. They had never caught the like here before and thought it was perhaps a southern fish from the coast of Spain or Portugal. It was almost half a yard long, very thick and heavy *and* of a red-brown or purple colour. The body was broad and flat at the bottom, the transverse section being something like the figure at A, the eye was very prominent like a red bead, *there were* spines like a carp down the back, sides and lower

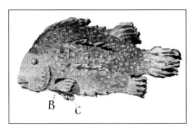

SECTION.

82/4/12 (Diary)

corners and lumps or tubercles on the back diminishing downwards. The rough sketch is mostly from memory. There was a curious circular sucker at B under the body about as large as a crown piece between the pectoral fins with a fringe round it, the hinder edge of which is seen hanging down at C. I believe *it to be* a northern fish of Greenland, green when young. (*Diary*).

Well fed. *Thursday May 25, 1882.* Unhappy young man that I am, to get two invitations to dinner on the same day. But the trial proved that it was not difficult to do. I dined early with the Buttemers at the Elms and late with Hine-Haycocks at Belmont, where I met the party from Core Hill. (*Diary*).

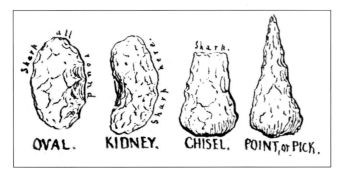

82/4/12 (Diary)

Flints in Exeter Museum. *Monday June 12, 1882.* Went down to Dawlish for a few days *and* took my enhydrite with me into Exeter (see September 26, 1881). I intended it for Exeter Museum in Queen Street some day, but fearing lest it might get accidentally injured I thought it better to deposit it there at once. This therefore I did. Mr D'Urban, the curator, then opened a case and showed me a number of large palaeolithic implements of flint and chert from the gravel pits at Broom, near Axminster. Their chief forms I give in the margin. They range in size from five to nine inches long. He told me they can only be procured now by paying a pound a piece or more to the finders.

Passing through Starcross, I observed the Swan floating on the river (*see* August 2, 1872), and at Langstone Point I remarked that the head of the Elephant Rock is falling away very fast (*see July 30, 1879*). (*Diary*).

Sidholme. *Thursday June 22, 1882.* Had an early dinner with Mrs. Davidson, her three children and the governess at Sidholme, formerly Richmond Lodge, which her late husband bought of the Earl of Buckinghamshire and to which she has made great additions. There is a good copy of a nude group of children after Rubens in the dining room, I guessed the painter by the noses, *and* there are several good landscapes by our Devonshire painter, Widgery. She took me all over the house and it is very beautiful certainly, *but she* herself *is* the greatest ornament. (*Diary*).

Flint artefacts from Ireland. *Monday July 17, 1882.* The annexed beautiful thin worked flints I copied from the originals lent to me by Mrs. Cowell of The Grove; recently from the north of Ireland. (*Diary*).

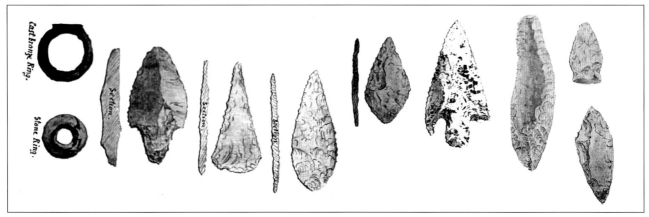

82/7/17 *Worked flints from near the Giant's Causeway, Ireland.* (Diary)

Horns of a dilemma. *Saturday July 22, 1882.* Walking down the road before Alma Place, a man with a basket of eggs on his arm was in advance of me *with* a large black dog running before him. A boy was driving a cow and her calf up from the town. The cow made a run at the dog, *which* ran behind the man's heels for safety. The cow followed up the charge and brought her horns to bear on his shins, *making him* caper and jump and scatter *some* eggs about the road and mash up the rest that remained in the basket. Then the cow came on towards me, so I got into a doorway not liking the appearance of things. The neighbours came out to discuss the situation:

'You can prosecute the owner of the cow and get damages'.
'No, you can't. You must prosecute the dog'.
'No you mustn't. The dog must prosecute the cow'.
I left affairs on the horns of a (cows) dilemma. (*Diary*).

82/7/22 (Diary)

Cat walk. *Thursday July 27, 1882.* Made a cat's ladder. My black tom cat Robbie has now three ladders on three different sides of the Old Chancel by which he can come in at the windows. (*Diary*).

Another enhydrite. *Saturday August 5, 1882.* On a visit to Sidmouth, Mr. Matchwick of the South Kensington Museum called and showed me a very pretty enhydrite looking like ground glass, smaller and flatter than mine (see September 26, 1881). He got it for a sovereign, *though* he told me that he had heard of a case where as much as twelve pounds had been given for one, and *in* another case fifteen pounds. He also showed me the half of one that had been accidentally broken. This is equally curious and as interesting as the whole one, as it showed the inside. Whereas the crystallisation of the outside is of the concentric or Bekeite type, on the inside a number of little prisms are visible. He also showed me a cairngorm having fluid and a moveable air bubble inside procured in Ceylon, *which* he got for three pounds. Likewise a transparent and colourless crystal of quartz, also containing fluid and an air bubble. (*Diary*).

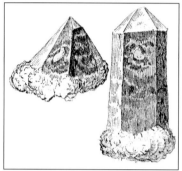

82/8/5 (Diary)

Church Lane cottages. *Friday September 1, 1882.* Dined again at the Toller's *where we were* six at dinner. I showed Mr Toller and friends over the church, knowing it well. The local Board has given £575 for some cottages above Church Lane to widen High Street. (*Diary*).

82/9/1 (Diary)

Old coins from Belmont. *Thursday September 7, 1882.* Mr. Hine-Haycock of Belmont showed me these old silver coins, dug up when altering the lawn in front of the house at Belmont in the spring of 1881. *They are* a Saxon one of Edward which I copy, a rather smaller one of Henry III and one of Elizabeth of 1575 of the size of the Edward. I must send an account of these to be preserved in the pages of the *Trans. Dev. Assoc.* (*Diary*).

82/9/7 (Diary)

Cockle's Bridge cross, Exeter. *Saturday October 14, 1882.* Went to Exeter by the 12.10 train *and* took two things to the Museum. One of them was the handsome Nepalese knife, a weapon that I have given to the Museum because it will be more accessible to the public and in an endowed building is likely to be well taken care of. The other is a sort of sword, like a saw, made of shark's teeth. William Hart, a sailor at Sidmouth, brought it from the Fiji Islands and gave it to me.

I walked down over the bridge and out two or three hundred yards beyond St. Thomas Church, to look again at the old granite stone or cross a yard high, built into the brick wall of a house that juts out. I came out and sketched it in June 1868. A person called Nicholls now occupies the house *and* I went in to make enquiries. The

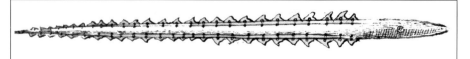

82/10/14 *Figi sword.* (Diary)

82/10/14 *Old granite stone cross, if such it be, built into the front of a brick house in St. Thomas's, Exeter. The house is 200 or 300 yards beyond St. Thomas's church and on the same side. Sketched Oct. 14, 1882.* (DRO, Z19/2/8F/33)

woman told me that though the street is now even and level, she understood that before the house extended out so far and when it was a country district, a brook or open stream used to run across the road (and might yet pass under it for all she knew), over which there was a bridge. That latterly the bridge went by the name of Cockle's Bridge and a court in the corner near the house, Cockle's Court. That the old cross is said to have stood on or near the bridge, that the land was enclosed and the bridge destroyed *and* that the father of the present owner built the house and, finding this old stone lying about and taken no account of, he built it into the wall to preserve it. (*Diary*).

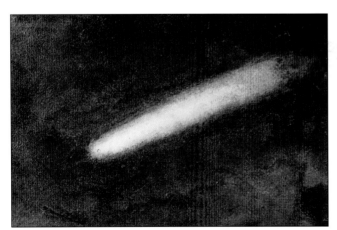

82/10/23 *Crul's comet.* (Diary)

Crul's comet. *Monday October 23, 1882.* Saw the comet at last! I believe it is the finest we have seen since 1861. I happened to wake this morning at 5.20, so got out of bed for the sky was clear. The nucleus is circular and apparently has concentric rings of light around it. Measuring rather roughly, it was about eighteen degrees above the horizon: the tail, sloping upwards at an angle of about twenty-five degrees, *was* about nineteen or twenty degrees long. Some have spoken of the tail as being curved, but if so it was scarcely perceptible. The comet, we are told, in passing round the sun almost brushed its surface, and that at its next perihelion it will probably plunge into it. I left off looking before six when the first faint indication of daylight was beginning to appear.

A lady writing to me from Exeter says the tail looked as if it were ten inches broad, and a friend in my house, speaking of the size of the whole affair, said it appeared large enough to cover the door. These measurements are worth recording as they may be useful to astronomers. (*Diary*).

Wreck of the Lady Elizabeth. *Wednesday November 1, 1882.* The boisterous, showery and unsettled weather has continued all over the country, the lowlands have been much flooded and the trains stopped. *There was a* violent wind from the south today and a heavy sea on the beach. A 'billy-boy', a vessel somewhat of the Dutch build and schooner rigged, was driven high and dry onto the rocks some three miles east of Sidmouth, at Longebb so-called. She came out of Exmouth yesterday in ballast to go up Channel, but she was caught by the violent southerly wind, which was too much for her. The Exmouth lifeboat went off but the Sidmouth one did not, *as* it is extremely difficult to launch anything from the open beach in rough weather. The vessel is called the Lady Elizabeth, is a hundred tons burden so I am told, and her crew of three men got safe on shore. *There is* small hope of saving her. (*Diary*).

Guy Fawkes Day 1882. *Monday November 6, 1882.* The two gentlemen represented opposite called upon me this morning. The 5th this year fell upon a Sunday, so that the Gunpowder Treason display of Old Popes and fireworks took place today with much vigour. When I was a lad, I used to hear the boys sing the lines *below*, *though* they now shout parts of them in a fragmentary way, having learnt them only imperfectly.

82/11/6   (Diary)

> Remember, remember
> The fifth of November
> The gunpowder, treason and plot.
> I see no reason
> Why gunpowder treason
> Should ever be forgot.
>
> Holla boys!   Holla boys!
> God save the King.
> Holla boys!   Holla boys!
> Make the bells ring.
> Up with the ladder and down with the rope
> Please give me something to burn the Old Pope.

The High Church or Ritualistic Party are now beginning to poo-poo this demonstration and say it is high time that it should be put down, *and* the Roman Catholics say the same. The Roman Catholics may take things complacently for they are increasing in England very fast, and they declare with a chuckle that the clergy of the Ritualistic Party are preparing the way for them. It is not hard to read the signs of the times, or to predict by an arithmetical calculation what this will ultimately lead to. Guy Fawkes will be sympathised with and Ridley and Latimer laughed at. (*Diary*).

82/11/17   *The comet again.*
(Diary)

Renegade nun. *Wednesday November 8, 1882.* Edith O'Gorman, now Mrs. Auffrey, who escaped from a convent and whose book I read last May, gave two lectures today at the London Hotel, Sidmouth. I went to one of them. Didn't she give it to the priests! (*Diary*).

Crul's comet again. *Friday November 17, 1882.* My birthday. I woke quite by chance before daylight on both these mornings. In one case the comet was rising and was behind the church tower from the Old Chancel, with the tail sloping more upwards. The other morning *it was* higher with the tail more horizontal, just as we sometimes see the three stars in Orion's Belt rise almost perpendicularly, *become* horizontal in the zenith and nearly perpendicular again when setting in the west. A few sleepy observations comprised all that could be done on a cold night by a person in his nightdress at a chilly window. (*Diary*).

Wrapping up warm. *Monday December 11, 1882.* The pump frozen *and* great consternation below stairs. I got some hot water and thawed it *and* then took a large piece of matting *kept* in reserve for the purpose which I bound round with a cord. Pumps and men need overcoats in December. *(Diary).*

Writing wrongs. *Thursday December 14, 1882.* I wonder whether I am drifting into the compilation of a book? Ever since my late cousin J. H., one of the canons of Lichfield Cathedral, died (April 28, 1865), and indeed ever since he superintended the printing of Governor Hutchinson's third volume of the *History of Massachusetts* some fifty-four years ago, it had been intended to publish a volume or two compiled from the Governor's diary and letters from the period of the revolutionary war, but nobody has been able to find the time to attend to it. At J. H.'s death the collection of manuscripts was handed over to me. It was a mass of confusion, *with* bags and bundles of letters and loose fragments of diaries all mixed together. At odd times I looked them over, pasted and repaired, strengthened rotten paper with a solution of isinglass size, smoothed and ironed them, arranged them chronologically and finally bound them into volumes. Not till then could the contents be got at and understood. Having *finished* my *History of Sidmouth*, I looked closer into the subject and last Lady Day I set to work to make a regular beginning, hoping that by next Lady Day I might accomplish a volume of some 600 pages. I see I cannot, *though* I have got to about 390 which is not quite two thirds. Selections of these manuscripts ought to be published if only in the cause of truth. Hitherto the Americans have had all the say, and they have said everything to suit their own views, proclaiming a great deal of self-glorification and vilifying everything English. These papers would put the dispute between England and her colonies in a very different light *and* I hope I may live to do something with them. *(Diary).*

Christmas Day 1882. *Monday December 25, 1882.* The wind having got round to the south-west, it has become extremely mild. I disapprove of dining out on Christmas Day and yet I always do it. I received two invitations to dine but only accepted one. Our boiled turkey was so immensely large that I had the curiosity to ask what it had weighed? Nineteen pounds and a half. *(Diary).*

Duty calls. *Friday December 29, 1882.* Called at Oakland and passed half an hour talking with Mr. and Mrs. Toller. Morning calls run away with a good deal of time but one is obliged to do it to keep up friendships. *(Diary).*

Legless jackdaw. *Saturday December 30, 1882.* Amongst the wild rooks that come to be fed under my window, some of them wonderfully tame, there are three or four jackdaws that come I believe from the cliff of Salcombe Hill. One or two are as tame as the rooks. Last autumn some horrible boy shot off the left leg of one of them and for some weeks it was in a dreadful state, but it is now able to come with the others. It stands upon one leg, but frequently goes down upon the stump and even uses it in walking or hobbling along, sometimes assisting itself with its wings. *(Diary).*

82/12/30 *Jackdaw.* (Diary)

Sidmouth peal. *Sunday December 31, 1882.* Last day of the year *and* incessant bell ringing. The peal of bells in the tower, from the last addition now amounting to an octave of eight, are in the key of F, *but* being odds and ends they are very imperfect. In short, they are very much out of tune. Nothing proves this so clearly as playing psalm tunes on them, as I used to do. I told the vicar the other day that as soon as I had enough and to spare I would give him a new set of bells for the tower, *but* very few of us have got enough, and still fewer 'enough and to spare'. *(Diary).*

1883

Offprints. *Saturday February 10, 1883.* Twenty copies of my letter on the preservation of ancient ruins have been sent to me for distribution from the Society of Antiquaries of London. It is printed in their Proceedings, Volume VIII, Second Series, p.483. (*Diary*).

Bottle-nosed whale on Sidmouth beach. *Tuesday February 13, 1883.* A small whale *was* discovered on the Hook Ebb reef of rocks a mile and a half eastwards, apparently not quite dead. The sea *was* too rough to tow *it* home with boats, *so* by means of horses and ropes it was dragged all the way to Sidmouth. It was the Globicephalus melas, the Bottle nose or Pilot whale. *It has* a very peculiar rounded forehead *and is* nearly eighteen feet long. The men made a tent with the sails of boats and admitted the public for what they chose to give them. (*Diary*).

Thursday February 15, 1883. Went down and sketched the so-called whale today. (*Diary*).

Monday February 19, 1883. Mr. D'Urban, curator of Exeter Museum, and the Rev. T. Hellings came to me about the whale. I took them to the east end of the beach where they examined it well. Mr. D'Urban asked me to negotiate for the skeleton for the museum, limiting me to five pounds. (*Diary*).

83/2/13 Bottle-nose whale , or Pilot whale, the Globicephalus melas, nearly eighteen feet long. Found by the fishermen at Hook Ebb rocks, not quite dead, a mile and a half eastward. Towed to Sidmouth and hauled up on the beach. Sketched Feb. 15, 1883. The skeleton is in the Exeter Museum.
(DRO, Z19/2/8F/35)

Tuesday February 20, 1883). 'Supposing I could get you three pounds for the bones of that whale from one of the gentlemen that came down yesterday, wouldn't you be very glad to get it?' 'Well sir, there's thirteen of us part or joint owners, and 'tis a dirty and difficult job to take them out without breaking and boil 'em all. Perhaps you could get us a trifle more?' (*Diary*).

Wednesday February 21, 1883. 'Will you undertake to get them all out carefully without losing or cutting any, if I can get you four pounds?' (*Diary*).

Thursday February 22, 1883. 'We have consulted together sir, and shall be very glad of four pounds, and will do our best'. So that was a bargain. The Board of Trade had laid claim to it, but eventually a message came down to say it was not the species they reserved to themselves and that the men could have it. I never heard of this before, *and* in short, it is only within recent times that any claim to the foreshore has been set up at all. (*Diary*).

Monday February 26, 1883. The whale being now given up, they cut off the blubber and sold it for ten shillings a hundredweight, *and* then proceeded with the skeleton. (*Diary*).

Tuesday February 27, 1883. They continued all last night boiling the bones. Not to keep them waiting, I paid them the four pounds. (*Diary*).

Wednesday February 28, 1883. Mr. D'Urban sent me a cheque for four pounds. The bones were packed in three hampers and sent in. Wrote an article on the whale for Lethaby's Journal next month. (*Diary*).

83/3/14 *Section.* (Diary)

Geological query. *Wednesday March 14, 1883.* Mr. T.V. Holmes of Crooms Hill wrote to me to enquire whether there are any holes in the soil and strata here like some near Blackheath, and Mr. Spurrell of Lessness wrote a couple of months ago on the same subject. I sent an answer and made some sketches. (*Diary*).

There are, or have been, circular holes in the fields on several of the hills surrounding the valley of Sidmouth, which, when they have been first discovered, have caused considerable alarm among the country people. From having examined some of them, I have no doubt they are only subsidences where springs have washed away the fox-mould and then a mass in the form of a cone has sunk down for want of support. They are dangerous to approach because the earth caves in underneath (as the accompanying section may show), but still, they are not deep. (*History of Sidmouth I, 18a*).

83/4/16 (Diary)

Escaped bear. *Monday April 16, 1883.* My servant Ann Newton has told me a curious story about a bear. She said that her mother's father, John Carslake, keeper of the turnpike gate at Trow, near Slade about the time of the Battle of Waterloo, had two or three daughters, her mother being one. Her mother's younger sister Elizabeth, who may have been sixteen or seventeen years old about this period, went one day from the tollgate to see a relation, *going* down a trackway, across some fields and by a sort of copse or wild district to the east of Knowle towards Harcombe. I

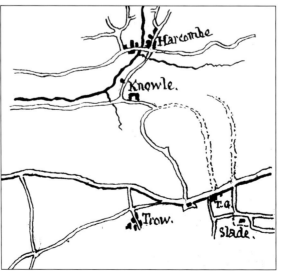

think I know the spot. Some years ago when enjoying a summer picnic at Knowle, we rambled out that way, and I have also been down one of the trackways from the tollgate side. Going along by the copse, her attention was arrested by a growl and a sort of roar such as one may hear at a wild beast show, and on turning round and looking towards the bushes, she saw a bear. She was dreadfully frightened as there was no shelter or protection in the open fields through which she was passing, but she started off and ran with all speed, expecting the animal would pursue her. She succeeded however, in getting to Harcombe, and bursting into the cottage fell on the floor in a faint. They were much alarmed, but on her recovering she described what she had seen *and* Harcombe was soon in an uproar. It was rumoured that a bear had been lost by its keepers from some show at Sidmouth and no one knew what had become of it. Report said that a party of Harcombe men shot it. (*Diary*).

83/5/18 *Starfish.* (Diary)

Starfish. *Friday May 1, 1883.* The fishermen dredged up and brought ashore a starfish I have not often seen before. Dr. Pullin showed it to me and said he was going to send it to the Exhibition of Fisheries, now open in London. Sketching from recollection, it was something like what is in the margin. (*Diary*).

Voracious pig. *Wednesday May 2, 1883.* Mrs. Mortimer, aged 71, came to be paid. She told me an extraordinary story about her late mother, who lies in the cradle as here represented in the annexed sketch, with her right arm hanging out over. The father and mother of the infant were called Newton and they lived at Norman's Town (so pronounced), a hamlet at the bottom of Newtonpoppleford Hill two thirds of a mile south of Harpford. One day when the father was out at work, the mother left the cottage to fetch a 'range' or hair sieve to sift ground corn to make bread, leaving the child in its cradle in the kitchen. She believed the door was shut when she went out and that some neighbour entered the house during her absence and omitted to fasten it on leaving. Anyhow, a large sow or pig wandering about the village at last came to the door, and pushing it open with is snout entered the kitchen. Coming to the cradle and finding the child's hand hanging out over, it bit off the arm halfway between the wrist and elbow and, munching it up, walked out. The mother took no notice of the pig as she returned, but coming to her own door she heard the baby crying violently. She was in a state hard to describe on going in and discovering what had happened, and there was no small stir amongst the inhabitants when the particulars of this occurrence became known. When the father returned, he seized a pitchfork *and* ran about the village looking for the pig *but* some of the neighbours shut it up and it was afterwards taken away into the country by a farmer. The mother started off for Sidmouth three miles away to seek some medical man, carrying the baby and running nearly all the way, and for some time afterwards she had to take the child into town until the arm was well. A brother of this child, baptised John, became the father of my servant Ann Newton and she also told me this story. The child recovered and lived to grow up and eventually married a man called Carslake. She was brought to the occupation of mantua making and needlework and was very clever at stay making. This took place about 1777, but there is nothing new under the sun and very possibly similar things have happened before and never recorded. (*Diary*).

83/5/2 *The pig bit off the child's right hand.* (Diary)

83/5/15 (Diary)

Geological drawings. *Friday May 11, 1883.* The Rev. W. Downes, curate of Kentisbeare, came over about some geological drawings which I am going to do for him. They will be lithographed and illustrate a paper for the next meeting of the Devonshire Association at Exmouth in July. (*Diary*). *Three sections along the line of the upper Exe valley railway by Hutchinson duly appeared in Downes' article 'Geological Notes upon the Exe Valley Railway' (Trans. Dev. Assoc. XV 1883).*

Statue of Venus. *Tuesday May 15, 1883.* Finished and sent off the three diagrams for Mr. Downes *and then* did some carpentry work at the back of the house during the morning. If I had had to earn my bread by manual labour, I should like to have been a carpenter. I called on Mr. and Mrs. Ede at Lansdowne and again examined their very pretty white marble statue of Venus. The annexed horrible outline will give an idea of the attitude. The figure is about three feet six inches high and the pedestal nearly as much. It was made in Rome near forty years ago by Mr. Holme Cardwell and exhibited at Manchester in 1857. One of Mrs. Ede's brothers, Mr. Openshaw, bought it for £200, and as he died recently it has come by bequest to Mrs. Ede. There is a small crack in the left instep, probably done by a jolt in travelling. The original model was destroyed by an inundation at Rome. (*Diary*).

New book completed. *Thursday May 31, 1883.* At last, after fourteen months work, I have got to the end of my book (volume one of the *Diaries and Letters of Governor Hutchinson*) of rather over 600 pages. It may be 620. I must now go over the whole of it again and revise it, and improve, and re-write those parts I can alter for the better, and this will probably take a month or more. (*Dairy*).

83/6/11   *Fish caught at Sidmouth.*
(Diary)

Rare fish. *Monday June 11, 1883.* Frederick Smith, son of my late father's groom, brought me a beautiful little fish to look at, of which the attempt in the margin gives but a wretched idea of the original, and said it had been pulled up in a net along with others but that none of the old fishermen knew what it was. I could not tell him. The fins and tail were so delicate and transparent that they were like glass. The colour was a soft green and the spots black. It is in some degree like the fish of May 17, 1880, that being full size. I have only done the *annexed* from memory. (See also May 17, 1882 *and May 31, 1886*). (*Diary*).

Erosion. *Sunday June 22, 1883.* After church, I took a turn up the lanes then out onto the hill above Peak House and down by the edge of the cliff. Every time I look at the cliffs after an interval, it is manifest that they are continually crumbling and falling away. (*Diary*).

Devonshire Association meeting at Exmouth. *Tuesday June 31, 1883.* Went to Exmouth to attend the meeting of the Devonshire Association, which meets this year at that place. The Imperial was full so I went to the Beacon Hotel. (*Diary*).

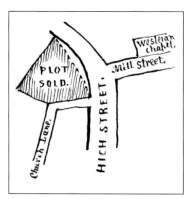

83/7/17   (Diary)

Church Lane sale. *Tuesday July 17, 1883.* On May 31st I got to the end of my American book. Since then, being some six weeks *and* amid many interruptions, I have gone over the whole and made several corrections and alterations and re-written some of the earlier parts. But I am not yet satisfied. I wrote my History of Sidmouth three times over, and I am quite sure that every book ought to be passed three times through the sieve. Even then, another revision or two would be sure to further improve the style, phraseology and arrangement, for perfection is never attained. I shall skim it over again, for I see several places where notes and annotations can be advantageously added.

I went to the London Inn, to the sale of a piece of land opposite Mill Street (so recently called) on which some old cottages had stood (*see September 1, 1882*). The local Board bought the cottages for £575 last year to pull down in order to promote a street improvement, the road being narrow just at the turn. They have pulled down all the cottages, marked off a greater width for the street and now offer the plot of land for anybody to build on. There is about 85 feet frontage. People thought it might be worth from £200 to £300 but the bidding went up to £370. We were told the plot had been bought to build a new Wesleyan chapel on. A quantity of old brick and stone lying on the ground was afterwards sold for £5. (*Diary*).

Illness of Mr. Heineken. *Sunday August 12, 1883.* Parish church *and* had tea with Mr. Heineken. After a severe illness for a man of 83, he seems to be gaining strength, and I hope his health may be soon re-established. (I did not know this was the last time I should see him). (*Diary*).

Seeing the publishers. *Monday August 13, 1883.* Went to London about my book and put up at the Charing Cross Hotel, where I have been twice before. (*Diary*).

Publishing agreement. *Friday August 24, 1883.* Signed an agreement with Messrs. Sampson Low, Marston, Searle and Kevington of 188 Fleet Street, to publish my book. They have written to their agents in Boston, Massachusetts, and I have also written to Dr. F. E. Oliver of the same place, to get as many authentic English copies as possible introduced into that country. (*Diary*).

Mr. Heineken's death. *Saturday August 25, 1883.* *I received a* telegram announcing Mr. Heineken's death this morning. (*Diary*). *Hutchinson returned to Sidmouth on the following Wednesday.*

Death of the executioner. *Wednesday September 5, 1883.* Marwood the hangman, or public executioner, died yesterday. Report says he was proud of his office, considering himself a respectable and highly important government officer. Ideas of respectability differ. When not hanging, he worked at his trade as a shoemaker. (*Diary*).

Willing recruits. *Wednesday September 19, 1883.* Strange indeed! What fascination can belong to the office of hangman, and what can we think of the mind and sensibilities of the person who can desire it? That twelve hundred people in England could apply for *the job* is astonishing. Applications have been made to the Home Secretary but he has made it known that he has no power *in the matter* - it is the Sheriff's *responsibility*. (*Diary*).

New Guide. *Thursday October 4, 1883.* I have recently been asked to write another little book about Sidmouth., to be circulated in the midlands and northern counties to make the place better known at a distance to bring visitors down here. I have just finished it and have given it the following startling and portentous title; *A History of Sidmouth from the Triassic Period to the Completion of those New Buildings.* (*Diary*).

Odd embellishments. *Sunday October 7, 1883.* Parish church. Frost last night *but* a beautifully quiet *and* sunshiny day. Took a sauntering walk on the beach over to Chit rocks this afternoon at low water *and m*easured the great oblong block of stone (9 ½ ft x 4 ½ ft and nearly 3 ft. out of the sand), being the foundation stone of the eastern pier of the harbour projected in 1836. I looked with wonder at what Miss Rastrick has been building against the cliff opposite the Chit Rocks to shore up the crumbling red rock; towers and buttresses and staircases, a boat house, a flag staff, etc., without any premeditated design (as she told me), allowing her nephew Mr. Temmet to amuse himself in such strange and expensive fancies. And it is all destined to come down some day. (*Diary*). *Hutchinson sketched these embellishments some years later (see May 1888).*

Domesday Committee. *Friday October 12, 1883.* Went into Exeter to attend a meeting of the Domesday Committee. Since the translators finished their portions, they have not been able to see their way to compare, collate and harmonise them together as they live so far away in different parts of the country. After much discussion, we at last decided as a preliminary step on having a dozen copies of part of the commencement printed and then circulated among the members for their consideration. I think there are now nine members on the committee and seven attended. I took the opportunity of carrying in and giving my puttah or gauntlet sword to the Exeter Museum and four books to the library. At the Institution in Cathedral Yard, I was shown a Bible of Milton's, and on the flyleaf were entries of the births of his children etc., in his own hand. (*Diary*). *This version of the Devonshire Domesday record was eventually published in two volumes by the Devonshire Association in 1892.*

Friends. *Thursday November 1, 1883.* The pears on my tree near the front door of the Old Chancel, a very late sort, are now picked in so that my friends the boys cannot steal them (they are very friendly at this time of year), and my other friends the starlings cannot peck them. On a late fig tree there were two or three figs remaining which I went to seek, but some of these 'friends' have walked off with them. The experience of this life teaches that if one does not always live in an attitude of strict defence, one's neighbours would soon pick and steal everything till they left nothing but one's bones. (*Diary*).

83/11/21   (Diary)

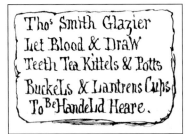

83/12/26   (Diary)

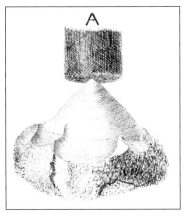

83/12/27   *Conchoidal fracture.*
(Diary)

Mr. Heineken's legacy.   *Wednesday November 7, 1883.*   Mr. and Mrs. Lloyd and their cousins, some of the Horsfall family, having proved Mr. Heineken's will are now in Sidmouth arranging affairs - packing up what they mean to take away, distributing some things among friends and probably there will be a sale of the rest.   *His* fossils, pebbles and notes of our journeys *have been* sent to me. (*Diary*).

Rebus.   *Wednesday November 21, 1883.*   As I had deciphered and translated some parts of Domesday Book, I have been asked to decipher the adjoining inscription. (*Diary*).

Final proof.   *Monday December 3, 1883.*   Corrected the press of the last sheet of my book *and* there now remains only the title page, preface and index.   The index I have preferred to make, though rather a troublesome thing if one is not a little indoctrinated, but as I have made the index to the Transactions of the Devonshire Association for the last dozen years the thing comes easily enough.   A book in the present day is scarcely looked upon as complete without an index. (*Diary*).

Old sign board.   *Wednesday December 26, 1883.*   Some short time since, a photograph of a decayed board was shown to me which had been found behind some old panelling in a house at Ottery.   It was secured by Mr. Brand, the dentist of the Cathedral Yard, Exeter, who buys up all kinds of curiosities and has a house full.   I have seen it in the papers, or was informed at the time, that he has presented it to the Dental Hospital in Leicester Square, London.   It is well known that barbers formerly combined the practise of bleeding and drawing teeth with shaving, but for a glazier to combine these arts with glazing windows is something new.   Perhaps buckelis is buckets.   (*Diary*).

Conchoidal fracture.   *Thursday December 27, 1883.*   The 'conchoidal fracture' of a flint – for the flint amongst stones seems to be the most given to it - does not occur often.   Perhaps when a man hits a flint with a hammer, it does not occur once in a hundred times, and when it does it occurs by accident.   Possibly study and practice might enable a man to do it on purpose.   I have had several specimens of conchoidal fracture at different times in my possession, but the one I here sketch was amongst the fossils and other things of Mr. Heineken which have been given to me.   When a man takes a hammer, as at A, and strikes perpendicularly down upon a flint pebble, he generally breaks it in half.   But it happens once in a thousand or ten thousand times that instead of so breaking, the splinters fly off all round leaving a well-formed core with the point to it under the hammer head.   I think I remember seeing a man do it who was cracking stones by the roadside, but he was quite as much surprised as I was at what he had done, and was unable to do it again.   (*Diary*).

1884

New Years Day 1884. *Tuesday January 1, 1884.* The first day began by ringing a peal of unruffled bells soon after midnight, and then all decent people went to bed. (*Diary*).

Treasure from the sea. *Thursday March 6, 1884.* The recent storms and gales have caused the sea to yield up some of its rich treasures. A boy found the top object in the margin. It is solid gold, weighs nearly a sovereign and a half and has markings on it like the knots on a branch. Each end is smooth *and was* perhaps part of some ornament. *It was* bought by Mr. Uglow, watchmaker, where I saw it. Also *found were* three silver oval discs about as thick as a sixpence, *one with* a loose rivet at A. They had been offered to me but I did not buy them, though I bought a silver sixpence of King George II bearing date 1757, found on February 15. An old half crown was found on the same day and sold for 3/6. (*Diary*).

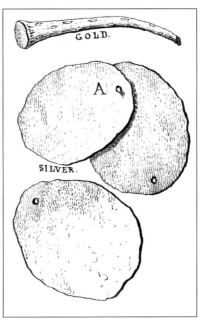

84/3/6 *Found on Sidmouth beach.* (Diary)

Box from Sidmouth beach. *Saturday March 8, 1884.* A girl called Dean brought me a box which she said her brother had picked it up on the beach, a sketch of which is given in the margin. The sides are brass or copper gilt, much worn, and the hinge injured. The top is a thick slice of semi-transparent calcedony bevelled and polished, and the bottom is of opaque agate apparently. She was glad to get a shilling for it. I have now been shown a similar one, half as large again and fitted up as a match box. Such boxes are made in Germany and sell for three or four shillings. (*Diary*).

84/3/8 *Box found on Sidmouth beach.* (Diary)

Clerical garb. *Sunday March 23, 1884.* At the parish church. Mr. Jenkinson the curate *was* assisted by the stranger, in a long black petticoat down to his heels looking like a Roman Catholic priest. Such clergy are doing their best to pull the church to pieces and get it disestablished. What with the like inside and the Dissenters outside, the fabric cannot stand long. There is no enemy so dangerous as one inside the camp. (*Diary*).

April Fool's Day 1884. *Tuesday April 1, 1884.* People are becoming so well bred that the old custom on this day of making their neighbours 'April Fool' is falling much into desuetude. (*Diary*).

Primrose Day. *Saturday April 19, 1884.* The anniversary of the death of the Earl of Beaconsfield. It is said he was fond of the primrose and so the Conservatives have adopted that flower as a badge and wear it in their buttonholes. He was a truly great statesman, without any fuss, mob oratory, chicanery, sophistry or something worse, and a gentleman and man of honour and principle as far above Mr. Gladstone, our present Prime Minister, as heaven is above the earth or the place below it. (*Diary*).

Critical acclaim. *Thursday April 24, 1884.* Two or three reviews of my book have appeared, both in the American and the English journals. On the whole they are very favourable. The reviewers here and there give vent to a few snappish remarks as is common with these censors, for nobody likes to be wholly satisfied or pleased, but they approve of the main point and that is all I care about. They say that the book is a valuable contribution to the period of the revolutionary war and some say they hope I shall publish another volume. Not likely! I never had any idea of that. It seems to be selling better than I expected and fifty more have been telegraphed for to go out to America, and I have heard through a private channel that Mr. Lowell, the American ambassador in London, has one. However, though I shall not live to write another volume, there is no harm in beginning it now the subject is well in my head to assist those who may, so I began to do this today. (*Diary*). *Hutchinson not only lived to finish a second volume but had it published as well. See December 21, 1885.*

84/5/12 (Diary)

Ingrowing horn. *Monday May 12, 1884.* Mr. Bolt, my butcher, who rents my field and also Mr. Ede's field between the Old Chancel and the church, has recently bought a very pretty cow. On feeling her head I found that the left horn was growing round over the left eye, and the point was so close that I could not put a penny piece between it and her head. I called Mr. Bolt's attention to this and warned him of the consequences if something was not done speedily. He said that it had been sawed off once or twice already and that he would attend to it at once. (*Diary*).

Weir on the River Sid. *Tuesday July 15, 1884.* Rain all the morning and St. Swithins too! In the afternoon I walked to Sid, or Seed, through the Salcombe fields *and* looked at the new weir. The section of the new work is like the annexed. The backing above the balks of deal is composed of a few stakes and stays as well as gravel and clay, and this raises the surface of the river by more than five feet so that it flows into the millstream on the further side of the river. The surplus runs away over the top balk and down the long steps, five or six feet each and composed of fir poles laid close together forming a sort of corduroy floor. In spite of the backing however, a certain amount of water percolates through. (*Diary*).

84/7/15 *Section of weir.* (Diary)

Sketch of Salcombe Hill. *Tuesday July 22, 1884.* Dined at Lansdowne with the Edes. Mr. Ede and myself then walked to the cemetery where I made a sketch of Salcombe Hill showing Mr. Scriven's cottages and his new purchase. (*Diary*).

Devonshire Association meeting 1884. *Monday July 28, 1884.* To Newton Abbot to attend the meeting of the Devonshire Association at that place *and* got a drawing room and bedroom at 5 St. Paul's Road. I called on Mr. R. W. Cotton at Woodleigh Villa whom I have long known, and then on Mr. and Mrs. Fisher who used to live near me at Blackmore Hall in Sidmouth. (*Diary*).

Stover Park and Lustleigh. *Friday August 1, 1884.* A charming expedition was organised for the members and about a hundred started at ten o'clock in seven or eight carriages. We first drove to Stover Park, the Duke of Somerset having expressed his willingness that we should see the house. As the Park is on Bovey Heathfield, I expected a dead flat, but the undulations are many and the house is on the crown of a considerable elevation. *A short description of the house follows.* James Templar, a poor boy born in Exeter in 1722 bound apprentice to a carpenter, ran away, got to India, made great wealth, returned, bought Stoford or Stover soon after 1765, pulled down the old house and built the present one and died in 1782. His eldest son James made the canal from Bovey to Newton but it did not pay as expected. His son and heir, George, hampered himself by making the railroad from Heighton and sold Stover to the then Duke.

84/8/1 *Font in Lustleigh church. Aug. 1, 1884.* (DRO, Z19/2/8F/43)

Thence we proceeded to Lustleigh where we stopped two hours *and* had a cold dinner at the Inn. Some ran off to Cleeve (Cliff ?) but as I had been there before I sauntered about the neighbourhood and examined the church. *There is* a peculiarly shaped old font, three recumbent figures in white stone - a female and two warriors, *and* an oak screen, partly old but well restored. *The* wagon roof *is* in fairly good keeping but the curious and interesting block of granite with its brief inscription DXX TUIDOC CONHINOC, supposed to be of Romano-British time as the letters are Roman (the letters DXX indicating the year 520) still remains as the sill of the south door, to be run over and obliterated by all the hobnails in the parish. Strange infatuation in the Rector to persist in keeping it there. It was placed there in ignorance, but better education ought to remove it to a safer place. It ought not to be set upright but horizontally, because the inscription so reads, *and* bedded on a stone shelf within the church some four or five feet from the ground. I called attention to this state of things in the Exeter Gazette of January 1871, and I think I must recur to it. *Which Hutchinson did, in a letter to the Exeter and Plymouth Gazette of August 14, quoting with amusement from the Rector of Lustleigh's lofty reply to his first letter: 'I rather fear however, that a writer who recommends the removal of the stone from its present position, a position it has occupied for 450 years and upwards, is scarcely likely to be a very competent judge on such matters'.* The door opens in two halves divided perpendicularly, the left hand *door* being shut and the other open for admission of the public. One glance serves to show how much more the inscription has been worn at the open end. A mat has been thrown over the stone to hide its shame but this is only a slight and perishable protection. The 'Bishop's Stone' is in the hedge opposite the hotel. (*Diary*).

338 84/8/1 *South door, Lustleigh.* (Diary)

Moretonhampstead Cross. *Saturday August 2, 1884.* Took the rail to Moretonhampstead, never having been higher than Lustleigh before. I expected to have found this place on the edge of the open moor, but to my surprise all the land is divided by hedges into as well-cultivated fields as they are in the valley. I lingered about the church and churchyard. The masonry is of granite, as all the churches are hereabouts. In the street near one of the entrances to the churchyard, on a platform that apparently once served as a broad base for a wayside post, is the head of a large granite cross with a T cut on the face of it. The block of stone, fixed upright, seems to be upside down judging by the moulding and the dowel hole in the top, but if it were turned over the T would then be upside down. I have put a coloured sketch of it in my sketchbook. Finding Moretonhampstead not on the open moor, I took the rail back to Newton Abbot earlier than I had expected. (*Diary*).

84/8/2 *Part of old cross, Moreton Hampstead. Aug.2, 1884.* (DRO, Z19/2/8F/43)

Return home. *Monday August 4, 1884.* After a tiring but very agreeable week I returned home. (*Diary*).

Weaver fish. *Tuesday August 12, 1884.* Made a coloured drawing of a fish called the weaver, caught here. (*Diary*). Not common. There is a dangerous fin on the top of the head. Sailors generally cut it off, as they did this, for it has four or five spines that are liable to wound the hand severely that ventures to grasp them. They are some-

84/8/12 *Weaver fish, caught at Sidmouth.* Not dated. (DRO, Z19/2/8F/45)

times eaten *and* are of different kinds, as: Trachinus draco – dry in eating, T. araneus – better eating, Scorpaena porcus – said to be of good flavour.   (*Sketchbook F*).

84/9/6   (Diary)

Thirsty rooks.   *Saturday September 6, 1884.   I have been* amused at the rooks drinking drops of rain, hanging under the top bar of the iron hurdles in front of the window of the oak room of the Old Chancel.

There is a review of my book in the Times today, page 6.   (*Diary*).

Sinking feeling.   *Monday September 8, 1884.*   Having been asked by a committee of the British Association to report on the amount of erosion of the cliff and some other things pertaining to the coast of Sidmouth, I have now completed it and sent it in.   The coast is receding by the advance of the sea but at various rates according to the softness of the rocks.   From long observation, from the stumps of trees of the submerged forest under the beach opposite Fort Field and from the foundations of some old buildings thirty feet outside the esplanade opposite Portland House and Marlborough Place, I have long had a growing feeling that the land is going down in the south of England.   At what rate it would be hard to say exactly, but I may venture to guess at perhaps about ten inches in a century. (*Diary*).   *See October 23, 1886.*

More fossils to the Museum.   *Tuesday September 16, 1884.*   Fine again.   Mr. Dallas the new curator of the Exeter Museum, his predecessor Mr. D'Urban having resigned, came down and spent the latter half of the day with me to look over my chalk and Greensand fossils and some other things, as I wish to give the best to the museum. (*Diary*).

Hangman dismissed.   *Wednesday October 8, 1884.*   The papers say that Binns, who was appointed this time last year to the office of hangman or executioner, has been dismissed.   He is a low, drunken fellow *and* bungled once or twice at executions, being the worse for drink.   (*Diary*).

Jenny Pine's Corner.   *Thursday October 23, 1884.*   Walked to Broadway *and* then to Knowle.   Called on Mr. and Mrs. Tyerman, had a long chat *and* bespoke a copy of his poems now in the press.   Walked on and had a look at the new nunnery.   Who would have thought such a building would ever have been built at Sidmouth!   Walked on to the carfoix, or four-cross way, long known as Jenny Pine's Corner.   Jane

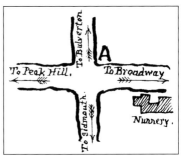

84/10/23   *Jenny Pine's Corner.* (Diary)

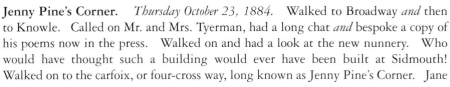

84/10/23   *Jenny Pine's Grave, or Jenny Pine's Corner commonly so called, as the scene looking towards Peak Hill appeared in 1826, and some years after.* (Hist of Sid. II, 125)

Pine cut her throat with a knife in a cottage at the back of the Anchor Inn in 1811. The wife of my late father's carpenter named John Ebdon told me some thirty years ago that, hearing the alarm *he* ran in and found the dying woman in a chair bleeding, with two fingers of her left hand thrust into the gash she had made. In the excitement of the moment, she cried out 'How could you be such a fool as to do that?' but was too far gone to speak *more*. She was a young woman of weak intellect. And John Ebdon told me that, as it was decided to bury her at this distant spot, a mile out of town and without funeral rites, he went up at night by torchlight with a posse of low, noisy and blaspheming boys and men and buried her in the middle of the four-cross way. At my earliest recollection of the spot the lanes used to be very narrow, but they have been much widened. There was a pollard oak at the north-east corner, at A, removed when the road was widened, on the trunk of which were cut the letters I.P. I suppose her bones rest there still. I have known the spot for near sixty years, since my father and mother came to Sidmouth in 1825 *and* I feel certain her remains have never been disturbed. I think I should have heard of it if they had. (*Diary*).

Worldly goods. *Monday November 17, 1884.* My birthday. No one could be more surprised than I am at finding that I have reached the age of 74 and yet feel so well. I have been much favoured in having been allowed to reach this age rather than to have been called away in the thoughtless years of youth, by which I am enabled to train my mind to a more wholesome, regular, reflective and profitable frame, the full sense of which is vividly before me. In common reason I cannot expect to have many more birthdays, and perhaps not another, from which conviction I feel that the great change cannot be very far off, though I contemplate it with the calm resignation that belongs to every Christian believer. If I am permitted to go through another year, I should like to finish and publish the rest of Governor Hutchinson's diary as an act of justice to him, and I have now written a quarter of a second volume. I have a great desire to place either a brass or some such memorial to his memory in Croydon church, a duty too long neglected. As for my houses here at Sidmouth, I am now utterly indifferent to them and all they contain, and the Old Chancel on which I have devoted so much labour and amusement, I do not care to finish or spend more money on, as I have no wife or children to leave it to. All these are perishable articles. (*Diary*). *In fact, with another thirteen years to live Hutchinson had plenty of time to complete his projects. He designed the brass to his great-grandfather Thomas Hutchinson and had it placed in Croydon church in July 1885 and recommenced building work at the Old Chancel on June 21, 1889.*

Babbacombe murder. *Friday November 21, 1884.* The papers have been full of the circumstances of a terrible murder of a middle-aged lady, a Miss Keyse of the Glen in Babbacombe, about one or two o'clock in the morning of last Saturday the 15th and then the house set on fire. Her head had been beaten in with three blows from the back of a hatchet and then her throat cut *whilst* she sat up late writing. One of the maidservants awoke smelling smoke, and opening her bedroom door raised the alarm. The fire was subdued by themselves and some people they called in. There were no traces of anybody having broken into the house *and* a young manservant of twenty called John Lee who slept in the house is arrested on suspicion. He had been several times before the magistrates and I suppose will soon be committed for trial. (*Diary*).

Rough justice. *Monday November 24, 1884.* The case of Adams v. Coleridge has astounded everybody, or rather the unexpected termination of it has. Mr. Adams was engaged to be married to the Hon. Mildred Coleridge, only daughter of Lord Coleridge. The Hon. Bernard Coleridge, the lady's brother, wrote his sister a letter defaming Mr. Adams in the grossest terms, *and the latter* brought an action against young Coleridge laying the damages at £10 000. *The case* was tried on Saturday, Mr. Justice Manisty being the judge. Evidence was brought that all the charges in the letter were false and had all the appearance of being actuated by malice. The Times newspaper speaks of the 'brutal tone' of the letter which was the cause of the action, and most of the newspapers of the day condemn it in strong terms. The judge summed up with an evident leaning towards the defendant *but* the jury brought in a verdict for the plaintiff with £3 000 damages. Upon this the judge immediately declared he did not see any malice in the letter, he overruled the finding of the jury, declared for the defendant and ordered Mr. Adams to pay the costs. It was plain this was done to swamp and ruin Mr. Adams. Mr. Justice Manisty works in the same court as the Lord Chief Justice, the defendant's father, and the Attorney General who was on the same side is of the same politics. Mr. Pitt Lewis, an attorney also in court and a protege of the Coleridge family, is frequently in Devonshire canvassing Exeter for the votes of the electors at the next vacancy. Mr. Adams was a bold man to plead his own cause in person against this powerful clique of lawyers, yet he got his verdict. Notice of appeal was given, so the affair is not over yet, *but* they will try to ruin him if they can. Mr. Coleridge, the defendant, kept out of sight, afraid probably of being cross-questioned by Mr. Adams. If the law is to be administered as it was in this case, goodbye to the security given us in our boasted trial by jury, goodbye to all respect for upright judges and goodbye to our liberties. (*Diary*).

Fishermen's complaint. *Monday December 22, 1884.* An immense number of herrings *have been* caught. For the past few weeks they have been taking more than they ever remember at one time. I will not talk of numbers for possibly they are spoken at hazard, *but* one boat was so full that the fishermen were obliged to transfer *part of* her freight into others to keep afloat. A few years ago they followed the plan of *launching* their boats about three in the afternoon and steering some miles east or west according to the set of the tide, and in fine weather it was a pretty sight to see twenty or more boats launched in twos and threes as fast as the men could get them

84/12/22 *Which is which? Some say t'other.* (Diary)

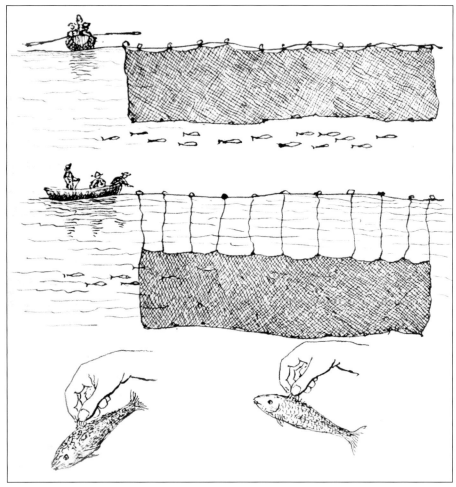

into the water. Arrived at the desired spot, they threw out the nets *attached to* a boat or two *and* drifted back with the tide, shivering or benumbed with the cold as there was then no work to be done for an hour or two. They filled up their time telling stories, 'beating the booby', lighting their pipes or tapping a stray keg of brandy. Sometimes, if they thought fish were about, they would haul up the nets and take out what fish were in them, but if fish were not plentiful they would drift on into the small hours and in certain cases stay out nearly all night. I am told they now follow a different and preferable plan. They cast their nets nearer to Sidmouth, but instead of staying with them, they anchor the nets and then come ashore and get a comfortable night's rest at home. After breakfast they go off and take them in.

The quantities now secured are a great boon to the fishermen and to many others, but the *former* are such a degraded and drinking set that the majority would be better off without money. When they get it, it is wasted on eating and drinking, so that their improvidence soon makes them poor men again. A month to six weeks ago they were preparing their fishing tackle anxious*ly* as the mackerel season in the summer had not been very profitable, *and* as the herrings were rather slow in coming they began to complain bitterly that they should all be starved in the winter. The common price for herring is about a shilling a dozen, though less sometimes for those who fetch them or to the poorer classes. *They are* three shillings a hundred to send away, though these things vary much and just now they are so abundant that every needy family can buy any amount at three pence a dozen. The wholesale dealers are buying them at seven shillings a thousand to retail in the inland towns or send to London. A month ago the fishermen were complaining loudly that there was no prospect of any fish and that they should not have a farthing in their pockets to provide for the necessities of winter, and now I am told they are complaining as loudly that there are too many and that they are selling too cheap! This is a new grievance. Ungrateful people.

Formerly they used to float the higher edge of their nets at the surface of the water by a series of corks, the lower edge being kept down by lumps of lead, but it was found, especially in deep water, that the fish frequently passed under them and were lost, as in the upper sketch. They now sink the net so many feet or yards by suspending it on ropes, as shown in the second sketch. The third sketch is more erudite. Some say that half the herrings sold in the market are pilchards. Who knows the difference between a pilchard and a herring? A fisherman told me last week that he could tell the difference in the dark – that the pilchard is a harder and firmer fish in the hand and that the scales of the herring are thin and soft but in the pilchard are of a thicker and stiffer nature so that they almost cut the skin if grasped firmly. I alluded to the old belief that *when* suspend*ed* by the back fin, the head of one of them will outweigh the tail whereas the tail of the other is the heaviest. I asked him which was which? He said he had heard the assertion but had never tried and did not know. I have asked many people in my time but no person could ever tell me. (*Diary*).

Bird brain. *Saturday December 27, 1884.* There was an active game of football opposite my window. I am however, quite sorry that the games are scaring my rooks and making them lose their tameness. I was much amused the other day, as indeed I have been many times before, at seeing one of my tamest hide some food he could not eat. It may have been a piece of potato or meat or a crust, but being already too full he took it into the field *looking for* a suitable tuft of grass, *and* into the middle of this he thrust it. Having pushed it as low as he could, he pulled the grass over it as much as the winter growth would allow and then looked about for a dead leaf or weed. Having found one, and I have seen both used on different occasions, he put it in place and pressed it down so as to make all secure. There was a great deal of intelligence in all this. (*Diary*).

Mr. Gladstone's birthday. *Monday December 29, 1884.* Mr. Gladstone is 75 today. Some people are never old enough to learn discretion. (*Diary*).

1885

Smallpox. *Tuesday January 6, 1885. There is* great alarm about smallpox in the parish. The schools have been shut and the children are not to come for a month. There have only been one or two deaths, but it has aroused the community. They are vaccinating all round, purifying the dirty cottages and are now running up a temporary building a mile out of town at Lower Woolbrook under the name of a smallpox hospital, to which infected persons may be moved. I hear they are going to provide for six patients. The disease is said to prevail at Honiton, Ottery and in most parts of the county. (*Diary*).

Trial of John Lee. *Wednesday February 4, 1885.* The trial of the young man John Lee for the murder of Miss Keyse at Babbacombe in November (see November 21), after occupying the court in Exeter for three days, terminated today in a verdict of guilty. He has shown much ingratitude to a good friend. He had been in her service as a boy, then was in several other places in one of which he was punished for theft and sent to prison, *but* afterwards Miss Keyes took him again, giving him a chance of retrieving his character. It might be asked what motive he could have for entertaining any ill-feeling towards her, but that he did so may be inferred by his having said to his half-sister, who was a servant in the house, and to the postman who called there, even eight or ten weeks before the commission of the deed, that 'he would serve her out' or that 'he would do for her', or words to that effect. Yet I think he had no other grievance against her except that she had talked of reducing his wages by six pence a week. I see no chance of reprieve for him. (*Diary*).

More donations to Exeter Museum. *Thursday February 12, 1885.* Last Wednesday I sent my brass gun, which was taken by my late cousin Lieut. John Roberton from a pirate on the coast of Borneo (see August 24, 1854) as a present to Exeter Museum, having no children to leave it to. Today I sent there three boxes of Greensand fossils of my own collecting in the cliffs east of Sidmouth, together with a number of the late Mr. Heineken's given me after his death. (*Diary*).

Elizabethan coin unearthed. *Wednesday February 18, 1885.* Called by appointment on Mr. Scott of Blackmore Hall. He showed me a silver coin of Elizabeth dated 1590 dug up in the garden. He is a very good turner, carpenter and mechanic and has a capital workshop. I asked him to come and look at my oak carving in the Old Chancel. *(Diary)*.

Hold up. *Friday February 20, 1885.* A curious story is going about Sidmouth, if it is true. Lethbridge, a grocer etc. of Exeter, has two branch shops in Sidmouth, one in Fore Street and the other in New Street kept by a Mrs. Casson, and other branch shops elsewhere. His man travels about in a van or covered light wagon, which I often see in Sidmouth. Returning to Exeter, I think last Monday the 16th, going up Aylesbeare hill, he was hailed by a woman who asked him for a lift in his van. He stopped and said she might get up, but whilst she was doing so he noticed a man's trousers below her petticoats. Not liking the look of this, he dropped his whip on the footboard as if he had lost it and asked the stranger to be so good as to step down and pick it up for him. The stranger however made excuses but as the driver pretended he could not leave his horses, the suspicious passenger, putting a leather bag and a parcel in the van, got down. The driver immediately urged his horses to their best speed, leaving the stranger behind. On approaching that well-known wayside Inn half way between Sidmouth and Exeter where all the coaches used to stop, known as the Halfway House, two men came out and tried to stop him, but he lashed his horses and knocked one of them down and hurried on. These men were supposed to be confederates of the other. On reaching Exeter he went to the Police Station at the Guildhall, told his story and gave up the goods. *Report* says there were two 'pig knives' in the parcel and four pistols, revolvers, in the leather bag, *and* some say dynamite. How much of this may be true I know not as people are very fond of the marvellous, but perhaps I may hear in a few days. *(Dairy)*.

Escape from execution. *Tuesday February 24, 1885.* Shocking news from Exeter. The young man John Lee was to have been executed for the murder of Miss Keyse (February 4) yesterday morning. Three attempts to do it failed as the drop would not act and the convict was taken back to his cell. The executioner is Berry, the former man Binns having been dismissed as a low drunken fellow. A new drop and gallows were erected in Exeter goal *but it* is said that the parts fit too closely, *though* they all worked well on Saturday when examined by the hangman. Lee was placed on the drop three successive times, but when the bolt or lever or whatever it may be was withdrawn, the platform on which he stood would not fall. Strange as it may seem, it has been ascertained by experiment since that it acts very well when there is no weight upon it, yet gets jammed in some way when there is. The travelling joints are too fine and the parts fir too close, and it is supposed that the wood had swollen by damp between Saturday and Monday as the weather has been wet lately. Everybody was shocked and horrified at these occurrences. The Under Sheriff lost no time but immediately started for London and laid all the particulars before Sir William Harcourt, the Home Secretary. He laid them before the Queen *and* not long afterwards it was made known that a respite and commutation of the sentence had been sent down. *There was* much excitement in Exeter, *with* people moved by various passions and opinions. Some assert that nothing ought to defeat the full carrying out of the sentence, whilst others feel that what he had to go through, together with the singularity of the case, may permit a leaning to the side of mercy. A searching enquiry will be made into all the circumstances. *(Diary)*.

C. F. Williams the artist. *Thursday February 26, 1885.* For more than fifty years I have had by me some early water colour drawings by C. F. Williams, done when we were boys. His father lived at Sidmouth and he was learning drawing of Mr. Haseler, a German artist I believe. There is great merit in them but old association enhanced their value in my eyes. Feeling that their value would be further increased if his name was put to them, I sent four over to Bath Cottage at Bittern near Southampton and received them back today, duly signed and dated. I have another early one of his of which he took no account, a view of Sidmouth beach looking west with the sun setting

85/2/26 *View of Sidmouth by Mr. C. F. Williams, a pupil of Mr. Haseler. I procured this drawing, one of his early ones, from Mr. Williams before he left Sidmouth, about 1832.* (Hist of Sid. V, 118)

beyond High Peak Hill. I could not send this for it is pasted into the fifth volume of my ms. *History of Sidmouth*, p.118. When returning my four drawings, I was much gratified at finding that he had sent me another dated 1880, a harvest field landscape with an ominous black thundercloud rising in the distance. The sky is beautifully stippled giving a soft aerial effect. When he was a lad a soft effect in the distance was produced by nearly washing out two or three times and then doing it again, but now stippling is employed. I have an account of Williams at October 8, 1872. (*Diary*).

85/2/27   *Rose Mount Cottage,*
Sidmouth, Devon. June 1836.
(DRO, Z19/2/8A/135)

Nutmeg rent. *Friday February 27, 1885.* Called again at Belmont about Mr. Williams's drawings, gave one of his prospectuses to Miss Hine-Haycock *and then* called on Madame de Rosen at Rosemount. She says her house is on a curious tenure. A lease was granted some two or three centuries ago by John Harlewyn for two thousand years, the acknowledgement being two nutmegs a year if demanded. I said I was curious on points of Sidmouth history so she said she would try to procure more definite information. *Baroness de Rosen did indeed write to her solicitor for further information and his reply confirmed the nutmeg rent for three thousand years granted by the Harlewyns (letter bound into the History of Sidmouth). Hutchinson's black and white drawing depicts Rose Mount Cottage as it was in 1936.*

News arrived of a terrible explosion at Shoeburyness. A group of officers and men were yesterday fixing a fuse into a shell when it burst. Several had their limbs blown off and their bodies much mutilated, among them Col. Fox-Strangways of Rewe near Exeter. (*Diary*).

Bound manuscripts. *Tuesday March 10, 1885.* Had the ms. of vol. 1 of my book bound in Exeter *and* got it back today. At first I was going to burn it all as useless, but then I thought I would save it. (*Diary*).

On the house. *Tuesday March 24, 1885.* A new kitchen grate from Exeter *was* put in No. 4 Coburg Terrace today. If you want to spite a friend, give him a house. (*Diary*).

Proposal for a new vane. *Tuesday March 31, 1885.* Called at the vicarage and showed them a model in paper for a new vane which I want them to put on top of the church tower. Anything in short rather than the present old one, which is so rusted that it sometimes sticks in the same quarter for a month together. The fly of the present vane has the date 1809 cut through the metal and this part I would retain to utilise again. (*Diary*).

85/4/1   (Diary)

Shadows on the church. *Wednesday April 1, 1885.* At three o'clock this afternoon, as I sat in the Oak room of the Old Chancel, the shadow of one of the pinnacles and two battlements of the church tower, fell upon the roof of the north transept, as represented in the sketch. It now wants 82 days to the longest day on the 21st of June, and perhaps at 82 days after the solstice, which will take us to September 11th, the shadow will be the same, but we shall see if we should live so long. (*Diary*).

Laureston Kneller. *Friday April 10, 1885.* Mr Laureston Kneller surprised me with a visit. I had not seen him since his late father, who was said to be a great-nephew of Sir Godfrey Kneller the painter, lived here more than forty years ago. The great-nephew was famous for running through big fortunes, of which he had two or three according to common report, and at last he was missing from Sidmouth one fine morning, having forgotten to square up with all his humble friends in the town. Lord Viscount Bolinbroke, who was a very retiring and shy man with limited means, then lived here (at Bedford House) with one son and three daughters, the Hon. Miss St. John the eldest being a fine young woman with a pair of handsome black eyes but not the meekest in expression. She had a very bold and independent temperament that rather scared reasonable men. She set her eyes upon John Walcott, a young man *and* the heir of Knowle in Sidbury parish, and gossip said she used to go out alone and cross his path on Peak Hill and other places when he was out shooting. But John's mother was afraid of her and, though a Lord's daughter, persuaded him against the match. The said John afterwards married the eldest daughter of Archdeacon Moore-Stevens, with whom at Knowle, and Mrs Theophilus Jenkins, I used to take the flute part in trios – she harp and Mrs J. piano – but he played away his means, and Knowle with the other estates were sold to the late Stephen Cave M.P. 'What happens is the unexpected'. Laureston was on the point of sailing for India. He had got his outfit as I remember, and told me he had even taken his passage, when somehow or other a match was knocked up between him and Miss St. John, and they were married at Sidmouth. It was said they went to Canada. I did not ask too many questions today. He lost his wife twenty years ago. He has five or six sons and two or three daughters grown up, scattered about over the world in professions and pretty well off his hands, so being alone and not so young as he was, he lives a great deal in Italy. (*Diary*).

Sidmouth Guide. *Saturday April 11, 1885.* Mr. Lethaby the bookseller here and owner of the copyright, tells me that the sixth edition of my *Sidmouth Guide* printed in 1879 is exhausted. At his request, I have looked it over and made certain alterations so as to bring it down and accommodate it to the present time. I originally wrote it so long ago as 1857. (*Diary*).

Devon arms. *Friday April 17, 1885.* The discussion on the subject of the coat of arms for the County of Devon has been carried on in the papers, but no one has gone sufficiently far back in their authorities. They will not get an older example than that of Vortigern. (*Diary*). *Hutchinson entered the debate with a letter published in the Exeter and Plymouth Gazette (April 14th).*

Letter writing. *Thursday April 23, 1885.* I dislike letter writing but I like working at my book *and* am about two-thirds through the second volume. My correspondence has fallen into arrears and I have now the disagreeable duty of working up lee-way. (*Diary*).

Sidmouth Church weather vane. *Saturday April 25, 1885.* The old vane of the church tower with the date 1809 cut in the metal is now taken down and I understand a new one is to be made. I have expressed a strong hope the old plate may be preserved. It is gilt on, I presume, a sheet of copper and if so it can be easily used again. (*Diary*).

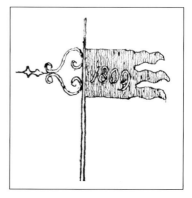

85/4/25 (Diary)

85/5/22 (Diary)

Ten shilling return. *Friday May 1, 1885.* A trifling sort of little guide book or account of Sidmouth might have been the joint property of Mr. W. Harding Warner and myself, as I wrote it and he illustrated it, if I had not often given him all my rights, title and ownership in it, both by word of mouth and by letter. as too small to care about He nevertheless desired to have it legally made over to him *and* what I have given already I have no objection to confirm by law. I have received from him a regular conveyance in which I sell him all my rights, title, ownership, etc., in the said book in consideration of the sum of ten shillings, the receipt of which I now acknowledge etc., etc. I signed it and Mr. Ede of Lansdowne witnessed my signature. We were both much amused *and* I am glad to be free of what is worth nothing. I took the ten shillings as proof I have sold it. If this book is not tampered with or altered, it will not clash with Mr. Lethaby's *Sidmouth Guide* which I wrote in 1857, the seventh edition of which is now in preparation (see April 11) and which I *also* gave away by word of mouth when I wrote it. (*Diary*).

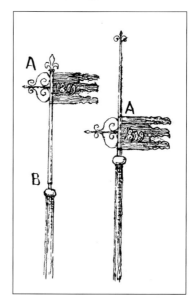

New vane on Sidmouth Church tower. *Friday May 22, 1885.* The new vane *was* put up on the tower today *but* they have not followed my model. They have re-gilt the fly with the date. The fly is soldered onto a tube stopped at the top either with a piece of brass, bronze or gun metal or with an agate or other hard stone, and supported on the point of a steel rod. The plug is at A, and I put but a small ornament over it so as not to make the vane top-heavy and a rather long though light tube down to B, hanging from the top like a pendulum to steady the vane and keep it from wobbling. As far as I can see with a telescope, there is no tube below the vane in the new one and there is a long rod over the plug. (*Diary*).

King Charles's Day at Tiverton. *Friday May 29, 1885.* King Charles's Day, as some call it. When I was a lad this used to be a great day in Tiverton. Men used to carry about a little boy seated in a bower made of oak branches and leaves and sang loyal and patriotic songs, which group represented Majesty and King, the king of course being the young King Charles II. Cromwell and republicanism were represented by a rough-looking man with face and hands blackened with soot and grease and having a long rope tied round his waist dragging behind him like the tail of the evil one. He was called 'Old Oliver'. He would now and then pretend to threaten the young king in the oak and have a hand to hand fight with sticks with the group who carried him. 'Old Oliver' would then make a dash into the crowd who fled in horror, smitting all he could catch. Such a mode of celebrating the day I do not recollect having heard of elsewhere. (*Diary*).

Looking for lodgings. *Saturday May 30, 1885.* Went by rail into Honiton after breakfast, to look for lodgings for self and servant for a few weeks. *There was* difficulty in getting any, as it is not the practise as it is by the seaside. Looked at two or three in the street but the rooms were too much piled one over the other. I was told of a house in the country half a mile north on the road to Awliscombe, *where there was* more space, *a* nice garden *and* much better, *so* I think I shall go there. The orchards in full bloom everywhere. (*Diary*). *Hutchinson went back to stay for a few weeks in Honiton, mainly to concentrate on working on the second volume of Governor Hutchinson's diaries and letters.*

85/6/16 *Stoney Bridge (so called) over the River Otter, near Tracey, Honiton. Coloured on the spot June 16, 1885.* (DRO, Z19/2/8F/49)

Mr. Newman of Tracey. *Tuesday June 9, 1885.* Finished a little article on 'Honeyditches' which I hope to read out at the meeting of the Devonshire Association in Seaton at the end of July. Walked through the streets of Honiton *and* towards evening had *another* walk on the Awliscombe road over the Otter by the old stone bridge covered with ivy, past the lodge entrance to Tracey, which I believe is the freehold of Mr. Newman. The mansion and park had belonged to the family of Lot the bankers, but when the firm of Flood and Lot went smash some thirty years ago and ruined hundreds, the estate was on the market. The only time I ever saw Mr. Newman was at the meeting of the Devonshire Association in July 1868, when he read a very well delivered paper on railways, he being a civil engineer as was said. He married a lady with a very long purse, the daughter of a distiller or cotton lord I was told, whose widowed mother for some time rented Mr. Marker's place at Combe and whose money bought Tracey. As money is the great power of this world, it got him seated on the magistrate's bench as well as housed in a comfortable manner. (*Diary*).

Honiton, Stoney Bridge. *Monday June 16, 1885.* Went down over the stone bridge and turned into the meadow on the left opposite the lodge of Tracey and made a watercolour sketch of the bridge. (*Diary*).

Salvation Army in Honiton. *Sunday June 21, 1885. Hutchinson was in Honiton, watching an inspection of the Artillery who were passing through the town on their way back from training on Dartmoor.* Scarcely had the band stopped when I heard a big drum in another direction, and I waited to see. It was the 'Salvation Army', a new sect started about ten years ago by a man called Booth which I had never seen before as they have not been to Sidmouth.. They copy the general arrangement of a military body, having generals, colonels, majors, captains, lieutenants and non-commissioned officers, women as well as men, and have now got detachments in many towns in great Britain and even on the Continent. They have to a great degree sought publicity and notoriety – perhaps it is part of their system, and they may think that it will make them better known and gain converts. A part of their military display is to march through the streets before they hold their services, with flags, music and singing, as in the sketch. All this has given the opportunity to the evilly disposed amongst the mob to jeer at them, and even to obstruct and hustle them, so that there have been no end of cases of assault and battery before the magistrates and Honiton has frequently been in an uproar. The procession *depicted* is as I saw it this morning.

First there marched a man carrying a flag, red with a blue border and a large eight-pointed star in the middle. Next followed two men dressed with some slight additions to their every-day dress to look like uniforms, scarlet shirts or jerseys with their coats over *so that* the fronts looked like scarlet waistcoats. The man who appeared to be the Captain or leader came next and he frequently turned round and walked backwards, singing and clapping his hands to keep time. Many of the others joined in the clapping. This man had on a scarlet jersey with nothing over it and I think a military cap, *with* the words 'Salvation Army' worked on the fronts of them in yellow worsted. Then *came* a man with a big drum and, I think, another with a cornopean, *followed by* four young women, one rather tall, with tambourines playing and singing. They were all dressed alike in blue dresses of serge or cloth and queer-shaped bonnets of what looked to me like black straw *tied* with dark blue ribbon. They conducted themselves modestly enough. After them came friends and supporters marching two and two, being members who had been duly admitted. They require certain promises from candidates, one being to forswear strong drink.

I had a curiosity to go to their service. They met in King Street. It is hard to describe what it is, it was so irregular – made up of singing hymns and addresses, not only from the chief members such as the band, but from some among the congregation. Then a hymn and a chapter in the New Testament *was* read and expounded by the man in the scarlet jersey, which seemed to be orthodox and spiritual, and then one of the young women would get up and either lead the voices in a hymn without music or commence an address herself. In making these addresses, which consisted of a revelation of their own religious thoughts, convictions and experiences, the

85/6/21 March of the Salvation Army at Honiton. (Diary)

speakers generally began in quiet tones but warming to their subject they ran on with the greatest volubility, sometimes with eyes shut and voice increasing almost to a scream, *before* ending rather abruptly and sitting down.   During a hymn, a man went round with a money box *and* I put in a shilling, probably the largest coin there for the worshipers were of the poorer classes.   After singing, the service ended with a Blessing something like that in church.

I am glad I went, because they have made a noise and caused great disturbances. All they want however, is to be let alone.   Disturbers have often gone to their services to jeer, laugh, smoke, read the newspaper and interrupt them, and collisions frequently occur in the street, *though* there were no disturbances at the service today. If they are let alone, I am persuaded they can do no harm.   Their style of worship would not suit the educated, but among a certain class they may catch those who never go anywhere, and consequently may do good in that direction. (*Diary*).

85/6/29   Font, St. Michael's Church. (Diary)

From top: 85/6/29   *Blagdon* (Diary); 85/6/29   *Marwood.* (Diary); 85/6/29   *Honywood* (Diary)

Right: 85/6/29   *West door, St. Michael's Church.*   (Diary)

Honiton, St. Michael's Church.   *Monday June 29, 1885.*   Walked up to Honiton old church, half a mile south of the town.   *It is* curious that the parish church should be so far from it, *but* they tell you that the town was once up there and that the chief thoroughfare east and west was then near it.   The stream that rises in Ring-in-the-Mire on the hill *to the* south and passes under the street in the lower part of the town on its way northwards, falling into the Otter just below 'Stoney Bridge' near Tracey, is called Giseage, from Gitt's hedge (as in Farquharson's *History of Honiton*).

But I went up to see the inside of the church.   The woman at the neat and pretty cottage (the cottage was prettier as a cottage than the woman as a woman), went with me and opened the door.   I fancied that the flagstone floor of the middle aisle gradually ascended from west to east.   I think Payhembury and some others do the same. The font in the tower is a somewhat curious structure, built up of Beer stone and Purbeck apparently.   The church was partly restored three or four years ago, *with* new glass in the east and south-east windows of better quality.   The great beauty is the oak screen across the church, the design of the carving *being* first class when examined critically.   I have carved oak enough myself to know how to appreciate this work and despise my own.   The horizontal string courses over the upper front are gilt, not too bright but only enough to enrich the oak and improve the general effect.   This splendid screen used to be blue or grey, if I remember right, having had plenty of coats of lead-coloured oil paint with white veins to imitate stone or marble.

I copied a few coats of arms.   On the floor towards the south-east is an old one to John Blagdon, 1694, incised on a flagstone.   Some say that Blagdon is only a contraction of Blackdown.   The name of Marwood is an old one hereabouts, which has merged into that of Tucker and others.   On one of the monuments is that of Honywood, in which the tincture of the bird's heads is faded and indistinct.   There is a monument in the south-east corner to Sir James Shepherd *who* gave the yew trees from his garden that make such a beautiful avenue in the churchyard.   I glanced at the tomb of James Rodge, 'bone-lace siller', dated 1617.   *There is* an alter tomb twenty-four feet north-east of the chancel to Nathaniel Knott, 1684, ditto Edward Searle 1607, twenty feet north of the north porch, etc.   A very pretty churchyard. (*Diary*).

Sidbury Church tower transmogrified. *Monday July 6, 1885.* Mr. Spencer's carriage came over from Sidmouth to Honiton and took me and my servant back. The weather was fine, the views all round when passing over the intervening Gittisham Hill and Honiton Hill were beautiful and I wished the journey of nine miles had been doubled. There is a long descent of nearly two miles, at the bottom of which is Colford where Mr. Bailey lives, and soon after *we* pass*ed* through Sidbury. *Here* I caught sight of the church tower, which has just been so strangely metamorphosed in the hands of the restorers that I did not recognise it. From a plain Norman tower with a pyramidal roof covered with shingles, we have now got an ornamental battlement, pinnacles and the top half of a spire, though I do not see how it is supported unless it is made of very light wood. The circular-headed Norman windows of the bell chamber remain. I reached home by five in the afternoon. (*Diary*).

85/7/6 *Sidbury church tower transmogrified.* (Diary)

Map of the Axe valley. *Wednesday July 8, 1885.* *Spent* the greater part of the day drawing a map of the valley of the River Axe from Seaton to Axminster, to illustrate a paper on 'Honeyditches' which I intend to read at Seaton about the 22nd. It is going to London to be lithographed and seven hundred copies taken. (*Diary*).

Sunfish caught at Sidmouth. *Sunday July 12, 1885.* This afternoon *there* was a great stir on the beach among the fishermen. They saw the back fin of a great fish moving about above the water and thought it belonged to a shark. They put nets around it and got it on shore, it did not resist much, *and then* put boat sails round it and admitted such of the public as gave them a few pence. They sent up to me *and* I went down and made a sketch of it. The sun fish, though not common on this coast, is occasionally met with. There is a large one preserved in Exeter Museum, but not so large as this, *which* is six foot six inches long, three foot eight inches high and from twelve to fifteen inches thick. (*Diary*).

85/7/12 *Large sunfish caught at Sidmouth, Sunday July 12, 1885.* (DRO, Z19/2/8F/51)

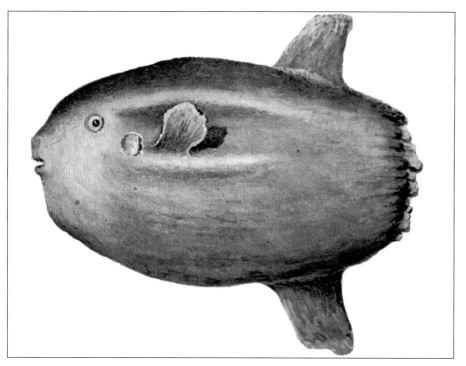

85/7/12 (Diary)

Monday July 13, 1885. I did not hear of the sunfish till this morning or go down to see it, though I have put the particulars under yesterday. (*Diary*).

Tuesday July 14, 1885. Went down to the beach after breakfast to put what may be termed a few finishing touches to my sketch of the sun fish, when I learnt that he had been too strong for his guardians. They reminded me of the present heat of the weather, that he was a fish out of water, that the sun was bright and hot, that so far from attracting visitors they rather preferred making a wide circuit round him, and that, as regarding themselves, they did not want to be poisoned. So they once more launched him into the deep and set him adrift. (*Diary*).

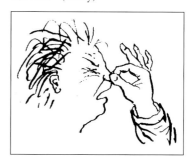

Devonshire Association meeting 1885. *Monday July 20, 1885.* Went to attend the meeting of the Devonshire Association at Seaton. There was great difficulty in getting a lodging in the town as we are now in the period of the year when people are enjoying their 'summer outings' as they term them, so I lodged in Honiton and went down by rail every morning. (*Diary*).

Rock fall at Beer. *Tuesday July 21, 1885.* Though I took up my quarters yesterday at Honiton, I did not go down to Seaton till today, when the work begins. I attended a meeting of the council at two *but* did not care about the general meeting at four so I sauntered about the beach. I went and laughed at the word MORIDUNUM inserted in black flints in the concrete wall outside the earth mound at the eastern half of the beach. The old notion that Moridunum was at Seaton is quite exploded. In Robert's *History of Lyme* or in another of his amusing books, he says that this is an artificial mound thrown up and a battery with guns erected on the top of it in or about (I think) the reign of Henry VIII to keep off pirates. *I then* walked half a mile westwards of the town and made a rough coloured sketch of the chalk cliffs looking towards Beer. Last Friday a quantity of the face of the 'White Cliff' fell into the sea, and there it lies at its base. Returned to Honiton in the evening. (*Diary*).

85/7/21 *White Cliff from Seaton looking towards Beer. Coloured on the spot July 29, 1885. There had been a great fall a few days before.* (DRO, Z19/2/8F/53)

Paper on Honeyditches. *Wednesday July 22, 1885.* Went down again. Read my paper on 'Honeyditches', a word supposed to have been corrupted from Hanna, the name of a Danish chieftain who landed on the coast, and ditches in allusion to the earthworks he threw up to fortify himself on Little Cooch Hill where a camp remained down to Stukeley's time. It was a roundish oval about three acres in area. Returned. (*Diary*).

Honiton fair. *Friday July 24, 1885. It was* Honiton fair this week. I did not think there was a fair in the country kept up as this one is. The noise, the crowds of people, the shows, the booths and the excesses in eating and drinking would be much better put an end to. The fair is proclaimed in the morning about eleven or twelve o'clock by a man who carries a large glove nearly half a yard long, tied on a pole in a bunch of laurel or suchlike evergreen. *He* is accompanied by a man who rings a bell, or does it himself, *and* is generally followed by a bevy of children. He occasionally stops, rings the bell and proclaims the fair open in the following words, or words to their effect:

Oyez! Oyez! Oyez! The fair's begun
No man can be arrested till the fair is done.

We are told that, by virtue of an old charter, all felons and debtors can come freely and without fear of arrest as long as the fair lasts, which is until noon on Friday. A policeman to whom I was talking on the subject told me however, that a soldier had at all events been arrested for desertion. The glove is said to typify fair dealing.

There is one custom at Honiton fair that ought to be put down because it encourages unconscionable gourmandising and drinking. Most of the tradesmen have a good and substantial meal laid out, of joints of meat, vegetables, bread, etc., and when a customer has paid his bill he goes in to the back parlour 'to take a little refreshment'. I have been told of cases where a man will spend sixpence on goods and then eat two shillings worth of dinner, *and* some customers are so dishonest as to bring friends with them to feast who have spent nothing. What I am informed is often the case *is that* after they have feasted at one house, they will go and do the same thing at another. In primitive times the hospitality may have been kind and commendable, but now they stuff from one house to another until some of them can scarcely move, so that it has become a monstrous abuse which everybody acknowledges but nobody has the courage to resist. Returned to Sidmouth. (*Diary*).

85/7/24   (Diary)

Bicton Cross. *Wednesday August 19, 1885.* Drove to Budleigh, took my servant and stopped at the house of her sister Mrs. Knowles. Went and had another look at Budleigh Church, which was open for work was going on in the tower. I again looked over the oak bench ends. Beside the Raleigh arms in the centre aisle, I observed the St. Claire arms with its quarterings in two places in the south transept. Outside I examined the new vestry and organ chamber in the northeast corner *and* sauntered around the large and beautifully situated burial ground, having an unusually large number of handsome monuments. The slab of Radulphus Node which was near the south iron gates, I remarked some years ago has been reprehensibly destroyed.

After an early dinner I walked to the vicarage of Bicton and called on the Rev. A. Kempe, who was at home. I then examined Bicton Cross, of which I made an outline sketch some years ago in one of my sketchbooks. The text or scripture on the upper part is now worn and illegible from the ground. The lower division has square stones inserted in the brickwork on the four faces, that on the eastern towards Sidmouth being here sketched in the margin, with the date. All these serve to direct travellers. I then proceeded to the field where the obelisk is. Some thirty or forty years ago it was struck by lightning and some of the stones displaced *and* I remember it in that condition. It was subsequently repaired and an iron conductor placed down the north side. It is built of white Beer stone, or at all events the outer casing is, *but* not very correct architecture – an Egyptian shaft with a Roman base and mouldings. (*Diary*).

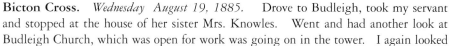

85/8/19-2 (Diary)

Left: 85/8/19
Bicton Cross, Devon. 1848.
Done 37 years earlier.
(DRO, Z19/2/8D/135)

Rock fall disaster. *Monday September 7, 1885.* The unfortunate affair at Dawlish on Saturday forenoon the 29th of August, when the cliff fell down on a group of people who were enjoying themselves on the sand at half tide, seems to have made a profound sensation all over the country. I know the place where it happened well of course, having been familiar with the town and beach from my childhood. From what the papers say, the ladies, nursemaid and children were at A, in front of the wall and cavern as shown in the first figure. The strata are considerably inclined and the red rock is a hard and coarse conglomerate at the lower half of the cliff, which is about 170 feet high at this place, but the upper part is loose sandstone and earth. The railway tunnel is only about 30 feet from the cavern, and when I have been walking on the wall,

85/8/19 Obelisk. (Diary)

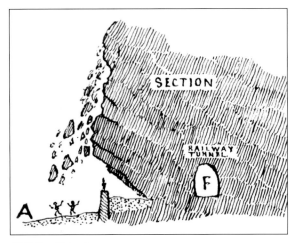

85/9/7   (Diary)

85/9/7   (Diary)

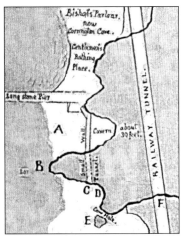

85/9/7   (Diary)

which is two or three feet wide, I could hear a train pass and feel the cliff tremble. I never felt myself safe there. The second figure is an imaginary section showing the strata, the cavern now half full of sand which the waves have at times washed over the wall, the wall built to protect the cliff and also the tunnel of the railway. The small tunnel C was made some ten years ago for the convenience of bathers. The low hole E used to be closed at the top but not now *and* from this to the tunnel C the papers say a bridge or gangway has been made since I was last there. Everybody is abusing everybody in Dawlish and casting blame pretty freely. (*Diary*).

Sidbury Church re-opened. *Thursday September 10, 1885.* Sidbury Church opened after having been restored *but* I did not go. I care very little about hearing bad intoning. (*Diary*).

Shadow again. *Friday September 11, 1885.* There now! The shadow on the church roof seems exactly the same as it was on the first of last April. (*Diary*).

Suffrage. *Wednesday September 30, 1885.* The new act of Parliament passed by the radicals shortly before the last ministry went out will cause a great revolution in the representation of the people, as the lowering of the qualification will add about two million voters to the list. As they are amongst the lowest and most ignorant in the country, the effect may be guessed. (*Diary*).

Guy Fawkes Day 1885. *Thursday November 5, 1885.* Windy, stormy weather *on* Guy Fawkes Day. A figure representing a disgraceful old clergyman residing here was paraded about to be burnt this evening on the bonfire (*see July 24, 1886*). Also a young man dressed up in woman's clothes with a veil and carrying the effigy of a baby. (*Diary*).

Death of Lady Rolle. *Saturday November 21, 1885.* It is reported in Sidmouth that Lady Rolle died last night at Bicton (corrected *later to* about four in the afternoon). This will probably make some difference at Bicton, *but* she would be more regretted if she had had a more heavenly temper. (*Diary*).

Geological drawings. *Wednesday November 25, 1885.* The Rev. William Downes of Combe Rawleigh has a paper on the geology of the district between Honiton and Axminster and I am making him some pen and ink drawings to illustrate it. He came over today, we had an early dinner together and then a conference on the drawings. They are a section from near the Honiton railway tunnel eastwards to Trinity Hill, Axminster, and a coastal section from Beer to near Lyme. (*Diary*).

General election 1885. *Thursday November 26, 1885.* The General Election for the new Parliament has now fairly begun and I never remember the country in such a state of political excitement as it is now. The gross falsehoods circulated by the low liberals and radicals in order to catch votes, especially from the nearly two million new electors whose ignorance makes them an easy prey (which was the reason for admitting them) are quite disgraceful in those who utter them. The late Prime Minister, Mr. Gladstone, is again speechifying in Midlothian, and with as much truth as he was five years ago. He is one of the most dangerous of men that ever had power in this country. He appears to be utterly without principle, intent only on political power and the emoluments belonging to it. (*Diary*).

Miscalculation. *Wednesday December 2, 1885.* The papers mention a horrible occurrence at Norwich. A man named Robert Goodale was condemned to be hanged for the murder of his wife. The attempt was made yesterday but the jerk of the drop pulled off his head in an instant, and his body and head fell to the ground together. Goodale stood five feet eleven inches and weighed fifteen stone, and the drop was six feet. (*Diary*).

Volume II completed. *Monday December 21, 1885.* This evening I finished the second volume of Governor Hutchinson's Diary and Letters. I got to the end a month ago but I have been going over it again to revise, put in finishing touches and fill in a few blanks left open for verification. The labour has been a pleasant amusement for about fifteen months. (*Diary*).

1885.

1886

Mock funeral. *Friday January 1, 1886.* A curious story came from Torquay last week. Last spring a Mrs Sutton residing at Bath lost a child, which was put in a wooden shell *within* a lead coffin, an outer wooden one and buried. She afterwards decided to live at Teignmouth or Shaldon and desired to take the remains of her child with her and inter them there. After a deal of trouble she got leave from the Home Secretary and a faculty from the Bishop to exhume the body and brought it to Devonshire. The maidservant, who it appears had nursed the child, persuaded her mistress not to bury it but to keep it to look at. Mrs Sutton followed this advice, and the two together opened the outer coffin and took the lead one out. They then filled the empty coffin with bricks, applied to the clergyman and had a mock funeral, he not knowing what he was burying. They then cut a hole in both *remaining* coffins and put in a glass window. The mother strewed the grave of bricks with flowers to keep up appearances. She *again* altered her plans however, and resolved to live in Torquay and engaged a house there. She procured an empty pianoforte case in which she and her servant packed the lead coffin and contents and took them there, *but* after a little time she *became* unable to meet her engagements with her landlord and under distress he seized her goods. He sent people to appraise the furniture, etc., and in going over the house they came upon the pianoforte case. Suspecting some goods might have been secreted there for the purpose of clandestine removal, they forced it open. As soon as Mrs Sutton heard what they had discovered, she absconded and kept out of the way, nobody knowing what had become of her. The men at once informed the police who took the coffin away. A post mortem examination was made and an inquest held, and Mrs Sutton, gaining courage, came back and told the whole story. The surgeon was satisfied from the appearance of the mouth and throat that the child had not been poisoned but decay had gone so far that he could not be sure of its age or sex. She stated that it was a boy eighteen months old and gave its names. The coroner told her she had been highly indiscreet in what she had done, *but* that there would be no punishment if she followed his directions. The law required that the dead must not be kept above ground to the injury of the living and that she must undertake to have it buried within two days, as if not done it would be carried out by his order and the expense charged to her. At the expiration of the time it was found that she had not complied and was asked for an explanation. She excused herself by saying that she wished to bury it with the other coffin but could not command the money. She was asked whether she had any friends who could help her, *and* she said her mother was living and if they would grant her a few days more she would apply to her and endeavour to get it done. As nothing has happened in the papers since, the bricks are probably taken up and the child put in their place. She is the wife of a photographer and farmer now in Canada. (*Later note:* The papers since say it has been buried at Shaldon). (*Diary*).

Devon earthquake. *Monday January 4, 1886.* This forenoon about 10.20, the sensation of an earthquake was sensibly felt by many persons along the line between Dartmouth and Kingsbridge. Some say it was no great shakes. (*Diary*)..

Proof reading. *Sunday January 16, 1886.* Received the first proof sheet of sixteen pages of volume two of the diaries and letters of Thomas Hutchinson. The publishers hope to get the book out by Lady Day but I am sure it cannot *be done.* Three hundred copies *are* already bespoken by the Americans. (*Diary*).

Gunboat design. *Tuesday January 19, 1886.* Found the gunboat *plans shown on November 4, 1854* in an old portfolio. It was a design of mine made more than thirty years ago before ironclads were known, for making a gunboat with eight guns entirely invulnerable. She was to have no rigging whatever, her smooth deck slightly convex and her sides sloping at an angle so that every shot that hit her must necessarily glance off. At each end of the deck (as in the plan) there was to be a large hatch flush with the deck when shut, strongly hinged at the outer end but which could be raised at the inner so that an enemy *in* possession of the deck could be cleared off it with rifles. I thought I should like to steer her through the fleet and beg them to fire twenty shots at me, to see if they could produce any effect. (*Diary*). *For Hutchinson's gunboat design, see November 4, 1854.*

Thoughts on ankles. *Monday January 25, 1886.* When walking behind people of both sexes it is impossible to avoid noticing their ankles, *and* in so doing, I have often been struck by their different shapes. The best formed ankles we see are those which tend in line with a straight leg, as in the first sketch. The second form belongs more to females, although this shape, which bears more or less decidedly on the inside of the foot, varies greatly. I have known some strong minded or masculine minded women whose ankles were as straight as in the upper figure, *among whom* I may mention the Miss Osbornes, daughters of Lord Sidney Godolphin Osborne. In young girls under the age of puberty, their legs and ankles do not differ from those of a boy, but in numberless instances where I have seen the daughters of my friends grow up, I have observed that the ankle changes its form as in the second figure at about the period when womanhood comes on. I believe that sculptors speak of this as beauty in women, *though* I should rather call it a peculiarity. As to the two lower figures, they are simply examples of a bow-legged and a knock-kneed man, each form of leg giving an idea of weakness. (*Diary*).

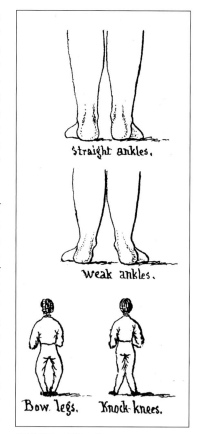

86/1/25   (Diary)

Idea of a bookcase. *Friday February 6, 1886.* Mr. S. G. Percival suggests to me that the books I intend to leave to the Free Library in Exeter would be better in a small bookcase. *Taking up* this idea, I have measured my materials, thought of a design and begun to make a small wooden model, for nothing shows a thing like a model. (*Diary*).

Wedding presents. *Monday February 8, 1886.* Gave Sarah Jane May, the daughter of my milkman, two tea trays of different sizes as a wedding present *as* she is to be married in a few days. That class may as well marry young *for* they have no expectations to wait for. I disapprove of wedding presents among the better classes *but* the practice has now become a fashion. The bride is taught to be covetous of a large number and vain when she displays them on a side table, vexed and envious if she does not get as many as her neighbour and proud if she happens to get more. The fashion has reached monstrous proportions and is quite a tax upon mere common acquaintances. The majority who give do so 'because I thought I must give something' or 'I couldn't very well avoid it'. I have long felt that if I were going to be married I should wish to make it known among my friends that they should not tax themselves on my account, if I could do it without offence. I have heard of a gentleman who did not like collective presents and resolved never to receive any 'except from one person' at a time. (*Diary*).

Roman tiles. *Thursday February 11, 1886.* Sent two Roman roofing tiles to the Museum in Exeter for Mr. Spencer G. Perceval. They were dug up at the ruins of a roman villa near Seaton many years ago by his uncle, the late Sir Walter Trevelyan, Bart. Sketching from memory, I have put them in the margin. See the article 'Honeyditches' in Trans. Dev. Assoc. XVII, 277. (*Diary*).

86/2/11   *Roman roof tiles.*   (Diary)

London riots. *Wednesday February 17, 1886. There have been* riots in London for the last day or two by the unemployed, led on by socialists and agitators. Windows *were* broken indiscriminately and *there were* many robberies with violence. Many houses of the nobility and the wealthy *were* assaulted simply because they were rich and the robbers poor, *but* they forget that it is by the rich they live and what would they do without them? *There is* great outcry against the new Ministry, just settled in their places, for allowing the mob to run riot for a couple of hours with no force sent out to check them. (*Diary*).

Dull days. *Saturday February 27, 1886.* Black, cold, leaden sky again. That 'all flesh is grass' is a piece of ancient wisdom, and as the grass on my lawn grows when the weather is warm and is retarded by cold, so I find with the beard on my chin. I have been surprised to observe how seldom I need shaving whilst this cold weather lasts. (*Diary*).

86/3/16   (*Diary*)

Lapwings. *Tuesday March 16, 1886.* I pity the birds this winter. The numbers that are about here now all seeking for food are very remarkable *and* until this winter I never saw peewits in the valley before. In former years they used to frequent the top of Salcombe Hill in flocks and hover round one's head with their screaming note. The hard weather has driven them to the valley where the ground is not frozen *and* for several days there have been three or four as well as the thrushes searching for food. I have been spying on them with an opera glass and made the *annexed* sketch, though I could not see details clearly. (*Diary*).

Bookcase for Exeter Library. *Wednesday April 28, 1886.* Called on the vicar and on Mr. Ede at Lansdowne. When I came back, I went to my carpenter to superintend the making of a small bookcase of Gothic design, the plain part of which is being made from my drawings, and a small wooden model, whilst I mean to carve the ornamental portions. It is in wainscot oak. I intend it for my ms. *History of Sidmouth, Diary, Sketchbooks,* etc., which I leave to the Free Library, Exeter. Mr. S. G. Percival put the idea into my head (see February 6). (*Diary*).

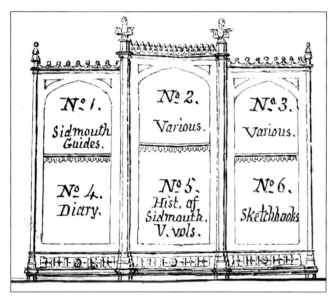

86/4/28   *Carved oak bookcase and stand for the free library in Queen Street, Exeter.* (Diary)

Young lumpsucker. *Monday May 31, 1886.* Mr. E. Chick brought *me* a beautiful little green fish *speckled* all over *with* black spots, about four inches long with a blunt head. It probably belongs to a more southern latitude. Made a drawing of it in my sketchbook. (*Diary*). Three have been caught here within my memory. It is the Sea Owl, Lump Sucker, etc., *but is* not known to the fishermen. The *annexed* is a young fish, transparent green when young becoming dark crimson when old. It is a Greenland fish and is eaten there. *Its* extreme length *is* sixteen inches *and* it feeds on small fish. On two occasions I have seen full grown ones at the fishmongers in Sidmouth for sale, but not caught at Sidmouth. Though we live close to the sea, it is rather strange that most of our supply comes from Grimsby, brought in there by the North Sea fisherman. (Sketchbook F).

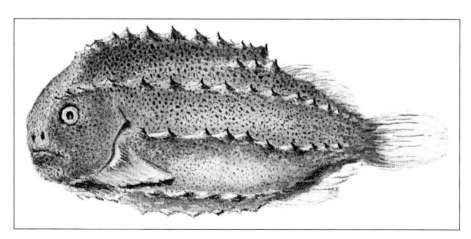

86/5/31   *Fish caught at Sidmouth, June 2, 1886.* (DRO, Z19/2/8F/55)

Stay in Honiton. *Wednesday June 16, 1886.* Went over to Oakmount near Honiton for a change as I did this time last year, taking my elder servant with me. (*Diary*). *Hutchinson stayed there for a month, mostly walking in the district.*

Trumpet involuntary. *Monday June 21, 1886.* Walked due south across the town of Honiton, under the railway and on towards 'Round Ball Hill'. More than twenty years ago, I came over with the Sidmouth Volunteer Artillery in which I was then a lieutenant (Gustavus Smith, J.P., being Captain), bringing our carbines. We had a friendly shooting match with the Honiton Rifles somewhere against the flank of Round Ball Hill, and I came out today to try and find the place. I had some difficulty, owing to the length of time, but the Honiton Rifles still shoot there and the targets were pitched. Whilst we were shooting, our trumpeter got jolly drunk in the town, and when he mounted his white horse to ride home with his trumpet slung over his back, he got up on one side and off on the other in the street with the trumpet under him and squeezed it flat. *Afterwards*, when anybody blew into it, it only groaned like the muffled bray of a donkey. The Captain reprimanded him and stopped back a guinea of his pay. (*Diary*).

86/6/21 (Diary)

Parliamentary election. *Friday July 2, 1886. It was* nomination today of candidates for Parliament for the south-eastern or Honiton division of the county, *so* I went to the Town Hall. Sir John Kennaway came in with Mr. R. Coleridge of Salston and some others, *and* he came over to shake hands and had a chat. No one on the Liberal side came forward to oppose Sir John so there was no contest, *and* after waiting a sufficient time and a few legal forms having been gone through, he was officially declared to be duly elected. I happened to have my badges in my pocket which I affixed to the left lapel of my coat. The first is the new Union Jack badge, worn not only by Conservatives but by those Liberals who have deserted Mr. Gladstone for his alliance with the Irish disaffected party and consider that the integrity of the Empire is endangered. Hence all those who have joined the consti-tutional party are called Unionists. The second is the Primrose badge in honour of the late Earl of Beaconsfield. They are both enamel and gilt. (*Diary*).

Above: 86/7/2 *Badge of Primrose League.* (Diary)
Left: 86/7/2 *Union Jack badge.* (Diary)

86/7/2 *John Cammell, Maltster, 1762. Head of a tombstone in Honiton churchyard about 30 or 40 feet north of the church. Sketched July 2, 1886.* (DRO, Z19/2/8F/43)

Plague of jellyfish. *Thursday July 15, 1886.* Called on the Buttermers at the Elms. They spoke of the dreadful smell of the decayed jellyfish on the beach whilst I was away, *of which* I had heard. In the calm hot weather, the sea as smooth as a pond, the water was full of jellyfish which were left on the beach when the tide receded. The edge of the water was an offensive black. Nearly all the south coast of England, report says, has been the same. I remember a similar occurrence took place many years ago, some say in 1851 or 52, *and* I went out in a boat with some friends. The sea was as smooth as a lake and multitudes of jellyfish were floating about. (*Diary*).

Disagreeable neighbours. *Saturday July 24, 1886.* A disagreeable affair has been the talk of Sidmouth for the last year or two. The Rev. Olmius Morgan, formerly a chaplain in the Royal Navy now near seventy, who, with his wife has lived some ten years in Sidmouth, bought No. 3 Coburg Terrace two years ago. He has for some time promoted a servant girl of low repute in the house to the place of her mistress and the old man and this servant have for more than a year been in the habit of persecuting Mrs. Morgan. Not only have they compelled her to do the housework, but they have frequently dealt her a bloody nose and black eyes, until she considered her life in danger. At last she applied to the magistrates for protection, and on Thursday the parties went to Ottery where Mr. Morgan was bound over in the sum of fifty pounds and the girl in ten pounds to keep the peace for twelve months towards the wife. My tenants in No. 4 are much shocked by the vileness of his language, which they hear so near them. (*Diary*).

86/8/4 (Diary)

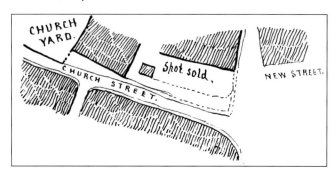

Sale of Church Street plot, Sidmouth. *Wednesday August 4, 1886.* Went to the London Hotel to see the sale by auction of the water mill by the river and the adjoining property, *but* no bid. Also the piece of land at the bottom of Church Street abutting on the Market Place, where the old cottages were pulled down. They are going to widen Church Street to thirty feet and sell a plot for three houses measuring sixty-two feet by thirty-two, *or* 1984 square feet. It was bought by Morton for Gliddon for £425, which is at the rate of 4s 3d a square foot. (*Diary*).

86/9/8 (Diary)

Ordnance Survey poles. *Wednesday September 8, 1886.* Went over to Beer in Spencer's large carriage to see C. J. Williams, the water-colour artist. I saw and passed several markers put up by the Ordnance surveyors, now engaged in the triangulation of the country for new maps on a large scale. There is one on the top of Sidmouth church tower. These marks, which have been put up since June, consist of a stout square stake or scantling perhaps six feet long or more, on the top of which are four projecting boards like the arms on a direction post. This is surmounted by a thinner staff bearing a little square flag *and* the whole affair is white, flag and all.

I found *Mr. Williams* and Miss Traies at the Dolphin *and we* walked down to the look-out station. *There was* a strong south wind *and we* saw five boats successively run in before it *onto* the beach, a very pretty sight. Dined with them at the Inn and then looked over his recent pictures, mostly beautiful coastal scenes. *I had* carried over my two volumes *as* I wished them to see the three portraits in volume two done in America . I had tea with them, left at 6.30 and was home by 7.30, a very pleasant day. (*Diary*).

Arms of Devon. *Thursday September 16, 1886.* Sent off an article on the *Arms of Devon* to the 'Western Antiquary', Plymouth. (*Diary*).

Court Rolls. *Thursday October 14, 1886.* Finished my report on the Court Rolls of Sidmouth for the Society of Antiquaries of London and sent it to the Secretary. Finding that it would comprise more matter than I had at first expected, I wrote it in a quarto blank book and it has filled more than fifty pages. I inserted a coloured map of the parish. (*Diary*). *Manuscript 309 in the Library of the Society of Antiquaries contains much of the material from volumes II and III of the History of Sidmouth.*

British Association Proceedings 1885. *Sunday October 23, 1886.* Finished skimming through the thick volume being the Report of the Proceedings of the British Association for 1885, recently issued. The march of modern science and the wonders of modern discovery are truly remarkable. Among other interesting subjects I may allude to the triangulation of India, the measurement of arcs to determine the curvature of the earth, the meteology on top of Ben Nevis, the origin of the fishes in the Sea of Galilee and many others. At page 417 I was surprised to see my report on the changes going on along the coast within my memory. I was asked for some kind of report from my long knowledge of the cliffs and the sea shore, *but* had no idea what was to be done with it. (*Diary*). *See September 8, 1884. The British Association had circulated a detailed questionnaire to local correspondents in the maritime counties, in an attempt to determine the nature and extent of coastal changes. Hutchinson had been allocated the south-east Devon littoral.*

Letter on Court Rolls. *Wednesday October 27, 1886. There is a* letter of mine in the Devon and Exeter Gazette about the Court Rolls. (*Diary*).

Tregoney charter. *Monday November 1, 1886.* A few days ago Mr. John Pole, or De la Pole, brought me an old deed to look at and decipher. It proves to be an original charter of incorporation, *written* in Latin duly abbreviated according to custom, granted by James I to the mayor and burgesses of Tregoney in Cornwall and dated 1622. It consists of two sheets and a half of parchment measuring 31 inches wide by 25 deep fastened at the bottom with a plaited silk cord, to which is attached the remains of a large seal, much broken. The initial letters are very elaborate and there is a recognisable portrait of James, the face about the size of a halfpenny, done with pen and ink and heightened with shading. How the Tregoney people got rid of this document may be a question *and* I must enquire how *it* got alienated. Mr. De la Pole tells me that it was given to him by Mrs. Jewell, the widow of Dr. Jewell who died here a few weeks ago to whom he had shown some kind attention during his last illness. Mr. De la Pole was informed that Dr. Jewell had resided at Tregoney, that he had lent the Mayor and Corporation money or somehow had a claim against one or more of them, and that one or more of their old deeds *along* with the silver mace if not other articles of Corporation plate were given him in part payment. If this is really so, it seems very irregular. Even if the Corporation has been dissolved, of which I know nothing, this property was not theirs to give away. Perhaps if I put a question in the 'Western Antiquary' I may get an answer or an explanation. As to the silver mace, the widow, a comparatively young woman and Dr. Jewell's second wife, having wound up her affairs here has taken it away with her. *She* has gone to her father who is said to be a gentleman's servant residing in the midland counties. (*Later note:* In the 'Western Antiquary' for January 1887 my article appears). (*Diary*). *No answer was published, but the Charter eventually found its way back to Cornwall and is now lodged in the Record Office in Truro.*

Thumbs down. *Thursday November 18, 1886.* I have recently been studying the hands of some of my friends. We sometimes speak of the effects of labour on the human frame and hear people talk of 'patrician' and 'plebeian' hands, and certainly there is a great difference between the two, chiefly manifest in the thumb. Of the first examples, the patrician's thumb has the end joint long and oval and thin below the neck, the nail being oval or almond shaped with the point turned down, as in profile number 2. The plebian thumb as in 1 and 3, is stumpy and shapeless, the nail round and thin and turned up at the end, looking more like the scale of a fish than anything else. Another peculiarity of the plebian thumb is this, that *in pressing* anything hard as in figure 6, the joint A bends inwards and joint B outwards producing a most inelegant form. The patrician hand holds an object, a coin for instance, as in 4, *and on pressure* would dig the point of the thumb into it, bending joint A outwards but not joint B. This is shown in the whole hands 7 and 8. We are told that it takes three generations to make a gentleman in mind and education, but I never heard how many it takes to form a patrician hand. (*Diary*).

Talented ladies. *Tuesday November 30, 1886.* Had an early dinner at St. Kilda with Mr. and Mrs. Cowan, Miss Gilcrist, Miss Lowan and Miss Scarth. I looked over Miss

86/11/18 (Diary)

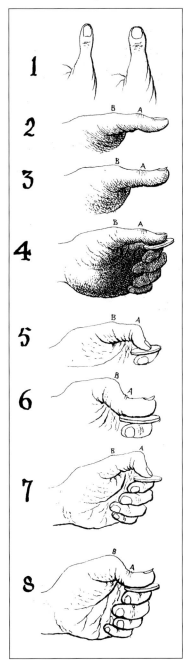

Gilcrist's watercolours *and could see* she has great talent and has been well taught. I then went to Miss Cowan's. She has filled it with an abundance of cabinets, drawers and boxes full of fossils, rocks, minerals and cut pebbles of her own collecting. She has a good specimen of a water-stone, the ripple marks very perfect, which she found on the beach under Salcombe Hill near a fall down of the cliff. We talked away the afternoon till dusk. (*Diary*).

Claims of the griffin. *Wednesday December 15, 1886.* In the current number of the Western Antiquary there is another article of mine on the arms of Devon. I continue to advocate the claims of the griffin. (*Diary*).

Index for the *Transactions* 1886. *Thursday December 16, 1886.* Finished the index to the Transactions of the Devonshire Association and sent a fair copy to the Secretary. I think this is the sixteenth or seventeenth year. (*Diary*).

Christmas begging. Tuesday December 21, 1886. Shortest day. The old practise of troops of antiquated females going about from house to house on this day to beg for something 'gin Christmas' or 'gin St. Thomas' as they expressed it, has happily pretty well died out. There is now no necessity to beg as there are so many active charities in Sidmouth, and I doubt the wisdom of giving money when I see how much of it is spent on gormandising and strong drink at this season of the year (gin = against). (*Diary*).

Emblem of Devon. *Wednesday December 29, 1886.* In the current number of the 'Western Antiquary' there is another paper by me urging the claims of the old griffin to be the rightful badge, ensign and armorial bearing of the county and of the early Earls of Devon. (*Diary*).

1887

Wreck of the Elizabeth Mary Ann. *Tuesday January 11, 1887. There was a* furious gale from the south with rain and mist and a raging sea. A schooner in the offing, *being unable* to weather the headlands, drifted towards Chit Rocks *and* made signals of distress, it being nearly low water in the afternoon. I heard two reports as signals from the Preventive Station. *There was a* heavy sea on the beach *and* whilst the lifeboat was preparing the crew got from the vessel onto Chit Rocks with great difficulty and were saved. The schooner was from Antwerp to Topsham with a cargo of superphosphate manure *and* was totally wrecked on the Rocks. The crew was English except for a black man *and* they mistook Sidmouth for Teignmouth. (*Diary*).

Wednesday January 12, 1887. Beautiful bright and calm sunshiney day, the sea smooth. I went and looked at the fragments of the wreck scattered all over the west end of the beach. The hull was split in pieces, half of her on the rocks and parts of the rest under the cliff. People *were* collecting the pieces and *others were* there looking on. (*Diary*).

Women doctors. *Friday January 28, 1887.* Beautiful day like spring, *the* thermometer *standing at* 50 degrees out of doors. Mr. Ede asked me to go to Lansdowne and take an early dinner with him. He is alone, two of his sons *being* in Paris, the third gold digging in South Africa and his daughter in London studying for the medical profession. Many and various are the opinions on this course. In the present day women are advancing fast *and* I see no harm in it myself. Some think they can never make such efficient practitioners as men *and* perhaps not in difficult cases, but I imagine their own sense would make them refrain from undertaking surgical cases not suited to their sex. If this be so, *and* few would have the nerve to attempt operations, they will be very efficient in the sphere of practise best suited to them as women. (*Diary*).

Death of Mr. Ede. *Friday April 1, 1887.* My friend Mr. Henry Ede of Lansdowne died this morning about half past four o'clock from disorder of the liver, after an illness of six or seven weeks. (*Diary*).

Water pitcher from Salcombe. *Monday May 2, 1887.* The sketch represents a 'clome' or red-ware water pitcher, found some years ago at the bottom of an old well in the village of Salcombe Regis by a mason of Sidmouth named Watley. I examined and measured this curious vessel of antique form. It is six and three-eighths inches high without the handle, the base four inches in diameter and the circumference of the swell eighteen inches. *It was* perhaps dropped by some child, *but* as it fell into the water it did not break or sustain any kind of injury. (*Diary*).

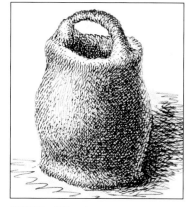

87/5/2 (Diary)

Bookcase finished. *Wednesday June 8, 1887.* At last my little bookcase is finished, the three doors having been glazed today. Taken at odd times, it has been a year in hand. I made it to give to the Museum Library in Exeter along with some books. (*Diary*).

Hedgehog. *Wednesday June 15, 1887.* The clear sky and burning sun fall upon us. After six in the evening I made a fire in the field of the dry trimmings of my shrubs cut in the spring. I collected some *with* a pitchfork that had been thrown close to

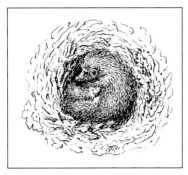

87/6/15 *Hedgehog's nest.*   (Diary)

the north side of the Old Chancel and scraped away some weeds and dead grass.   To my surprise I uncovered the nest of a hedgehog, about the size of the inside of a man's hat.   There lay the hedgehog, curled up in a ball with her face visible but ready to hide it if I had not stopped, alongside two or three young ones about the size of large mice.   The quills on the backs of the youngsters were nearly white, *though* brown on the mother.   I was afraid to look too closely but I drew my finger down the side of the mother.   She did not move or try to escape but lay quiet with her *family*, though I suppose cringing with fear.   I carefully covered it up again, replacing the grass, weeds and leaves and left it quiet. (*Diary*).

'We donkeys' in Sidmouth. *Saturday June 18, 1887.*   Miss Gibbons of Budleigh Salterton, who for the last three seasons has been making tours on Dartmoor and other places in a small carriage drawn by two donkeys, has just made another. Having visited Sidmouth and the neighbourhood, *she* has requested me to look over the proofs referring to this place and the district.   I received the first slip today and when done I sent it back. (*Diary*). *Hutchinson does not mention that Miss Gibbons had come to tea and he had shown her over the Old Chancel, a visit she described in 'We Donkeys on the Coast of Devon'.*

Jubilee celebrations. *Monday June 20, 1887.*   Today all Sidmouth is very busy decorating the town with flags, arches of laurel etc., across the streets for the Jubilee tomorrow. (*Diary*).

Tuesday June 21, 1887.   The Queen succeeded to the throne on the 20th of June, 1837, but as the 20th this year fell on a Monday it was thought that Sunday militated against making the necessary preparations, especially in London *where* the due celebrations were to be on a most imposing scale.   It was therefore held on the 21st. I shall only jot down a few particulars relative to Sidmouth.   We were awoke in the morning by bells ringing and guns firing making a great noise.   I hoisted a Red Ensign on the Old Chancel and many other people extemporised flags and streamers of various descriptions to display their loyalty and set off their buildings.   In the forenoon there was a short service at the parish church to which I went *and then* a cold collation in the ballroom of the London Hotel.   After this, all parties repaired to the Fort Field and places adjacent, to organise a long procession made up of the Band and Volunteers, the Committee of Management, gentry, lifeboat men, coastguards, sundry Friendly Societies, schools, etc.   *The procession trooped off around the town to the beach where the National Anthem was played and then returned to the Fort Field.*   All round the field a sort of course had been marked off with posts and ropes in which running and bicycle races took place.   There was a rather amusing game called the 'obstacle race', the contending boys having to cross a large open netting hanging loosely from poles and then run to several empty barrels with the heads and tails knocked out

87/6/21 (Diary)

suspended from ropes about two feet from the ground.   These they had to creep through, no easy matter, and then back again and once more across the netting, no easy matter either, to the *finish*.   In the evening, fireworks amused us from ten till past eleven and were very good.   A novel feature of the display was the bonfires on the hills.   It had been arranged that Lord Clinton, the Lord Lieutenant of the County, should send up a rocket and light the first fire on one of the hills on his property in north-west Devon *as* the signal for the lighting of others.   I was on the esplanade near Fort Cottage looking at the fireworks *when* very shortly after ten I saw one after another make their appearance on the headlands up and down the coast. They blazed out on Salcombe Hill immediately to the east, on Peak Hill a mile west and on Core Hill a mile and a half inland. The fire on Salcombe Hill, close to the edge of the cliff, was a very large one and so bright that though a mile off it shed so much light on the esplanade as to make our shadows clearly visible. There was a fine one above Budleigh Salterton, several away towards Torbay and distant specks of light like stars about Start Point. Some sailors who had been out fishing reported that they counted twenty-two, *but* from the tops of the hills many more than that were within sight.

There are about 3 400 people in the parish of Sidmouth. It had been given out that one pound of beef, one pound of bread and three pence in money would be given to any person residing in the parish without distinction above the age of fourteen, and half that quantity to those under and a new penny. Although it was intended for the poor, it was impossible to draw the line and anybody could apply at their discretion. As 2 290 portions were taken (two thirds of the population of the parish) it may be inferred that many applied who could afford to buy. About £220 had been given and I was anxious that half of it should be put aside for the production of some permanent memorial in bronze or stone, but they have been intent on eating and drinking it all. (*Diary*).

Unexpected remuneration. *Sunday June 25, 1887. Having completed the two American volumes, Hutchinson had sent the original manuscripts to the British Museum.* I received intelligence that the Trustees of the British Museum *at* a meeting on the 10th had decided to give me £100 for the old diaries and letters from which I compiled my two recent volumes. (*Diary*). *Hutchinson later heard that the American agent for the Washington Libraries would have* offered twice the sum *for the manuscripts*. If he wanted the manuscripts to send out of England, I would not have parted with them for any sum he could have offered me. It is well known that they buy up all such commodities, and at high prices too, and then suppress or destroy all such parts as militate against the measures they took at the time of the Revolutionary dispute. (*Letter to Perceval dated August 31, 1887*).

Stay in Exeter. *Tuesday June 28, 1887.* Went in a carriage into Exeter for a week or two, taking my servant Ann Newton and boxes with me. Lodged at 8 Peamore Terrace, St. Davids. (*Diary*).

Offering to the Queen. *Sunday July 2, 1887.* Extremely hot, the wind feeling as if it came from a furnace. The papers say that in the procession in which the Queen went on Jubilee Day to Westminster Abbey there were present sixteen kings, queens and next heirs to the various thrones of Europe. The women's offering to the Queen has reached £80 000, Devonshire contributing £2 228. The rule was 'not less than a penny or more than a pound'. (*Diary*).

Courtenay arms. *Monday July 13, 1887.* Sketched the coats of arms around the base of the Courtenay tomb. The more I consider them, the more I feel sure that they are far from correct. (*Diary*). The absolute correctness of this series of armorial bearings is looked upon with some doubt by archaeologists. No one would be capable of ensuring its true and certain correctness unless he were first to make himself master of the history of the Courtenay family and of the various alliances, foreign and English, into which its members have at different periods entered. One omission to me is very apparent and that is the absence of the golden griffin on a red ground. Whilst the heralds tell us that Hengist bore a white horse on a red ground, they also inform us that his contemporary and friend Vortigern, then king of the Dumnonii, bore a golden griffin on a field of the same colour. Seventy years after this, the West Saxons who were turning Dumnonia into Devonshire, adopted this native badge and continued with it 547 years till the Norman Conquest. After the Conquest, the same device was assumed by the family of de Redvers, and according to Mr. Planche, at least four generations used the griffin as their coat armour for the space of another hundred years. Then Richard de Redvers, about 1167, married the heiress of Ralph de Dol whose coat was a blue lion on a golden field. Though this last was only a new importation, the griffin began to fall into abeyance, yet all the evidence goes to show that the griffin was not only a principle quartering in the

87/7/13 *Coats of arms round
the base of the Courtenay alter
tomb in the south transept of Exeter
Cathedral.   Not dated.*
(DRO, Z19/2/8F/59)

Courtenay shield but was also the ancient ensign of Dumnonium and Devonshire. The subject is treated of in the *Western Antiquary VI, 23, 156*, etc.   (*Sketchbook F, 59*).

Plympton Castle.   *Monday July 25, 1887.*   Started for Plympton to attend the meeting of the Devonshire Association.   Went into Exeter by rail and then took the South Devon line via Dawlish, Teignmouth, Newton, Totnes, etc., to Plympton, *where I* lodged nearly opposite the Guildhall.   I called on Mr. Brooking Rowe, *who* took me up and showed me the remains of the castle and invited me to breakfast next morning. (*Diary*).   *The accompanying sketch of Plympton Castle seems to be dated a year out as Hutchinson was attending the Devonshire Association meeting in Exeter this date in 1888.   The small building just showing in the ditch below the motte has now gone.*

87/7/23 *Remains of Plympton
Castle from the castle area, looking
east.   Sketched on the spot July 28,
1888.*   (DRO, Z19/2/8F/61)

Breakfast at Mr. Rowe's. *Wednesday July 27, 1887.* While I was dressing at my lodging, a message came from Mr. Brooking Rowe to say I must go to his house to breakfast. On going there I found Sir John Phear who is staying at the house and Mr. Elworthy, famous for his studies in west of England dialects. After breakfast we went to the Town Hall to hear the reading of the papers. (*Diary*).

Return from Plympton. *Friday July 29, 1887.* There was a long excursion organised for today, but I made my excursion by returning home. I came by taking the route along the south coast and I returned by Lydford, Okehampton and Crediton, thus making the circuit of Dartmoor. At Sidmouth junction I was surprised to see flags of all kinds and colours fluttering in the breeze. The Rifle Volunteers were assembling and pitching their tents in a neighbouring field for a week's drill. (*Diary*).

Fatal accident. *Sunday July 30, 1887. There was a* terrible accident today, ending in death. Mrs Grose, a partly paralysed old lady living with her sister Miss Skinner at Sid Abbey a mile off in the parish of Salcombe Regis, was taking an airing this forenoon in a three-wheel chair drawn by a donkey. Her sister was with her. They were passing through Mill Lane, now called All Saints Road, between Rose Lawn and Oakland and near The Elms, the parsonage and All Saints Church. The gardener at Rose Lawn was engaged with a beehive taking some honey, *though* one would suppose that it was a most ill-chosen time in the heat and bright sunshine to meddle with bees when they are lively and active. The usual time is in the cool of the evening before dusk when they are quiet. The bees were much enraged at being disturbed and as the donkey was passing many of them settled on its head and stung it. The donkey became restless, further accessions from the swarm arrived and attacked not only the donkey but the old lady and Miss Skinner. Mr Reed, the gentleman now occupying Rose Lawn, came out to render assistance, *but* the bees so maddened the donkey that it ran round and round and tried to lie down in order to rub them off. In doing this it upset the carriage, threw Mrs Grose out onto the road, dragged the carriage over her and trampled upon her, breaking her bones. A letter carrier came by and he and Miss Skinner tried to hold the donkey to extricate the unfortunate lady. Then a man with a pipe in his mouth came down the road and they appealed to him for help but he kept aloof and went on, for which he was severely reprimanded at the subsequent inquest. At last they got Mrs Grose clear of the encumbrances, carried her into Rose Lawn and sent for Dr Pullin, *but* she had been so much injured that she was taken to Sid Abbey on a stretcher. (*Diary*).

Monday August 1, 1887. Mrs Grose died this morning. People say she had one leg broken (some say both), an arm, a collar bone and some ribs. At the inquest the verdict was 'accidental death'. (*Diary*).

Genealogical article. *Saturday August 13, 1887.* Finished another article for the 'Western Antiquary' on the arms of this county, but this time it is rather an enquiry into the arms and descent of the De Redvers and Courtenay families. I have added a tabular pedigree to make things clearer and have sent three pen and ink sketches of the Redvers seals bearing the griffin for woodcuts (*see November 4, 1887*). (*Diary*).

Tunnel noise. *Monday August 15, 1887.* Went to London by the 12.10 train. After passing Honiton the line goes through a tunnel *which* is acknowledged to be the most noisy, screaming and disagreeable tunnel train ever went through. Some echo, reverberation or acoustic property may be the reason. After going partly through, the rattle and screaming increase and run through one's head. Some of my friends have told me they found it so unbearable that they stopped their ears, and a gentleman with whom I was travelling did so today. People with weak nerves probably feel it most. I think the tunnel inclines downhill going eastwards and so perhaps the pace is accelerated, for in returning the speed is slower and the noise not so great. (*Diary*). *Hutchinson went on to Hertford to see his cousin Mrs Oliver and returned to Sidmouth three days later, not having enough money for a longer stay in London.*

William Wallis. *Wednesday August 24, 1887.* Mr. William Wallis who is just now in Sidmouth had tea with me. We used to play ball together in the Fort Field some sixty summers ago. (*Diary*).

87/8/28   (Diary)

Curve of the earth. *Sunday August 28, 1887.* Heard a good sermon from the vicar this morning, *and* later in the day I took a look at the sea. There was a large barque 'hull down' in the offing going up-Channel, illustrating very clearly the roundness or sphericity of the globe on which we live. More than forty years ago, *when* my brother went out with Sir John Hindmarsh (the first Governor) to found the colony of South Australia, my father's groom called Wellington Smith was told they had gone to the other side of the world. He thought the world was flat like a plate and he enquired what they did when they came to the edge? He supposed they would fall off, and he may have concluded that they would fall for nine days as Milton says Lucifer did. (*Diary*).

Exeter theatre fire. *Tuesday September 6, 1887. There are* accounts of the burning of Exeter's new theatre at the top of Longbrook Street last night. *It is* supposed to have originated in the 'flies' at the side of the stage *when* there were about eight hundred people in the building. The bodies were removed to the yard and stables of the London Inn close by, *and* before midnight there were eighty-five laid out and twenty injured persons sent to the hospital, of whom three or four soon died. It is said that a hundred and eight *have perished* but accounts are not made up. A man called Fish from the York Hotel in Sidmouth had gone in and it was feared that he might be *amongst them* but he proved to be safe. Several people went in by train this morning to enquire for friends, but none were missing. The old theatre was burnt in 1885 and this one has been built since. (*Diary*).

Thursday September 8, 1887. We hear from Exeter that the dead are being continually dug out of the ruins and eight have died at the hospital. My baker's errand boy who brings the bread to my house has gone in to Exeter to attend the funeral of his sister who was burnt there. (*Diary*).

Saturday September 10, 1887. The talk of the week in Exeter has been constantly on the fire and the work arising out of it. Inquests have been held *and* the unrecognisable remains have been buried first. Those recognisable have been buried by their friends or by the city in the upper or lower cemetery. About a hundred and thirty dead have been removed from the ruins but the work of excavation is still going on. (*Diary*).

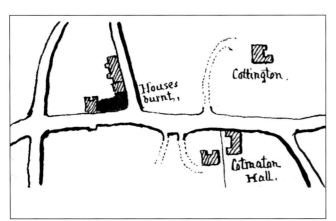

87/10/6   (Diary)

Fire at Cotmaton. *Thursday October 6, 1887. There was a* fire last night soon after eleven in the hamlet of Cotmaton. Last year Mr Walter Sellek, the butcher, built some cottages at the corner on land rented from the Manor. The most westerly was rented by a man named Cosins, the next by Barnard and his wife and the one at the corner by a Mr or Captain Elliot. The fire occurred at the first named, which was burnt out, all but the outer walls. Everything *was* insured. Barnard's furniture *was* not insured and he lost nearly everything, *and* the corner house was not quite so badly burned and a few things were saved. The fire is said to have originated from some sticks put in front of the grate to dry, which got ignited. (*Diary*).

County Arms again. *Monday October 24, 1887.* My last article on the Arms of the County of Devon, this month in the Western Antiquary, rather deals with the pedigrees of the De Redvers and Courtenay families and the descent of the griffin as a heraldic bearing. The editor has sent me six copies of the article, which I can give away. (*Diary*).

Drunken tramp. *Thursday November 3, 1887.* Depredators about. A few days ago a drunken tramp made his way into Sid Abbey late at night and thrust his head through a glass door, cutting himself severely. *He* said he had come to beg *but was* too drunk to know what he was about *and* used violent and disgusting language to those whom he had called out of their beds. Finis – fourteen days in Exeter jail. (*Diary*).

Courtenay griffin. *Friday November 4, 1887.* The three seals annexed illustrate my last paper in the 'Western Antiquary', advocating the claims of the griffin to a place on the Courtenay coat of arms. The De Redvers family bore the griffin for four successive generations until Mary De Redvers, who had no brother, eventually *became* heiress *and* married Sir Robert De Courtenay. The seals are attached to old charters granted by members of the family not long after the Conquest, and though rude and the strange animals misshapen, they are nevertheless perfectly authentic (see December 29, 1886). (*Diary*).

87/11/5   (Diary)

87/11/4   (Diary)

Guy Fawkes day 1887. *Saturday November 5, 1887.* Two or three strange gentlemen like the sketch annexed paid me a visit during the forenoon, but the boys who carried them seem to have quite forgotten the integrity of the verses they used to recite (see November 6, 1882) and *are* utterly ignorant of the origin or meaning of the celebration. The lure of gunpowder makes it popular. There was a torch-light procession down the town and a bonfire on the beach after dark this evening, but the rain came on and damped the ardour of the sport. (*Diary*).

Wincanton stone. *Thursday November 17, 1887.* Another birthday and I feel wonderfully well, except for a continuous hissing and singing noise in my head and a tender throat that advises me to keep house in cold weather. I should enjoy a good walk over the hills but it is frosty and cold with a cutting north-east wind. I tell my friends that I am fourteen today, and I prove it thus: $7+7=14$. *Some friends call and bring him presents of fruit.* One of my domestics gave me a teapot and milk jug to commemorate my birthday and the other worked the initial letters of my names in Honiton lace.

I made the *annexed* sketch from a photograph given me by a stranger who had been to Wincanton and called on me here. He told me the stone was near two feet square. On considering the incongruous and obscure subject *of the carving*, I recollect that St. Dunstan is said to have practised the blacksmith's art, and that one day whilst he was at work at his forge the Evil One intruded, and that the angry saint caught him by the nose with his red hot tongs. (*Diary*).

87/11/17   *Sculptured stone found in the wall of the church, Wincanton.* (Diary)

Sidmouth haunting. *Wednesday November 23, 1887.*   Rev. Mr. Jenkinson, now again our curate, called *and* among sundry things he told me was a curious story for the age in which we live.   At a house called Balsters, but now recently Hoptouns, where two ladies live, there has been great alarm for some time, there being no doubt as the ladies think that the house is haunted.   It seems that a door between a bedroom and a dressing room, though well fastened at night, is always found open in the morning (perhaps it needs a new catch).   They fancy they have seen the mysterious figure of an old gentleman pass through the doorway *and* this was too much for them.   Anyhow, the ladies are very much frightened, so much so that they have given up the house and are going, or have already gone away.   The house is a little above the vicarage, between the Hermitage and the house next to the entrance to the Elysian Fields.   (*Diary*).

Old spring gun. *Friday November 25, 1887.*   Two young men brought me something the other day which at first I could not make out, but examination suggested that it was an old spring gun.   The construction is very ingenious.   A blunderbuss barrel with a flintlock is fixed in a stock and a perpendicular spike underneath enables the whole affair to turn about like a swivel gun.   A horizontal rod under the stock is connected with the trigger by a bent arm or lever, and if this rod is jerked forward the gun is fired.   Another contrivance turns the barrel towards the *victim*. At the outer end of the rod there are three loose rings, to each of which a long cord may be tied.   Suppose then that the owner of a garden finds that his fruit is stolen at night.   The spike is put into a hole in the top of a post so the gun will turn about. At the top of the spike there is a hinge by which the muzzle can be adjusted to any elevation and there fixed, and the three cords are laid across the garden in any direction.   A trespasser would be sure of catching his foot in one of them, when the pull

87/11/25   (Diary)

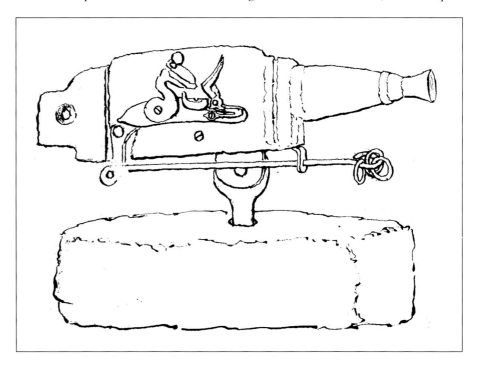

would bring the muzzle round to bear upon him and fire.   The mechanism is simple but certainly clever.   The young men knew nothing of its history *beyond that* it was found amongst some rubbish at the back of Little Belgrave, behind Belgrave House. They wanted to sell it and were happy in getting half a crown.   Spring guns are now against the law.   (*Diary*).   *Hutchinson thought this mantrap worthy of an article in 'Notes and Gleanings' for March 1888.*

Loss of the Albany. *Thursday December 8, 1887.*   A brig, having lost her way in the Channel owing to the thick and heavy weather, has run upon the reef at Long Ebb four miles east of Sidmouth and is likely to become a total wreck.   The crew numbered eleven *and all* got ashore.   She is the Albany *out of* Greenock *and* is nearly new and copper bottomed.   She has come from La Plata in South America laden with hides and horns and was to call at Falmouth for orders but missed her port.   They hope to save the cargo if they cannot save the ship.   *(Diary)*.

Index to the Transactions.   *Sunday December 17, 1887.*   Finished and sent off the index to Volume XIX of the Transactions of the Devonshire Association to be printed.   *(Diary)*.

Pugilism in France.   *Thursday December 22, 1887.*   The newspapers have an account of one of the longest and severest pugilistic encounters that has ever taken place in the annals of fighting.   To avoid the penalties of the law, the parties went to France last Monday and met on an island in the Seine twenty miles from Rouen.   There were eighty-three persons present to witness it.   On one side *was* Jack Kilrain, an American Irishman, and on the other Jem Smith, an Englishman.   Stakes were £1 000 a side.   They fought in a most determined manner for two hours and a half and accomplished 106 rounds, both being dreadfully punished when darkness came on and they were obliged to stop.   They agreed to consider it a drawn or undecided battle.   I thought that prize fighting had been stopped but it is being revived again with some zest.   Among those who were present were Lord Churston, Captain Grenville, Lord de Clifford, Colonel Browne, the Marquis of Queensbury, Lord Mayo, and so on and so on.   Some few years ago I saw in the papers a strange account of the Marquis of Queensbury burying his deceased wife in a grass plot near his house, and I am not sure he did not lend a hand with the shovel.   The public press made some remarks upon this, which called forth an angry letter from him justifying the act, and also betraying some very loose religious sentiments - with the word 'religious' left out.   *(Diary)*.

1888

Eclipse of the moon. *Sunday January 28, 1888. There was a* splendid eclipse of the moon this evening *which* began about 9.30 PM, the moon having been up some hours. It was quiet with a gentle breeze from the north and not a cloud. A considerable time before the shadow touched the moon there was a long extended penumbra spreading over its south-east side, striped like mares–tail clouds of a cold grey colour *as* I have endeavoured to show in the first figure. The second figure exhibits the moon nearly half eclipsed at about 10 PM. The shadow was of the same blackish-grey, and I mention this because it was very different afterwards. Total obscuration was effected at 10.31, but the third figure represents it at 11.02 when it was at the middle. Here it was a deep brown, more intense towards the centre *and* the cold grey had changed to a warmer colour. Perhaps the bright half had dazzled the eye

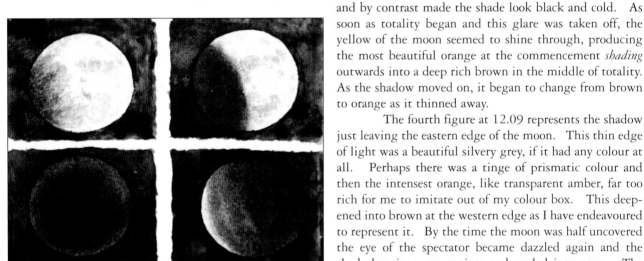

and by contrast made the shade look black and cold. As soon as totality began and this glare was taken off, the yellow of the moon seemed to shine through, producing the most beautiful orange at the commencement *shading* outwards into a deep rich brown in the middle of totality. As the shadow moved on, it began to change from brown to orange as it thinned away.

The fourth figure at 12.09 represents the shadow just leaving the eastern edge of the moon. This thin edge of light was a beautiful silvery grey, if it had any colour at all. Perhaps there was a tinge of prismatic colour and then the intensest orange, like transparent amber, far too rich for me to imitate out of my colour box. This deepened into brown at the western edge as I have endeavoured to represent it. By the time the moon was half uncovered the eye of the spectator became dazzled again and the shade lost its warmer tints and cooled into grey. The

88/1/28 (Diary)

eclipse was entirely over at ten minutes after one and I watched it to the end. It was the finest I remember to have seen, though my glass was small and the moon inconveniently high overhead. It is stated in some of the public prints the eclipses of a similar nature and number generally occur at intervals of eighteen years and eleven days, and that in 1870 the aspects were the same as this year. (*Diary*).

88/1/31 (Diary)

Triptych for sale. *Tuesday January 31, 1888.* Mr. Tinley, a dealer of 51 Paris Street, Exeter, brought me a small triptych of carved oak. The centre piece, a plaque resembling enamel, represented a woman on her knees with perhaps an attendant standing behind her, a priest or saint before her with uplifted right hand and holding a torch in the left, a man behind him and above her the words ENGVERRAND de MARIGNY. There were narrow plaques inside the doors with quarter circles over and a half circle above the centre, all painted. He said the plaques were enamelled on copper, which I rather doubted, thinking they might be glass burnt in. The work was old and apparently foreign. He wanted to sell it but as I am situated without wife or family, I buy but little now-a-days. (*Diary*).

W. C. Borlase. *Monday February 20, 1888. There has been* another bankruptcy of a lamentable kind. Some weeks ago the affairs of Mr. William Copeland Borlase, late M.P. for St. Austell and an Under-Secretary of State in Mr. Gladstone's ministry a few years ago, were under investigation as published in the papers. I think his place in the west of Cornwall is called Castle Horneck. In a literary and antiquarian light his name is of repute in those parts and I presume he is a man of cultivated mind, having heard of his collections of books, curiosities and works of art and having observed his name on the list of vice-presidents of the Society of Antiquaries of London. The first thing that attracted my attention was seeing an advertisement some months ago announcing his collection was to be sold, and later I heard that he had resigned his seat in Parliament. I was astonished *and* expressed my surprise to Mr. Franks when he was with me, who knew him well. He said there was a dark-eyed lady in the case. At the public examination it was stated that his liabilities were £42 653. 8s. 8d. and his assets £6 371. 0s .4d. Madame de Quiros, a Spanish lady, received judgement against him for over £4 000. He ascribed his bankruptcy to his expenses in Parliament and to the persecution he had suffered recently from Madame de Quiros, because he refused to settle £1500 a year on her. Some people go uphill and some go downhill, but downhill is the quickest. (*Diary*).

Blizzard in New York. *Wednesday March 14, 1888. There are* terrible accounts of a violent gale of wind and snowstorm in New York last Monday, the like *of which was* never remembered before. The Americans call such a storm a 'blizzard'. Queer English over there. (*Diary*).

My bookcase. *Friday May 18, 1888.* Finished carving the Gothic ornamental parts of the stand for my bookcase, the perpendicular octagonal legs being covered with a leaf or scale pattern and the horizontal bars with a Gothic edging. The bookcase amused me for a year and the stand since last autumn. The cabinet maker may do the plain part and put it together. (*Diary*).

Old limekilns, Sidmouth, 1888. *May 1888. No Diary text accompanies the latest sketch of the old limekilns at Sidmouth, depicting Miss Rastrick's recently constructed embellishments on the cliff opposite Chit Rocks (see October 17, 1883).*

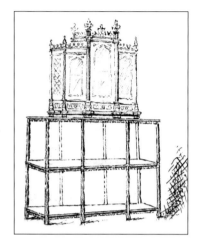

88/5/18   (Diary)

88/5/?   Remains of the old limekilns altered and fancifully built over, being in private grounds. Sketched on the spot May 1888. (DRO, Z19/2/8F/63)

Thoughts on resignation. *May 29, 1888. Hutchinson considers resigning from the Society of Antiquaries, having been Local Secretary for Devonshire since 1865 (see April 17, 1889).* To C. Knight Watson, Esq.. Dear Sir. I regret I am not the active boy I was a few summers ago, having some winters back got an attack of something like bronchitis from thoughtless exposure, and I cannot now defy the elements as I used to. But I should like to see an active local secretary in Exeter. The old city is a rich mine. Scarcely is a hole made or a foundation dug but something of interest comes to light, Roman, Greek, Egyptian, etc. Last summer considerable Roman remains were met with in the city when clearing the ground for new buildings, and when digging a trench for a drain in a field once belonging to the ancient priory of Cowick half a mile west of the city the workmen came upon a perfect stone coffin with indications of others. This made a considerable amount of talk but I do not think much notice was taken of the circumstances beyond two or three not very complete accounts in the local papers and magazines. But considering that there are some gentlemen living at hand who put F.S.A. after their names, a local secretary ought not to be needed. I asked one of them why he did not collect all the particulars with sketches etc., when discoveries were made and send them to the Society of Antiquaries, but he said 'it was not in his line'. He searched registers, charters, etc., and has written some good accounts of one or two parishes and several of the old churches, but I thought that F.S.A's. didn't draw lines. As I live fifteen miles from Exeter I do not hear of a find until the crock has been broken by the eager workmen and half the coins stolen. I beg to remain *etc.* P. O. Hutchinson. (*Letter dated May 29, 1888, preserved in the Library of the Society of Antiquaries*).

Devonshire Association meeting 1888. *Wednesday July 25, 1888.* Went to Exeter, the meeting of the Devonshire Association being held this week in the City, *and* took my servant Ann Newton with me. (*Diary*).

Thursday July 26, 1888. Went to the large room in the Museum to hear the papers read. I read nothing and probably have read my last, *as* I have grown indifferent of late. (*Diary*).

88/8/1 *Elephant carved under one of the misereres in the choir of Exeter Cathedral. It is number 27, on the northern side. It is early work, about 1350. Sketched Aug. 3, 1888.* (DRO, Z19/2/8F/65)

Exeter Cathedral miserere and other sketches. *Wednesday August 1, 1888.* During my stay in Exeter I have been often at the Museum and Free Library *and* copied some particulars about the Courtenay pedigree during one of my visits to the Institution in the Cathedral Yard. Copied an elephant under one of the misereres, No. 27, on the north side of the choir in the Cathedral. Went down to Dawlish and sketched the Old Maid rock (*see November 9, 1878*) which lost its head last winter and then walked a mile eastwards as far as Langstone Point and sketched the Elephant Rock, which I observed as I came down by the train had lost its head by the falling away of the cliff. In my sketchbooks I have now got three sketches of three different aspects of this rock, the first being a very good representation of an elephant. The cliffs are always falling away on this coast. The Parson and Clerk will go some day. *The Old Maid has been further reduced to a featureless stump and Elephant Rock is now unrecognisable.*

Went into Exeter to look at old St. Pancras Church, which is being restored *and* also out to Heavitree to look at the new tower they are now building to Heavitree Church. I see that the tombstones of Thomas Hutchinson and Henrietta are now close against the north wall of the church, removed from the west wall of the churchyard, but the yard has been somewhat enlarged on that side. (*Diary*).

New servant. *Tuesday August 21, 1888.* Alice Godfrey, a young servant I got from an Institution in St. Bartholomew's Yard, hoping she will be more steady, honest and economical than the general run of older ones, came from Exeter today. (*Diary*).

Tuesday September 18, 1888. Made a fire in the field and burnt the dry trimmings of my shrubs. Alice Godfrey left. (*Diary*).

88/8/1 *The Old Maid Rock,*
Dawlish Beach. The top fell off last
winter. I believe it was assisted off
as it was dangerous. See back
August 2, 1879. Sketched July 31,
1888. (DRO, Z19/2/8F/69)

88/8/1 *The Elephant Rock*
with the head fallen off. Coloured
on the spot July 31, 1888. (See
back July 30,1879, and May 4,
1868.) These changes shew the
constant wasting of the cliff. The
waves have made caverns and passages
underneath its body and between
its legs, through which I have
walked and come out the other side.
(DRO, Z19/2/8F/67)

Thursday September 27, 1888. I was busy writing in the Oak Room of the Old Chancel *when,* on raising my head, I saw a lady and two girls with their faces close to the glass looking into the room. On seeing me they withdrew *and* afterwards asked my housekeeper whether the building was a church? I am accustomed to such visits from strangers. (*Diary*).

Jack the Ripper. *Friday September 28, 1888.* There are strange occurrences in the world. Just now London is in a state of the greatest excitement and alarm from the affair of three or four murders of women, accompanied by unusual and horrible circumstances. They have been killed by having their throats cut or by strangulation and then the uterus and accompanying parts have been cut out and carried away. The coroner at the inquest of one told a strange story. He said that it had come to his knowledge that some time ago a man had called at several medical establishments asking if he could be supplied through the means of the London hospitals or otherwise with such specimens, *for which* he would give twenty pounds each. If so, they should not be put in spirits but in glycerine as the flaccidity would be better preserved. In answer he was told that it would be quite impossible to supply him with any such specimens. The man was an American *and* this story caused a great sensation. Could the specimens have been wanted for the American market? No English practitioner would buy them, certainly not now. It is alleged that no common murderer committed these crimes, for the parts have been cut away with sufficient dexterity to prove that he, or they, had a certain knowledge of anatomy and were possibly not unacquainted with the dissecting room. (*Diary*).

Tuesday October 2, 1888. Two more murders in London! (*Diary*).

Tuesday October 27, 1888. Finished an article for 'Notes and Gleanings' of Exeter. (*Diary*).

Wednesday October 28, 1888. Finished some particulars about the Harlewyn family of Sidmouth for Lieut. Col. Vivian, who is preparing a work on genealogy. (*Diary*).

Upturned wagon. *Friday November 23, 1888.* The flood in the river has been higher than ever known *and* exceeded seven feet perpendicularly. Two men drove a wagon drawn by two horses laden with coals through the ford opposite the mill, a little above the National School. They delivered their coal and tried to come back the same way, but the wagon was now light and when the body *of the cart* touched the water it floated like a boat and was carried down. People on the banks saw the danger. The horses had lost their footing and would have been drowned, but ropes were thrown over them from the bank, the harnesses *were* cut and they were got out. The men had a narrow escape but were saved. The wooden bridge for foot passengers had already been carried away and washed out to sea in fragments. The wagon was turned over and driven against the eastern bank under the great tree *where* it was turned over and stuck fast, or otherwise it would probably have gone to sea too. I got a sketch of the wagon as it lay there. (*Diary*).

88/12/3 *Six feet long.* (Diary)

Large catch. *Monday December 3, 1888.* Some sailors brought in a great fish rather more than six feet long, something like this sketch in the margin done from memory. It was blue-black on the back and white underneath. It got entangled in a herring net and that is the way they secured it. They said they did not know what it was, but I took it to be a species of porpoise *as* I have the jaws of a Bottle-nose porpoise very like this. (*Diary*).

Index to the Transactions 1888. *Saturday December 8, 1888.* Finished the index to Volume XX of the Transactions of the Devonshire Association and sent it to the editor. (*Diary*).

Projected pier. *Wednesday December 19, 1888.* A younger generation who cannot remember and have never read about the many attempts to make piers or harbours in Sidmouth, or the failures and monstrous losses of money attending them, is agitating to *have* a pier *constructed.* Since 1811, I make out that at least £40 000 have been

88/11/23   No title.
(DRO, Z19/2/8F/71)

utterly wasted by mismanagement or on ill-judged projects, for which the place has received no kind of benefit whatsoever.   I have a letter in the 'Sidmouth Observer' today and *another* next week about it.

Received the twelfth and last number of *Notes and Gleanings,* the last that is of the first volume.   My seventh and concluding article on the Cartulary of Otterton and Sidmouth is in it.   (*Diary*).

1889

Devon County Council. *Thursday January 24, 1889.* The new County Council for Devonshire, the elections for which have much occupied the electors of late, met in Exeter for the first time today. All except two of the seventy-eight elected were present. Lord Clinton, the Lord Lieutenant of the County, was appointed provisional chairman. (*Diary*).

Demon drink. *Saturday February 16, 1889.* Last Thursday, at a sale of farming stock at Mincombe in Sidbury, two young men were nearly killed by drinking raw spirits. It seems that at these sales spirits are given away freely to anybody. George Berry, aged seventeen, drank more than half a pint *and* about a quarter of an hour afterwards he suddenly dropped down. He was picked up insensible and carried to a cottage on Honiton Hill, but was dead before he arrived there. Another called Lockyer *who* drank pretty much the same helped carry Berry, and all the men were very drunk. Dr. Pullin was sent for *and* he tells me that he found Berry propped upright in a sitting posture on a seat quite dead and Lockyer in convulsions lying in the middle of the floor, kicking so violently that everybody was afraid to touch him. He would have died too if the spirit could not be got off his stomach. One of the men and the doctor held him and with difficulty forced some mustard and water into his mouth and got him to swallow, and after a time he was sick. The effect of the scene was heightened by the hysterical screaming of the two mothers. Lockyer was put in bed and before the night was over he recovered consciousness and was able to answer Pullin's questions. At the subsequent inquest some strong things were said to the publican and the attention of the magistrates was called to these abuses. (*Diary*).

Torquay gold rush. *Thursday April 4, 1889.* Gold is said to have been discovered in the rocks of Daddy Hole Plain, Torquay, and a company is being formed to work it. (*Diary*). *This appears to be the first of the many recorded 'discoveries' of gold at Torquay. The Torquay Gold Prospecting Syndicate sunk a shaft on Daddy Hole Plain but operations ceased after only a few months without locating workable deposits.*

89/4/17 (Diary)

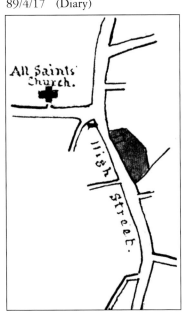

Treasure wrecks. *Wednesday April 15, 1889.* A prospectus containing particulars of a curious project has been sent to me. A company has been formed for the purpose of trying to recover a quantity of treasure supposed to be in the hulls of several ships lying on the sea bed in Aboukir Bay, sunk by Nelson's fleet at the Battle of the Nile. The Frenchman's flagship is said to have £600,000 in specie *aboard* to pay Bonaparte's troops in Egypt, and two silver gates and other things taken from a monastery in Malta. There are three or four ships lying there in only seven or eight fathoms, and they can be seen in quiet weather. Divers have recently been down and examined them. I have no money for speculations of this nature, but I should like to go out and watch the operations. (*Diary*). *The French flagship L'Orient and two more of the four French ships sunk during the battle were relocated again in 1983. Along with numerous artefacts, human bones, etc., a vast quantity of gold and silver coins have indeed been recovered.*

'Myrtles', Sidmouth. *Wednesday April 17, 1889.* Resigned my honorary post as Local Secretary to the Society of Antiquaries of London, *to which* I was appointed in June 1865. I find I am not the boy I was.

Walked through the High Street to look at the spot tinted red in the annexed plan. The old house called 'Myrtles', once belonging to Mr George Manning and then to Mr Cutler, has been bought by the local board *in order* to widen the street in that place. The outer wall, the house and everything are down and they are removing the old materials. They will put the wall back and then sell the land in lots for building houses on. In my manuscript *History of Sidmouth, Vol. 5 p.63*, there is a coloured aquatint of the house from the lawn drawn by H. Haseler and aquatinted by D. Havell dated 1817. The house had its end against the street. (*Diary*).

Wooden model. *Thursday April 18, 1889.* Fine and hot, the first really spring-like day. I finished carving a small design about four inches long as a pattern for a friend who wants to take up wood carving. (*Diary*).

89/4/18 (Diary)

Excessive testimonials. *Monday May 6, 1889.* People have been testimonial mad here lately. Since last June there have been - for Mr. Lethaby £63; for the Rev. Mr. Jenkinson who was leaving £55; for Mr. J. G. Radford because he has been married fifty years (which seems to be a great advantage to a man) £141 and £96 from the town's people; for Miss Thompson the voluntary organist at All Saints Church and at Choral Society meetings etc. £67; and for Dr. Harding the organist at the parish church *who was* leaving £212. Some of the money was given in silver plate, etc. Besides this, as free gifts, £55 to a popular missionary preacher, £50 to the cottage hospital which was low in funds and £3 for a lamp. All these sums added together amount to £742, a large sum for a small place not very thriving, *when* most of those who gave could ill afford it. I am no great advocate for these subscriptions *and* to my certain knowledge the majority gave unwillingly. Frequently, a few zealous people take up a thing as a whim of the moment and force it upon their neighbours *who* find it difficult to refuse. What is the consequence? The vicar has just preached a begging sermon because the accustomed contributions to keep up the church are so short. People can't give to everything. (*Diary*).

Staircase addition. *Friday June 21, 1889.* The stone for the new staircase in the Old Chancel having a few days ago arrived from Portland, the steps are now being made in a shed I have had put up in the field. For some years I have been wishing to have this staircase made but the expense scared me. Whilst the two volumes of the Governor's Diary were in hand, I could not think of it *as* they cost me £800, but that large sum has now come back. (*Diary*).

Elephantine neighbours. *Thursday July 11, 1889.* Sanger's great show of beasts and performances visited Sidmouth and bivouac'd in the Blackmore Field close to the Old Chancel. Soon after breakfast a man came to the door in a fluster and said I had better come out as the elephants were pulling my hedge to pieces and eating the bushes. Upon this I went out and there I saw nine elephants walking about the field, one with long curly tusks, a number of horses and many men busy erecting tents for the performance. The weather was fine and it was a very pretty sight to see so many huge creatures *ambling* about the field at their ease. There were two or three elephants by the railings reaching across the path, pulling away at the thorn bushes, brambles and weeds in my hedge and I was rather amused at seeing them put all this rubbish, thorns and all, into their mouths and masticating it. One of them, taking the grass, pulled up the turf with roots and earth and this went into his mouth altogether, but he spat out what he didn't like. When the procession went round the town, all nine elephants were yoked in tandem or in single file to one of their large carriages. (*Diary*).

Corbels in the Old Chancel. *Wednesday August 7, 1889.* Finished carving the first corbel of Bath stone, twenty-five inches long, on which the arch over the stone stairs will be turned when the second is done. (*Diary*).

Tuesday August 20, 1889. And I finished the second today, having been much interrupted by visitors. (*Diary*),

Thursday August 22, 1889. And today they were put up in their places and fixed. (*Diary*).

89/8/7 (Diary)

Miniature skewers. *Wednesday September 18, 1889.* Mr J. Y. A. Morshead of Salcombe Regis having sent me a brace of partridges they were dressed for dinner, and whilst carving one of them I was reminded of a story the vicar told me a year or two ago. The circumstance was the subject of remark at the vicarage, if it did not occur there. A Mrs. . . . . was a professed cook and she was occasionally engaged to

89/9/18 (Diary)

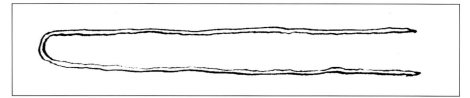

dress dinner at houses *for* parties, suppers, entertainments etc. I have had her for weeks at a time when I needed additional help and a very good cook she was, barring the drawback that the spirit bottles in my chiffonier (which I never locked) leaked very fast from some unexplained cause and the contents of my larder went too fast, to feed her relations. Well, one day at a dinner party, where among other things she had sent up a brace of partridges, it was discovered that she had trussed and skewered them with her hair pins which she had not taken out, much to the horror of the carver. But there is nothing new under the sun *as* I have discovered that my present cook has done just the same thing. Women's hair pins are made of a piece of bent wire lacquered in black like the shape here annexed. She had broken them in two and used the halves as skewers but omitted to take them out. Some time afterwards I took her to task about this new fashion and her excuse was that the ones she had in the kitchen were too large for such small birds. I said I would get others. (*Diary*).

Guy Fawkes Day 1889. *Tuesday November 5, 1889.* After dark this evening *there was* a torchlight procession down through the town to the beach, fireworks *and* a bonfire. Happily *there were* no riots or damage as too often *happened* on some occasions in former years. It was a quiet night *with* a clear sky and the moon nearly full, too light for fireworks. (*Diary*).

Friday December 13, 1889. Finished the index to Vol. XXI of the Transactions of the Devonshire Association. (*Diary*).

1890

Curious moon. *Friday January 17, 1890.* Woke this morning about a quarter or perhaps half past seven when it was just getting daylight. Looking towards the church tower, there was a curious effect with the nearly ended moon, for it will be new moon in three days. The thin crescent was bright on a deep blue clear sky, the light convex side *being* towards the east where the sun would rise a few minutes before eight. I dozed off again and forgot all about moons. (*Diary*).

Repairing the church clock. *Sunday March 29, 1890.* All week the clock in the church tower has been under repair and they are also re-gilding the figures outside. For this purpose a stage about six feet long and three wide has been made, *into which* a man gets and is hauled up to the clock face. The face is not solid *since* the figures, ten inches long, are of open ironwork fixed a few inches off the wall. Having gilt the north side, the stage has been moved and the face on the south side is in hand. (*Diary*).

Old glass from Salcombe Regis Church. *Wednesday April 16, 1890.* Mr J. Y. A. Morshead of the adjoining parish of Salcombe Regis called and showed me some old glass once in the east window of the north aisle of his church. (*Diary*).

Carved banister end. *Thursday April 17, 1890.* Finished carving the model in deal of a bunch of grapes for the lower end of the banister rail in the Old Chancel. (*Diary*).

Electrocution U.S.A. *Monday August 11, 1890.* The papers are full of accounts from America in which a man named Kemmler was executed for murder by electricity. It took place at Auburn jail in New York State. He sat in a chair strapped hand and foot *and* two electrodes *were* applied, one to the top of his head *making* contact by a wet sponge *and* the other to the small of his back. When the current was turned on *there were* great contortions of body and limbs. After an interval of a minute or two he was pronounced dead, the current *was* turned off and the electrode on his head was loosened, when he began to struggle violently. Doctors and many persons present *were* horrified at the scene *and* two fainted and were carried out. The electrode *was* re-applied and the intensity augmented. Everybody *was* paralysed with horror and the public with indignation, the doctors and others present declar*ing that* they would never assist in such a thing again. The theory of executing criminals by electricity has been discussed in America for some time *but* one attempt at the practice is perhaps enough. They seem to have done it by a current of galvanism, *though* I thought it would have been *better* done with a sudden shock so as to kill instantly, like a flash of lightening. Perhaps there is no way more merciful than the English mode of hanging by a drop. (*Diary*).

90/1/17 (Diary)

89/9/18 (Diary)

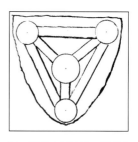

From top:
90/4/16 (Diary);
90/4/17 (Diary)

90/8/23 *Snakes eggs.* (Diary)

90/8/23 (Diary)

Snake's eggs. *Saturday August 23, 1890.* Mr and Mrs Heaven (cousin of the owner of Lundy Island) and *their* three daughters, who are just now *living* in my house No. 4 Coburg Terrace, had afternoon tea with me. Whilst they were *here,* two men called and said they had something curious to show me. One *of them* opened a paper and displayed several bunches of ovoid bodies, like grapes but opaque white, which were snake's eggs. They were not covered with a hard shell but with a tough skin like paper or the leather of white kid gloves. They were digging beside a bank in the neighbourhood when a snake about two feet long *slithered* out and escaped *but* they perceived a hole full of eggs, which they took out. They opened one or two to show me and my company, *one of which contained* a young snake about four or five inches long, alive but not too lively. They asked me whether I would like to have the eggs as curiosities. 'No, thank you all the same. Perhaps they will hatch *out and* I don't want a house full of snakes'. I gave them a shilling to take them away. (*Diary*).

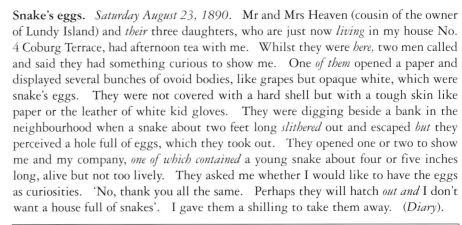

Circus at Sidmouth, 1890. *Friday September 12, 1890.* A short time ago there was a wild beast show at Sidmouth. I always go to them as it is the only chance stay-at-homes have of seeing rare animals alive, and I saw one or two that were new to me. Part of the entertainment was the silly and cruel practice of a man going in with the lions and knocking them about with a stick, some saying that there was a sword inside it and a loaded revolver in his pocket. Let me see a lion tamed by kindness, as glad to see his keeper as a dog is to see his master, *for that* would be a pleasing sight. Then we saw a kind of leopard *sitting on* the flat saddle of a horse and trotted about. Children rode on the backs of elephants, and one of these performed that most difficult feat of stepping from an inverted tub on to a cylindrical barrel, rolling it forward with its feet and then stepping off onto another tub. We had a tune on the organ and a 'dance', one elephant turning the handle of the organ with his proboscis whilst another on his tubs lifted his feet alternately as if dancing, and *kept it up* as long as the music lasted. (*Diary*).

From top:
90/9/12 (Diary);
90/11/15 (Diary)

Friendly fly. *Sunday November 15, 1890.* As the weather is getting cooler, I have a very sociable fly that lives constantly in my room. It walks over my book as I read and my paper as I write and over my hands and face. It breakfasts, dines, teas and sups with me. It is amusing to see it wash its hands and rub its head with its long forelegs. Its neck looks no thicker than a piece of sewing cotton. (*Diary*).

Honiton lace. *Friday December 12, 1890.* Finished reading, making notes and writing out a fair copy of the index to Vol. XXII of the Transactions of the Devonshire Association for the press. Yesterday was buried Mrs. Treadioun of Exeter, and I think once of Honiton, *who* has for some years been the chief dealer of Honiton lace. Though decidedly out of my line I admire Honiton lace as I would admire anything that is pretty and ingenious. It is certain however, that Honiton lace is doomed *as* it does not pay, *and* that fact is enough to annihilate any trade or occupation. Times are changed, wages have advanced and machinery has been so much improved that it can now do almost anything that hands can do. Formerly when driving through Branscombe, in passing the open doors of the cottages I could see regular schools of girls being taught to make lace, but now they are taught other trades that pay better. I saw the lace handkerchief given by the Marquis of Lorne to the Princess at their marriage, *and* another time in Sidmouth I had in my hands yards of the deep flounces made for the Queen (the price 300 guineas). (*Diary*).

1891

Short cut. *Friday February 6, 1891.* Very ingenious! A project has lately been put forwards to make a ship railway from Bridgewater in the north to Seaton in the south, with a branch turning off to Weymouth. Ships with their cargoes are to be supported on sacks full of water carried on railway trucks and then go merrily on to the next port across the county. Will the passengers be sea-sick? (*Diary*).

Missing robin. *Monday March 9, 1891.* I am afraid that the robin that has been on my windowsill twenty times, more or less, every day since last autumn has come to some misfortune. It suddenly ceased coming one day last week and I have seen nothing of it since. It *had* got extremely tame and would flutter against the plate glass as if it wanted to come into the room, and if it had not been so cold I would have opened the window. I suppose I distributed every day nearly as much food as would have kept one person amongst the rooks, starlings, sparrows, chaffinches, etc., and one meal all day long for the robin. In the severe weather in January my carpenter caught a fine male blackbird, put it in a cage and probably saved its life. When better weather arrived and we felt as if spring was upon us and the birds began to sing in the trees, it was lamentable to see that unhappy blackbird shut up in a cage, looking through the bars at others enjoying their liberty. I took the carpenter to task for his thoughtless cruelty, *and* asked him how he would like to be shut up in a cage the size of his parlour and hung on a nail outside his house? And I wound up by asking 'What crime has it committed that it should be sentenced like a felon to imprisonment for life? This shamed him, *for* the next morning in the sunshine he opened the cage door and gave it its freedom. (*Diary*).

91/3/9 (Diary)

Waste of money. *Monday March 30, 1891.* Easter Monday. The great increase in the wages of the working classes seems to have done them no good. Their increased resources seem to go mostly on feasting and rioting. (*Diary*).

Tail of the dog. *Tuesday April 21, 1891.* A boy of nine, instigated by an older one who lent him a knife, came into my garden and cut off the tail of my 'Green Dog', as he is commonly called. Some seven years ago, more or less, I planted four young box trees for the legs and by constant trimming, pruning and clipping with scissors I have fashioned an animal something like a dog. I have not had much difficulty in forming the head, the greatest difficulty being to make the hind and fore quarters grow over to meet in the middle and form the body. The young culprit has expressed so much regret and the parents have offered so many apologies that I am mollified, and think I shall be able to develop a new tail from the side shoots at the stump. (*Diary*).

Not bad for eighty. *Wednesday September 2, 1891.* Up in the chestnut tree for an hour, carving and chopping off the redundant branches. Not bad for 80. (*Diary*).

91/10/6 (Diary)

Portuguese man-of-war. *Tuesday October 6, 1891.* Two fishermen brought to the door one of those curious things commonly called a 'Portuguese man-of-war' to show me, which they found on the beach cast up by the rough sea. I remember seeing another here many years ago. This was in a bowl of water. The bladder was about six inches long and fully extended, and a number of veins and arteries of a pink or crimson shade ramified about it. Underneath, the shapeless body was of a purple colour like a piece of raw meat.   I have sketched *it* from memory only *and* the colour of the bladder is too yellow.   (*Diary*).

Plucky shot.   *Tuesday November 3, 1891.*   The papers say that last Friday the gunboat Plucky commanded by Lieut. Freemantle put two shot, one after another, through two fishing smacks anchored outside Plymouth breakwater.   *There were* two men in each *and both* boats were sunk.   Three of the men jumped overboard and were saved but one was either killed by the shot or drowned.   A great stir *is* made about it.   (*Diary*).

Thinking ahead.   *Tuesday November 17, 1891.*   I am 81, but well as I feel I cannot in common reason expect to be spared much longer.   Indeed, my recent building operations at the Old Chancel, some necessary work long needed, was only an effort to 'put my house in order' preparatory to leaving it altogether.   Two or three years ago I had my shroud made and it is in a drawer in one of my bedrooms, which is an anticipatory move in the same direction.   (*Diary*).   A person may with advantage sometimes be his own executor, at all events to a certain degree.   He who is solicitous in his later years to set his house in order is likely to be predisposed in that direction.   What a man can do whilst he is alive will release his executors from doing it after he is dead.   My small oak bookcase, the carving of which gave me much amusement for a considerable time and which contains a collection of books almost all relating to Sidmouth, is given in my will to the use of the Free Library at Exeter Museum, but I have decided to send it there during my life and this step will save others the trouble of doing so.   (*Colophon to Diary*).   *When the bookcase and its manuscripts were received by the Museum, the curator, Mr Dallas, wrote back 'I can safely say that during my term in office, no donation has been the subject of so much interest'.   (Letter to Perceval, December 10, 1894).*

91/12/21   (Diary)

Sunrise on the shortest day.   *December 21, 1891.*   The shortest day.   Beautiful clear sky but hard frost.   At half past eight by the parish church clock (professed to be set to Greenwich time) the disc of the sun began to appear above the ridge of the house, as in the annexed sketch.   I was in the Oak Room of the Old Chancel looking south-eastwards over the churchyard, soon to have breakfast.   The sexton's house in the churchyard is the one with the tallest chimney near the rising sun in the middle of the picture.   (*Diary*).

1892

Another moon eclipse. *Wednesday May 11, 1892.* The beautiful eclipse of the moon this evening was well seen, for the sky was cloudless and the night was calm. The obscuration began at 9.10 with a brush or diffused penumbra, as shown in number 1 of the different phases sketched in the margin. Number 2 represents the appearance at about 9.45 *and* number 3 at 10.10. Number 4 *was* as it appeared at 10.40 when the whole disc of the moon could be seen, the shadow gradually losing its cold grey and becoming a warm brown tint as the light portion grew less and less. Number 5 was the greatest obscuration at 10.53, when nothing but a thin line of light remained and the shadow at the edge assumed a beautiful yellow tinge passing into orange and then brown. In this it resembled the changes of colour which I copied on the night of January 28, 1888 at the total eclipse then occurring. As the shadow then began to pass off, it lost its brown tint and returned to the cold grey as the light got stronger, as in number 6. In number 7 at about 11.45 one half of the moon was in light and the last brush of the penumbra finally left it at 12.37. I watched it to the end. (*Diary*).

Controversial confirmation. *Wednesday April 6, 1892.* The Bishop of Exeter has conferred the rite of confirmation on thirty-eight idiots now in the asylum at Exminster and a great controversy on the subject has arisen in the neighbourhood. (*Diary*).

Lord Tennyson's death. *Thursday October 13, 1892.* Lord Tennyson, the Poet Laureate, died about 1.30 AM on the 6th at Aldworth, Hazlemere, and was buried yesterday in Westminster Abbey. The small fry of poets are in a flutter discussing who is to be appointed next, *but* public opinion is rather against appointing anybody. Times are changed, education has advanced *and* monarchs don't require paid poets to sing their praises. Let it drop. (*Diary*).

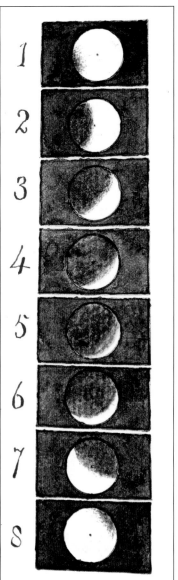

92/5/11 (Diary)

The way they draw at 5 years old.

The way they draw at 82.

92/?/? Presumably this sketch was done in 1892. (DRO, Z19/2/8F/73)

1893

Recovery from an illness. *Sunday January 1, 1893. At the beginning of the previous November, Hutchinson was struck down with a severe influenza-like illness that kept him in bed for some weeks. The daily visits of the doctor and the attentions of his many friends near and far cheered him up enormously however, and by January he had recovered sufficiently to be able to thank them. Much touched by their kindness, Hutchinson composed a verse recording his progress and had fifty copies printed off. One was sent to his friend Mr. Keily, dated January 1, 1893:* In the enjoyment of excellent health and spirits and without any act of imprudence on my part that I can recall to memory, the baleful finger of influenza, or something of this nature, touched me in the beginning of November, and I was cast down on the bed of sickness. The remembrance of kind sympathies and amiable attentions of many friends now outweighs the remembrance of the dismal ordeal of the sick-bed, and to take this opportunity of returning them my sincere and hearty hanks seems but a poor and paltry acknowledgement –

> Good friend – good friends – though poor the offering be,
> Accept my grateful thanks – accept I pray,
> For all those kind attentions showered on me,
> When on my dismal couch so long I lay.
> Those happy courtesies administered just then,
> Have brought me back to my good health again.

(*Dawson Papers 63*).

Indexing again. *Monday January 16, 1893.* After making the index to the yearly volumes of the Transactions of the Devonshire Association for somewhere near a quarter of a century, this time my illness prevented me. I have always begun in November, just when I was taken ill. I have now informed the Secretary that I thought I was well enough to do it, *and as* he has not been able to secure another hand I set to work. (*Diary*).

Friday February 17, 1893. Finished and sent off a fair copy of the index, twelve foolscap pages. (*Diary*).

Grotesque. *Friday April 21, 1893.* Finished carving in oak the grotesque head to go under the mantel shelf in the small room at the end of the passage upstairs in the Old Chancel. (*Diary*).

William Widgery. *Tuesday May 16, 1893.* William Widgery died on the 8th of last month. From being a common mason, he became by his native talent a clever and noted painter in oils, his chief subject representing the wilds of Dartmoor. *He was* born in North Molton in 1827. (*Diary*).

93/4/21 (Diary)

Change of air. *Monday May 29, 1893.* After I got well of the influenza I was much troubled with flying rheumatic pains all over me. As they did not seem disposed to leave me I was advised to try a change of air, so I went into Exeter today for three or four weeks. (*Diary*).

Recuperation in Exeter. *Monday June 26, 1893.* Returned from Exeter stronger but *the* rheumatism not much better. I amused myself there with copying sundry papers, in writing sundry letters I could not find time to do at home, in taking two walks every

day and sketching *the* contorted cliff opposite Head Weir and the two Russian guns now in the Bonhay little park, visiting the Cathedral, St. Petrock, St. David, St. Michael, St. Pancras, etc.   Mr. Winslow Jones showed me the collection of books in the Chapter House *and* I was quite astonished.   At the Museum two or three times.   Exeter languishing for rain.   (*Diary*).

93/6/26   Geological section of the cliff in the Bombay road, under Mount Dinham and opposite Head Weir on the River Exe.   Sketched on the spot June 6, 1893. (DRO,Z19/2/8F/76,77)

93/6/26   The two Russian guns taken at Sebastopol in 1855. When first brought home they were placed on Northernhay close behind the law courts at the Castle of Exeter, and there I first saw them: then they were removed to the half moon grass-plat in front of the Rougemont Hotel, but across the road: and now they are in the Bonhay playground near the river. They are nine feet long and the bore is six and five eighths inches. The furthest gun has a piece knocked out on the right side of the muzzle. The boy's hand points to the spot. June 8, 1893. (DRO, Z19/2/8F/79)

Near miss.   *Friday September 1, 1893.*   He fired right into the middle of the covey, but the astute birds flew off in radii and eschewed the charge of small shot. (*Diary*).

93/9/1   (Diary)

West end of Sidmouth beach.   September 1893.   The *accompanying sketch*, done from memory in September 1893, represents the west end of the beach as I remember it to have been some sixty-five years ago.   (*See sketch on September 15, 1881*).   Clifton Place

93/9/?   (Hist of Sid. IV, 167)

(then Heffer Row) had only a red earth bank between it and the sea. Number 1 was a small circular house. At a later period they built a square house in the place of it. (*History of Sidmouth IV, 167*).

Wedding presents. *Tuesday September 19, 1893.* Miss Arnold *was* married today to the Rev. Breasby *and I* gave her a piece of silver plate. Wedding presents have become quite a tax. I have heard of a single gentleman who declared that he was determined to get married some day if it were only to get back his money's worth for what he had given away. (*Diary*).

1894

New Years Day 1894. *Monday January 1, 1894.* Like an old garment the late year has ceased to occupy our thoughts, so we will now see with some interest to the new one and how it will suit us. (*Diary*).

Fighting robin. *Tuesday January 9, 1894.* As I have been in the habit of feeding the birds for more than thirty years, I have many visitors. A robin (not the one of March 9, 1891) was eating food on the window sill when a thrush flew in to share it with him. They pecked together for a short time when the robin, seeing that the bigger bird was devouring 'the lion's share', suddenly lost all patience, and ruffing up his feathers in a great passion flew at the face of the thrush with claws, open beak and much twittering. The latter was so taken by surprise that it started back, sitting on its tail feathers and putting itself in an attitude of defence. After further altercation, but no closing, they both flew off. I was much surprised at the courage of the little robin *whose opponent* was three or four times larger than himself. (*Diary*).

Far left: 94/1/9 (Diary)

Left: 94/5/1 (Diary)

94/6/9 (Diary)

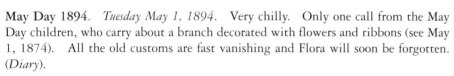

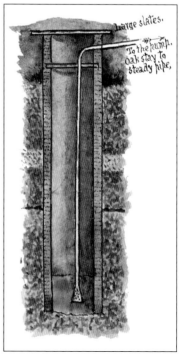

May Day 1894. *Tuesday May 1, 1894.* Very chilly. Only one call from the May Day children, who carry about a branch decorated with flowers and ribbons (see May 1, 1874). All the old customs are fast vanishing and Flora will soon be forgotten. (*Diary*).

Garden well deepened. *Saturday June 9, 1894.* During the past week men have been at work on the old well in the field behind the Old Chancel. It was made twenty-five years ago, as recorded February 23, 1869, and has done well till lately when the water began to get scarce. I have had all the brick work taken up, which was not set in mortar, and the well deepened four or five feet when they *found* plenty of water. The same coarse alluvium of loam, gravel and flints are as mentioned before and I am surprised they did not reach the red rock. The whole has been bricked up again and, except *for* the three feet at the bottom, the bricks are all bedded in cement. The geological appearance of the succession of deposits suggests that the valley of Sidmouth was once a vast lake, *which* was probably tapped and drained by the advance of the sea. (*Diary*).

94/8/1 (Diary)

Stolen boat. *Saturday August 1, 1894.* Yesterday, the first, (when Mr Smith went out to knock down a partridge only the gun kicked him backwards) four apprentice boys at Brixham stole a small yacht and put to sea in her. Although the weather was fine, they got stranded on Sidmouth beach *and* the vessel is much damaged. They said they wanted to get to Portsmouth. The police took charge of the lads and they have been sent back to Brixham to be dealt with there. (*Diary*).

Pig meat. *Friday September 8, 1894.* A concrete wall near the gas house fell out upon a pig's shed in which were fifteen pigs belonging to Mr. Holmes, my butcher. Two were crushed so that they had to be killed and thirteen were smothered and suffocated under the debris of the wall. Mem. – don't order any pig for a month. (*Diary*).

Last entry. *Saturday September 29, 1894.* Michaelmas Day. Fine but autumnal in feel. I have decided not to continue my Diary any further. Though remarkably well for my age, I think I may as well end this record. If I live until November 17, I shall reach 84. I was born November 17, 1810 and baptised at Heavitree October 22, 1811. (*Diary*). *Peter Orlando Hutchinson still had three more years to live, but true to his resolution he added no more entries to his Diary. He died on October 1, 1897 and was buried in Sidmouth cemetary, where his tombstone can be seen beside the path below the chapels.*

References

Allen, J. and Timms, S. 1996 'Treasures of Ancient Devon'. *Devon Books.*

Bateman, T. 1861 'Ten Years Diggings in Celtic and Saxon Grave Hills'.

Clements, H. 1903 'A Local Antiquary'. *TDA Vol. 35.*

Cresswell, B.F. 1908 'Exeter Churches'

Davidson, J. 1833 'The British and Roman Remains in the Vicinity of Axminster'.

Davidson, J. 1861 'Notes on the Antiquities of Devonshire'.

Fox , A.., Ralegh Radford, C., Rogers, E.H., Shorter, A.H. 1949 'Report on the Excavations at Milber Down, 1937-8'. *DAES Vol. 4.*

Grinsell, L.V. 1983 'The Barrows of South and East Devon'. *DAS, No. 41.*

Holbrook, N. 1987 'Trial Excavations at Honeyditches and the Nature of the Roman Occupation at Seaton' *DAS No. 45.*

Holbrook, N. 1989 'Roman Lead Sling-shot and an aureus from near Hawksdown Hill Hillfort, Axmouth' *DAS No. 47.*

Jones, A.M. and Quinnell, H. 2008 'The Farway Barrow Complex in East Devon Reassessed'. *DAS. No. 66.*

Lewis, V. 1997 'Satan's Mistress'. *Nauticalia Ltd.*

Obituary Notice of Peter Orlando Hutchinson. *TDA Vol. 30 1898.*

Pollard, S. 1965 'Neolithic and Dark Age Settlements on High Peak, Sidmouth, Devon'. *DAES, No. 23.*

Pollard, S 1966 'Seven Prehistoric Sites near Honiton, Devon'. *DAES, No. 24.*

Pollard, S. and Luxton, S. 1978 'Neolithic and Bronze Age Occupation on Salcombe Hill, Sidmouth'. *DAS, No. 36.*

Rogers, W.H. 1867 'The Sepulchral Effigies in the Parish Churches of South Devon'. *Trans. Exeter Dios. Arch. Soc.*

Tilley, C. 2009 'Jacob's Well, Black Hill: A Bronze Age Water Shrine on Woodbury Common'. *DAS No. 67.*

Todd, M. 1992 'The Hillfort of Dumpdon' *DAS No. 50.*

Westcote, T. 1845 'View of Devonshire'.

Whitton, E.E. and Lane, R.H. 1997 'Sidmouth Parish Church' guidebook.

Young, A. and Richardson, K.M. 1953 'Report on the Excavation at Blackbury Castle'. *DAES Vol. V.*

Index